The Gospel of

JOHN

Also by James Montgomery Boice

Witness and Revelation in the Gospel of John
Philippians: An Expositional Commentary
The Sermon on the Mount
How to Live the Christian Life (originally, *How to Live It Up*)
Ordinary Men Called by God (originally, *How God Can Use Nobodies*)
The Last and Future World
John: An Expositional Commentary (5 volumes)
"*Galatians,*" in the *Expositor's Bible Commentary*
Can You Run Away from God?
Our Sovereign God, editor
Our Savior God: Studies on Man, Christ and the Atonement, editor
Does Inerrancy Matter?
The Foundation of Biblical Authority, editor
Making God's Word Plain, editor
The Epistles of John
Genesis: An Expositional Commentary (3 volumes)
The Parables of Jesus
The Christ of Christmas
The Minor Prophets: An Expositional Commentary (2 volumes)
Standing on the Rock
The Christ of the Open Tomb
Foundations of the Christian Faith (4 volumes in one)
Christ's Call to Discipleship
Transforming Our World: A Call to Action, editor
Ephesians: An Expositional Commentary
Daniel: An Expositional Commentary
Joshua: We Will Serve the Lord
Nehemiah: Learning to Lead
The King Has Come
Romans: An Expositional Commentary (4 volumes)
Mind Renewal in a Mindless Age
Amazing Grace
Psalms: An Expositional Commentary (3 volumes)
Sure I Believe, So What!
Hearing God When It Hurts
Two Cities, Two Loves
Here We Stand: A Call from Confessing Evangelicals, editor
    with Benjamin E. Sasse
Living by the Book
Acts: An Expositional Commentary
The Heart of the Cross, with Philip G. Ryken
What Makes a Church Evangelical?

The Gospel of

JOHN

Volume 3

Those Who Received Him

John 9–12

JAMES
MONTGOMERY
BOICE

Baker Books

A Division of Baker Book House Co
Grand Rapids, Michigan 49516

© 1985, 1999 by James Montgomery Boice

Published by Baker Books
a division of Baker Book House Company
P.O. Box 6287, Grand Rapids, MI 49516-6287

Previously published by Zondervan Publishing House

Second printing, December 2001

Printed in the United States of America

Library of Congress Cataloging-in-Publication Data
Boice, James Montgomerty, 1938–
    [Gospel of John]
    The Gospel of John / James Montgomery Boice.
        p.   cm.
    Includes bibliographical references and indexes.
    Contents: v. 3. Those who received him, John 9–12.
    ISBN 0-8010-1087-X (hardcover)
    1. Bible. N.T. John Commentaries. I. Title.
    BS2615.3.B55   1999
    226.5'077—dc21   99-22764

For current information about all releases from Baker Book House, visit our web site:
http://www.bakerbooks.com

To him who came
to call not the righteous but sinners to repentance

Contents

Preface

It has been more than thirty years since I began to study the Gospel of John in a serious way and nearly twenty-five years since my studies of the Gospel began to appear in print. They have been out of print for some time. So it was with much gratitude that I learned of Baker's interest in reissuing them in this revised and attractive version. This version matches the format of the other sets that Baker has published: *Genesis* (3 volumes), *Psalms* (3 volumes) and *Romans* (4 volumes). It also matches the single volume studies of *Acts* and *Ephesians*.

This is the third volume of a five part work. The first volume dealt with Jesus' coming into the world and the reactions of a few representative persons to him. It covered chapters 1–4. The second volume dealt with the origins of the hostility to Jesus that began to develop among the religious authorities early in his ministry. It covered chapters 5–8. This volume covers chapters 9–12 in which Jesus turns to those whom the Father has given him out of the world and begins to teach them.

Volumes 4 and 5 complete the series. Volume 4 (chapters 13–17) is concerned with Jesus' final private teaching of his disciples, usually called the final discourses, and with his powerful high-priestly prayer recorded in chapter 17. Volume 5 deals with the culmination of Christ's earthly ministry, centering in his betrayal by Judas, his arrest, his trial by the Jewish and Roman authorities, his death, and his resurrection (chapters 18-21).

As with previous volumes, I have occasionally deviated from a strict verse-by-verse exposition to deal with a particularly important theme in greater depth than would be possible by the verse-by-verse method. The clearest example is the study of John 11:35, the shortest verse in the Bible ("Jesus wept"), to which I have devoted four studies. I have also devoted six studies each to the themes of the Good Shepherd (John 10:1–21) and suffering and death (John 11:4–26). In earlier volumes extensive study was given to the themes of baptism, witnessing, the Sabbath, and the authority of the Scriptures. Echoes of three of those subjects—witnessing, the Sabbath, and the Scriptures—occur at appropriate places in volume 3.

Some of this material has already appeared in print, although with limited circulation. The most widely circulated piece was the message on "How to Save Your Own Life" (John 12:24–26), which was printed in the *Christian Observer*, a paper which has since gone out of business. Material from chapter 20 ("Word of the Living God," John 10:35) appeared long ago in a small pamphlet by the same title. Several of the messages on suffering were published in a special premium booklet offered to listeners to the *Bible Study Hour* during the spring of 1976. The *Bible Study Hour*'s regular publication, originally called *Bible Studies Magazine* (now *God's Word Today*), circulated each of these studies as they were aired.

It is impossible adequately to express a debt to all, both living and dead, who have been a help to me in my preparation of these studies. The footnotes will reflect my strong debt to Charles Spurgeon, Arthur Pink, Donald Barnhouse, and Alexander Maclaren, but dozens of other commentators were regularly consulted. I still believe that Leon Morris's volume, *The Gospel According to John*, is the best of all recent commentaries. As with most of my books, Miss Caecilie Foelster, my secretary, joined me in careful editing of the manuscript and in seeing it through the stages of its original production. I owe a debt as well to the Session and congregation of Tenth Presbyterian Church who encourage me to spend much of my time in such serious Bible study and writing.

To God be all glory, for this and all other spiritual endeavors by his elect people. Amen and amen.

James Montgomery Boice
Philadelphia, Pennsylvania

Those Who Received Him

112

Christer and a Man Born Blind

John 9:1

As he went along, he saw a man blind from birth.

There are verses in the opening chapter of John's Gospel that provide an outline for the first twelve chapters of the book and are, therefore, important at this point as our study of the Gospel enters upon a new section. These verses speak of the coming of the Light into the world and say of that Light, "He came to that which was his own, but his own did not receive him. Yet to all who received him, to those who believed in his name, he gave the right to become children of God" (1:11–12). The coming of the Light aptly describes the content of the first four chapters of John's Gospel. That "he came to that which was his own" describes the content of the next four chapters. The chapters we are about to study, chapters 9 through 12, deal with "all who received him," for in these chapters we see that the emphasis is on Jesus calling out a people of his own in the midst of, and in spite of, growing hostility from the authorities of Judaism.

This new section differs from the one before it in that in the old section we see Christ being rejected by his own people, while in this section Christ, being rejected by his people, begins to call out a new people. This is first exemplified by the story of the call of Jesus to the man who had been born blind.

"I Am the Light"

The contrast between these two sections—section two (composed of chapters 5 through 8) and section three (chapters 9 through 12)—may be pointed up in another way also. In chapters 8 and 9 there is an "I am" saying of Jesus that is repeated twice, once in each chapter. The saying is the same—"I am the light of the world"—but the contexts are different; this is illustrative of the difference between the two sections.

In John 8 Jesus' saying occurs in the twelfth verse, just after he had dealt with the accusers of the woman who had been taken in adultery. It refers to the effect of his testimony upon these men. They had come to Jesus after having just trapped the poor woman. They said, "In the law Moses commanded us to stone such women. Now what do you say?" (v. 5). They were not interested in the law. They were only figuring that if Jesus consented to the requirement of the law and had the woman stoned, then they could ridicule him as the One who invited sinners to come to him but then dealt harshly with them. On the other hand, they reasoned, if he overlooked the law and gave a judgment of mercy, then they could say, "What kind of a prophet is this who advises laying aside the law of Moses?" Jesus dealt with these men by suggesting that the one who was sinless cast the first stone. At this point, as the light of his righteousness shone upon them, the accusers began to slip away one by one, beginning with the eldest. At last Jesus, being left alone in the midst of the crowd with the woman, uttered his saying.

What did he mean when on this occasion he said, "I am the light of the world"? To have an answer we need only think of the effect of light on something that has been shielded from light a long time. Imagine a board out in a field. Kick it over and immediately all the bugs and other squirmy things begin to slither away into dark areas. This is what happened when Jesus spoke to these leaders. Jesus turned over a board, and away went those Pharisees! They could not stand before the light, and they hated Jesus for it. It is not surprising, therefore, that the chapter ends with an attempt by these men to stone Jesus.

On the other hand, light also has another and entirely different effect upon some things that are exposed to it. Take the ground that was covered over by the board. When the board is first turned over the bugs run for cover. But leave the board off that patch of ground for awhile, and soon the same sun that made the bugs run for cover will begin to make the seeds in the ground grow. In a short time that patch of earth will be covered with grass or flowers, just like the growth in the field that surrounds it. This latter effect gives us the meaning of Christ's second "I am the light of the world," in John 9. In chapter 8 the Light made the creatures of darkness run. In chapter 9 the Light begins to call forth life and produce growth in those within whom God has planted the seed of saving faith. In this sense John 9 is the story of the sovereign and electing grace of God in salvation.

Arthur W. Pink, a valuable commentator on this Gospel, captures the differences between chapters 8 and 9 (hence also between sections two and three) in this manner: "In John 8 we behold Christ as 'the light' exposing the darkness, but in John 9 He communicates sight. In John 8 the Light is despised and rejected, in John 9 He is received and worshipped. In John 8 the Jews are seen stooping down—to pick up stones; in John 9 Christ is seen stooping down—to make anointing clay. In John 8 Christ hides Himself from the Jews; in John 9 He reveals Himself to the blind beggar. In John 8 we have a company in whom the Word has no place (v. 37); in John 9 is one who responds promptly to the Word (v. 7). In John 8 Christ, inside the Temple, is called a demoniac (v. 48); in John 9, outside the Temple, He is owned as Lord (v. 36). The central truth of John 8 is the Light testing human responsibility; in John 9 the central truth is God acting in sovereign grace *after* human responsibility has failed."[1]

No Frustration

If this is the true contrast between these two sections, as there is every reason to believe, then the first and great lesson to be learned from chapter 9 is that *man cannot frustrate God.* Man's hatred cannot frustrate God. Man's sin cannot frustrate God. Rather, God accomplishes his purposes sovereignly, saving by grace those whom he chooses to call to himself.

The fact that man's hatred cannot frustrate God is seen clearly from the story and in particular from the fact that Jesus was not disturbed by the action of the religious leaders in their attempt to stone him. The stoning attempt was a serious incident. It would have created a great turmoil in the temple precincts. Nevertheless, a moment later, after Jesus had removed himself probably little more than a good stone's throw away, we find him stopping to fix his eyes on the blind beggar who had been sitting near the temple gate. Most of us in a similar situation would scarcely have had eyes for the beggar. We would be looking over our shoulder to see if we were being pursued, and we would be trying to put an even greater distance between ourselves and our enemies. Not Jesus! No doubt he felt the contradiction of sinners against himself. He even wept over Jerusalem at one point in his ministry. But this did not disturb him where his work was concerned. So we find him calm and self-possessed, acting with a profound disregard of his enemies and their hatred.

Jesus was not deterred from his work either, which we might well have been had we been in his place. He was the light of the world. He had just been rejected. Would it not have been reasonable for him to have returned at once to heaven, thereby turning his back on our sinful world? Would it not have been reasonable for him to have abandoned our race? Nothing is more reasonable from a human point of view. But Jesus had God's point of view, and it was God who was acting. Therefore, instead of accepting the no of sinful men, Christ simply persevered in his task and began to elect some to salvation. The Bible says, "I will have mercy on whom I have mercy, and I will have compassion on whom I have compassion" (Rom. 9:15).

This verse tells us about the God whom we serve, and we should know that nothing frustrates him. What do you think God is doing in heaven anyway? To hear some people talk you would think he is cowering behind a cloud somewhere, afraid of every new evil that man's rebellion might bring. At the height of the Watergate scandal, with its long series of damaging revelations, a cartoon appeared in which a man and a woman were cowering behind a chair that, in its turn, was facing a television set. They were holding onto each other and were shaking with fear as the newscaster said, "And now for the latest stunning development. . . ." We must not think that God is like that. Some people picture God as surprised when Adam sinned. God had created a perfect world. Adam spoiled it. So God is imagined to have said to himself, "Oh, my, the man and the woman sinned. They fell. Whatever will I do now?" Eventually God decides that he will send Jesus, but when Jesus is rejected he is puzzled again. God is not like that. That is not our God. Our God sees the end from the beginning and is not frustrated. Therefore, nothing defeats or will ever defeat his purposes.

Jesus said, "I will build my church." This is his purpose in this age, and he is building it. Therefore, all who are given to Jesus Christ by the Father will come to him.

We may make an important conclusion at this point, and the conclusion is this: If God's purposes cannot be frustrated—and they cannot be—then if we make God's purposes our purposes, we will not be frustrated either. Do you find life frustrating? Does it get you down? Do you seem to be getting nowhere? If so, make God's purposes your own, and you will find that frustration will disappear and life will receive new meaning. If you are working for God, then your work will bear fruit and Jesus Christ will be glorified.

The State of the Lost

We have seen that the hatred of man cannot frustrate God. We also need to see that the state of the lost cannot frustrate God either. Once again, this is made clear by our story.

Think for a moment of this poor blind man, and think of all he symbolizes. He symbolizes the state of the lost apart from the creative and transforming power of the Lord Jesus. On the one hand, we have the rulers of the people, the Pharisees, who can see physically but who are spiritually blind. On the other hand, there is the blind man. He cannot see physically, but Christ makes him see both physically and spiritually. By the end of the story we find him worshiping Jesus as the Son of God and the Lord.

What is the state of this man? For one thing, he cannot see, and this means that he cannot see Jesus. This is the state of the lost today. Jesus is preached, but they cannot see him. The gospel is explained, but they cannot understand it. Indeed, the Bible says that "the man without the Spirit does not accept the things that come from the Spirit of God, for they are foolishness to him, and he cannot understand them, because they are spiritually discerned" (1 Cor. 2:14). If there is to be spiritual sight, Jesus must first open blind eyes.

Second, because the man who had been born blind was unable to see, it was also true that he could not seek Jesus. Indeed, how can a blind man seek anything? In spiritual terms this means that a man is unable to seek God, which truth God tells us. For he flatly declares that "there is no one who . . . seeks God" (Rom. 3:11).

Third, if the blind man was unable to seek Jesus, it is also true that he was unable to find him. What is more, since he was a beggar, it is also obvious that he was unable to hire someone else to seek Christ and find him either. What a condition—unable to see, seek, or find Jesus, and unable to procure help in finding him. It is a sad state, but it is doubly sad in that it describes the condition of all men spiritually.

Have you ever noticed that all the miracles of healing in John's Gospel illustrate the truths of this story? Each one shows man to be helpless in his sin, but each also shows the grace of the Lord Jesus Christ triumphant. The first miracle is the healing of the impotent man, recorded in John 5. What is the point of this story? Why did John include it? Obviously, John included this healing to make the point that the man was unable to make the first move toward Jesus. Nor can we. If we are to be saved, Jesus must make the first move toward us and even give strength to respond to him. The story of the man born blind is saying the same thing in other ways, making the point that sinful men cannot see God's truth. But again Jesus makes the first step by restoring sight. Finally, a few chapters further on, we come upon the case of Lazarus, who had been dead four days before Christ came to him. He was utterly lost. Lazarus could not even call out to Jesus to say, "Master, help me." He was dead. But Jesus called him—"Lazarus, come forth"—and the call of the Lord of life gave life to Lazarus.

This is the gospel. It is the truth of God concerning the hopeless state of the lost and of the power of God to save such as he wills to save. God's purposes are not frustrated by either the hatred of men or the sin of the lost.

Sinner, Take Heart

Let me apply these truths in this way. First, if you are a Christian and have been witnessing to another person concerning Christ, you can be encouraged by knowing that God will never be frustrated by human sin. There may be much in the situation to frustrate you. You may seem to get nowhere. In fact, in a given witnessing situation there may be more to frustrate you than in any other situation in life. Still, God is not frustrated, and you should not be either. Instead, you should be encouraged by knowing that if God is working, nothing will hinder that working. If the light of God is shining, his light will make seeds grow. So, be bold! Witness boldly, and expect God to bring forth his harvest!

Second, if you are one who has not yet believed in the Lord Jesus Christ as your Savior, you too can take heart by seeing what he did in the life of the man who had been born blind. Think of what Jesus Christ did for him. For one thing, the story tells us that he saw him, that is, that he took notice of him. The blind man could not see Jesus, but Jesus saw the blind man; and that was the important thing after all. Moreover, when he saw him he saw him as a man who needed his help. Jesus alone saw him in this way. The disciples looked at the man and saw him as a sinner. "Who sinned," they asked, "this man or his parents?" The passersby looked at him as a beggar. "Isn't he the man who sat and begged?" The Pharisees saw him as a tool, for they wanted to maneuver him to trap Jesus. But Jesus—well, Jesus saw him as a man who needed help, and he saved him.

Moreover, Jesus took him in when all others had cast him out. His family had cast him out. His neighbors had no use for him. Even his pastors rejected him. Eventually, because of the excommunication, the nation had no room for him either. No family, neighbors, pastors, nation! Who was left? Only Jesus! It was Jesus who sought him out and received him when no one else would receive him or even rejoice in his healing.

Are you one whom this world has cast out? Do you feel alone and rejected? Come to Jesus! Jesus is the One who is altogether lovely. Let Jesus be yours. Say, "O Lord Jesus, I want you to be my Savior."

113

The Problem of Pain

John 9:2–3

His disciples asked him, "Rabbi, who sinned, this man or his parents, that he was born blind?"

"Neither this man nor his parents sinned," said Jesus, "but this happened so that the work of God might be displayed in his life."

Ⅰf God were good, he would wish to make his creatures perfectly happy, and if God were almighty he would be able to do what he wished. But the creatures are not happy. Therefore God lacks either goodness, or power, or both." This, as C. S. Lewis states in his small book, *The Problem of Pain,* is the problem of human suffering in its simplest form. And it must be admitted that if the Bible does not throw additional light upon this problem—if it does not reveal more about the nature and purposes of God than this statement of the problem leads us to see—then the problem is insoluable and life lacks meaning.

All Suffer

At some time or other every human being must experience suffering. A person causes pain by being born. Many live by inflicting pain. Most suffer pain. Eventually all experience death. It is true that believers who are alive at the time of Christ's return to this earth will be transformed in a moment and will not die. But with this exception, it is the lot of all to suffer and die. Eliphaz spoke truthfully to Job when he told the suffering patriarch, "For hardship does not spring from the soil, nor does trouble sprout from the ground. Yet man is born to trouble as surely as sparks fly upward" (Job 5:6–7).

There is a distinction to be made even at this point, however. For while it is true that all suffer, Christians as well as non-Christians, it is nevertheless not true that all suffering is alike. Seen from the outside, a Christian suffering from an incurable disease and a non-Christian suffering from the same disease may be supposed to be undergoing the same experience. But, according to the plain teachings of the Word of God, the two are not equal. From God's point of view the non-Christian is suffering without purpose. Or, which may sometimes be the case, he is suffering at the whim of Satan, who is merely doing as he pleases with a member of his own kingdom. In the case of the Christian, an all-wise heavenly Father is permitting suffering in a carefully controlled situation in order that he might accomplish a desirable purpose. The Book of Job alone teaches us about the latter.

But if suffering—that endured by a Christian—has purpose, surely we are not out of line in asking what that purpose is. If we are to learn from it, we must ask what it is we are to learn; if we are to profit, we must ask how. The answers to these questions are suggested to us by some of Christ's words uttered on the occasion of his healing of the blind man, recorded in John 9.

False Assumptions

We are told by the author that as Jesus passed by the gate of the temple, having placed himself out of reach of those leaders of the nation who were attempting to kill him, "he saw a man blind from birth." This man had begged at the temple gate for many years, and he was apparently known to the disciples. They would have walked on. But when Jesus stopped to look at this man, they stopped too and began to ask him a philosophical question: "Rabbi, who sinned, this man or his parents, that he was born blind?"

The question they asked was the age-old question of the problem of pain, the question we have been asking. But in their mouths it took a form that immediately reveals two basic (and erroneous) assumptions. In the first place, the question revealed the pagan assumption that suffering in this life often is retribution for sin committed in some previous life, conceived in the categories of a system of reincarnation. Such views were common in the first century, even in Judaism. Many religions and cults in our own day still hold to them. The Scriptures do not support this, however. Instead they teach that the issues of eternity are settled for each individual during his own, single lifetime.

The second erroneous assumption made by the disciples was that the suffering of the blind man had been caused by the sin of his parents. This, of course, was possible. Sins of parents can be visited upon children. Blindness can result from venereal disease, for instance.

In this case, however, Jesus replied that the man had been born blind, neither because of his own sin nor for the sin of his parents, but rather that the glory of God might be revealed in him. He said, "Neither this man nor his parents sinned, but this happened so that the work of God might be displayed in his life" (v. 3). This means—let us state it frankly—that God had allowed the man to be born blind so that at this particular moment in his earthly life Jesus might come upon him and cure him and that, as a result, God might receive glory. Having said that, Jesus then performed a miracle and restored the man's sight.

Here is our first great lesson from the story. *There are no pat answers to the question of human suffering.* There are answers, of course—we are going to see some of them—but there are no pat answers. Consequently, we cannot say, as some do, that it is the right of every believer to be healthy. This is nonsense. Or that suffering is always the direct result of personal sin. In some cases, suffering is corrective. It is given in order to get us back on the path that God has chosen for us. In other cases, it is constructive. It is given to build character. In still other cases, as here, it is given solely that God might receive glory.

We must not make the mistake of some people who imagine that if someone suffers some great natural catastrophe, it is because God has struck him or her down for some sin. These people imagine God to be a stern, implacable judge, who spends his time watching over people in order to catch them sinning. "I am watching you," God says, "and if you do something you are not supposed to do—whoops!—you did it! So 'BANG'—that's what happens to you." This is not true. What is more, it is a scandal on the name of God. One commentator puts it this way: "God is not up in heaven trying to hit people. God is love. Anyone could testify to the fact that many times he has sinned and has not reaped the fruits of that sin. God has been gracious in a wonderful way. How tender and patient He is with us."[1]

Do not ever imagine that this is God's way. For if you do, you immediately make yourself into a nasty little judge, trying to find out what another Christian has done instead of recognizing that in God's providence all things come to God's people, and that in many cases God simply sends suffering that he might be glorified. In these cases suffering is a great honor, and we should be humbled before it.

Three Errors

Calvin, the great reformer, has some wonderfully wise words for all of us who tend to judge others. First, we should note, he acknowledges that in one form or another suffering does come from sin. If there had never been sin, there would be no suffering. But when we go on from that statement to begin to link up particular suffering in some person with some particular sin, we generally err in one or all of three ways.

"Since everyone is a bitter censor of others," Calvin writes, "few apply the same severity to themselves as they should do. If things go badly with my brother, I at once acknowledge the judgment of God. But if God chastises me with a heavier stroke, I overlook my sins. In considering punishments, every man should begin with himself and spare none less than himself. And so, if we want to be fair judges in this matter, let us learn to be perspicacious in our own evils rather than in those of others.

"The second error lies in immoderate severity. No sooner is a man touched by the hand of God than we interpret it as deadly hatred, and make crimes out of faults, and almost despair of his salvation. On the other hand, we extenuate our sins, and are hardly conscious of faults when we have committed most serious crimes.

"Thirdly, we are wrong to put under condemnation all without any exception whom God exercises with the cross. What we have said just now is undoubtedly true, that all our distresses arise from sin. But God afflicts His people for various reasons. Just as there are some whose crimes He does not avenge in this world, but whose punishment He delays to the future life, to try them the harder, so He often treats His faithful more severely; not because they have sinned more, but that He may mortify the sins of the flesh for the future. Sometimes, too, He is not concerned with their sins, but only testing their obedience or training them to patience. As we see that holy man Job unfortunate beyond all others, and yet he is not beset on account of his sins; but God's purpose was quite different—that his godliness might be the more fully testified in adversity. They are false interpreters, therefore, who attribute all afflictions without distinction to sins; as if the measure of punishments were equal, or as if God regarded nothing else in punishing men than what every man deserves."[2]

God's Purpose in Suffering

There are, then, many false views of suffering, and they must be avoided. But, when that is said, we still want to know the correct views. We still want to know why Christians especially suffer. And, to make it very personal, we want to know why God permits us to suffer in any specific instance. Here only the Word of God gives guidance.

To begin with, we are told that some sufferings are corrective, that is, that God sends some pain in order to get us back on the path he has set before us. Spankings are an illustration here. If a child has done wrong, he needs a spanking; and if he has the right kind of father and mother, he receives one. Why? Because the father and mother delight to inflict pain? Because they do not love the child and therefore do not care about him? Not at all! In fact, the opposite is the case. If they do not love him, they do not spank him; if they do love him, chastisement follows when he has done wrong. Spankings are a necessary part of the child's training, for he must learn that an individual is not free to do whatever he wishes to do, irrespective of the wishes and sometimes the commands of others. Moreover, he must learn through obeying the parent to obey God. In the same way, some suffering is given to teach Christians that sin is wrong and to teach them obedience.

It is along this line that the well-known verses from Hebrews 12 were written. "My son, do not make light of the Lord's discipline, and do not lose heart when he rebukes you, because the Lord disciplines those he loves, and he punishes everyone he accepts as a son. Endure hardship as discipline; God is treating you as sons. For what son is not disciplined by his father? . . . No discipline seems pleasant at the time, but painful. Later on, however, it produces a harvest of righteousness and peace for those who have been trained by it"(vv. 5–7, 11).

The first thing we should do when we are confronted with suffering is to ask God whether or not it is intended for our correction. If it is, then we need to confess our sin or waywardness and return once more to the path set before us.

Constructive Suffering

Second, God sends the believer some sufferings that are constructive. It is by means of these sufferings that God is able to whittle away that which is unpleasing in our lives and form the character of the Lord Jesus Christ within us.

In one of his books, Donald Grey Barnhouse illustrates this process by the task of producing a statue. He writes, "The great artist Benvenuto Cellini tells us in his autobiography how he felt as he stood before a block of marble that had been brought to Florence for him to form into a great statue. Several chapters are devoted to the design and creation of the work of art which still stands in his native city as his greatest monument. Between the rough-hewn block of marble and the finished statue were all the love and care of the artist, and the infinite patience of releasing from stone the vision of beauty which he saw before he began to work. Thus the Heavenly Father is at work in the life of everyone whom he has foreknown as believing in the Savior. There is a difference between ourselves and a block of marble, however, in that we have feelings and can shrink from the strokes with which the divine Sculptor would cut away the marble so that the likeness of Christ may emerge in our lives."[3]

In David's great psalm about the importance of knowing the Bible, the great king tells us that before he was afflicted he went astray, but that after his affliction he obeyed the word of God (Ps. 119:67). Affliction was a factor in his growth. So it is in the lives of many of God's children.

Glory to God

Finally, as in the case of the man who had been born blind, some suffering is merely that the grace of God might be revealed in the life of the Christian. Job was such a person. Lazarus was another. Beyond any doubt, both of these men were sinners and both suffered corrective and constructive sufferings at many different times in their lives. Nevertheless, in the cases of their suffering that are recorded for us in the pages of God's Word (one in the Book of Job and one in John 11), neither constructive nor corrective sufferings are in view but rather that kind of suffering that brings glory to God. In Job's case glory was given in the demonstration, observed by Satan and all the angels, that Job did not love the Lord for what he could get out of him but because the Lord was worthy to be loved and obeyed. This was true regardless of what happened to Job personally. Ultimately Job was vindicated and received his reward.

Would God Almighty permit a man to be stripped of his family and all his possessions, to be struck with such illness that he would find himself sitting in ashes bemoaning that he had ever been born, just so that God himself might be vindicated? Would God permit a man to be struck with total blindness throughout the better part of his life so that in God's own time he might become the object of a miracle performed by the Lord Jesus Christ? Would God permit a child of his to die, bringing suffering not only upon himself but also upon his sisters who mourned for him, just so God could be glorified? In the light of the Word of God we answer not only that God would do such things but that he has done them and, indeed, continues to do them in order that he might bring victory for himself and all believers in that great and invisible war between the powers of good and of evil. Moreover, those who know God well know this and (in part) understand it. They know that God is both perfect and loving and that he does all things well.

When suffering comes we must therefore check out these three possibilities. One, is it corrective, sent by God to return us to the proper path? Two, is it constructive? If so, we should ask him to use it in making us more like Jesus Christ. And three, is it for his glory? If the latter is the case, we must ask God to keep us faithful so that Satan and his hosts may be discomfited and others may learn that we at least are delighted to have God do with us whatsoever he pleases.

114

Jesus, the Worker

John 9:4

"As long as it is day, we must do the work of him who sent me. Night is coming, when no one can work."

The subject of the following study is work, particularly Christian work. And the example for that work is none other than that great worker, the Lord Jesus Christ. In the words we are studying he speaks about his work and gives direction to our own. The text is the fourth verse of John 9: "As long as it is day, we must do the work of him who sent me. Night is coming, when no one can work."

To understand the force of this text we must take it in the context of the chapter, for it follows upon a speculative question that had been asked of Jesus by the disciples. The group had come upon a man who had been blind from birth, and the disciples had asked, "Rabbi, who sinned, this man or his parents, that he was born blind?" In other words, the disciples (who had not yet learned to look on men as Christ looked on them, as people to be loved) saw the man as a philosophical problem, and they were at once ready to debate it. Suffering is related to sin, they reasoned. The man is suffering; therefore sin is involved. So, whose sin is it? This was the line of their thinking.

To Jesus, however, the man was above all a man and, more than that, one on whom he had compassion. So instead of entering deeply into their question—he could have written a book about it—he answered them briefly, while at the same time setting about to heal the man born blind. It is in this connection that he spoke of his work, stressing that he must be about it. He added that the night was coming when no man could work.

We are to learn from this, as Spurgeon said, that "the Savior has a greater respect for work than he has for speculation." Questions are good. There are answers to such questions. Jesus gives them. But there is an eternity to ask and answer questions. What counts now is to work, for the working time is limited and the workers are few. God had sent Jesus to work. He was determined to do that work. If you are a Christian, God has also given you work to do. The conclusion is that you should set about doing that work with the same determination.

A Need to Work

The verse itself is most instructive, however, and the first thought it brings before our minds is the necessity of working. This is indicated by the first phrase, in which Jesus said, "We *must* do the work."

The necessity of working is something that is found throughout Christ's ministry, and it is related to the *will of God* for him. Indeed, it is almost a *leit motiv* of Christ's teaching. The earliest recorded utterance of Jesus makes this point. His parents had taken him to Jerusalem for the Passover when he was twelve years old, and when they left to return to Nazareth Jesus stayed behind in the temple. Joseph and Mary thought he was with the others in their company. When they discovered he was missing, they went back to Jerusalem and, after much searching, found him. He was discussing doctrine with the leaders of the people. "Son, why have you treated us like this?" asked his mother.

Jesus replied, "Why were you searching for me? Didn't you know I *had to* be in my Father's house?" (Luke 2:49).

Years later Jesus began his public ministry and, early in that ministry, came to Capernaum. In Capernaum he cast out demons and healed Peter's mother-in-law who was sick with a fever. As a result of these miracles, many in Capernaum and the area around it urged him to remain with them. But Jesus answered, "I *must* preach the good news of the kingdom of God to the other towns also, because that is why I was sent" (Luke 4:43). In other words, he felt the divine necessity to work in his preaching.

On another occasion a short man named Zacchaeus climbed a tree in order to see Jesus as the crowd in which Jesus was walking passed by. Jesus knew the need of this man's heart and soul. So he stopped at the tree, looked up, and said to the man; "Zacchaeus, come down immediately. I *must* stay at your house today" (Luke 19:5).

Jesus referred to the lifting up of the brass serpent in the wilderness in speaking to Nicodemus, saying, "Even so *must* the Son of man be lifted up"

(John 3:14). He said, "The Son of Man *must* suffer many things and be rejected by the elders, chief priests and teachers of the law, and he must be killed and on the third day raised to life" (Luke 9:22). Later he told his disciples, "Other sheep I have, that are not of this fold; them also I *must* bring, and they shall hear my voice; and there shall be one fold, and one shepherd" (John 10:16). From the beginning of his ministry to the end, Jesus felt a necessity of obedience to the will of God to be resting upon him.

There is another reason why Jesus felt compelled to work. The first was obedience to the will of God. The second, which is no less important, is the *need of men*. In John 8 we read about Jesus being driven out of the temple area. We would feel it to be all right if we found Jesus thinking primarily about his own needs and problems. But he is not. For as soon as he is outside the temple area, by the very gate of the temple, he spots a blind beggar and is immediately taken up with his need and problems. The heart of the Lord Jesus Christ went out to him. Moreover, it was always this way with Jesus. Wherever he looked there were sheep to be gathered and souls to be won. So he worked; the need of men compelled him to it.

It is no different today. Today the need is also great. Men and women are perishing in our time without the gospel and without Christ. They fill our cities and our countryside. There are the poor, the lonely, the outcasts of our society. The need is there. Who will reach them? Will you? Do you feel that you must work? Jesus felt it and, as a result, was a blessing to all who knew him. What have we done to be a blessing to those who are in need?

A third source of the necessity that Jesus felt to work was undoubtedly the *love for others* that filled him. Jesus loved others; hence, he had to go out of his way to work for them.

Do we love others? Or do we see them only as problems, as the disciples saw the man who had been born blind? Do we love others enough to help them? Or do we merely give lectures? There is an illustration of what ought to be done in Christ's story of the loving father and the prodigal son. The son had taken his share of the father's inheritance and had gone off to another country where he had wasted it on low living. When it was gone he returned home and found his father waiting. He said, "Father, I have sinned against heaven and against you. I am no longer worthy to be called your son." The father said—well, what did the father say? Or, to make it more personal, what might we have said had we been the father? Is it not true that we would have been ready first of all to give lectures and to ask questions? "Where have you been?" we might have asked. "What have you been doing? What happened to your good clothes? And where is your money? Don't you know that you have wasted it all, and that it was half of my estate? Waste is not good. You have not played the role of a good steward, even less that of a faithful and loving son. What are we to do with you? What could you possibly expect to receive from me now?" These are the questions and comments we might have made, but this was not the course taken by the father. Instead, he threw his arms about the neck of his son and kissed him—he knew it all anyway, you see—and said, "Bring the best robe and put it on him. Put a ring on his finger and sandals on his feet. Bring the fattened calf and kill it. Let's have a feast and celebrate. For this son of mine was dead and is alive again; he was lost and is found" (Luke 15:22–24).

The story is given to show the love of God the Father and of the Lord Jesus Christ for sinners, and it should be our pattern. Is the man or woman who is steeped in sin repulsive to you? His sin is no less repulsive to the Lord Jesus. Jesus loves him anyway, even to the point of having died in his place. This love should move us. The love of the Lord Jesus Christ should constrain us. It should constrain us to work for the other person's salvation.

Specialized Work

There is a second lesson that comes from Christ's words about work. It is the specialized nature of the work, which Jesus indicates by the next phrase in the sentence. "I must do *the work of him who sent me.*" It was the work of God (and only that) that Jesus felt compelled to do, while it was yet day.

There are many people who can take the first part of this verse and say with great honesty and enthusiasm, "I must work." But there are few who can say, "I must do the work of him who sent me." Take as an example a man who is determined to get ahead in business. He rises early in order to get to the office before most of the other employees. He puts in a long day, skipping coffee breaks, even having his lunch sent in to him. After the others leave, he stays; it is late when he finally starts home. At night he is thinking about his business and planning for the next day. What time and what skill he puts into getting ahead in his work! How strong is his desire! It is a proper desire, of course. If a man wants to get on in the world, he must work. Hard work is good for a person. We would never want to encourage any active man to be idle. And yet—this is the point—Jesus came into the world not to get ahead in business or to get rich, but rather to do the work of him who sent him. It was upon this that he set his desire and bent every activity.

Do we apply the same discipline and enthusiasm that we have in other areas of our lives to the work of God?

Moreover, notice that Jesus was not selective in the works he felt compelled to accomplish. He did not pick and choose. Rather, he said, "We must do the *work* of him who sent me." That is, "We must do all of them." There were works of preaching and of praying, of rebuking and of suffering, finally, even of dying. But whatever they were and whether they were either personally appealing or unappealing—we remember that in the Garden of Gethsemane he sweat as it were great drops of blood as his soul shrank in horror from the spiritual suffering of the cross—Jesus determined to do all of them. Have we? Or have we pulled back from that which is distasteful? There is no doubt that much Christian work remains undone simply because of this: that all Christians have not yet learned that each believer is personally to do the works—all the works—of him who sent him.

Shortness of Time

Third, Christ's words about work also teach us about a limitation of the time allotted to work and, therefore, also about time's shortness. Jesus indicated this by saying, "*As long as it is day,* we must do the work of him who sent me."

These words are striking in the mouth of the Lord Jesus Christ, much more so than if they had been spoken by any mere man or woman. Christ is the timeless God. He lived in eternity past and will be living throughout eternity future. If anyone could have postponed work, surely it was the Lord Jesus. Yet we see him concerned for the moment and aware that the moment was passing. If that is true for Jesus, how much more true is it for us who are entirely creatures of time and for whom time is quickly passing!

Time is passing for ourselves, first of all. We are here today, studying our Bibles, listening to a radio broadcast. But there is not an ounce of assurance that we will be here tomorrow. Death may come. At the very least sickness may be upon us, and the opportunities for service that we have today may be over. Or, again, even if we remain in good health, the time of opportunity may pass for the one to whom we should be bringing the gospel or whom we should be serving.

Are you a preacher? If so, you will not preach to that same congregation for long. Some will die this year, more the next. What are you waiting for? What hinders you from preaching the full counsels of God with all the depth, maturity, and enthusiasm of which you are capable? Richard Baxter once said, "I preach as though I ne'er might preach again, and as a dying man to dying men." That should be your standard.

Are you a Sunday school teacher? If you are, the principle applies to you also. You will not have your children long. You have them for a little less than sixty minutes a week and for less than a year. What will you teach them in that time? What will they learn? For some it may be the only time in their lives in which they will have opportunity to hear about God's love for them in Christ and of his great plans for them. For some it may be the only time in which they will have an opportunity to memorize Scripture.

Are you a mother or a father? Then these truths are for you also. Now is the time to train your children. You must begin while they are young. You will not have them for more than twenty years, and they will be malleable to your teaching for even less than that. You must lead them to faith in the Savior. You must teach them the ways of God with men and help them to develop Christian character. God will not hold you guiltless if you fail to do this; for you are responsible for them, and the time is passing. In this as in other areas "night is coming, when no one can work."

The Night, the Night

Finally, and as a result of this last phase, we must consider the end of things historically. True, there is an end of life for each of us, for those to whom we witness and for ourselves. But it is also true that the night comes in history, so that opportunities for work that a particular age offers can be ended. Today there are great opportunities. How long will they last? Who knows but that a new dark age may soon be upon us?

In an address given on the occasion of his installation as Visiting Professor of Theology at Eastern Baptist Seminary in Philadelphia, Dr. Carl F. H. Henry spoke of the frightening rise of a new barbarianism in our age. "The barbarians are coming," said Henry, as he likened today's onrush of paganism to the barbarian conquest of Christian Rome. They are coming in science, through the misuse of new discoveries. They are coming in communications, as men discover ways to manipulate public opinion for bad ends. They are coming in the religious realm, as institutional Christianity increasingly gives way to the occult, the cults, and Satanism. "Obscure the vitalities of revealed religion," said Henry, "detour churchgoers from piety and saintliness, and in the so-called enlightened nations not only will the multitudes soon relapse to a retrograde morality, but churchgoers will live in Corinthian immorality, churchmen will encourage situational ethics, and the line between the Christian and the worldling will scarce be found."[1]

The night is coming. Jesus said it is coming, and we can sense that it is so. But this is not all we can say. The night is coming? Yes! But Jesus is also coming. And so, the barbarians do not have the future to themselves. The Lord is returning to judge the barbarism and receive his own. One day we must stand before him. That is our hope. We rejoice! At the same time we recognize that it is also a day of reckoning. Have we worked for Jesus? Have we invested those talents that he has given us? God grant that we may and that one day we may hear him say, "Well done, good and faithful servant."

115

The Sixth Miracle

John 9:5–12

"While I am in the world, I am the light of the world."

Having said this, he spit on the ground, made some mud with the saliva, and put it on the man's eyes. "Go," he told him, "wash in the Pool of Siloam" (this word means Sent). So the man went and washed, and came home seeing.

His neighbors and those who had formerly seen him begging asked, "Isn't this the same man who used to sit and beg?" Some claimed that he was.

Others said, "No, he only looks like him."

But he himself insisted, "I am the man."

"How then were your eyes opened?" they demanded.

He replied, "The man they call Jesus made some mud and put it on my eyes. He told me to go to Siloam and wash. So I went and washed, and then I could see."

"Where is this man?" they asked him.

"I don't know," he said.

The miracles recorded in John's Gospel have been chosen with a view to the spiritual lessons they can teach. There are only seven of them—the changing of the water into wine, the healing of the nobleman's son, the curing of the impotent man at the pool of Bethesda, the feeding of the five thousand, Christ's walking on the water, the restoring of sight to the man who had been born blind, and the raising of Lazarus. Many more could have been included. But these were chosen—John says so explicitly—in order that those who read about them might be led to faith in Jesus Christ as the Messiah and the Son of God (20:31).

In John's mind, then, these miracles are particularly significant. They are significant precisely because they teach spiritual truths.

This has been becoming more and more obvious as our study of the miracles has proceeded. The first miracle pictured Jesus at a wedding, making wine. Clearly this reveals him as One who enters into human joys and who actually gives joy; but it is not a terribly profound lesson. Other people could be said to do that. In later miracles, however, we see him as the One who is able to restore lost health, provide for all human needs, and even save people when people do not desire saving. In these later miracles we learn of our terribly lost condition, of God's unmerited election of sinners to salvation, and of the irresistible nature of Christ's grace.

In the sixth miracle—the miracle of the restoring of sight to the man who had been born blind—this is no less true. Hence, we are able to turn to the story, not only for the story itself (it is a very good one) but also for what it has to teach about the nature of our salvation. To do this we look first at the blind man; second, at Jesus; third, at the means employed by Jesus in the miracle; and fourth, at his command. The conclusion is that we are to be saved from our spiritual blindness in the same manner.

The Blind Man

We begin, then, with the blind man. Indeed, it is a pitiable place to begin. There is not much we can say in favor of him at the moment in which Jesus found him. Later he becomes quite tenacious in hanging onto what he knows about Jesus. This is praiseworthy. But at the beginning of the story he is only a blind beggar, condemned by his condition to a life of hopeless deprivation and suffering.

He could not see Jesus, of course. Jesus could see him; but he could not see Jesus, even, we might add, when Jesus stood directly in front of him looking down on him as he sat begging. Perhaps he sensed that someone was there. But he did not know who was there or what his presence signified. It is likely that the man did not greatly value sight, for he had been blind from his birth and hardly had an idea of what it meant to see. Had he lived with good sight for thirty or forty years and then lost it as the result of an accident, or some such thing, we might expect him to have been bemoaning his loss. But he knew none of the world as we receive it through our vision and, hence, could not fully value vision. He knew that he was missing something, of course. But how could he value it properly, having never seen? Finally, notice that he also did not pray for sight. At least, we are not told that he did. He was a beggar. It is a beggar's task to beg. But he did not beg for sight. His condition was hopeless, and what is the use of asking for something that everyone knows cannot happen! The blind man certainly did not expect the miracle that was about to be performed by Jesus.

No, little can be said in favor of this man at the moment Jesus found him. Yet, to be perfectly fair, there is at least one thing. The one circumstance in favor of the blind man is that he was at least in the place where Jesus was likely to go. He had not planned it that way. He sat at the gate of the temple because thousands of people passed through the gate of the temple and he could ask them for alms. Yet, whether he had planned it or not, this was where Jesus passed by. And Jesus found him.

I wonder if that might not describe many who will read these words. I am sure that it will at least describe some. You are like the blind man. To begin with, you cannot see spiritual truths. You have heard the gospel preached— perhaps you have even been reading the Bible as well as Christian books— but you cannot understand what is said, and you cannot see Jesus. Moreover, you do not even properly value what you are missing. Since you have never understood spiritual truths, you hardly have a sense of what they are and therefore cannot value them. Then, as a consequence of this, you have not prayed to understand them. So far as you are concerned, your condition is as it is, and it will never be changed by anything.

What can be said for you in your condition? There is hardly a good thing that can be said. You are lost and blind, and your condition is hopeless— apart from the Lord Jesus Christ. Yet, like the state of the man who had been born blind, there is this at least to be said: you are in a place where Jesus is likely to go. You have not planned it that way, but, nevertheless, you are there. You are reading these words. Perhaps you have been attending a believing church. Perhaps another member of your family has been converted. These are good signs; and I at least am encouraged by them. You cannot see Jesus. But if you are one such as I have been describing, Jesus is seeing you. He is looking down on you, searching you out from head to foot, and thinking of what he is about to do in your life and what he will make of you.

Are you such a one? Then you are just whom he wants. Jesus said, "I am the light of the world" (John 9:5). It is with your darkness that he wishes to deal.

The Man Jesus

Second, I want you to look at the man Jesus. I call him "the man Jesus" because this is what the man who had been born blind called him. After he had been healed by Jesus, the neighbors of the man asked, "How were your eyes opened?" They were not even sure that the healed man was the right man; for, although they thought he was the man who had been born blind, he seemed different and they were unable to account for the miracle. "How were your eyes opened?"

The man replied, "The *man they call Jesus* made some mud and put it on my eyes. He told me to go to Siloam and wash. I went and washed, and then I could see" (v. 11).

Jesus is more than a man. The fact that he healed the man who had been born blind is proof of that, and there are many other proofs as well. Jesus is also God. He is the Alpha and the Omega, the beginning and the end. He is the King of kings and Lord of lords. He is the Ancient of Days. He is Jehovah-jireh, El Elyon, Adonai. He is the Lord of hosts. He is the Savior. Jesus is all these things. And yet—it is also his glory—he is a man, and this is not at all a bad place at which to begin to know him.

What a man he is, this man Jesus! He is a man's man. J. B. Phillips, the author of one of the modern paraphrases of the Bible, sensed this keenly in his translation work and has written of it. "I had deep respect, indeed a great reverence, for the conventional Jesus Christ whom the Church worshipped. But I was not at all prepared for the *unconventional* man revealed in those terse Gospels. No one could possibly have invented such a person: this was no puppet-hero built out of the imaginations of adoring admirers. 'This man Jesus,' so briefly described, rang true, sometimes alarmingly true. I began to see now why the religious establishment of those days wanted to get rid of Him at all costs. He was sudden death to pride, pomposity, and pretence.

"This man could be moved with compassion and could be very gentle, but I could find no trace of the 'Gentle Jesus, meek and mild.' He was quite ter-rifyingly tough, not in a Bulldog Drummond-James Bond sort of way, but by the sheer strength of a unified and utterly dedicated personality. He once (at least) walked unscathed through a murderous crowd. I have known a few, a very, very few, men who could do that. But then I find that this sheer strength was still His after hours of unspeakable agony in the garden of Gethsemane. Those who were sent to arrest Him 'fell back to the ground.' . . . Jesus was a man of such stature and quality that he could remain in com-mand of a situation even when the odds were heavily against him."[1]

This is the kind of man we meet in John 9. Thus, it is no surprise to find that, after his healing, the blind man had thoughts only for Jesus. To this man, Jesus had become the most important person in existence. He did not know much about him; he only knew that he was "the man called Jesus." He had not even seen him; for Jesus had sent him away to the pool of Siloam, where the healing took place. Still, Jesus was closer to him than his neighbors, fam-ily, or the Pharisees.

Moreover, his talk was all about Jesus. He told how Jesus had made the clay, how Jesus had anointed his eyes, how Jesus had sent him to wash in the pool of Siloam, and how (as the result of what Jesus had done) he came see-ing. Indeed, in one sense, the miracle was not complete until he had been found by Jesus the second time and had come to worship him as Lord.

So it will be with you, if you are found by Jesus. You may not know much about him, but for you it will be "Jesus only." You will be able to sing:

> Jesus paid it all,
> All to him I owe;
> Sin had left a crimson stain,
> He washed it white as snow.

May Jesus do for you now that spiritual work that will enable you to see him, believe on him, and, as a result, be able to sing his praises forever.

The Humble Means

Third, there are lessons to be learned from the humble means that Christ employed to perform the miracle. The story tells us that Jesus spit on the ground, made clay from the dust and saliva, and then anointed the sightless eyes of the blind man. Does that offend you? Does it seem inadequate and even foolish? Does it seem harmful? In one sense it probably should; for the gospel, through which God gives spiritual light and sight, is all these things to the unconverted.

It is evidently offensive. For when we speak of it there are those who turn away as though it were coarse, old-fashioned, or beneath their dignity. To these men the age-old gospel of salvation through faith in Christ, who died for our sin, giving his blood as propitiation of God's just wrath—to these men all this seems hopelessly old and irrelevant. It is offensive to some minds. But offensive or not, it is by these means that God saves lost and sinful men. Clay? Yes, but it is clay made by Jesus. Saliva? Yes, but from his mouth. In the same way it is by the gospel declared in the words of Scripture—which came from the mouth of Christ—that God calls men and women to repentance. And it is even by preaching. For, as Paul writes, "God was pleased through the foolishness of what was preached to save those who believe" (1 Cor. 1:21).

There are others—we must admit it—to whom the gospel is not so much offensive as it is inadequate. They point to the deep personal and social needs of men and turn from the gospel, trying rather to meet the need through psychiatry, politics, social action programs, and other devices. Well, let them try. It is good to have workers in all fields. Let them do everything they can. Still, while wishing them well, we will not abandon the gospel; for, simple though it may be, the gospel of salvation through faith in Jesus Christ, believed and acted upon, has transformed millions. The gospel has made countless numbers of men and women into new creatures and, through them, has transformed their environment.

Finally, to some the gospel appears worse than inadequate. It actually appears harmful, just as the anointing of the blind man's eyes with clay might have been supposed to have hindered rather than aided his sight. To such the news of salvation through the unmerited grace of Christ seems actually to encourage sin. For, as they said in Paul's day, "Let us sin, that grace may abound." Is this true? Does our gospel encourage sin? Not at all! On the contrary, the gospel is the greatest purifying power in human life, as every true believer knows. This simple means has been a channel of great blessing and of displaying God's glory.

Will you accept this gospel? If you are still drawing back from it as the leper Naaman drew back from the water of the Jordan River, thinking it to be beneath him, then you have not yet seen your plight to be as desperate as it really is. But if, like the blind man, you know it to be desperate, if you sense that there is no hope for you unless Jesus himself comes into your life and does a miracle—if that is the case, then you will not draw back at the simplicity of that which is preached to you but rather will go on to accept whatever Christ offers and do as he tells you.

The Command

This brings us to our final point: the command. What was it? It was simply, "Go, wash in the pool of Siloam" (v. 7). It was simple; it contains only seven words. It was personal; it was directed to the blind man and to him alone. It involved the test of obedience; for it involved a response to the Lord Jesus Christ. In the same way, the gospel that comes to you is simple—"Believe on the Lord Jesus Christ and you will be saved." It is personal; you must believe. Above all, it is a test of obedience; for the question is, "*Will* you believe? Will you trust Jesus?"

If you are hesitating, the blind man can be your guide. For if you are hesitating, you are blinder than he was by far. What did he do? He was blind, but as the old Puritan divine John Trapp quaintly observed, "He obeyed Christ blindly." As a result of his obedience he immediately received physical sight and entered upon a pathway by which he eventually received true spiritual sight in addition.

What a wonderful thing the Lord Jesus Christ did for this man! What a wonderful thing he is prepared to do for all who obey him! Will you obey him? If so, he will begin by giving you spiritual sight and will end by making all things new.

116

"He Is a Prophet"

John 9:13-17

They brought to the Pharisees the man who had been blind. Now the day on which Jesus had made the mud and opened the man's eyes was a Sabbath. Therefore the Pharisees also asked him how he had received his sight. "He put mud on my eyes," the man replied, "and I washed, and now I see."

Some of the Pharisees said, "This man is not from God, for he does not keep the Sabbath."

But others asked, "How can a sinner do such miraculous signs?" So they were divided.

Finally they turned again to the blind man, "What have you to say about him? It was your eyes he opened."

The man replied, "He is a prophet."

I would like you to imagine for a moment that someone you know has just recently become a Christian and then ask yourself these questions: (1) From whom is the new Christian likely to receive the most encouragement? and (2) From whom is he likely to hear the most disheartening remarks?

Most of us would probably agree that the answer to the first question is: those through whom he became a Christian in the first place; for they naturally have joy in his having believed on Jesus. I am not sure that we would come up with an answer to the second question so easily. What would you say? Many, I am sure, would think that his greatest discouragements would come from those who are avowed enemies of the gospel, perhaps from skeptics or hedonists. Actually, it is probably true that his greatest discouragements would come from those who are outwardly religious, but who do not have the truly transforming love of the Lord Jesus Christ in their hearts.

One commentator says, "The ones who will treat worst the young believer are not open infidels and atheists, but those who are loudest in their religious professions."[1]

Let me give you the following example. A number of years ago my wife and I worked with an older woman who became a Christian at about fifty years of age. She had been a faithful church woman for most of her life, but she had never actually understood the gospel or placed her faith in the Lord Jesus Christ. When she finally understood what it was all about and became a Christian, she found herself filled with joy and her life almost completely transformed. She wanted to tell her minister what happened; so she did. She went to him joyously, thinking that he would rejoice with her. But his reaction was not one of joy. Rather, it was a grim and deflating response. He urged her not to become emotional and above all not to do anything foolish. Later the relationship deteriorated to the point at which he actually asked her to leave his church, and she returned to the small fellowship of people who loved her and through whom she had been saved.

It would be nice if this were a single and unique incident. But, unfortunately, it is not. Instead, it is more like a pattern, and the discouraging words are often sharp barbs and the opposition intense. What about such circumstances? Should the new Christian be encouraged or discouraged? Strengthened or confused? There is a great deal of light to be thrown on this situation by the story of the confrontation between the man who had been born blind (but who had been healed by Jesus) and the Pharisees who were offended by his healing. The conflict was lopsided—between the simple beggar and the self-righteous and cocksure Pharisees. It was intense. But it ended, in spite of the man's excommunication, in his triumph. In short, it was a case of the triumph of fact over theory and of true spiritual experience over closed minds.

The Sabbath Problem

On the surface at least the problem was the old sabbath problem that had arisen early in Christ's ministry.[2] That the man had been healed would have been bad enough, given the facts that he had been healed by Jesus and that the Pharisees hated Jesus for his exposure of their sin. But that he had been healed on the Sabbath and by means of clay that Jesus had made from his spittle and dust—well, this was intolerable!

There was no doubt at all that Jesus had broken the Sabbath—at least as they conceived it. What is more, he had done so previously in the case of the impotent man at the pool of Bethesda (John 5:1–16) and in other instances. In this case there were at least three ways in which he had broken the sabbath laws. First, by making clay he had made himself guilty of working on the Sabbath. The law clearly said, "Remember the Sabbath day by keeping it holy. Six days you shall labor and do all your work, but the seventh day is a Sabbath to the LORD your God. On it you shall not do any work, neither you, nor your son or daughter, nor your manservant or maidservant, nor your animals, nor the alien within your gates" (Exod. 20:8–10). The rabbis had defined this as meaning that a man could not carry a handkerchief from an upstairs room to a downstairs room; that was carrying a burden, and carrying a burden was work. A man could neither light nor extinguish a lamp. He could not cut his fingernails, nor pull a hair out of his beard. Most certainly he could not spit in the dust to make clay; for making clay was manual labor.

Second, Jesus had broken the Sabbath by healing the blind man. According to rabbinic maxims, it was all right to practice medicine if life was in danger; that is, it was permissible to try to keep the patient from getting worse. But on the other hand, it was forbidden to do anything to make him get better. A doctor could not treat toothache, for instance. A person could not put cold water on a sprain. Clearly, since the man who had been born blind was in no danger of dying from his handicap or of getting blinder, Jesus broke the sabbath laws when he healed him.

Finally, as regards the actual method of healing, the law clearly stated that "as to fasting spittle, it is not lawful to put it so much as upon the eyelids." So, since Jesus had done this, he was obviously guilty on this count also.

Jesus was guilty of breaking the sabbath laws as the rabbis of Israel had constructed them. But these were man-made regulations; and Jesus, who understood God's law perfectly, knew it, and simply disregarded them. Moreover, they were actually harmful. For they were means by which those who were fundamentally incapable of keeping God's true law nevertheless buttressed themselves up in the conviction that they were doing all right as religious people, that they were going to earn heaven. They also convinced themselves that they did not need God's grace. If they were doing all right, they did not need a Savior. They did not need Jesus. Besides, within their system they could do almost anything they wished—so long as they did not violate the sabbath laws. Thus, they were ready to kill Jesus for breaking the Sabbath, but they were not prepared to let him heal on it. Later they would be ready to have him crucified, so long as the execution took place before sundown on Friday evening.

This was a horrible system. Religious formalism is always horrible. Yet, it was this that confronted the poor beggar when he was ultimately brought before the Pharisees by those neighbors of his who had witnessed the miracle. We can see it now—the leaders, elegant in their robes and secure in their positions, and the beggar, inelegant and insecure—save in Jesus. We can sense the tension. The man was healed. He had been blind for the whole of his lifetime, and now he was healed! We might expect the leaders to have rejoiced with him. But did they? Not at all! Instead, we see them dredging around in the dark recesses of their minds to discover what they can do about this unfortunate event. Can they discredit the miracle and thereby brand the carpenter from Nazareth a fraud? Or—this would be better yet—can they maneuver the testimony of the blind man to trap him?

As a blind man and as a beggar, this man had no interest for the Pharisees. They would have stepped on him as they made their impressive prayers on the street corners. But now, as a healed man, he was interesting in a negative sort of way. Perhaps he could become their tool to trap Jesus.

A Sharpened Testimony

So they began to ask questions, and the first was how he had received sight. Apparently they had already heard the story; the text says, "The Pharisees *also* asked him how he had received his sight." But this was a formal hearing, perhaps even something of a cross-examination. Would the blind man say something contradictory and thus discredit himself and Jesus? Would he say something that could be used against Jesus? "Tell us again," they said. "Let's hear it from the beginning."

I can almost see the blind man's eyes narrowing as he replies to their question somewhat warily now and quite tersely, "He put mud on my eyes, and I washed, and now I see."

I find this very interesting. For the fact that the man who had been blind replied in such terse language shows that *his testimony to the Lord Jesus Christ was sharpening*. Notice that this version of his testimony is shorter than the version in verse 11. I can imagine that both are shorter than the story he told earlier in the day. Shortly after the healing the man might have told about it with many interesting but irrelevant details. "There I was, sitting by the temple gate," he might have said. "You know, the big one where so many people go in and out. I had gotten there a bit late because there was an unusual number of people on the streets. In fact, back on the other side of the square the crowd was so thick I actually got knocked down. Well, as I was saying, I got there late and took my usual place. You know—off to the right, near the bakery. Then, no sooner was I there than I heard this commotion in the temple courtyard, a great commotion. There was shouting. Someone was yelling, 'Stone him! Stone him!' I listened anxiously. Then the shouting died away and after awhile. . . ." Well, the story might have gone on like that for a long time with much irrelevant detail. But that would have been earlier in the day. Here, when opposed by the Pharisees, the man does not ramble but instead tells his story pointedly. There was much the Pharisees could question. Much might even be uncertain. But this much was at least clear: Jesus had put clay on his eyes; he had washed; he had come away seeing.

Learn that this is what opposition should do to your testimony. It should sharpen it up. When you have great leisure and are among friends, no one will mind (and it may even be quite interesting) if you tell your story with many subjective details. That is all right in those circumstances. But when there is opposition, then something quite different is called for. Your words must count. You must stress basics. What has Jesus done?—that is the important thing. And—equally important—what happened when you obeyed him? If you are giving such a witness, then your words will be effective. We might even say that it is to develop such an ability, in part at least, that God permits opposition to the Christian's testimony.

Growth in Perception

But there is another reason also, as we will see in the story. The man who had been born blind had given his testimony, and the first thing we notice is that it had been effective. The rulers had begun by questioning him. Now they turned to each other, some at least apparently accepting the reality of the miracle. "This man is not from God, for he does not keep the sabbath day," some said. Others replied that he must be of God because it would be impossible for a man who is not of God to do such miracles. They were clearly divided. So the only thing they could think of was to question the blind man again. They asked him for his opinion about Jesus. "What have you to say about him? It was your eyes he opened."

"He is a prophet," the man answered.

Now here is the second thing we notice. It is the second reason why God often permits opposition to the new Christian's testimony. As a result of the conflict *the man had grown in faith*. He had grown in his perception of Jesus. In his first testimony the man had called Jesus only a man. "The man they call Jesus made some mud," he said. He was quite a man, but still the beggar knew no more than this. By the time we come to this point in the story, the man had come to see that calling Jesus a mere man was not enough; hence, he called him a prophet; that is, one who speaks and acts for God (v. 17). Later he advances to the thought that Jesus is One who is worthy to be a teacher and to have disciples (v. 27), then to the perception that he is "from God" (v. 33). Finally, he comes to believe on him as "the Son of God" to whom worship should be given (v. 38). By contrast, the Pharisees start from the view that Jesus is *not* from God (v. 16), question the miracle (v. 18), call Jesus a sinner (v. 24), acknowledge their ignorance (v. 29), and at last are by Jesus pronounced both blind and sinful (v. 41).

Opposition led the blind man into new understanding, and this should be the effect of opposition on us all—if we are faithful in giving our testimony. If a believer is faithful according to the light that he has, more is given to him. As Jesus said, "Therefore consider carefully how you listen. Whoever has will be given more; whoever does not have, even what he thinks he has will be taken from him" (Luke 8:18). In other words, if you would grow in your knowledge of Jesus, tell others what you know already and do not be afraid of opposition.

Be Bold

We have come to the end of our exposition of these verses, and a few words should be said by way of summary and conclusion. There are three main points and one conclusion. First, if you are a genuine believer in the Lord Jesus Christ, conflict will come. You will not always have conflict, but sooner or later in one form or another you will be opposed for the sake of the gospel. So do not be surprised when it happens. Remember that the Bible says, "In fact, everyone who wants to live a godly life in Christ Jesus will be persecuted" (2 Tim. 3:12). It also says, "For it has been granted to you on behalf of Christ not only to believe on him, but also to suffer for him" (Phil. 1:29).

Second, even though conflict will come, you can know that God will not abandon you in the conflict—any more than he abandoned the man who had been born blind. When he was challenged concerning his opinion of Jesus, the man suddenly answered, "He is a prophet." He may not have been able to say that a moment before, but he did in that instant. In his hour of need divine grace did not fail him but rather enabled him to witness a good confession.

Third, when faced with such situations, you can know that God has his purposes in them and you should be encouraged by that knowledge. There may be many purposes, but among them are at least those two that we have seen in the case of the blind man. Opposition will (1) sharpen your testimony and (2) lead you into a deeper understanding of the gospel.

Finally, we may conclude that we, no less than the man who had been born blind, should be bold in our testimony. If the blind man, who had hardly met the Lord Jesus and knew little about him, was bold, why should we not be? On this point Calvin has written wisely, "If he, who did not yet know that Christ was the Son of God, courageously and freely confessed He was a prophet, how shameful is the treachery of those who out of fear either deny Him or are silent, though they know that He sits at the right hand of the Father and from thence will come to be the judge of the whole earth! If this blind man did not quench his tiny spark of knowledge, we should endeavor that a frank and full confession should blaze forth from the full brightness which has shone in our hearts."[3]

117

We Know, We Know

John 9:18–33

The Jews still did not believe that he had been blind and had received his sight until they sent for the man's parents. "Is this your son?" they asked. "Is this the one you say was born blind? How is it that now he can see?"

"We know he is our son," the parents answered, "and we know he was born blind. But how he can see now, or who opened his eyes, we don't know. Ask him. He is of age; he will speak for himself." His parents said this because they were afraid of the Jews, for already the Jews had decided that anyone who acknowledged that Jesus was the Christ would be put out of the synagogue. That was why his parents said, "He is of age; ask him."

A second time they summoned the man who had been blind. "Give glory to God," they said. "We know this man is a sinner."

He replied, "Whether he is a sinner or not, I don't know. One thing I do know. I was blind but now I see!"

Then they asked him, "What did he do to you? How did he open your eyes?"

He answered, "I have told you already and you did not listen. Why do you want to hear it again? Do you want to become his disciples, too?"

Then they hurled insults at him and said, "You are this fellow's disciple! We are disciples of Moses! We know that God spoke to Moses, but as for this fellow, we don't even know where he comes from."

The man answered, "Now that is remarkable! You don't know where he comes from, yet he opened my eyes. We know that God does not listen to sinners. He listens to the godly man who does his will. Nobody has ever heard of opening the eyes of a man born blind. If this man were not from God, he could do nothing."

We live in an age that places great value on knowledge. Since Christians have always done the same we might think that ours would be a great age for Christianity. Actually, this is not the case.

711

Christians claim that they know many important things. They *know* whom they have believed (2 Tim. 1:12). They *know* that their Redeemer lives (Job 19:25). They *know* that they have passed from death to life (1 John 3:14). They *know* that all things work together for them for good (Rom. 8:28). They *know* that when the Lord Jesus Christ returns they shall be like him (1 John 3:2). But such claims generally do not mean much to our contemporaries, and Christians often find themselves asking: Do we indeed know what we claim to know? What do we know? Do we know it for certain? And how is it that we know it?

The basis for our study is the report of the interrogations of the parents of the man who had been born blind and the man himself by the leaders of Judaism, as recorded in John 9. The theme is suggested by the interesting fact that each of the parties is said to have claimed both to know something and not to know something. And since the claims and the reasons for the claims differ, the contrasts afford a means for examining the various types of knowledge, particularly Christian knowledge, as exemplified by the statements of the man who had been born blind.

The parties in the debate are the parents of the man, the Pharisees, and the man himself. We need to look at the claims of each one.

The Parents

The first people who are interrogated are the parents of the man whom Jesus healed. The questioning was an obvious attempt by the Pharisees to discredit the man's testimony; for if they could have gotten the parents to say that the man was not their son or that he was not really blind, then they could have branded the healing a fraud and have attacked Jesus. So they asked, "Is this your son? Is this the one you say was born blind? How is it that now he sees?" (v. 19). The overtones of the question were that the parents were to stop lying and come clean.

They answered, "We know he is our son, and we know he was born blind. But how he can now see or who opened his eyes, we do not know. Ask him. He is of age; he will speak for himself" (vv. 20–21).

Notice that the parents affirm two things: (1) that the healed man was indeed their son and (2) that he was born blind. This was part of what they knew, and they were not afraid to affirm this. On the other hand, there were also two things they denied knowing: (1) how he came to see and (2) who did the miracle. This latter part was not entirely truthful, as is evident even from their testimony. For if they did not know how he was healed, then they would not have known that any person ("who") was involved. That they spoke of a person shows that they had at least heard the story and knew of Christ's role in it.

Why did they not acknowledge what they knew of Christ's role in the healing? John gives the answer when he says that "they feared the Jews." For, he says, they knew that the leaders had already agreed to excommunicate anyone who should confess that Jesus was the Messiah. In our terms we would say that the parents simply did not want to get involved. *They knew, but they did not want to know.* They were afraid to acknowledge what had been revealed to them.

This is an accurate picture of many in our age. The truths of Christianity have been proclaimed to them—perhaps by their parents or friends, or through their church. Intellectually they know and even believe such things. But they do not come out and say so. Were the parents of the blind man true followers of Jesus? We do not know. We can hope so. Failing that, we can hope that they became followers later. But we do not know from the story. Like many today they were afraid to acknowledge Christ for fear of the consequences.

The Pharisees

The second group was composed of the Pharisees who were conducting the interrogation. They also say "we know" and "we do not know." Since they had been unable to extract damaging testimony from the parents of the man who had been blind, they again called the man and began to interrogate him more thoroughly. He apparently had not been present during the questioning of his parents, for when he came back the leaders attempted to finesse a damaging admission out of him by pretending that they had learned the true story during his absence. "Give glory to God," they said. "We know this man is a sinner" (v. 24). There was an exchange of comments, and then they amplified their position. "We know that God spoke to Moses, but as for this fellow, we don't even know where he comes from" (v. 29).

Here is another situation in which a group of people claim both to know something and also not to know something. They claimed to know: (1) that Jesus was a sinner, and (2) that God had spoken through Moses. They claimed not to know Christ's origins. Interestingly enough, however, what they claimed and what they denied were contradictory. For one thing, in claiming not to know Christ's origins they contradicted what they are reported to have said earlier—"We know where this man comes from" (John 7:27). For another, even these statements were contradictory; for if they did not know Christ's origins, they could not know whether he was a sinner or not.

What can describe these men? Unlike the parents, who can be said to have known the truth but were unwilling to admit it, these men can be said to have thought that they knew the truth but actually to have been ignorant of it. *They wanted to know.* They wanted to be known as those who knew. *But where Jesus was concerned they knew nothing.*

Unfortunately, this too describes many in our age, particularly those pseudo-scholars and pseudo-leaders who claim to know all about Christ and Christianity but who have never really come to know Christ personally. This is true of many who write popular books about Jesus, for instance. Every year a number of these books appear, each one pretending to tell the truth about

Jesus because the "truth" has become known through some manuscript discovery or some scientific advance. In one, Jesus will be pictured as a Messiah who planned a crucifixion from which he was to be saved in order to convince his followers that he was fulfilling the Old Testament prophecies. In another he will appear as the leader of an ancient drug cult. Such books are based on distortions of the most flimsy evidence, while at the same time they neglect the weighty evidence of the Gospels. Do these men know Jesus? Not at all. They are modern-day Pharisees; for although they claim to know and want desperately to know, they know nothing.

The Man Born Blind

The third party in the story is the man who had been born blind. What was his testimony? Quite simply, he readily acknowledged that there was much that he did not know—"Whether he is a sinner or not, I don't know" (v. 25). But then he added, "One thing I do know. I was blind but now I see" (v. 25). He could not tell his interrogators everything about Jesus. In fact, he was unable to debate the matter of his person. But one thing he did know and that was that Jesus had changed him; and because he knew it and really knew it, no one was going to shake him from his position.

In this the blind man becomes a type of those who are genuine Christians. *They do not know everything*—the finite cannot exhaust the infinite—but *what they do know they know truly.* And they know it because they have met Jesus personally.

Lack of Knowledge

This is worth some reflection. We have summarized the positions of the parents, the Pharisees, and the man who had been healed. What is it that makes the testimony of the healed man different? Why is his approach to knowledge to be emulated?

First, we notice that he, unlike the others, began with *his limitations in knowledge.* That is, he began humbly. Each of the parties in this report said both "we know" and "we do not know." But both the parents and Pharisees said "we know" first and, only after that, acknowledged that there was something they did not know. The parents said, "We know he is our son, and we know he was born blind. But how he sees now . . . we don't know." The Pharisees said, "We know that this man is a sinner. . . . We know that God spoke to Moses, but as for this fellow, we don't even know where he is from." Both of these groups were most interested in what they did know, and as a result were either cowardly or else knew nothing. The man born blind began with an admission of his ignorance but went on to affirm what he did know as the result of God's revelation.

Here is a great biblical principle. It is that no one can know God by means of the mind or by any other human instrument. The Book of Job asks, "Can you fathom the mysteries of God? Can you probe the limits of the Almighty?" (Job 11:7). The answer that our hearts must give is no, for "the man without the Spirit does not accept the things that come from the Spirit of God, for they are foolishness to him, and he cannot understand them, because they are spiritually discerned" (1 Cor. 2:14).

In Christianity we begin with our ignorance, just as we begin with our sin. We acknowledge both our inability in spiritual things and our shortcomings. Thus, we acknowledge that unless God chooses to reveal himself—which he has done in his Word and in Jesus Christ—we can know nothing.

Second, we notice from what is told us of the blind man that, starting from his own lack of knowledge, he was thereby prepared to recognize *the absence of knowledge in others.* In this case, he recognized the great ignorance of the so-called educated ones, the leaders of the people. This is the most humorous part of the controversy. The Pharisees had come to him with great claims— "we know, we know"—and they had spoken disparagingly of Jesus. "But as for this fellow, we don't even know where he comes from." But this was a fatal admission before their very shrewd witness, and he at once seized upon it.

"Now that is remarkable," he said sarcastically. "You don't know where he comes from, yet he opened my eyes" (v. 30). They did not know even the most basic things about Jesus, and the man who had been healed at once saw this—because he had recognized his own limitations.

This sounds contradictory, and yet it is true. Who are those who are most likely to be taken in by authority? We answer: the foolish. But who are the foolish? The answer to that question is not necessarily "those who are uneducated" and most certainly not "those who are aware of their own lack of knowledge." The answer is those who are overly sure of what they think they know. Thus, you will find professors being swept up into foolish theories by other professors, and ministers being led into nonsense concerning Christ by doctors of theology.

Third, having eliminated a false self-confidence as well as an unjustified confidence in the Pharisees, the man who had been born blind was left with *what he truly did know.* "Whether he is a sinner or not, I don't know. One thing I do know. I was blind but now I see" (v. 25). He had eliminated the fringe areas, you see. Oh, he would get to these later. In fact, he would become quite sure of some of them later on. But here, in the midst of the debate, he took his stand upon the certainties; and for him the certainty was that he had been healed by Jesus.

What are your certainties? Do you have any? You do, if you have been touched by Jesus. In this regard I think of Martin Luther. Luther was not always the great victor in debates that we sometimes imagine him to be. He was sometimes pressed into making admissions that he did not intend to make when he first entered the discussion. At Leipzig, in a debate with John Eck, Luther came to admit that the Hussites and other early reformers "were not all wrong." At Worms he admitted that the councils of the church had erred. At times Luther admitted his own lack of knowledge, for, as he said, he was "only a man and not God and was liable to make mistakes." Nevertheless, the more he was pressed, the more certain Luther became of that which he did know—namely, that salvation was by grace through faith and that the Word of God was powerful and would ultimately prevail.

If you are uncertain about spiritual matters, then you need to get your eyes off yourself and others and onto Jesus. What has he done? What has he said? What has he revealed about God? What has he made known to you? Spiritual knowledge is based upon the intervention of God in history and the personal revelation of God by the Holy Spirit to the human soul.

Knowing More

Finally, we notice that what the man who had been born blind truly knew (even though it was small) became the basis upon which *he went on to learn more*. His starting point was only this: that Jesus had healed him. But he went on to develop that point so that he came to know that Jesus was no mere man, but was God.

What the man comes to see in this final exchange with the Pharisees is remarkable—actually, the basic tenets of revealed religion. The Pharisees had argued that Jesus was a sinner, and the blind man had declared himself unable to argue with that proposition. He only knew that Christ had healed him. As he thought about it, however, he found that he could say more. First, he knew that God does not hear sinners; that is, that sinners have no claim upon him. This point involves the whole doctrine of man's spiritual depravity, his hopelessness in sin. Second, he declared that God does hear those who do his will; that is, those who are in a right relationship to him. This is a declaration of the fact that God has revealed his will and that salvation is possible. Finally, the man argued that since God had heard Jesus in the matter of his own healing, Jesus must be in God's will in a special way and must therefore be "of God." In other words, Jesus becomes the Savior of man because of who he is and of his origins.

So it is for all Christians as they grow in knowledge. They do not know exhaustively, but they do know truly because they know on the basis of God's written and incarnate revelation—and they grow in knowledge. The Scriptures say, "The path of the righteous is like the first gleam of dawn shining ever brighter till the full light of day" (Prov. 4:18).

118

Last Resort of the Unconverted

John 9:34

To this they replied, "You were steeped in sin at birth; how dare you lecture us!" And they threw him out.

The last resort of the unconverted is, simply, to refuse to listen. The subject comes to us from John 9:34. This verse concludes the report of the conversation between the man who had been born blind (but who had been healed by Jesus) and the Pharisees. The man who had been blind had seen the true purpose of the Pharisees' questioning—they were trying to trap Jesus—and he had begun to rebuke them for their unbelief. They were offended, naturally. So we read, "To this they replied, 'You were steeped in sin at birth; how dare you lecture us!' And they threw him out."

This is our text. It teaches that being defeated by the man's arguments, the Pharisees tried excommunication rather than acknowledge Christ's claims.

This is something that often happens. Sometimes it is official, as in this case. At other times it is more disguised. Not long ago I heard of a couple who were witnessing to one of their relatives by sending him books and other Christian literature. The material was received for a time, but eventually the answer came back—"I am glad to receive letters from you, but I am tired of receiving the literature. Please stop." They had to stop; but, fortunately, the relative later became a Christian through other channels. In many instances a person does the same thing by changing the subject whenever spiritual matters are brought up. To give one final example, I learned of a case in which a woman was witnessing to a certain man who became so exasperated by her witness that he knocked her down. In this case the man himself did not become a Christian, but another man who saw the incident began coming to church as a result, and eventually believed on Jesus.

There are many different ways of closing one's mind to the gospel; and it is one of these, a means often used by religious leaders, that we find in our story. The blind man was excommunicated. We also find this repeated many times in church history.

Four Attempts

To understand this fully we need to understand that excommunication was only the last of four attempts by the Pharisees to avoid the supernatural support that the miracle of healing gave to Christ's claims. The Pharisees did not refuse to listen at first. They began by trying to discredit the miracles, or, as they would have said, to uncover the true story. When that failed they tried to separate the miracle from Jesus; that is, they did not deny that the healing had taken place, but they denied that Jesus was the cause. Third, they retreated into law—"We know that God spoke to Moses." It was only at the last, when these attempts had proved inadequate, that they threw out the blind man.

The most interesting thing about these attempts to avoid the force of Christ's claims is that they are precisely the attempts that have been played out in church history.

Take the first one. This was the attempt to uncover the "true" story behind the healing and so do away with the miracle. It was what was involved in the early questioning of the man and his parents. We see this particularly in the nineteenth century. This might even be called the history of the nineteenth century so far as biblical scholarship is concerned. In the nineteenth century, rationalists, who had become rationalists as the result of their secular educations, confronted the obviously supernatural element in the biblical narratives. These men called themselves Christians, which meant that they had to have some well-thought-out relationship to the Bible. But here were books, claiming to be by eyewitnesses of the events of biblical history, in which the supernatural was prominent. What were they to do? The only thing to do was to attempt to discredit the miracles. So, many years were spent in trying to explain how what seemed to be miracles actually happened. Thus, we find men writing that, in the incident referred to in John 6, Jesus was not actually walking upon the water but rather was standing in shallow water at the lake's edge. He was thought to be walking on water because the night was dark and cloudy and the disciples thought that they were still far from land. Or again, the miracle of the multiplying of the loaves and fishes was said to be accomplished through the foresight of the disciples who had stored sufficient food in a cave and who passed it up secretly to Jesus who, thereby, seemed to be making it multiply. Others suggested that what actually happened was that all the people, moved by the generosity of the young lad, shared their lunch.

It is hard to believe today that such theories were actually taken seriously. But they were, and in some cases they were obviously made in good faith. The men who made them thought that by stripping away the supernatural they would get to the true heart of the story, like getting to the nut after taking off the shell. What they found was that they were dealing with something more like an onion than a walnut. What happens when you take away the outer layer of an onion? You find another layer inside. Take away that layer, and another layer is visible. By the time all the layers are removed there is nothing left. This is precisely what happened in biblical scholarship. The supernatural was removed, but there was nothing left—at least nothing that was even vaguely reminiscent of Christianity. To summarize: the scholarship of the nineteenth century resulted in this, either a supernatural Bible with a supernatural Christ or no Bible and no Christ at all. The interesting thing is that in following this line of study it turned out to be the scholars themselves (like the Pharisees), rather than the miracles, who were discredited.

The second attempt by the Pharisees was to separate the miracle from Jesus. That is, they accepted the miracle—they could hardly deny it—but they denied that Jesus (whom they hated) was the one responsible. The argument went: "Give glory to God. We know this man is a sinner" (v. 24).

Unfortunately, this too has been played out in history. One example is theological. Following their failure in the nineteenth century to discredit the miraculous, scholars tried to divorce the so-called heart of Christianity from anything objective; that is, to divorce Christian experience from the actual life, death, and resurrection of Jesus of Nazareth. It is not so much what Jesus actually said and did that is important, we were told, but rather what Jesus means to Christians today. It would not matter if the body of Jesus should be found as the result of some archaeological expedition, so the argument went. That would disprove a literal, bodily resurrection. But the important thing is that what Jesus stood for continues to live in our hearts. That would continue in spite of the discovery. The answer to this argument is that it would not continue. In fact, if it were not for the literal resurrection of Jesus, there would be nothing to continue, for Christianity would have been forgotten about and buried long ago. No one can successfully separate cause from effect. So if there is a genuine Christian experience, there must be a genuine Christ, the Christ of the Gospels, to account for it. Without this cause there is no valid experience and no Christianity.

The attempt to separate Christianity from Christ is done in less scholarly ways whenever a person attempts to explain away conversion to Christ by calling it the product of wish-fulfillment, escapism, high-pressured sales techniques on the part of an evangelist, or some such thing. This is an attempt to separate the results of conversion from the Christ who has produced the conversion, and this too is foolish. Besides, it will never have much effect on the one who is converted. If he has really met Christ, he knows that the historic, objective Christ is inseparable from the experience.

Third, the Pharisees retreated into law or, as we could equally well say, into tradition. They could not discredit the miracle. They could not separate the miracle from Jesus. So they said in effect, "We do not know how this happened or what part Jesus may have had in it, but we do know that God has spoken to us through Moses; and this is all we need to know. So don't bother us. We are all right with our traditions." It is sad but true that traditions, even good traditions, have closed many hearts to the gospel.

The blind man also challenged this attempt to escape Christ's miracle. For he pointed out, rightly, that even the principles of the law encourage belief in Jesus. Would they retreat into traditions? Well, the best of these traditions should have caused them to be looking for Christ, to have recognized him when he came, and to have followed him and to have believed on him as the Savior. At this point, the Pharisees simply closed their ears and had the man removed from their assembly.

Strong Testimony

This brings us to the excommunication itself and to the fact that it often is the inevitable result of strong testimony. Fail to confess Christ, go along with the world and its values, compromise the standards of Christian conduct, and the world will welcome you. But confess Christ boldly, live as a Christian, and you will soon find yourself unwelcome in the world's assemblies.

A number of years ago, during the First World War, Donald Grey Barnhouse had the opportunity of leading the son of a prominent American family to the Lord. The young man was in the service. So when he professed to accept Christ as his Savior, he immediately made public testimony to that fact among the soldiers of his company. In time the war ended and the day came when he was to return to his prewar life in the wealthy suburb of a large city. He talked to Barnhouse about it and shared his fears that he might soon slip back into his old habits among his old friends. Barnhouse told him that he would not have to give these people up. Instead, they would give him up—if he made public confession of his faith in Jesus Christ. As a result of their conversation the young man agreed to tell the first ten people of his old set whom he met that he had become a Christian.

The soldier left his unit and went home. Almost immediately—in fact, while he was still at the suburban station at the end of his return trip—he met a girl whom he had known. She was delighted to see him and asked how he was doing. He told her, "The greatest thing that could possibly happen to me has happened."

"Oh," she exclaimed, "you're engaged to be married!"

"No," he told her. "It's even greater than that. I have taken the Lord Jesus Christ as my Savior." The girl's expression froze; she mumbled a few polite words and quickly went on her way. A short time later the new Christian met a young man whom he had known. The young man informed him that there would be some good parties now that the soldier had returned. "I've just become a Christian," the soldier said. Again it was a case of frozen smiles and a quick change of conversation. After this the same circumstances were repeated with a young couple and with two more old friends. By this time the word had gotten around, and soon friends stopped seeing him. He had become peculiar, religious, and—who knows?—they may even have called him crazy! What had he done? Nothing but confess Christ! But the same confession that had aligned him with Christ had separated him from those who did not want him.

So it will be for all who are faithful in their testimony. If you are a Christian, it is not good to be spoken well of by everyone (Luke 6:26). All will not believe. And yet, you are to bear a testimony so that by the grace of God you might win some.

The Arms of Jesus

Finally, we need to see the results of the Pharisees' action upon the man who had been blind. In the first place, it was a great honor for this man. He might not have felt it and was probably a dejected man when Christ later found him and revealed himself to him. Nevertheless, it was an honor to him to be ejected from the company of those who would not have Jesus.

So it is today. Believe me when I say that it is an honor to be thrown out of some churches. It was an honor when Martin Luther was expelled from the Roman Church in the sixteenth century. It was an honor when Calvin was forced to leave France for Geneva because of his testimony. Thus were the Waldenses, Huguenots, Covenanters, and Puritans treated. Thus are some treated today, and it is not tragic. It is an honor, as I have said. In many cases excommunication has been the brightest moment of some Christians' careers.

But then notice what the excommunication did. The gospel tells us that the Pharisees cast the man out. This was true. But to what did they cast him out? They cast him into the arms of Jesus. If there had been no one waiting, this might have been bad. It would have been bad to have been alone—without family, friends, spiritual counselors, or the benefits of the synagogue. But to be cast into the arms of Jesus—well, what could be better than that? His are great arms. In his arms we can each find all we need. Do you need strength? The arms of Jesus are strong arms. Do you need love? The arms of Jesus are loving arms. Do you need comfort and protection? You will find comfort and protection there. Jesus is waiting. Do not be afraid. The Scriptures say, "Though my father and my mother forsake me, the LORD will receive me" (Ps. 27:10).

It is easy to apply these truths to each person who is reading this book. If you are a Christian, first of all, do not be afraid to witness. Be bold in your witness. The worst that can happen is that you will be rejected, but that is not bad if at the same time you are received by Jesus. So do not hesitate to be identified with Jesus. Speak and allow him to use your testimony. Tell what you know and allow God to use that in bringing many others to the Savior.

Finally, if you are not yet a Christian, why should you not learn from this story? I do not say that you have been doing all that the Pharisees did, or, if you have been doing these things, that you have been doing them consciously. Yet this may be the case. You may have been trying to deny the miracles. That is why those popular books that seek to explain the "true" origins of Christianity appeal so strongly to you. Perhaps you have been seeking to detach the fruit of Christian experience from Jesus. That is why you are so concerned to prove that a Christian you know has become a Christian only because someone has pressured him into it or because he is seeking to fulfill some inner need. Perhaps you have been retreating into tradition. Perhaps you are just refusing to listen. I do not know where you stand, but if you stand here, do not refuse to listen any longer. Open your ears. Hear the voice of Christ. Believe him. Turn to him. Throw yourself upon him. Receive him as your Savior.

119

A Question for Everyone

John 9:35–38

Jesus heard that they had thrown him out, and when he found him, he said, "Do you believe in the Son of Man?"

"Who is he, sir?" the man asked. "Tell me so that I may believe in him."

Jesus said, "You have now seen him; in fact, he is the one speaking with you."

Then the man said, "Lord, I believe," and he worshiped him.

We have already studied the story of the man who had been born blind sufficiently to be aware of the situation at this point. The man had been healed by Jesus. But as the result of his healing and of his testimony before the Pharisees, the man had been rejected, first by his family and friends, then by his church and nation. The man was undoubtedly dejected. Yet, this man, who had been rejected by everyone else, was not rejected by Jesus. We read that Jesus, when he heard that the man had been excommunicated, sought him out and asked him a question. It is unlikely that there are many reading this who have literally been excommunicated, though there may be some. Nevertheless, I am sure that many are in a similar condition. You feel cut off from other people and perhaps from God. It may even be that you have cut yourself off, for the knowledge of what you have done burns in your conscience, telling you that there is no hope for you of God's pardon. If that is the case, then you must listen to this great question and answer it. It is a question by which God can do you good.

Notice that this was Jesus' purpose in asking the question of the man who had been born blind. Unasked, he had been healed by Jesus. Unsought, he had been found by Jesus. Now, by this question he is helped to make a considerable advance in his faith. The man knew something about his benefactor already. He knew that he was a man called Jesus (v. 11). He had come to see that he was a prophet (v. 17). Later he began to understand that Jesus was from God; for, as he said, "If this man were not from God, he could do nothing" (v. 33). Nevertheless, the man who had been blind still did not know all that Jesus intended for him to know. So Jesus came with a question that was to bring him to the place where he was able to fall down and worship him—"Do you believe in the Son of Man?"

This was the question by which Jesus sought to do the man good, and it is the question by which I seek to do you good at this moment. Will you ask it of yourself? There is no more important question that can either be asked or answered.

An Important Question

Let me justify the fact that this is an important question. It is important, first of all, because it concerns salvation, and salvation is important. Here is a picture of Jesus coming to a man whom he had helped physically (he had enabled him to see) and whom he had also helped intellectually. But these two areas of life were relatively unimportant compared with the salvation of the man spiritually. So Jesus asked a question designed to quicken his faith and lead him to place his trust in Jesus himself regarding salvation. The situation is repeating itself today. There are many things in your mind that you think are important and that the world judges to be important, but none of them are as important as the great matter of salvation that I am pressing upon you. Do you believe on Jesus? The Bible stresses the importance of this matter when it asks properly, "What good is it for a man to gain the whole world, yet forfeit his soul?" (Mark 8:36).

Second, the question is important because it concerns the only way of salvation. It is not the case that there are many roads, all of which lead to heaven. Many believe this, but it is not true. It is not the case that there are many ways by which a man can become right before God, but rather that Jesus is himself "the way and the truth and the life" (John 14:6). It is because of who Jesus is that he is able to save sinners. He is God and, as God, is able to die for an infinite number of sins. He does what no mere man can do. Therefore, salvation is by him, through him, in him, of him. Indeed, as the Scriptures say, "Salvation is found in no one else, for there is no other name under heaven given to men by which we must be saved" (Acts 4:12).

In Christianity salvation is something achieved by Jesus. Hence, Jesus is at the center of Christianity as no other individual is in any other religion.

When Buddha, just prior to his death, was asked by his disciples how best they might remember him, Buddha replied that they were not even to trouble themselves by such a question. His point was that it did not matter whether or not they remembered him. What mattered was his teaching, his teaching of the *Way*. In this respect, his teaching had the characteristics nearly of a truth of science, which exists entirely apart from the one who discovers it. This is not the way of Christian truth, for Jesus pointed men and women to himself. In our text he asks, "Do you believe in the Son of Man?" Later he instituted the Lord's Supper with the words, "This is my body, which is for you; do this in remembrance of me. . . . This cup is the new covenant in my blood; do this whenever you drink it, in remembrance of me" (1 Cor. 11:24–25).

A person can gain a better feeling for the importance of Jesus as the sole way of salvation by imagining how the situation with the man who had been healed might have been approached by someone from another religion or with another commitment. If this had been Buddha himself or another teacher of an eastern religion, the teacher might have spoken to the man of the unimportance of the details of this life. The important thing is peace of mind, he might have been told. Therefore, the proper course is detachment as a first step in attaining to the divine life. If this had been one of our modern churchmen, the churchman might have been distressed by the rupture between the man who had been born blind and Judaism. Without Judaism he was cut off from the sacraments of Israel. Hence, the proper course (the man would have been told) would be a reconciliation with the religious leaders. If the man had been approached by one of our modern pastors, the kind who feels that pastoral counseling is more important than a proclamation of the Word of God, the healed man might have been asked to explore his own feelings and see whether he might not be able to accept the situation. This was not Jesus' way. Jesus was concerned with the man's salvation, and he knew that the man's salvation depended at its base upon the man's relationship to himself. Did he believe on Jesus? That was the question. So Jesus comes asking him about it—"Do you believe in the Son of Man?"

Do you believe in the Son of Man? The question is important because it concerns salvation and because it concerns belief in the Lord Jesus Christ as the sole means of salvation.

No Substitute

Third, the question is important because of the fact that no other experience eliminates the need to answer it. Think of this man for a moment. Think of all that he had already gone through. First of all, he had already been *obedient* to Jesus. Jesus had found him by the temple gate, had made clay of the dust, and had anointed the blind man's eyes. Jesus had said, "Go, wash in the Pool of Siloam." This the man did. We are told that as a result of his obedience he found himself seeing. Moreover, we do not read even of any hesitation in the man's obedience. He might have hesitated. He might have argued that the pool was far away and that nothing was to be gained by washing, so far as he could discern. But he was not another Naaman, who hesitated on the banks of the Jordan—"Are not Abana and Pharpar, the rivers of Damascus, better than any of the waters of Israel?" (2 Kings 5:12). The blind man obeyed immediately and without quibble. Still the Lord came to him with the great question, "Do you believe in the Son of Man?" The question needed to be asked even though the blind man had been unhesitatingly obedient.

It is the same with many. You may not have been obedient to what you know of Christ's teachings; if so, it is a fault. But you may have been obedient, and even then you need to face this question: "Do you believe on Jesus?" No religious observances, however perfectly carried out, can save you. You must believe on Jesus.

Then too, the man had passed through considerable *experiences* as the result of his obedience. He had been born blind, but as the result of Jesus' intervention in his life he had come to see. How could he forget the long years of darkness? He had lived in the dark throughout his youth and through much of his manhood. But now Jesus had healed him, and the light that he had never known before streamed in upon him. Here was a great change. It was a great experience. Still he needed to answer Christ's question: "Do you believe in the Son of Man?"

In the same way, the question needs to be asked of such persons today. Are you one who has tried to substitute religion, even Christian experience, for true faith? Perhaps you have been to a meeting in which the preaching has been eloquent and the spirit enthusiastic. Perhaps you have been moved to tears in such a meeting. Perhaps you have even come forward in response to an invitation. Perhaps you have received the so-called baptism of the Holy Spirit so that you have been able to speak in tongues or some such thing. Even you need to face this question. Experiences do not save anyone. Only Jesus saves. Consequently, you need to examine your relationship to him. Do you believe on Jesus? Jesus knows that changes have taken place in your life, just as he knew that changes had taken place in the life of the man who had been born blind. Yet he presses this question upon you.

Notice also that the blind man had borne a courageous *testimony* for Jesus, yet he still needed to answer this question. And what a great testimony he gave! It was not more than he knew. It was all that he knew. It was so well grounded in fact and so well supported by reason that it confounded the arguments even of the religious leaders of his day. Yet Jesus seeks him out and asks him this question. Are you such a one? Perhaps you have grown up in a Christian church and have even been asked to give a testimony on occasion. You have done it. You have spoken of the blessing of God in your life. You have spoken of Jesus, perhaps even of the fact that he died on the cross and that you are thankful that he loved you enough to do it. Yet you have never really believed on him. Such things are possible. And since they are possible the question I am asking is for everyone. Do you believe on Jesus? This question is for elders. It is for deacons. It is for Sunday school teachers. It is for parents, grandparents, and children. Do you believe on the Son of God? God grant that you may be able to answer that affirmatively and with full confidence.

Finally, notice that the man had also *suffered* for the cause of Christ. He gave his testimony to Christ and then had been thrown out of the synagogue. He was a dejected man when Christ found him. Still Jesus asked this question. In the same way, you may have suffered for Christ's cause and still have failed to believe on him unto salvation. Have you believed? Do not fail to ask yourself this question today and do not fail to answer it as Jesus wants you to do. Say, "Yes, Lord, I do believe on you. I believe that you died for my sin, and I do place my faith in you for salvation."

An Inescapable Question

A few more things need to be said in conclusion. First, you need to know that if you do not face this question now, you must face it later; for the question itself is inescapable. The very nature of the question makes it inescapable. Your answer must be a yes or a no. A maybe is a no. A delayed answer is a no. Even to fail to answer it entirely is a no. So if you have heard it, you must answer it. In addition, however, it is also true that you must answer it in the day of God's judgment, even if you have tried to avoid it in this life. This will be the basis of God's judgment. Have you believed on Jesus? If you have not yet believed, now is the time to do so.

Second, you should know that the question can be settled now. Perhaps you have agreed with me that this question is important, and you want to believe. Well, then, you can, In one of his messages, the great Baptist preacher Charles Haddon Spurgeon tells of a pastor whom he knew who had become converted suddenly in the midst of one of his own sermons. The pastor was much like the man who had been born blind. He had obeyed Christ. He had passed through considerable spiritual experience. He had witnessed for Christ. He had even suffered for him to some degree. Nevertheless, he was not converted. One Sunday as he was preaching he was taken up with the truth of the gospel. He was so taken up with it, in fact, that it affected his normal mode of speaking and he found himself declaring the truth concerning Christ's death with utmost conviction. The congregation began to notice the change. At last a Methodist, who was in the church, shouted out, "The preacher is converted; hallelujah!"

The others said, "Well, we believe he is too."

The pastor stopped preaching and added, "I believe you are right. Something wonderful has happened to me. I do believe on Jesus." Then all together they stood and sang "Praise God from whom all blessings flow." The question can be settled now. It can be settled instantly.

Finally, you should know that if you are having difficulty answering this question, you can have help from Jesus. You may be saying, "I would like to answer yes to this question, but I do not know that I can. I am not sure that Jesus is the Son of God or that I can believe on him." If that is the case, do what the man who had been born blind did. Ask Jesus to help you.

The man had been cast out, and Jesus had come to him asking, "Do you believe in the Son of Man?"

The man did not know whether he did or not because he did not know who the Son of Man was. So he turned to Jesus and asked him, "Who is he, sir? Tell me so that I may believe in him" (v. 36).

At this point Jesus revealed himself to the blind man. He answered his question, "You have seen him now; in fact, he is the one speaking with you" (v. 37). As a result the man born blind believed and worshiped him.

If you are having difficulty with these matters, turn to the One who helped the blind man. He has already helped you much or you would not even be considering the question. You would not even understand what it means unless he had already given you understanding. Well, then, turn to him. Ask him, "Who is he, Lord, that I should believe on him?" If you do, he will point you to himself and will lead you to true faith. Do you believe in the Son of Man? Let your heart say, "Yes, I believe." Then tell someone else about it.

120

Are We Blind Also?

John 9:39–41

Jesus said, "For judgment I have come into this world, so that the blind will see and those who see will become blind."

Some Pharisees who were with him heard him say this and asked, "What? Are we blind too?"

Jesus said, "If you were blind, you would not be guilty of sin; but now that you claim you can see, your guilt remains."

I am fairly certain that the biblical writers never heard a joke in the "good news/bad news" category. But I am equally certain that the apostle John would have understood if someone had told him that parts of his Gospel have those characteristics. A good news/bad news joke is one like that involving the captain of a slave galley. The captain comes to the slaves one morning and asks them to put down their oars. Then he says, "Gentlemen, I have some news for you. Some of it is good and some of it is bad. I'm going to give you the good news first. Tomorrow we're going to dock at Caesarea, and you will all be getting shore leave. There will be plenty of parties, and you can all do anything you want. Now, the bad news. Today, the admiral wants to go water skiing."

Parts of John's Gospel have those characteristics. Thus we find a statement of the best news—that anyone who believes on the Lord Jesus Christ will be saved—followed by the worst, namely, that any who do not believe not only will be condemned but are condemned already. The difference lies in the fact that in John's case the good news/bad news is not funny.

This comparison is seen in the third chapter between verses 16 and 18—"For God so loved the world that he gave his one and only Son, that whoever believes in him shall not perish. . . . Whoever does not believe stands condemned already." The contrast appears in chapter 12, in the words of Jesus—"I have come into the world as a light, so that no one who believes in me should stay in darkness. . . . There is a judge for the one who rejects me, and does not accept my words" (vv. 46, 48). The same is found in our text. In the verses we have just looked at we have discovered a great question used by Jesus to assist the growth in faith of the man born blind—"Do you believe in the Son of Man?" Now we see the dark side of the matter, as Jesus declares, "For judgment I have come into this world, so that the blind will see and those who see will become blind" (John 9:39).

Christ's Present Judgment

The way in which the statement is put should at once show us the nature of the present judgment about which Christ is speaking. It should also help us understand why there is no real contradiction between this verse and others in which Jesus says that he has not come to judge. In 12:47 Jesus says, "I did not come to judge the world but to save it." But that verse obviously is speaking of the immediate object of his coming—to die for our sin. In our text he is speaking of the indirect moral effect on everybody of his presence in the world, according to which some believe on him and others reject him.

We are helped to understand the nature of this effect by the illustration regarding the sun's light that we used earlier.[1] The purpose of the sun is to warm things and make plants grow. Coupled with the effect of the warm spring rains the sun will make seeds germinate and will bring plants to flower and trees to foliage. At the same time, however, the light will also drive away the creatures of darkness, so that bugs and crawly things will slither away into dark places if the light of the sun is suddenly made to shine upon them. These were precisely the effects that the Lord Jesus Christ had on his contemporaries. He was the light of the world, as he said (John 8:12; 9:5). As the light of the world he caused faith to sprout and that which was alive spiritually to grow. A perfect example is the growth of the man who had been born blind. On the other hand, he also repelled the religious leaders who, as creatures of darkness, hated him and wished to extinguish his light.

In these concluding remarks on the incident of the healing of the blind man, Jesus says this in terms of blindness and sight. To some, like the man born blind, he was the restorer of spiritual sight. To others, like those who thought they could see, he caused an even greater darkness.

Moreover, if this was true of the moral effect of his life (which it is), it is more true of the effect of his death by crucifixion; for it is at the cross that the division concerning Christ is most apparent. Most persons do not have trouble accepting Jesus of Nazareth as a teacher. There have been many teachers in the long course of the world's history. There will be many more. We would be badly off without them. Hence, Jesus as a teacher is not offensive. But Jesus crucified—well, that is another matter. For a Jesus crucified speaks of man's inability to save himself, of the supremacy of Jesus by which he alone is able to make atonement for sins, of the truth that there is only one way of salvation, and that there is a future judgment against sin for any who reject him. Because of these truths the cross is indeed a stumbling block to the Jews and foolishness to the Greeks, as the apostle Paul discovered through his preaching (1 Cor. 1:23).

Years ago, on a trip through the western part of the United States, I visited a point along the Continental Divide high in the Rocky Mountains of Colorado at which the waters of a small stream separate in order to begin two long and very diverse journeys, one leading to the Atlantic Ocean on the eastern coast of the United States, the other to the Pacific Ocean on the west. The dividing point is a rock in the middle of the stream. One drop of water striking that rock might turn west, with the result that it would flow into a small stream that in turn flowed into another one and another one until it entered the White River of Utah, then the Grand River, followed by the Colorado, the Gulf of California, and eventually the Pacific Ocean. Another drop, turning east, would flow through various small streams into the North Platte River and from there into the Missouri, Mississippi, Gulf of Mexico, and the Atlantic. The destinies of the two drops are entirely different, though the turning point is a very small one at the rock. In the same way, the cross of Jesus is the rock that is the true turning point in man's destiny. Those who believe enter into eternal life and go on to eternal happiness in the presence of God. Those who reject Christ reject God and go on being separated from him forever.

So the conclusion of the first part of the study is this. Take heed to your relationship to Christ. Your relationship to him is not inconsequential. How you respond to him determines your destiny. Will you reject him? Or will you believe? The story of the blind man is told so that you and I might be like the blind man and believe on Jesus, rather than being like the Pharisees.

Those Who Are Blind

The verses we are studying also give indication of what is wrong with those who will not believe on Jesus. That is, it reveals their characteristics.

One characteristic is that they have no sense of need. They are all right by their own standards, and since they do all right by their own standards they imagine that they will do all right by God's. This is the point of the question that the religious leaders asked Jesus. He had just stated that one purpose of his coming into the world was to cause those who see to become blind. He did not mean by this that those who rejected him could actually see spiritually, but rather that they thought they could see (though actually blind) and therefore would not come to Jesus. But this offended them more. So they asked—we must understand the question to have been asked sarcastically—"Are we blind too?" (v. 40). The point of the question was to highlight how ridiculous the teaching of Jesus was in their opinion. How could he suggest that they might be blind? If he did, his opinion could hardly be taken seriously. Pharisees blind? How hilarious! Yet they were blind, and they showed it nowhere more strongly than in their total absence of a sense of need.

The second characteristic of these men was that they considered the teachings of Jesus foolish. They had dismissed them as foolishness before—"Aren't we right in saying that you are a Samaritan and demon-possessed?" (8:48). They would do so again—"Many of them said, 'He is demon-possessed and raving mad. Why listen to him?'" (10:20). But they considered Christ's teachings to be foolish because they did not want to hear him and because their own judgment had been blinded by sin.

Finally, these men were also characterized as being guilty for their sin in rejecting Jesus. There is an interesting twist to the conversation that indicates this. When the Pharisees asked sarcastically, "Are we blind too?" they undoubtedly expected Jesus to answer that indeed they were. This was only what they could expect from one whom they had opposed so forcefully. But Jesus does not say this. It is true that in one sense they were blind. The story of the healing of the blind man is told to make this point among others. Nevertheless, Jesus does not actually say this in his reply. He turns it a bit and, instead of saying, "Yes, you are blind," he says that if they actually were blind, they would be guiltless. That is, they would have an excuse. But they were not totally blind. They knew the Scriptures and therefore were guilty. In the context of this discussion Jesus can only mean that they are guilty before the law, for it is a sin for men who know the law to act as they do. Leon Morris, one of the best commentators on John's Gospel, says, "His meaning is that they have enough spiritual knowledge to be responsible. Had they acted on the best knowledge they had they would have welcomed the Son of God. But they did not act on this. They claimed to have sight, but acted like the blind. Therefore their sin is not taken away. It remains with them."[2]

Those Who Come

These, then, are the characteristics of those who are offended by Jesus. They are unaware of their need. They consider the teachings of Christ foolish. They are guilty before the great God with whom they have to do. How different are the characteristics of those who come to him!

First of all, these admit their need. They cannot see, but, like the blind man, they know they cannot see. They know that their case is hopeless unless the God of miracles should help them. Second, they have all met Jesus and have found his teachings both comforting and reasonable. There may be much they do not understand, but what they do understand makes sense. Therefore, they want to learn more. Third, they have obeyed Jesus. He has anointed their eyes, and they have gone to the source of living water, the Word of God, with which they have washed the clay away and then have returned seeing. Finally, and as the result of these things, they have found themselves growing in the knowledge of him and have found themselves worshiping at his feet. None of this has been due to themselves or to their spiritual ability—they have none—but solely to the grace of God that sought them out and healed them unasked. Such are God's children. Such are those who believe and whose guilt is washed away by Christ's blood.

Jesus died for these people. His death was the atonement for their sins so that the guilt of their sin might never rise up before them again. As a result of that death their sin has been removed as far as the east is from the west. It is blotted out as with a thick cloud. It is buried in the depths of the sea. It is forgiven, forgotten, and gone. As a result of Christ's death God is able to clothe these, his people, with the robes of Christ's righteousness, so that they might stand before him as acceptably as Jesus himself. He has made them heirs with Christ of all his riches. He has made them a kingdom of priests unto himself forever.

In which camp are you? Which way have you turned at Christ's cross? Is the gospel good news or bad news for you? If you have not yet believed, then the fullest extent of the good news is to be found in the fact that it is not too late for you to believe on Jesus. Believe on him. Even now you can find him to be the doorway to salvation.

A Future Judgment

We could certainly stop at this point, and it would be nice to do so. But since we are thinking of Christ's role as a divider of men, it is only honest to point out that his greatest acts in filling that role are yet future. They are those associated with his role in the final judgment, spoken about in many places in Scripture.

One such reference is from Acts. In that book, in the seventeenth chapter, there is a report of one of Paul's great sermons delivered on Mars Hill in Athens to an assembled crowd of Greeks. First, Paul speaks of the Greeks' obvious awareness of a divine being. He adds to this that they are also obviously unsure of who God is and of his nature. They worship him ignorantly, Paul says; and God has been patient. In these days, however, God calls upon all men to repent—that is, to turn from sin and to take sides with Christ—declaring that they must do so in that "he has set a day when he will judge the world with justice by the man he has appointed. He has given proof of this to all men by raising him from the dead" (Acts 17:31). It is possible to repent now, says Paul, but it will not always be so. For one day the same Christ who is an indirect divider of men now will be directly active in judgment, sin will be punished, and those who will not repent will be separated from God forever.

Are you saying as you read these words, "What are you trying to do, frighten me?" If you are saying this, I must admit that in a sense I am; for I could desire so to frighten you that you would turn from your sin and blindness to Christ, becoming God's son or daughter, and thereby not be frightened in a greater sense in the day of Christ's last judgment.

Suppose that a group of criminals has kidnapped your son and is holding him hostage. They think they cannot be discovered. But through the work of the police their hideout is detected and the building surrounded. Suddenly in the midst of their supposed peace and safety, the door bursts open and you and the armed officers enter. There is your son, and there are the gangsters. What is the attitude of each? The attitude of your child is one of delight and love as he immediately springs from his corner and rushes toward you. The attitude of the gangsters is of fright and a knowledge of their certain doom. So it will be at Christ's second coming to render his permanent judgment. Therefore, if the Bible and those who teach it do speak of judgment, it is that you might fear that greater fear and turn to the Lord Jesus Christ while there is hope.

Today the hand of God is extended toward you in grace. Will you not take that hand and receive the amnesty God offers? The doom of future judgment is one we all deserve, but it is one that Jesus has taken on himself for all who will trust him. Trust him, and ask him to be your Savior.

121

The Parable of the Good Shepherd

John 10:1-6

"I tell you the truth, the man who does not enter the sheep pen by the gate, but climbs in by some other way, is a thief and a robber. The man who enters by the gate is the shepherd of his sheep. The watchman opens the gate for him, and the sheep listen to his voice. He calls his own sheep by name and leads them out. When he has brought out all his own, he goes on ahead of them, and his sheep follow him because they know his voice. But they will never follow a stranger; in fact, they will run away from him because they do not recognize a stranger's voice." Jesus used this figure of speech, but they did not understand what he was telling them.

John 10 is a wonderful chapter in this most wonderful of books, rightly beloved by Christians everywhere. The reason lies in its striking portrait of Jesus Christ as the Good Shepherd and of ourselves as his sheep.

That this portrait has been beloved by Christians from every culture and from every period of history is easy to demonstrate, for the evidence abounds in Christian art and literature. A number of years ago on one of my trips through Italy, I had opportunity to visit Ravenna and spend some time among the masterpieces of Byzantine art and architecture to be found there. I thought that one of these was particularly interesting. On one of the walls of the burial chamber of Galla Placidia, a sister of one of the early Byzantine emperors, there is a mosaic portraying Christ as the Good Shepherd. He is seated on a low outcropping of rock, holding a shepherd's staff in the form of a cross, while the sheep gather around him. He strokes the head of one sheep. One sheep looks on. Another seems to be wandering away. In the background, water bursts from a rock in the midst of a verdant garden. The whole is composed of the softest shades of blue, green, yellow, and gold. No one who has seen that picture can miss the thought that the one who follows Christ will not lack any good thing. The artist seems to have been saying of him:

> The LORD is my shepherd; I shall not be in want.
> > he makes me lie down in green pastures,
> > he leads me beside quiet waters,
> > > he restores my soul.

Christ's sheep will indeed be provided with all good things and will dwell in the house of the Lord forever.

It is not just in the Twenty-third Psalm that this image is found, however. It is found in many places throughout the Old and New Testaments. The psalmist wrote, "We are his people, the sheep of his pasture" (Ps. 100:3). Isaiah declared, "He tends his flock like a shepherd. He gathers the lambs in his arms and carries them close to his heart; he gently leads those that have young" (Isa. 40:11). Mark wrote that Jesus had pity upon the crowds because "they were like sheep without a shepherd" (Mark 6:34). Before his crucifixion Jesus referred to Isaiah's prophecy of the suffering servant, saying, "You will all fall away, . . . for it is written: 'I will strike the shepherd, and the sheep will be scattered'" (Mark 14:27). The author of Hebrews spoke of Jesus as the "great Shepherd" (Heb. 13:20). Peter saw him as the "Chief Shepherd" to whom the undershepherds are responsible (1 Peter 5:4).

From this rich mine of biblical imagery the parable of the Good Shepherd, which begins the tenth chapter of John's Gospel, is taken. "I tell you the truth, the man who does not enter the sheep pen by the gate but climbs in by some other way, is a thief and a robber. The man who enters by the gate is the shepherd of his sheep. The watchman opens the gate for him and the sheep listen to his voice. He calls his sheep by name and leads them out. When he has brought out all his own, he goes ahead of them, and his sheep follow him because they know his voice. They will not follow a stranger; in fact, they will run away from him because they do not recognize a stranger's voice" (John 10:1–5).

The image speaks to us of the underlying sympathy between the shepherd and his sheep and of the unfailing love and vigilance of the Great Shepherd.

Shepherds, Thieves, and Sheepfolds

In view of the wide use of the shepherd theme throughout the Bible one would think that the shepherd parable in John 10 would be easy to interpret. But this is not the case, if we are to judge by the various interpretations given to it. In one interpretation the sheepfold is the world. In another it is the church. In a third it is heaven. In one interpretation the sheep are all mankind, in another only the Jews. All would agree that the shepherd is Jesus. But who is the porter? Who are the thieves? And how can Jesus be both the shepherd and the door of the sheepfold at the same time?

I believe that these diverse views arise from a failure (1) to take the story in context and (2) to recognize that Jesus is playing upon various aspects of the shepherd imagery, much as a composer might develop variations upon a musical theme.

The greatest failure is to neglect to take the story in its context. It is to be found in the preceding chapter in the story of the man born blind and in his mistreatment by those who were the leaders of the people. This is obvious because of the absence of any transitional words at the beginning of chapter 10. When John indicates a transition either geographically or in time he usually says something like "after these things," "after this," "on the next day," or "as Jesus passed by." Here the words of Jesus flow on immediately after his comments about the Pharisees at the end of chapter 9 and therefore are related to them. This does not mean that they were necessarily spoken on the same occasion. They may have been spoken later; in fact, they probably were. But it does mean that Jesus had the incident of the blind man in view as he told the parable.

As soon as we recognize this, we recognize that the thieves and robbers must refer to the false shepherds of Israel (the Pharisees) and that the sheepfold represents Judaism. The ones who hear Christ's voice and respond to his call are those of his own who are within Israel, of whom the man born blind is an example.

This understanding of the parable is further encouraged when we recognize the particular aspect of the shepherd imagery upon which Jesus is playing in these first verses—which, by the way, is not the same as that used later. In this chapter there are two kinds of sheepfolds. The first kind of sheepfold was that found in the countryside. It was nothing more than a circle of rocks into which the sheep could be driven. There was no door, just an opening across which the shepherd would place his body. This is the kind of sheepfold that Jesus is thinking about when he says, "I am the gate for the sheep," just a verse or so later. The other kind of sheepfold was more substantial. This kind was found in the towns and villages and consisted of a room or enclosure with a regular gate or door. Into such an enclosure many shepherds together would drive their flocks when they returned to the village at night, and at such a place at night the sheep would be in the care of a porter. In the morning each shepherd would come to the fold, call his sheep by name—they, incidentally, literally knew his voice and would respond to his call—and then lead his own sheep out to pasture. This is the kind of sheepfold about which Christ is thinking in this parable.

What is the sheepfold then? It is not heaven, for thieves and robbers do not climb up into heaven. It is not the church, for the shepherd does not lead his flock out of that, as he does here. The sheepfold is Judaism, as we have already been led to suspect from the context of chapter 9; and the point is that Jesus presented himself to Judaism in order to call out from that body those whom God had given him. Later he says that he will soon call out sheep from other folds that there might be one great flock, the church, and one shepherd (v. 16). The porter—if we must identify him—is God, or God's Holy Spirit, who opens to Christ and releases the sheep to Christ's call.

The Shepherd and His Sheep

Having understood the parable of the sheepfold, sheep, porter, and thieves, we can now reflect upon it for what it teaches spiritually. What are the lessons of this parable?

First, the parable teaches that *the Lord Jesus Christ knows his sheep* and that it is a wonderful thing to be known by him. This truth is implied in verse 3 ("he calls his own sheep by name"). It is stated even more explicitly in verse 14 ("I am the good shepherd; I know my sheep and they know me"). Moreover, according to the further teaching of this chapter, the sheep are known to Christ because they have been given to him by the Father (v. 29), and it is for these and not for all sheep that the shepherd dies (vv. 14–15). What a wonderful collection of truths this is! God has given a certain number of individuals to Christ. Jesus knows who they are. And he dies for them in order that the way to heaven might be provided for them and that they might be safe.

Have you ever noticed that all this is done on behalf of God's chosen ones, even though God knows they are sinners and do not deserve it? Jesus not only knows us; he knows us as we are, and yet he died for us. Here Paul's words in Romans throw light on Christ's teaching. In the wonderful section of Romans 5 in which Paul writes of the results of our justification, there is a parenthetical statement saying that Christ died for us even though we were sinners: "When we were still powerless, Christ died for the ungodly. Very rarely will anyone die for a righteous man, though for a good man someone might possibly dare to die. But God demonstrates his own love for us in this: While we were still sinners, Christ died for us" (Rom. 5:6–8). These verses are intended to help us to get our minds off ourselves and instead to rest in Christ's love.

While we were sinners, Christ died for us. That is a great truth; for if it were otherwise—if Christ did not know us or does not now know that we are sinners—we might fear that some fresh revelation of sin in us might discourage him and weaken his love. "As it is," says Bishop Brooke Foss Westcott, "nothing in his flock is hidden from him: their weaknesses, their failures, their temptations, their sins, the good which they have neglected when it was within reach, the evil which they have pursued when it lay afar. All is open before his eyes. He knows them . . . and he loves them still."[1]

Second, the parable teaches us that having known them, *Jesus calls his sheep* and that he does so by name (v. 3). This is the doctrine of election, which is so prominent in John's Gospel. It is not liked. It is not often preached. But it is in Scripture and must be preached, above all by anyone who is serious about expounding this Gospel. For what is the central point of Christ's parable? Election! That is the point. It is that God has given some sheep to the Lord Jesus and that Jesus comes to the door of the sheepfold and, knowing his sheep in advance, calls to them and leads them out. Not all people are saved. Jesus did not call the Pharisees. But all those are saved whom God has given to Jesus. Indeed, these shall never perish, never be taken from Jesus (v. 28).

This is not an impersonal, still less an arbitrary decree, however, though some have charged this. It is a very tender and personal thing, for Jesus says that the shepherd calls his own sheep *by name*. Being called by name, they follow him. In his commentary Arthur W. Pink points out a number of illustrations throughout the Gospels. "'And as Jesus passed forth from thence, he saw a man, named Matthew, sitting at the receipt of custom; and he saith unto him, Follow me. And he arose, and followed him' (Matt. 9:9). Here was a lone sheep of Christ. The Shepherd called him; he recognized His voice, and promptly *followed* Him.

"'And when Jesus came to the place, he looked up, and saw him, and said unto him, Zacchaeus, make haste, and come down; for today I must abide at thy house' (Luke 19:5). Here was one of the sheep, called *by name*. The response was prompt, for we are told, 'And he made haste, *and came down*, and received him joyfully' (v. 6).

"'The day following Jesus would go forth into Galilee, and findeth Philip, and saith unto him, Follow me' (John 1:43). This shows us the Shepherd *seeking* His sheep before He called him.

"John 11 supplies us with a still more striking example of the drawing power of the Shepherd's voice as He calleth His own sheep. There we read of Lazarus, in the grave; but when Christ calls His sheep *by name*—'Lazarus, come forth'—the sheep at once responded.

"As a touching example of the sheep *knowing* His voice we refer . . . to John 20. Mary Magdalene visited the Saviour's sepulchre in the early morning hour. She finds the stone rolled away, and the body of the Lord gone. Disconsolate, she stands there weeping. Suddenly she sees the Lord Jesus standing by her, and 'knew not that it was Jesus.' He speaks to her, but she supposed Him to be the gardener. A moment later she identified Him, and says, 'Rabboni.' What had happened in the interval? What enabled her to identify Him? Just one word from him—'Mary'! The moment He *called His sheep by name* she *knew* his voice!"[2]

This is the way it has always been, and it is how the call comes today. It is how he calls you. He knows you, of course, as we have seen. He knows you with all your failures and sin. But he also knows what he is going to make of you. As Paul writes, "For those God foreknew he also predestined to be conformed to the likeness of his Son, that he might be the firstborn among many brothers. And those he predestined, he also called; those he called, he also justified; those he justified, he also glorified" (Rom. 8:29–30). This is what he intends to do—make you like himself, glorify you. For this end you are called. Mary! John! Peter! Susan! James! Do you hear his call? It is a wonderful thing to be known personally by the great God of the universe, the Lord Jesus Christ.

Finally, the parable teaches us that having known his own sheep and having called them, *the Lord Jesus Christ leads them out* (v. 3). To what does he lead them? To his own great flock, the church, and into green pastures. From what does he lead them? The answer is from anything that would keep them from his pasture. We have already seen one example in this story. Jesus led the man who had been born blind out of Judaism. But there are other examples. Later he will speak of other sheep and other folds, and he will state his intention to lead those sheep out of those lesser allegiances. The lesser allegiances can be many things. Jesus had led some out of paganism. He has led others out of western materialism. He has led some out of communism, some out of the worship of knowledge, some out of the rat race generated by our competitive society. These are our sheepfolds, whatever they may be, and it is from these that Christ calls us. Perhaps he is calling you from some lesser allegiance at this moment.

Hearing the Call

The story tells us that when Jesus told this parable the first time "they did not understand what he was telling them" (v. 6). But you have no reason not to understand. Moreover, if you are hearing Christ's call, you should respond to him quickly. To hear Christ's call is not the same thing as responding to emotional pressure in an evangelistic service. It is not the same as agreeing to become a member of a church. It is not agreeing to do anything. It is hearing, hearing Christ deep within your own spirit and personality. I will tell you what it is like. It is, above all, arriving at the conviction that what the Bible says regarding your need and the love of the Lord Jesus in answer to that need is true and that you should respond to it.

Have you been sensing that? Have you been saying, "Yes, what I am hearing is true. I have been waiting all my life for this. This is that for which I have been made"? If you have, do not make the mistake of being slow to answer Christ's call. Respond immediately, as Zacchaeus did and many millions of others have done, and follow Jesus. He is the Great Shepherd. Those who follow him do not want for any good thing.

122

"I Am the Gate"

John 10:7–9

Therefore Jesus said again, "I tell you the truth, I am the gate for the sheep. All who ever came before me were thieves and robbers, but the sheep did not listen to them. I am the gate; whoever enters through me will be saved. He will come in and go out, and find pasture."

The parable of the Good Shepherd is familiar and generally understood because it has been told so many times. But when the parable was spoken the first time, it was not understood. Thus, in developing the image, Christ changed it slightly, this time speaking of a second kind of sheep pen and of himself as the gate of the sheep rather than as the shepherd. This development throws more light on Christ's parable and prepares for the explicit identification of Jesus as the Good Shepherd (John 10:7–9).

A Rustic Sheep Pen

In our last study, as we began to talk about the ways of keeping sheep in Christ's day, we saw that there were two kinds of sheep pen. The first is the kind in view in the opening verses of this chapter. This kind of sheep pen was in the cities and villages. It was fairly large, large enough to hold several flocks of sheep at any rate, and it was public. Moreover, it was fairly substantial. A sheep pen like this was in the care of a porter, whose duty it was

741

to guard the gate during the night and to admit the shepherds in the morning. The shepherds would call their sheep, each of whom knew his own shepherd's voice, and would lead them out to pasture. We saw from the context of this parable that by it Jesus was referring to his role in calling his own sheep out of Judaism.

The second kind of sheep pen was not public, nor was it in the villages. This sheep pen was in the countryside, where the shepherds would keep their flocks in good weather. Presumably this is where the shepherds were keeping their sheep at the time of Christ's birth when the angels appeared to them and invited them to Bethlehem. This type of sheep pen was nothing more than a rough circle of rocks piled into a wall with a small open space, a gate, through which the shepherd would drive the sheep at nightfall. Since there was no gate to close—just an opening—the shepherd would keep the sheep in and wild animals out by lying across the opening. He would sleep there, in this case literally becoming the gate. Clearly, this is the kind of sheep pen about which Jesus is speaking in the further development of the parable.

"I am the gate for the sheep." In this section Jesus is the gate. He speaks of leading his flock in rather than of leading them out. He talks about the church itself rather than about calling the church out of Judaism. In other words, he is dealing now with a particular body of people committed to his care and he is revealing the relationship in which he stands to them.

Only One Gate

What does this image teach us about Christianity then? What does the gate teach us about Jesus Christ? First, it obviously teaches that there is only one gate, meaning that Jesus is the sole way to God. This point is evident from the nature of the sheep pen that Christ had in view—if it had more than one gate, it would have been useless—and it is reinforced from many of Christ's other sayings. Thus, to give but one example, Christ says in the fourteenth chapter, "I am the way and the truth and the life. No one comes to the Father except through me" (v. 6).

This is crucial for Christianity. It is not so for other religions. It would make little difference to most of the world's religions if their founder were someone else, or even if they had no founder at all; for essentially they are collections of spiritual truths (or claims to truth) and methods, all of which could exist without their founder. They needed someone to discover them, of course. But the point is that anyone could have discovered them and that once they were discovered they existed in their own right much like scientific propositions. Besides, if they became lost, they could be rediscovered. This is the nature of the world's religions. Christianity is not in this category. Nor is Jesus like these other religious figures. Jesus did not claim merely to know the truth; he said that he is the truth. He did not merely show the way to God; he said that he is the way. Therefore, within Christianity, if there is no Christ, there is no way to God, no truth about God, and no vitality.

How could Jesus make such claims? If he were only a man, they are preposterous, of course. On the other hand, if he is who he said he is and if he did what he said he would do, they make sense. Jesus claimed to be God and to have come to earth to die for our sin. We deserve to die for our own sin, both physically and spiritually. We deserve to be separated from God. But Jesus died in our place. He who was sinless accepted the guilt of our sin and died for us. No one else could do it, but he could and did. Thus, he literally became the gate by which sinful people can approach God the Father. The author of the Book of Hebrews called him "a new and living way" (10:20). Paul wrote, "through him we . . . have access . . . to the Father" (Eph. 2:18).

We must admit at this point that the claim of Jesus Christ to be the gate is a contested claim, contested by those whom he terms "thieves and robbers." Yet, as Christians believe, it is a claim that can stand up to scrutiny.

There are two kinds of such men, and Jesus uses two different words to describe them. The first word is *kleptēs*, from which we get our word *kleptomaniac*. It refers to one who steals cunningly or by stealth. The other word is *lēstēs*, for which we have no English derivative. It refers to one who steals by violence. Thus, if we may imagine the first word to refer to someone who carries off department store merchandise under a coat, the second would refer to those who might use guns to rob a bank.

In the religious world both types are prominent. The first type uses cunning, as Satan did in his approach to Eve in the Garden—"Did God really say . . . ?" (Gen. 3:1). In this category are all who raise doubts in the minds of others—unbelieving ministers, Sunday school teachers, and professors of theology. By their questions they turn the minds of their learners away from Christ and instead cause them to rely upon the supposed wisdom of the teacher. These are those whom Paul terms "treacherous, rash, conceited, lovers of pleasure rather than lovers of God—having a form of godliness but denying its power." He advises, "Have nothing to do with them" (2 Tim. 3:4–5). The other type is violent, for he thrusts himself into a place of authority in the church and demands that others follow him. The Bible terms this ecclesiastical tyranny the doctrine of the Nicolaitans, which God hates (Rev. 2:15).

There is only one gate, according to Christ's image; and Christ himself is the gate. Many have found this claim to be valid and have been willing to be sheep in his pasture.

For Any Man

The first lesson of the image, then, is an exclusive one—there is only one door. But there is a second lesson that is correspondingly broad. It is that anyone may enter it. Jesus indicates this in verse 9: "whoever enters through me will be saved. He will come in and go out, and find pasture."

This verse has sometimes been taken in a way that contradicts John 6:44, which says: "No one can come to me unless the Father who sent him draws him." But those who dislike John 6:44 either completely disregard it or else try to use our text to overturn its plain meaning. Actually the two verses are not in conflict. John 6:44 looks at the matter from the Godward side and declares, rightly, that no man ever made the first move toward God. Men come to God only because God draws them. On the other hand, as our text from John 10 shows, God does not respect persons; therefore, any man, regardless of who he is or where he comes from, may be among that number. Let me put it this way: the call of God is not restricted by anything we can imagine. It is not restricted on the basis of race, education, social position, wealth, achievements, good deeds, or anything else. Therefore, there is no reason why you (whoever you are) should not be among the number of those whom God draws to Jesus.

Do you hesitate to believe that? If so, look at the state of the man who had been blind and for whose sake the parable of the Good Shepherd was told. He had nothing; he was a beggar. He was nothing; no one would have paid attention to him for more than a moment, and then normally only to push him out of the way. Yet this man, despised by every one else, was saved by Jesus. Certainly, if this beggar could have entered in, then any one can. You can. So can others.

You Must Enter

But you must enter in; this is the third lesson that Christ's image teaches. To enter, in this verse, is the same thing as to "eat" of Jesus, "drink" of Jesus, or "come" to Jesus, all of which we have looked at earlier. It means to believe on him or trust him and do this personally.

I am sure that this is precisely why Jesus calls himself "the gate for the sheep." As the phrase stands it is a bit peculiar. We might say, "the door through which the sheep enter" or "the door to the sheep." But "the gate for the sheep"—well, that is just not good English idiom. If we change this into another form, however, then I believe we can understand it. We can understand it if we say "the sheep's door." What is the difference? Only that this particular form of the phrase makes the door personal. It makes clear that we are not talking about an abstract principle or concept. We are not trusting an object. We trust a person, Jesus Christ. And, because Jesus gave himself for us by dying for our sin, we find that he becomes ours through our believing on him, just as surely as we have become his by the same act.

Have you believed on him? It is not hard. There is no complicated course to follow. If Jesus had compared himself to a wall we should have to climb over, it might be hard work. If he had compared himself to a long, dark passageway, we should have to feel along it; some might be afraid to try. But he is not a wall or a passageway. He is a gate, and a gate can be entered easily and instantly.

Let me demonstrate how instantly by this story. A number of years ago a woman sat in a pew in the Tenth Presbyterian Church in Philadelphia, which I now serve as pastor. At the time, the pastor was Donald Grey Barnhouse. He was talking about the cross and of the need to believe on the Christ who died upon it. The woman I am talking about was not a Christian. She had been raised in a religious home and had heard about Jesus. She had heard about the cross. But she did not understand these things and therefore obviously had never actually trusted in Jesus for her salvation. In order to make clear that for salvation only belief in Jesus Christ is necessary Barnhouse said, "Imagine that the cross has a door in it. All you are asked to do is to go through. On one side, the side facing you, there is written an invitation: 'Whosoever will, may come.' You stand there with your sin upon you and wonder if you should enter or not. Finally you do, and as you do the burden of your sin drops away. You are safe and free. Joyfully you then turn around and see written on the backside of the cross, through which you have now entered, the words 'Chosen in him before the foundation of the world.'" Barnhouse then invited those who were listening to enter.

The woman later said that this was the first time in her life that she had really understood what it meant to be a Christian and that in understanding it, she had believed. She believed right there—in that church at that moment. She entered the door. Moreover, the rest of her life bore witness to the fact that a great change had occurred and that she was God's child. I am certain of the facts of this story because that woman was my mother.

Three Benefits

Finally, I want you to see that these verses also speak of three great benefits of entering into God's flock through Christ. They are consequences of belief in one sense. In another sense they are inducements to come. Each begins with an "s," so I know you can remember them.

First, Jesus says that anyone who enters in will be *saved*. This promise is not the limited promise that we sometimes make it out to be. That is, it is not purely future, as if Jesus were offering a "pie in the sky by and by" salvation. Salvation is partially future; that belongs to it. But it is also past and present. It affects who we are and what happens to us from beginning to end. A better way of talking about it is in terms of sin's penalty, power, and presence. By entering in through Christ we immediately escape sin's penalty, so that we need not fear our sins will ever rise up against us. This is justification. Then, too, we also enter into a life in which we are increasingly delivered from sin's power. The Bible calls this sanctification. Finally, we look forward to a day marked by the return of Christ or else our passing into his presence through death, in which even the presence of sin will be gone and our salvation will be perfected. The Bible calls this glorification.

Second, Jesus promises that anyone who enters in will be *safe*. This is the point of his reference to going "in and out." If we did not know better from other references and from a knowledge of Hebrew and Aramaic idiom, we might think that this referred to entering and leaving the church or to salvation itself. But this is not what Christ means. To be able to go in and out means security (cf. Deut. 28:6; 1 Kings 3:7; Ps. 121:8), for in Christ's day when a man could go in or out without fear it meant that his country was at peace and that the ruler had the affairs of the nation under control. When danger threatened, the people were shut up in the cities under siege. Thus, Jesus promises safety for those who trust him.

Third, he also promised that they would be *satisfied*—saved, safe, and satisfied—for he said that they would be able to go in and out and "find pasture." Palestine is a barren land for the most part, and good pasture was not easy to find. Consequently, to be assured of good pasture was a wonderful thing. It spoke of prosperity and contentment, of health and happiness. It was in this sense that David wrote of the care of his Good Shepherd: "He makes me lie down in green pastures, he leads me beside quiet waters, he restores my soul" (Ps. 23:2–3). It was this that Paul wrote of when he told the Philippians, "And my God will meet all your needs according to his glorious riches in Christ Jesus" (4:19). This last verse does not speak of all our desires, of course. We often desire that which is wrong or is not good for us. It speaks only of our needs, but even in that form it is a great promise. It is the promise that the one who enters in by Christ will not lack any good thing.

God Provides

Finally, let me indicate one more verse by way of conclusion. It comes from the Old Testament, from a passage in which Moses is asking God to raise up a leader for the people. Moses is about to die, and he wants God to provide a person to succeed him. "Moses said to the Lord, 'May the Lord, the God of the spirits of all mankind, appoint a man over this community who will lead them out and bring them in, so the Lord's people will not be like sheep without a shepherd'" (Num. 27:15–17). In the context of this book God answers the prayer of Moses by choosing Joshua, who then goes on to lead the people in the conquest of the Promised Land. But in the longer view God answered that prayer through the coming of the Lord Jesus Christ. He is the Great Shepherd, our Savior. He leads us in, and he leads us out. Under his care we find pasture.

123

Life, More Life

John 10:10

"The thief comes only to steal and kill and destroy; I have come that they may have life, and have it to the full."

I am pausing in our study of the tenth chapter of John's Gospel to give particular attention to verse 10; for it contains an idea that has become popular in some Christian circles, and it is important that we understand it. The idea is that of the abundant life. Verse 10 suggests it: "The thief comes only to steal and kill and destroy; I have come that they may have life, and have it to the full."

What is the full or abundant life? It is not necessarily a long life, although there are verses that promise a long life to some, such as to those who honor their father and mother (Exod. 20:12; cf. Eph. 6:2–3). It is not necessarily a life free from sorrow or sickness either, although God certainly does spare us many sorrows that we might otherwise have and often preserves us from sickness. It is not a life of sickly piety, where everything is "beautiful" or "precious" or "just wonderful." The abundant life, as Scripture speaks of it, is, above all, the contented life, in which contentment comes from the confidence that God is equal to every emergency and does indeed supply all our genuine needs according to his riches in glory by Christ Jesus.

The contented life is the life of the sheep who finds himself in the hands of a good shepherd. There may be dangers; in fact, there *will* be dangers. There may be storms at times, even drought and famine. Still, in the hands of a good shepherd the sheep is content and life is bountiful.

Abundance

Contentment means satisfaction, and satisfaction means to have enough. This understanding is reinforced by the meaning of "abundance" in English and in most ancient languages.

Our English word "abundance" comes from the two Latin words *ab* and *undare* which mean "to rise in waves" or "to overflow." The first translation gives a picture of the unceasing rise of the waves upon a seashore. There the waves rise again and again. One wave surges forward and exhausts its force on the sand, but another follows and another and another. Thus it will continue as long as time lasts. The other picture is of a flood. This makes us think of a river fed by heavy rains, rising irresistibly until it overflows its banks. The abundant life is, therefore, one in which we are content in the knowledge that God's grace is more than sufficient for our needs, that nothing can suppress it, and that God's favor toward us is unending.

The Greek word for "abundance," *perissos,* has a mathematical meaning and generally denotes a surplus. In this sense it is used of the twelve baskets of food that remained after Christ's feeding of the five thousand, as related in Matthew's Gospel (14:20). It is translated "remains." The comparative is used to say that John the Baptist excelled the Old Testament prophets in dignity and importance (Matt. 11:9) and that love is more important than all sacrifices (Mark 12:33).

Made Alive

Before one can know the abundant life, he must first know life. That is, he must first be made alive through faith in Christ. Christ is speaking of this when he says, "I have come that they may have life." It is only after this that he adds, "and have it to the full."

Are you aware that you have been made alive spiritually? You should be just as certain of this as you are that you have been made alive physically. In fact, one whole book of the Bible has been written so that Christians (who have been made alive through the new birth) might be certain of it and might grow in Christ on the basis of that assurance. The book is 1 John, and John tells us that this is his purpose in writing. He says, "I write these things to you who believe in the name of the Son of God so that you may know that you have eternal life" (1 John 5:13). A few verses earlier he tells us that God has given life to all who believe on Jesus as God's Son and that they can be assured of this because God himself tells them that this is what he has done.

The Twenty-third Psalm

This brings us to the abundant life itself, and in order to discuss it in its fullest biblical framework I want to take you to the Twenty-third Psalm. This psalm is, above all, the psalm of the contented life. When it begins by saying "The Lord is my shepherd, I shall not be in want" this is precisely what it is talking about. Not to be in want is to be content, and this state can exist only when the sheep is in the care of a good shepherd. In the psalm David tells us that he is content in the Lord in reference to five things.

First, he does not lack rest. He indicates this by saying, "He makes me lie down in green pastures; he leads me beside quiet waters, he restores my soul."

In the small but very rewarding book, *A Shepherd Looks at Psalm 23,* author Phillip Keller, who was himself a shepherd, tells of the difficulty there is in getting a sheep to lie down. Sheep do not easily lie down, he says. In fact, "It is almost impossible for them to be made to lie down unless four requirements are met. Owing to their timidity they refuse to lie down unless they are free of all fear. Because of the social behavior within a flock sheep will not lie down unless they are free from friction with others of their kind. If tormented by flies or parasites, sheep will not lie down. . . . Lastly, sheep will not lie down as long as they feel in need of finding food. They must be free from hunger."[1] Freedom from fear, tension, aggravation, and hunger! These are the four necessities. And the important thing, as Keller points out, is that it is only the shepherd himself who can provide them.

This is an interesting picture. For when the psalm begins with the sheep at rest it begins with a picture of sheep who have found their shepherd to be a good shepherd, that is, one who is able to meet their physical needs and to provide them with release from anxiety. Moreover, it is interesting that it begins at this point. For the other advantages of the contented life—guidance, comfort, safety, provision, and a destiny—come only to one who has found the Lord adequate to his every need.

Guidance

Second, the psalmist tells us that he does not lack guidance. For "he leads me beside quiet waters" and "he guides me in paths of righteousness for his name's sake."

Sheep are stupid creatures. In fact, they are probably the most stupid animals on earth. One aspect of their stupidity is seen in the fact that they so easily wander away. They can have a good shepherd who has brought them to the best grazing lands, near an abundant supply of water—still they will wander away over a hill to where the fields are barren and the water undrinkable. Or again, they are creatures of habit. They can have found good grazing land due to the diligence of the shepherd; but then having found it, they will continue to graze upon it until every blade of grass and even every root is eaten, the fields ruined, and themselves impoverished. This has actually happened to sheep and the land they graze on in many parts of the world—Spain, Greece, Mesopotamia, North Africa, parts of the western United States, and New Zealand.

No other class of livestock requires more careful handling and more detailed directions than do sheep. Therefore, a shepherd who is able to give good guidance is essential for their welfare. He will move the sheep from field to field (before deterioration sets in) and will always stay near water. He will chase strays. He will plan the grazing to fit the seasons of the year. In the same way, we too need the Good Shepherd. We do not lack guidance if we will but have it.

Safety

Third, David tells us that he does not lack safety, even in the presence of great danger. "Even though I walk through the valley of the shadow of death, I will fear no evil, for you are with me; your rod and your staff, they comfort me."

This verse often has been taken as providing words of comfort for those who are dying; and it is not wrongly used in that way. God certainly is a source of comfort in death. Primarily, however, the verse speaks of the shepherd's ability to protect the sheep in moments of danger. The picture in this verse is of the passage from the lowlands, where sheep spend the winter, through the valleys to the high pastures where they go in summer. The valleys are the places of richest pasture and of abundant water. But they also are places of danger. Wild animals lurk in the broken canyon walls to either side. Sudden storms may sweep down the valleys. There may be floods. The sun does not shine so well into the valleys. So there really is shadow, which at any moment might become death's shadow. It is through such experiences that our Lord leads us in safety.

In the book that I referred to earlier, Keller notes how often Christians speak of their desire "to move on to higher ground with God," wanting to move above the lowlands of life and yet not realizing that mountaintop experiences are entered into only by passing through the valleys. Strong faith comes from having faith tested. Patience comes from having lived through tribulations. This means that life will not necessarily be smooth under the direction of our Shepherd. He will sometimes lead us through rough places. Nevertheless, as we go through them we can know of his ability to keep us from falling and to present us before the presence of his Father with great joy.

Keller writes: "The basic question is not whether we have many or few valleys. It is not whether those valleys are dark or merely dim with shadows. The question is how do I react to them? How do I go through them? How do I cope with the calamities that come my way? With Christ I face them calmly. With His gracious Spirit to guide me I face them fearlessly. I know of a surety that only through them can I possibly travel on to higher ground with God."[2]

Provision

Fourth, Psalm 23 speaks of the shepherd's provision for each physical need of the flock. "You prepare a table before me in the presence of my enemies, you anoint my head with oil; my cup overflows."

Keller thinks that the reference to preparing the table refers to the shepherd's advance preparation of the high tablelands or mesas where the sheep graze in summer. If so, it refers to the elimination of hazards, the destruction of poisonous plants, and the driving away of predators—all before the sheep arrive. If it does not refer to this, it must be taken merely of God's provision of peace and feeding even when enemies lurk nearby. In such a time, says David, God anoints him with oil and fills his cup of wine to overflowing.

In biblical imagery oil and wine speak of joy and prosperity; for the growing of olives and grapes and their transformation into oil and wine take time and gentle care. In times of domestic turmoil or war these tasks were forgotten.

Moreover, oil and wine well suited the inhabitants of a dry and barren land and were therefore highly valued. In Palestine, where the sun shines fiercely most of the year and the temperature continually soars up into the hundreds, the skin quickly becomes cracked and broken, and throats become dusty and parched. Oil soothes the skin, particularly the face. Wine clears the throat. Therefore, when a guest arrived at the home of a friend in Palestine in Christ's or David's day, hospitality demanded the provision of oil and wine so that the ravages of travel might be overcome and friends might make merry in each other's company. David spoke of this elsewhere when he prayed, "O LORD . . . let your face shine on your servant" (Ps. 31:14, 16). A shining face was the face of a friend. In another passage he thanks God for "wine that gladdens the heart of man, [and] oil to make his face shine" (Ps. 104:15).

David knew of God's great love and provision; his face shone, and his heart was made merry because of it. Oh for the shining face and the merry heart today! Far too many have scowling faces and gloomy hearts, but that is not what God intends for his children. Instead, if we will allow him to lead us to the high pastures of the Christian life we will find our table prepared, our heads anointed with purest oil, and our cups overflowing with the wine of joy.

A Heavenly Home

Finally, having spoken of all these provisions, David adds no less gladly that he does not lack for a heavenly home. He is blessed in this life, but it is not in this life only that he knows God's goodness. He will know it forever.

Thus he declares, "Surely goodness and love will follow me all the days of my life, and I will dwell in the house of the LORD forever" (Ps. 23:6).

To have a sure home is one of the great desires of the nomadic people who have generally occupied that area of the Near East bordered by the Mediterranean Sea, the Red Sea, and the great Arabian desert. T. E. Lawrence, who gained fame as Lawrence of Arabia during World War I, has written of this eloquently in his classic *Seven Pillars of Wisdom*. He tells in the opening pages of that book how, because of the geography of this area, one tribe after another came out of the desert to fight for the lush Judean highlands, which contained the best trees, crops, and pastures. The Israelites in their conquest of Palestine under Joshua were just one of these peoples. When one group (like the Israelites) succeeded, the conquered people generally moved just a bit south into the Negev (which was also good land but not quite as good as that to the north) and displaced others. Those who were displaced in turn displaced others, and those displaced still others, with the result that there was always a constant movement around the entire area. The last of the peoples would be forced back into the desert with nothing before them but Damascus. At some point all the peoples of the Near East had this background. So, for most of them, Damascus with its ample rivers and fields became the symbol of true abundance at the end of life's pilgrimage. It symbolized home.

For us who know the Good Shepherd there is also a similar longing; but the longing is not for Damascus or any other earthly home. Our longing is for that great and final home that the Lord Jesus Christ has himself gone to prepare for us. He has said, "I am going to prepare a place for you. And if I go and prepare a place for you, I will come back and take you to be with me that you also may be where I am" (John 14:2–3). With such a promise we know that we will dwell in the house of the Lord forever. Of our state in that home John the evangelist later wrote in the Book of Revelation: "Never again will they hunger; never again will they thirst. The sun will not beat upon them, nor any scorching heat. For the Lamb at the center of the throne will be their shepherd; he will lead them to springs of living water. And God will wipe away every tear from their eyes" (Rev. 7:16–17).

The blessings of this life and heaven too! Nor can we forget that this was achieved for us by One who himself became a lamb in order to die for us so that we might be able to enter into the fullness of such a great salvation.

124

"I Am the Good Shepherd"

John 10:11–18

"I am the good shepherd. The good shepherd lays down his life for the sheep. The hired hand is not the shepherd who owns the sheep. So when he sees the wolf coming, he abandons the sheep and runs away. Then the wolf attacks the flock and scatters it. The man runs away because he is a hired hand and cares nothing for the sheep.

"I am the good shepherd; I know my sheep and my sheep know me—just as the Father knows me and I know the Father—and I lay down my life for the sheep. I have other sheep that are not of this sheep pen. I must bring them also. They too will listen to my voice, and there shall be one flock and one shepherd. The reason my Father loves me is that I lay down my life—only to take it up again. No one takes it from me, but I lay it down of my own accord. I have authority to lay it down and authority to take it up again. This command I received from my Father."

The claim of the Lord Jesus Christ to be "the good shepherd" is the fourth of the "I am" sayings in John's Gospel. But if we were to order these sayings in terms of their popularity, I am sure that "I am the good shepherd" would be number one. It is not that we understand it so completely, for there is certainly much about shepherds and their care of sheep in Christ's time that we do not know. It is rather that there is so much in Christ's saying that our hearts know intuitively and for which Jesus is loved.

The Good Shepherd

For one thing, Jesus claimed to be the "good" Shepherd. And we know by comparison with other people—particularly with those who are in positions of responsibility, whether parents, pastors, or politicians—that he is uniquely good. That is, he is good in a way that they are not. The word "good" is itself interesting, and we sense its meaning even though we may never have heard of the Greek word it translates or what the Greek signifies. The word means "good" in the sense of being morally good; but it also means "beautiful," "winsome," "lovely," "attractive," or even "possessing all and whatever qualities make the object described a good thing or the person a good person." Moreover, if we compare Christ's "I am the good shepherd" with his parallel claims to be "the true bread" or "the true vine," we also see that the word means "genuine" or "true," as opposed to "false" or "artificial." But we all sense this; that is my point. At least, it is my point as regards all Christians. We sense that by this phrase we are to recognize Jesus as the good, beautiful, winsome, lovely, attractive, true, and genuine Shepherd.

Moreover, we understand that he is claiming to be that exclusively. For he is not *a* good shepherd, as though he were one of many in that class. He is *the* Good Shepherd. There have been other shepherds, of course. The Old Testament speaks of both good and bad shepherds of Israel. The New Testament speaks of shepherds for our day; for Jesus is termed the "Chief Shepherd" from whom the leaders of God's people, the undershepherds, have assigned responsibilities (1 Peter 5:4). But compared to Jesus, we who are shepherds in the lesser sense scarcely seem to be that at all. For who of us could call ourselves "a *good* shepherd," much less "*the* good shepherd." Yet we instantly confess that he is both and love him for it.

Why does he call himself the Good Shepherd? Or, to put it in other language, what is he like or what has he done that he should bear this title? The verses of John 10 answer the question in two parts. First, Jesus is the Good Shepherd because he lays down his life for the sheep. We find that in verse 11. Second, Jesus is the Good Shepherd because he knows his sheep and directs them properly. We find that in verse 14. In both of these aspects Jesus is above all other men or women.

His Death, No Tragedy

I am amazed at the amount of teaching about the death of Jesus that we find in verse 11, and the more so because the teaching is more or less incidental to Christ's statement. The point Jesus is making is that he can be called the Good Shepherd primarily because he gives his life for the sheep. This is obvious, first, because he repeats it four times—in verses 11, 15, 17, and 18—but also because it is emphasized in contrast to the hired hand who runs away when danger threatens. The good shepherd is the one who sticks by his sheep, who defends them, and who will even die for them if necessary. This is the main point. What is amazing is the amount of teaching about Christ's death that occurs over and beyond this.

First, we are led to see that the death about which Jesus speaks is *voluntary*. This is evident in two places: in verse 11, which says, "I am the good shepherd. The good shepherd lays down his life for the sheep," and in verses 17 and 18, which add, "The reason my Father loves me is that I lay down my life—only to take it up again. No one takes it from me, but I lay it down of my own accord. I have authority to lay it down and authority to take it up again."

We must never think, in contemplating the death of Christ, that this death was somehow an accident or, even worse, a tragedy. It may or may not have been a tragedy when Alexander the Great fell sick and died at an extremely young age, or when Keats died in his early twenties. But it was most certainly not a tragedy when Jesus died at approximately thirty-three years of age. This was no accident. This was and is the great turning point of history. It was planned before the foundation of the world, for Peter spoke of Christ, saying, "This man was handed over to you by God's set purpose and foreknowledge; and you, with the help of wicked men, put him to death by nailing him to the cross" (Acts 2:23). It was this for which Christ was born, for the angel told Joseph, "You are to give him the name Jesus, because he will save his people from their sins" (Matt. 1:21). It was this toward which Jesus' life consciously and deliberately moved, as these and many other sayings of the Lord indicate. Jesus did not have to come to this earth, any more than a man has to be a shepherd. He did not have to die. Nevertheless, he both came and died voluntarily for our salvation.

Second, we are told that his death was *vicarious;* that is, Jesus died not for his own sin—he had none—but for ours and in our place. He indicates this by saying, "The good shepherd gives his life *for the sheep.*"

I cannot understand why so many have been urged to deny this. The words are plain enough, both here and elsewhere. They tell us that Jesus died, not only *for* others in the sense of "on their behalf," but and even stronger than this, in the sense of "in their place." The Greek preposition is *hyper,* the sense of which is given beyond any doubt in Romans 5:6–8, where the same phrases occur: "When we were still powerless Christ died *for* the ungodly. Very rarely will anyone die for a righteous man, though *for* a good man some might possibly dare to die. But God demonstrated his own love for us in this: While we were still sinners, Christ died *for* us." The meaning is this: We are sinners; as sinners we deserve to die (both physically and spiritually); but Christ willingly died in our place, taking our punishment, so that we might be set free from sin and its penalty to serve God.

Third, the death of the Lord Jesus Christ was *specific;* that is, he died for a specified number of people designated in this verse as his sheep. We do not know who these sheep are, of course, and I am glad that we do not. If we could, we would be constantly prying into other persons' lives to see whether or not the other one is chosen; and in that case we would be little better than spiritual peeping toms. It is not for us to know. We cannot know. If we had lived in Sodom, would we have judged Lot, Abraham's nephew, to be a saved man? Probably not! Yet the New Testament tells us that he was accounted righteous in the sight of God, though he undoubtedly erred greatly in going to Sodom (2 Peter 2:7). Would we have considered Judas to be saved? Probably yes, in his case. But Jesus told us explicitly that he was a tool of Satan (John 6:70–71).

We cannot know precisely who these are for whom Christ died. But Jesus does know them and died for them. The result of this is that he literally paid the penalty for their sins and theirs only, with the further result that they are now fully justified in the sight of the Holy God and can stand boldly before him.

Finally, we are told the cause of the Shepherd's death for the sheep. It is because he cares for them (v. 13) or, as we should more properly say, because *he loves them.*

"What? Love sheep? Do you mean to say that you really love sheep, Jesus, and that you love them enough to die for them?"

"Yes, that is right," says Jesus. "I really do love them."

"But they are just sheep, and sinful sheep at that! We would understand if you should say that you felt pity for them, that you hated or were even grieved to see them torn by wild animals or scattered. But surely you would not go so far as to give your life for these poor silly creatures? Your love cannot be as great or as strong as that?"

"But it is," says Jesus. "I do love them. I love you."

"Me? Me, with all my sin?"

"Yes," says Jesus. "You are the one. I love you. I died for you. I want you to become a happy and useful sheep in my flock."

I do not know about you, but I cannot understand such love. I cannot fathom it. I cannot trace the reasonings of such love. But I do believe it and respond to it rejoicing. That is all we can do after all. David once wrote, "How can I repay the LORD for all his goodness to me?" He answered, "I will lift up the cup of salvation [that is, I will believe God concerning his offer of salvation] and call on the name of the LORD [that is, I will praise him for it]" (Ps. 116:12–13). And so we do, knowing that ours is the loveliest, most glorious song of the universe.

> Awake, my soul, in joyful lays,
> And sing thy great Redeemer's praise:
> He justly claims a song from me,
> His loving-kindness is so free.
>
> He saw me ruined in the fall,
> Yet loved me notwithstanding all,
> And saved me from my lost estate,
> His loving-kindness is so great.

Foolish men may be ashamed of such a song and of such great love. But Jesus is not ashamed of it. It is rather his boast and glory: "I am the good shepherd; the good shepherd lays down his life for the sheep." God forbid, then, that we should glory save in that which is his glory, even the cross "through which the world has been crucified to me, and I to the world" (Gal. 6:14).

Knowing and Known

In the second place, Jesus is the Good Shepherd because he knows the sheep and is known by them. There is comfort in that.

Why is that comforting? It is comforting because we long to be known and know others, and yet are basically incapable of it. It is true that there is a certain amount of knowledge of one another between human beings. Friends know one another. Parents know their children, children their parents. There is often a special and beautiful knowledge between husband and wife. But in spite of these things, for each of us deep in our hearts there is a hunger to be known better, to be known for what we really are, and to share a corresponding and similar knowledge of another. It exists on the human level. It exists above all on the divine level. For though we are sinners and in rebellion there is, nevertheless, a certain emptiness or hunger to know God and be known of God. Augustine called it restlessness, adding, "Our hearts are restless until they find their rest in Thee."

Moreover, there is comfort in the claim that Jesus knows his sheep because it is precisely as "his sheep" that he knows them. In other words, to be known of him is at the same time to be a member of his flock and thereby to be one for whom he died and who, as he says later, will never be snatched from his hand. This is a permanent relationship, then, and a personal one. I am his sheep? Yes, forever! Then he is my Shepherd, and that is forever too.

Finally, there is comfort in the fact that Jesus knows his sheep. I therefore need not fear that something about me might suddenly rise up to startle him and diminish his love.

There is a wonderful illustration of this point in the nature of sheep themselves. It is because of it, no doubt, that we find the image of the sheep and the shepherd so apt. Think of the characteristics of sheep. For one thing, they are all *different*. In our time, we are so oriented to mass-produced products and, even in ranching, to such large herds that we seldom think of differences. To us a sheep is a sheep, a cow is a cow, a dog is a dog . . . yes, even a person is a person. But sheep are different from each other, people are different from each other; and the Good Shepherd recognizes those differences. In fact, it is by their differences that he knows them. If they were all alike, they would be indistinguishable.

I sometimes think that half our problems in the Christian church come from our trying to be exactly like another person, or from other people trying to make us be like them. Sheep are different. Jesus made them different and knows that they are different. So, be yourself, and strive to become all that Jesus wants you personally to be.

Not only are sheep different, they also are *helpless*. Jesus knows they are helpless, and that is why he has become our Good Shepherd. Did you know, for instance, that a sheep will often get stuck on its back like a turtle, so that it is unable to move, and that in warm weather it can die in that position within a few hours? A sheep in that position is called a "cast" sheep, and it must be rescued. Or again, did you know that a sheep is undiscriminating in its choice of food, so that it will eat anything, even poisonous roots and weeds? Or again, that a sheep is helpless in the face of predatory animals, so terrified, in fact, that it often will simply stand there without uttering a bleat until it is attacked and killed? I see myself in these characteristics, and as I do I am even more grateful for my Good Shepherd.

Jesus knows his sheep! Well, then, he also knows that they are *wayward*. A sheep can have perfect pasture, all that it needs or can ever need; yet, if there is so much as a tiny opening in an otherwise secure fence, somehow the sheep will find the opening, wriggle through, and wander away to less ample fields and into danger. I am like that, and so are you.

> Prone to wander, Lord, I feel it;
> Prone to leave the God I love,

reads the hymn; and it is true. All we like sheep *have* gone astray yet in Jesus we have a Shepherd who is constantly on the alert to keep us from wandering and to seek us out when we succeed (as we often do) in going astray.

Finally, a sheep is useful. Each year, under proper management, it produces a valuable crop of wool. Thus, when we are told that Jesus knows his sheep, we know that he knows that of us also and that he desires to have us be useful both to himself and to others. I know that he does not need us. He who created the heavens and earth and all that is in them does not need sheep for what they can give him. He does not need our good works. He does not need us to convert people, or even to sing his praises. He has angels to do that. But the fact is: he has created us; he has called us into his flock; and he has given us work to do. How, then, will we do it? Will we be useful or useless? Industrious or lazy? Our attitude should be, "Lord, what would you have me do?" To be willing is to express gratitude to the One who is indeed our Good Shepherd.

125

The Chief Shepherd

John 10:11-18

"I am the good shepherd. The good shepherd lays down his life for the sheep. The hired hand is not the shepherd who owns the sheep. So when he sees the wolf coming, he abandons the sheep and runs away. Then the wolf attacks the flock and scatters it. The man runs away because he is a hired hand and cares nothing for the sheep.

"I am the good shepherd; I know my sheep and my sheep know me—just as the Father knows me and I know the Father—and I lay down my life for the sheep. I have other sheep that are not of this sheep pen. I must bring them also. They too will listen to my voice, and there shall be one flock and one shepherd. The reason my Father loves me is that I lay down my life—only to take it up again. No one takes it from me, but I lay it down of my own accord. I have authority to lay it down and authority to take it up again. This command I received from my Father."

The parable of the Good Shepherd is a parable in which believers can learn about the Lord Jesus Christ. But it is not only that. Like most passages of the Bible that tell us about the Lord Jesus Christ it also is one in which we can learn what *we* are to be as we are made like him. In other words, as Christ is the Good Shepherd, so, too, are we to be shepherds; and we are to find the standards for our shepherd work in his own.

The Bible points to this truth in an interesting way. Three times in the New Testament Jesus Christ is represented as the Shepherd, but in each case the word "shepherd" is preceded by a different adjective. In John 10, Jesus is called the *good* Shepherd, as we have seen—"I am the good shepherd. The good shepherd lays down his life for the sheep" (v. 11). Here the emphasis is upon the voluntary and vicarious death of the Shepherd. In Hebrews 13:20–21 Jesus is called the *great* Shepherd—"May the God of peace, who through the blood of the eternal covenant brought back from the dead our Lord Jesus, that great Shepherd of the sheep, equip you with everything good for doing his will, and may he work in us what is pleasing to him, through Jesus Christ, to whom be glory for ever and ever. Amen." In this verse the emphasis is upon Christ's resurrection and therefore also upon his ability to work through and accomplish his purposes in his sheep. The third passage speaks of Jesus as the Chief Shepherd and stresses his second coming to reward those who have served him as undershepherds. It is 1 Peter 5:4— "And when the Chief Shepherd appears, you will receive the crown of glory that will never fade away."

These passages highlight the focal points of Christ's ministry. As the Good Shepherd, Christ dies for the sheep. As the Great Shepherd, Christ rises from the dead so he might serve the sheep. As the Chief Shepherd, Christ returns to reward those who have been faithful in the responsibilities to which they have been assigned as undershepherds. It is the last of these that highlights the point I am making.

When Jesus described himself as the Shepherd he revealed many important aspects of what he is to us, but at the same time he also revealed what we should be to others. For we are all shepherds—if we are believers in Christ. To a greater or lesser extent we have all been given an oversight of others. Do we exercise our responsibility as Jesus exercised it—in the family, in business, in the affairs of the church, in government, or in other areas? Do we show Christ's self-sacrifice and sympathy? Are we faithful? Whether we are or not, we may improve our service by reflecting on the characteristics of the Good Shepherd.

Found Faithful

The first and most obvious characteristic of the Good Shepherd is that he is faithful; that is, he is faithful in his responsibilities, not only when the skies are sunny and the countryside is peaceful but also when times are hard and when danger threatens. This is apparent from Christ's contrast of himself to the hired hand who, unlike the Good Shepherd, "sees the wolf coming, . . . abandons the sheep and runs away. Then the wolf attacks the flock and scatters it" (v. 12).

The hired hand is one who is doing a job primarily for what he can get out of it rather than out of a true sense of responsibility toward the sheep. So the question becomes: Am I a hired hand in relation to those for whom God has made me responsible? Am I faithful or faithless? Do I stay with the work? Or do I abandon it when I see the wolf coming?

Before we try to excuse our conduct in this area (and we do try to excuse it), we need to hear one other thing said about the hired hand. It is in the next verse: "The man runs away because he is a hired hand and cares nothing for the sheep" (v. 13). At first reading this may seem trite, but it is not at all trite. It reflects a profound principle: a man does what he does because of what he is. Pink writes, "The drunkard drinks because he is a drunkard. But he is a drunkard *before* he drinks to excess. The liar lies because he is a liar; but he is a liar before he *tells* a lie. The thief steals because he is a thief. When the testing time comes each man reveals what he is by what he does. Conduct conforms to character as the stream does to the fountain."[1] Therefore, before we try to excuse ourselves, let us learn that our conduct in testing proves what we are. Let us ask God for the character that proves faithful.

There is much in the Word of God about faithfulness. Jesus spoke of stewards who proved that they were faithful by the way they handled their master's goods (Matt. 24:45–46; 25:14–30; Luke 12:42–43; 19:11–27). Paul wrote, "It is required that those who have been given a trust must prove faithful" (1 Cor. 4:2). He also encouraged Timothy to commit the gospel "to reliable men who will also be qualified to teach others" (2 Tim. 2:2). He calls Onesimus a "faithful and dear brother" (Col. 4:9). Peter calls Silvanus "a faithful brother" (1 Peter 5:12). In Revelation, Antipas is called "my faithful witness" (Rev. 2:13). Faithfulness is of primary importance in Scripture. So whatever good characteristics we may have, we will prove of little value to the work of Christ if we do not possess this primary and essential characteristic.

Hardworking

Second, we must be hardworking and diligent. Nothing worthwhile is done without hard work. Yet many Christians act as though they have been saved by Christ merely to be transported to heaven on "flowery beds of ease," as the hymn acknowledges. Our standard is to be that of the Good Shepherd who works hard for his sheep.

In our study of John 10:10 we had occasion to look at Psalm 23, which tells us that the one who has God for his Shepherd does not lack any good thing. Specifically, he does not lack rest, guidance, safety, provision, or a heavenly home. These provisions are worth reflecting on in themselves—we did reflect on them earlier—but they also lead us to ask: Why does the sheep of the psalm not lack them? The answer obviously is that the Shepherd provides them and that he does so through much diligence and hard work. The sheep does not lack rest because the Shepherd seeks out green pastures in which he may lie down. He does not lack guidance because "he leads me beside quiet waters" and because "he leads me in paths of righteousness for his name's sake." He does not lack safety because the Shepherd defends him against natural disasters and wild animals. He does not lack provision because the Shepherd finds all that he needs and spreads it before him. He does not lack a heavenly home because the Shepherd has gone to prepare it for him and will return to lead him to it. All these items are provided through the hard work of the Shepherd.

In the same way, the needs of God's people—whether in families, homes, or churches—are provided by the hard work of those whom the Lord has appointed as undershepherds. This includes most of us. If God's people do not receive good spiritual food, it is usually because some minister is not working hard enough to provide it. If a family lacks love and security, it is because the parents are not working hard to provide these things in the home. If the widows are not cared for, it is because the deacons are slothful. If the church is not given proper spiritual direction, the elders are failing in their responsibility. The list could be carried on indefinitely.

Are we diligent? Do we work hard? One very hard worker, Watchman Nee of China, once wrote, "Only a diligent servant is of use to [the Lord. So] do not let us regard this matter lightly. . . . We shall have to deal with ourselves unsparingly before the Lord if we are to become workers who are not 'unprofitable' in his service."[2]

Patient

Third, we need to be patient—not with ourselves, of course, but with the sheep. This arises from the fact that sheep are sheep and that they need to be dealt with patiently.

A Christian humorist once said, "To look at the behavior of some ministers you would think that instead of having said, 'Feed my sheep,' the Lord had actually said, 'Teach my trained dogs new tricks.'" This stimulates an interesting train of thought, for it is true that some regard God's people as anything but sheep. Some, as the humorist indicated, act as though God's people were circus dogs. Others act as though they were attack dogs; so they are always telling them to "Go, get the liberals" or "Go, get the Communists." Some treat Christians like horses, getting them to charge some obstacle. Still others regard them as robots—they don't have to think; they just need to be programmed. But we are not dogs or horses or robots. God calls us sheep, and sheep need patience.

Moreover, sheep are different, as I pointed out before. Some go too fast; we need to be patient with those. Others are too slow; we need to be patient with those who fall behind. In this as in other matters we need to learn from the Chief Shepherd.

A Good Example

Fourth, we need to be a good example. This is what Peter is talking about primarily in the verses in which Jesus is called the "Chief Shepherd." He is writing to elders in these verses, though his words also apply more widely. He says, "To the elders among you, I appeal as a fellow elder, a witness of Christ's sufferings and one who also will share in the glory to be revealed: Be shepherds of God's flock that is under your care, serving as overseers—

not because you must, but because you are willing, as God wants you to be; not greedy for money, but eager to serve; not lording it over those entrusted to you, but being examples to the flock. And when the Chief Shepherd appears, you will receive the crown of glory that will never fade away" (1 Peter 5:1–4). Are we like that? Are we examples of mature Christian understanding, faithfulness in the midst of persecution, Christian morality, love, joy, peace, patience, gentleness, goodness, faith, meekness, self-control, and all the other virtues? The point of these words is that we should be such and that we also should be examples in our careful feeding of the sheep.

Self-Sacrificing

A shepherd must be self-sacrificing. This is the fifth characteristic. What is it that characterizes the good shepherd in Jesus' description of him in John 10? Above all, that he gives his life for the sheep. We will never be able to give our lives as Jesus gave his life for us—he died for us as our sin-bearer— nevertheless, there are other ways in which we can give our lives for others. We can give our time in order to help them. We can sacrifice things that we would rather do or rather have in order to serve and give to others. In other words, we must put others ahead of ourselves. Our primary desire must be for their spiritual well-being and comfort.

The world says, "Me first; others second; God last." The order for believers should be, "God first; others second; myself last." It does not sound like a very attractive order to the natural mind, but the truth is that this is the way to a full life and a joyful existence. It takes self-sacrifice if a parent is to raise children properly, if a pastor is to guide and teach his people effectively, if a Sunday school teacher is to help her pupils, or if any worthwhile thing is to be accomplished. But it is rewarding. It is a source of great joy.

Moved by Love

Finally, the shepherd needs to be moved by love. Jesus loves us; he cares for his sheep. So ought we to love one another and care for one another. By this men should know that we are his disciples (John 13:34–35).

But where are we to learn this love? The only answer is: from Jesus. Therefore, we must learn to love him first of all, for it is only after this that we shall be able to love those whom he entrusts to our care. This was the last lesson the Lord Jesus Christ had for Peter. Peter had denied him three times, and the Lord wished to recommission Peter for service. So he came to Peter with the question: "Peter, do you love me?" It was repeated three times. On each occasion Peter answered, "Yes, Lord, you know that I love you," and Jesus then replied, "Feed my sheep." He knew that once Peter had come to love him he would love others also and would care for them.

So it is with all the lessons we are to learn. It is from Jesus himself that we learn them. Take the men from the Old Testament who are known as having been shepherds, and ask them where they learned to be shepherds.

Look at Jacob. He was not a particularly praiseworthy character. He was a cheat and a coward. But in one respect he was praiseworthy—he was a good shepherd. He was known for his faithful *care* of the sheep (Gen. 30:31; 31:36–42). Moreover, later (after the Lord had dealt with him), he was known for his care of his family in exactly the same way. We say to him, "Jacob, where did you learn to be a good shepherd? Where did you learn to care for the sheep?"

Jacob replies, "Well, it is true that I did care for the sheep; but I did not learn it of myself. It was not that I was faithful. I learned it rather from the Good Shepherd, the Shepherd of Bethel, who revealed himself to me and who cared for me during the years of my exile."

We turn next to Joseph and say to him, "Joseph, you too were a shepherd in your youth; it is said of you that you were faithful in *feeding* the sheep (Gen. 37:2). Moreover, you were used by God later to feed people; for as ruler in Egypt you were used to store up grain that helped preserve millions of people during a great famine. Where did you learn that? Where did you learn to be faithful in feeding the sheep?"

Joseph answers, "From the God of my fathers, who fed me during the years of my slavery and imprisonment."

"Moses, even you were a shepherd. You were raised in Egypt in the court of Pharaoh, but you spent the next forty years of your life in the deserts of Midian caring for the flocks of Reuel. It is said of you that you *watered, protected, and guided* the sheep (Exod. 2:16–17; 3:1), just as under God you later watered, protected, and guided the people of Israel during the forty years of their desert wandering. Where did you learn to do that? Where did you learn to give such care?"

Moses tells us that it was not from himself that he learned it, but rather from God's protection and guidance of him as he fled from Egypt.

Finally, we see David. "David, you are preeminently the shepherd of Israel, the great shepherd king. As a boy you cared for the sheep; for you were the youngest in the family, and it was the job of the youngest to care for them. During those years you showed prowess in *defending* the sheep, for we read that you killed both a lion and a bear in rescuing them (1 Sam. 17:34–36). Later you showed similar prowess in defending Israel against even greater enemies. Where did you learn such courage?"

David says he learned it from the Great Shepherd about whom he had written. "Even though I walk through the valley of the shadow of death, I will fear no evil, for you are with me; your rod and your staff, they comfort me. You prepare a table before me in the presence of my enemies" (Ps. 23:4–5).

Each one learned what he learned from the Shepherd of Israel. We can be good shepherds too if we can first say, "The Lord is my shepherd," and then learn from him.

126

One Flock, One Shepherd

John 10:16, 19–21

"I have other sheep that are not of this sheep pen. I must bring them also. They too will listen to my voice, and there shall be one flock and one shepherd. . . ."

At these words the Jews were again divided. Many of them said, "He is demon-possessed and raving mad. Why listen to him?"

But others said, "These are not the sayings of a man possessed by a demon. Can a demon open the eyes of the blind?"

In previous studies of the parable of the Good Shepherd in John 10, we have passed over one very important verse to which we must now return. It is a verse that deals with the church—for the first time in the Gospel—and that therefore sets the pattern for much of the teaching about the church that follows. It tells us about those who are members of the church, about how they become members, about the unity of the church, and about the Shepherd who is its sole head. In terms of the imagery involved, we may say that it teaches about the sheep, the flock, and the shepherd.

The verse is John 10:16: "I have other sheep that are not of this sheep pen. I must bring them also. They will listen to my voice, and there shall be one flock and one shepherd."

Other Sheep

The first part of the verse deals with "other sheep" who in the context of the parable are Gentiles. The opening verses of the chapter have already spoken of one pen, or fold. That fold was Judaism; it was Christ's teaching that he had come to call those who were his own out of Judaism. The man who had been born blind was one example. The disciples were others. In the next chapter Mary, Martha, and Lazarus also are seen to be Christ's sheep, similarly called out of Judaism. Now Christ teaches that there are other folds from which many more sheep must be called—the fold of the Greeks, of the Romans, the barbarian fold, and others. In each of these folds Christ has those who are his own, who have been given to him by the Father, for whom he was about to die, and whom he would call. These are now to form that one great flock, the church, of which he is the one true Shepherd.

What wonderful things Jesus says about these sheep. In the first place, he says that he *has* them—"I have other sheep"—that is, he says they are his already. If they were not, he would have had to say, "I will have other sheep" or "I hope to have other sheep," assuming that all things would go as he hoped they would go. But this is not the expression used. Jesus says they are his and he has them.

I am sure that as he said this none of these sheep were in the minds of the disciples. They were hoping that Jesus would become the Messiah of Judaism, and they probably hoped that many, if not all, of the Jews would believe on him. But did their minds stretch beyond the fold of Judaism to see that Christ had sheep in Samaria, Syria, Asia Minor, Greece, Macedonia, Rome, Gaul, Spain, or other countries of the then known world? I doubt it. I doubt if Peter or James or John ever thought of Rome or Greece as eventual recipients of the gospel. And yet, Jesus was thinking of these places even then and was teaching that he had those living in them who would believe on him.

Spurgeon once wrote on this theme, "Our Shepherd-King has greater thoughts than the most large-hearted of his servants. He delights to enlarge the area of our love."[1]

This verse reminds us of Christ's similar words to the apostle Paul recorded in the eighteenth chapter of Acts. On this occasion Paul was in Corinth, having come there from a not-too-successful preaching mission in Athens. Moreover, he had just experienced opposition from the Jewish population in Corinth. No doubt Paul was somewhat discouraged at this point. But here in Corinth, at this very point in his ministry, the Lord appeared to him by night in a vision and said, "Do not be afraid; keep on speaking, do not be silent. For I am with you, and no one is going to attack and harm you, because I have many people in this city" (Acts 18:9–10). Many people! What a comfort that must have been to Paul and how bold he must have been as he set out to find these sheep who belonged to the flock of the Great Shepherd.

There is also comfort for those of God's people who love their fellowmen and who wish to witness to them of Christ's love. I have been told, "If Christ already has his sheep, what is the use of witnessing to them?" But I say, "What is the use of witnessing if he does not?" It is the fact that the sheep are his that makes us bold in Christ's service. If they were the devil's sheep, I would not bother. The devil is stronger than I am. Besides, to steal his sheep would be wicked. But they are not his sheep; they are Christ's sheep. God the Father gave them to Christ. Christ died to pay the price of their full redemption. Therefore, I can be bold in searching them out. If they are Christ's, I can step to the very borders of hell to call them back to him.

Then, too, notice this saying. Jesus says he *must bring* them—"I have other sheep that are not of this sheep pen. I must bring them also." It would be a great enough encouragement were Christ to have stopped after the first statement, telling us that he had certain sheep. That is great, but when he tells us that he must bring those sheep—well, if the first statement is sufficient to get us witnessing, the second should literally propel us forward.

Years ago I preached a sermon entitled "The Musts of the Master." The message considered this verse and three others. First, "Just as Moses lifted up the snake in the desert, so the Son of Man must be lifted up" (John 3:14). This spoke of the necessity of Christ's death. Second, "Knew ye not that I must be about my Father's business?" (Luke 2:49 KJV). This referred to the whole of Christ's life. Third, "Zacchaeus, come down immediately. I must stay at your house today" (Luke 19:5). Here the divine necessity is applied to the calling of the individual. Then, our text, "I have other sheep that are not of this sheep pen. I must bring them also." Here the principle is applied to the calling of God's people throughout the world.

Most of us do not like the thought of necessity. We do not like to be told, "You must!" Kings certainly do not like necessity. Yet here is One who is a King of kings, above all kings, who nevertheless glories in the fact that he must bring these people.

Moreover, when Jesus says "must," things happen. When I say "must," things may happen, although not necessarily. When he says "must," difficulties vanish, mountains are torn down, life comes out of death, hell is vanquished, men believe. Do you not feel that you should have a part in that conquest? Do you not feel compelled to go out into the highways and byways and draw God's people to the wedding feast that the tables may be filled? If this does not move you, what will? If this does not encourage you, how can you be encouraged?

Then, too, notice that Jesus tells us how those who are to believe will come to him. It is *by hearing*—by hearing his voice, by hearing the gospel. There is no other way by which men and women can be brought to him. I believe that we should be alert to any means by which the gospel may be conveyed to people, and we should certainly be as clear and contemporary in our presentations as we know how to be. But we must not confuse our methods with the gospel, thinking somehow that it is the method rather than the gospel that saves people. It is by the proclamation of the cross that men and women are won (1 Cor. 2:1–5). It is through the foolishness of preaching that God saves some (1 Cor. 1:21). Speak the word of the cross, and some will believe. The word of Christ guarantees it. Moreover, the history of the church confirms the truth and wisdom of Christ's teaching.

One Flock

The second major subject in this verse is the flock, and it is the teaching of Christ that there is to be one flock for those whom he calls to himself. "There shall be one flock and one shepherd."

Here, of course, we must understand precisely what Christ says; for this verse has been both badly translated and misused, with the result that serious damage has been done to the church and to Christian thinking. The initial error can be traced to Jerome and the Latin Vulgate, for in that version Jerome failed to distinguish between a "fold" (which is mentioned in the first part of the verse) and a "flock" (which is mentioned later). There are two entirely different words in Greek, yet Jerome treated them the same, and many of our translations have followed him. The error is corrected in the RSV, NEB, NASB, and NIV. In Jerome's version, Jesus seems to be saying that there is only one organization, and the obvious deduction was that there could therefore be no salvation outside the formal organization of the Roman Church. This became official Roman teaching. Thus, Catholics were taught that Jesus was speaking of an organization and that, since there can be no salvation apart from membership in that organization, there could therefore be no salvation apart from the church of Rome. But all this is based upon a wrong translation, as I have said.

The church about which Christ was speaking is not an organization (though it obviously has organized parts) but rather the entire company of those who own the Lord Jesus Christ as their Shepherd. Thus, the unity comes not from the fact that the sheep are all forced into one organization but in the fact that they have all heard Jesus and have left lesser loyalties to follow him. Moreover, to the degree that they do follow him there is also a visible (though not necessarily a structural) unity that follows.

The question is: Do we truly acknowledge such unity? The answer, even for evangelicals, is that we often do not. The error of the Roman Catholic Church is the error of supposing that the Holy Spirit must work and, in fact, will only work along ecclesiastical lines. That is a real error. But precisely the same error exists within Protestantism. It is not so much that there are different denominations within Protestantism. That in itself does not bother me; for people are different, and there is no reason at all why there ought not to be different organizations with different forms of service and church government to express those differences. The fact that there are different denominations is not the problem. Indeed, to insist that there must be one great Protestant denomination (which some in the ecumenical movement insist on) is the precise error of Romanism. No, the problem lies along another line entirely. It is that believers within one denomination refuse to cooperate with believers within another denomination, justifying this on grounds that the other Christian is somehow contaminated by his associations, or is disobeying the Lord by remaining in his church, or is not actually (which is sometimes said) a Christian.

That is the problem. Evangelicals are more guilty of this than anyone, and I do not hesitate to say that this is the greatest single cause for the hindrance of the advance of the gospel in the world today—greater than liberalism, greater than humanism, greater than the materialism and rampant immorality of our time. Moreover, it is sin. We will not have great revival until true believers repent of this sin and ask God to cleanse them of it.

What are we to conclude about the church of the Lord Jesus Christ, then, on the basis of these and other biblical passages? I can state it in the following four principles:

1. According to the Lord Jesus Christ, there is one church to which all who confess him as Lord and Savior belong. Therefore, all who are Christians are one with all other true Christians and should acknowledge that to be true, even though the other believer is wrong about or denies what we consider to be important doctrines.

2. Nothing in the Bible tells us that there is to be or that we should desire one all-encompassing organization. As a result of this we may expect God to call people to faith in Christ within various organizations and to lead believers into Christian service within those organizations. We dare not say that another believer is out of God's will because he is serving there.

3. God's people need one another and must learn from one another. This does not mean that each of us will therefore think other believers are completely right in church matters or even in doctrine—we do not dare say that we are totally right—but it does mean that we need to learn something about the body of Christ and receive help for the body of Christ from all other Christians.

4. Because of the love that is to bind the true church together, we also have an obligation to demonstrate that love-unity tangibly, over and above denominational programs and concerns. Indeed, we must; for it is the indispensable basis for our mission. "By this"—your love for one another—"all men will know that you are my disciples," said Jesus (John 13:35).

One Shepherd

Is there a cure for such problems? Of course. It is to be found in the third great subject of this verse—the Shepherd. He is the source of our unity and its basis. Therefore, it is only in Jesus Christ that two men, or women, or races can ever become one.

In his commentary on this passage William Barclay tells of an incident from the life of Egerton Young, the first missionary to the Red Indians of Saskatchewan, Canada. Young had gone to these Indians with the message of the love of God the Father, and they had received it like a new revelation. When he told his message an old chief said, "When you spoke of the great Spirit just now, did I hear you say, 'Our Father'?"

"Yes, I did," said the missionary. "We know Him as Father because He is revealed to us as Father by Jesus Christ."

"That is very new and sweet to me," said the chief. "We never thought of the great Spirit as Father. We heard Him in the thunder; we saw Him in the lightning, the tempest and the blizzard, and we were afraid. So when you tell us that the great Spirit is *our Father,* that is very beautiful to us." The chief paused, and then, as though the glory of it were even then breaking over him, he asked, "Missionary, did you say that the great Spirit is *your* Father?"

"I did," said Young.

"And," said the chief, "did you say that He is the Father of *the Indians?*"

"Yes," said the missionary.

"Then," said the old chief, like one on whom the light had now burst, *"you and I are brothers."* [2]

This is the only possible unity for men on this earth. Nothing we ever do will abolish distinctions between nations. There will always be nations. Nothing (so far as I can see) will ever abolish denominations. But in spite of these things—in spite of race, nations, and denominations—there can be a real and visible unity for those who acknowledge the Lord Jesus Christ as their Lord and Shepherd. As Dr. D. Martyn Lloyd-Jones says in his volume on the second chapter of Ephesians, "We are all equally sinners. . . . We are all equally helpless. . . . We have all come to one and the same Savior. . . . We have the same salvation. . . . We have the same Holy Spirit. . . . We have the same Father. . . . We even have the same trials. . . . And finally, we are all marching and going together to the same eternal home."[3] It is a knowledge of these truths and, above all, of the love of the Lord Jesus Christ for us that will draw us closer to one another.

127

True Words Plainly Spoken

John 10:22–26

Then came the Feast of Dedication at Jerusalem. It was winter, and Jesus was in the temple area walking in Solomon's Colonnade. The Jews gathered around him, saying, "How long will you keep us in suspense? If you are the Christ, tell us plainly."

Jesus answered, "I did tell you, but you do not believe. The miracles I do in my Father's name speak for me, but you do not believe because you are not my sheep."

Several years ago, when I was speaking to someone about the gospel, the person to whom I was speaking replied that the discussion was merely a question of "semantics." I suspected that he had just learned that word, for he used it several times in the course of our discussion, in each case suggesting that there is no such thing as truth, that all ideas are relative, and that a person may therefore call himself a Christian while at the same time believing anything he wishes to believe. His reason was his feeling that language cannot be pressed to the point of precise definition.

I acknowledged that it is sometimes hard to define words, particularly theological words. Theology is the art of defining precisely what certain words mean and do not mean. But at the same time I denied that this was any excuse for failing to grapple with the precise demands of God made in Scripture or for refusing to alter one's life accordingly. The young man would not accept this, however. So he continued to use "semantics" as an excuse for failing to believe on Jesus Christ. He also, so it seemed to me, blamed

God for his problem, for he was suggesting that things would be very different had God only expressed himself more clearly.

To this person and to all who think that God has not been clear enough in his revelation, the verses in John's Gospel to which we now come should be important.

The Complaint

At this point the Lord Jesus Christ was approaching the end of his public ministry. He had been in Galilee and Judea for nearly three years and had been teaching publicly for that time. He had not often said, at least explicitly, that he was the Messiah—the people were looking for a political messiah—and if he had done that he would have raised false hopes. Still, he had been open in many claims, saying that he had a right to other persons' loyalties and was able to satisfy all legitimate wants and needs. He had healed the sick, given sight to the blind, and done many other things that were in fulfillment of the Old Testament prophecies concerning the Messiah. These were sufficient grounds for anyone to have recognized the nature of his claims or at least to have followed him in order to have learned more. But the people did not want this. So, rather than simply saying that they did not want it or did not want to believe Christ, they said that he had not taught them plainly.

The text says, "The Jews gathered around him, saying, 'How long will you keep us in suspense? If you are the Christ, tell us plainly' (v. 24).

We need to see, moreover, that in asking this question Christ's hearers were actually trying to place the blame for their lack of belief on Jesus. This is clear from the language; for they prefaced the complaint with the question: "How long will *you* keep us in suspense?" In other words, they were saying that their failure to believe was his fault, in spite of the fact that he had been clear in his teaching and had been doing miracles among them for three years.

That makes me think of the story from Genesis in which Adam tried to do the same thing. God had given the man and woman the greatest freedom anyone has ever known. They were free to subdue the earth, free to eat of any tree of the Garden. But there was one tree, a symbol of the fact that they were still God's creatures and were dependent on him, the fruit of which they were not to eat. God had said, "You are free to eat from any tree in the garden; but you must not eat from the tree of the knowledge of good and evil, for when you eat of it you will surely die" (Gen. 2:16–17). In other words, God had said, "You may eat of anything north of here, east of here, south of here, and west of here; but this tree is a symbol of your dependence upon me, and you shall not eat of it."

This bothered Adam. It did not bother Eve so much, for there is nothing in the Bible to indicate that she found God's command offensive. Eve, we are told, sinned through being deceived. The serpent told her that if she ate of the tree her eyes would be opened to discern between good and evil and that she and Adam would become like God. She believed the serpent, rather than trusting God; so she ate of the fruit. The Bible says, "The woman who was deceived . . . became a sinner" (1 Tim. 2:14).

On the other hand, Adam was not deceived. He sinned deliberately, saying in effect, "I do not care if I can eat of every tree north of here, east of here, south of here, and west of here; so long as this tree is forbidden to me I hate it, and I hate God who gave it." So Adam ate deliberately, understanding precisely what he had done.

When God came to them—this is the point for which I tell the story—he came to the man first (because his sin was greater) and found that Adam denied responsibility. When he turned next to the woman she admitted what she had done and did not attempt to excuse herself. She said, "The serpent deceived me and I ate" (Gen. 3:13). But Adam . . . Adam tried to escape his guilt by shifting it both to God and the woman. Adam said, "The woman you put here with me—she gave me some fruit from the tree and I ate it" (Gen. 3:12). In other words, Adam blamed the woman as a secondary cause; and he blamed God as a first cause because it was God who had given him the woman. This is what we are all guilty of, for it is the nature of sin to blame others. Thus, we find the people of Christ's day blaming him for their lack of belief and (in the same way) many in our day blaming him also.

Do you do this? If so, may I warn you of how dangerous it is. The Bible says, "If we confess our sins, he is faithful and just and will forgive us our sins and purify us from all unrighteousness" (1 John 1:9). But if we blame God, our hearts are hardened and the day of grace passes by. I am certain that John is suggesting that this was so for those who asked this question of Jesus. Here both the context and the language are important. The incident took place near the end of Christ's public ministry. It was winter. For these quibblers the summer of Christ's ministry was over and the warmth of his life and teaching was about to be withdrawn. As he gives these details John most certainly has these overtones in mind. So what can be said of these quibblers? Surely, as Jeremiah declared, "The harvest is past, the summer has ended, and we are not saved" (Jer. 8:20). I trust that this is not true of you. Unbelief may seem logical to our way of thinking, but it is not logical to God's way of thinking; and it is with his thinking that you and I have to do. According to him we have been told everything we need to know and are therefore without excuse if we fail to believe on Christ as our Savior.

Christ's Answer

This is precisely what the Lord Jesus Christ replied to these who had voiced their complaint, "If you are the Christ, tell us plainly." He said that he *had* told them plainly. Moreover, his works substantiated his teachings. He said, "I did tell you, but you did not believe. The miracles I do in my Father's name speak for me" (v. 25).

What gracious works these were and how richly they substantiate Christ's claims! The words alone had caused some to believe. It was the testimony of the Samaritans that they had believed Jesus because "we have heard for ourselves," rather than because of the testimony of the woman whom Jesus had met at the well (4:42). The nobleman who had his son restored to health by Jesus "took Jesus at his word" (4:50). Peter had testified, "Lord, to whom shall we go? You have the words of eternal life" (6:68). These had believed on the basis of the words alone. Yet, there were also Jesus' many works that substantiated them.

In John's Gospel the works are called "signs," as we saw in chapter 5. A sign is a symbol; that is, it points to something signified. The miracles are signs in that they point to the unusual ability or character of the one performing them.

There are seven great miracles recorded in the Gospel of John. The first is the miracle at Cana of the changing of water into wine (2:1–11). John tells us that this was the first of Christ's signs and that, as a result of it, the disciples believed on him. The second miracle is the healing of the nobleman's son (4:46–54). This work shows Christ's power to overcome sin and sickness and to instill peace and faith in the human heart. The third sign is the healing of the impotent man (5:1–16). The meaning of this is that all men are spiritually impotent—they cannot come to Jesus—but that Jesus acts in grace to call them to himself in spite of their inability. Fourth, there is the feeding of the five thousand (6:1–14). Here Jesus is revealed as the One who alone can satisfy the hunger of the human soul. Fifth, there is the walking of Christ upon the water in which his power over the elements is dramatized (6:15–21). The sixth miracle is the healing of the man who had been born blind (9:1–41). Finally, there is the raising of Lazarus (11:1–44). Each of these reveals something about Jesus that we would not have seen so clearly otherwise, and each supports his claim upon men's loyalty.

"But these are not enough," some say. "Let him do more." Well, says John, Jesus did quite a bit more. In fact, he says, if everything about Jesus was written that could be written, even the world itself would not be able to contain the books. This is enough—that is the point. These words and works are sufficient. Consequently, "These are written that you may believe that Jesus is the Christ, the Son of God, and that by believing you may have life in his name" (20:31).

To ask for evidence or for plain speech is a good procedure if evidence or plain speech is lacking. But if these are present, then to ask for more evidence or for plainer speech is only an attempt to avoid responsibility and shift the blame. Suppose that you are driving down a super highway at sixty-five miles per hour and that the speed limit is fifty-five. A policeman stops you and says, "What are you doing? Don't you know that the speed limit is fifty-five?"

"That's a good question," you say. "Actually, I was wondering about that. Is it fifty-five? Or is it sixty-five? I was going sixty-five."

"I'll say you were," says the trooper, "and sometimes it was seventy. Didn't you see that sign back there?"

"Oh! That sign!" you answer. "Well, actually I did see it; but that was a quarter of a mile back. It seems to me that if the state wants drivers to move along at that speed, it should mark the speed limit more plainly. There should be a sign here, for instance. And there should be one another hundred feet ahead, and another hundred, and so on."

What does the trooper do? Does he say, "I am so sorry that I stopped you. I see your point. There should be more signs. Go on your way. We'll put up a dozen new signs by next week"? Of course not! If you would answer a trooper like that, he would have you ticketed so quickly that you would hardly know what happened. The fault is not in the signs. The fault is in the driver who does not like to abide by regulations and who prefers to be his own authority.

Do not tell God that he has not revealed the truth plainly. Say rather that you do not like the truth he has revealed. And let that truth move you to repentance and faith in the Savior.

Do We Follow?

We must stop at this point for a few conclusions. But before we do, let me point out that what we have seen thus far is not the whole of Christ's answer to the demand that he speak plainly. His first answer, as we have seen, is that he had spoken plainly. He had said everything that could be said. He had done everything that could be done. If they had not believed by this time, nothing else he would ever say or do would move them. But they had asked him to speak plainly. So in the second part of his answer this is precisely what he does. It is a dangerous thing to ask Christ to speak plainly, for when he speaks plainly he *really* speaks plainly. He tells it like it is. In the verses that follow, and which we will discuss in our next chapter, Jesus gives the most highly condensed statements of the doctrines of grace in the entire Gospel, saying that in themselves men and women are unable to believe, that those who believe do so only because God acts in grace to elect them into the company of his people, that all whom God elects do, in fact, come and that none of those who comes is ever lost. These are the central doctrines of the reformed faith as it has been expressed by Jesus, Paul, Augustine, Calvin, and a host of others. If you want it plainly, this is it. This is pure biblical teaching.

At the same time we must add that the doctrines of grace cannot be used as an excuse to escape responsibility. It is true that we cannot choose God unless he first chooses us, doing a miracle in our hearts by which we understand these things and respond to him. But we are, nevertheless, responsible for the things we do choose and for the way in which we handle his revelation. What about Christ's words? What about his works? You cannot escape them. If they are true—and what possible reason do you have to doubt them save that someone has told you at one time or another that the Bible is not true, that it is only a collection of stories, and that without evidence—if they are true (I repeat it), then wisdom and simple honesty demand that you drop all lesser loyalties and follow Jesus. This is what he wants. He says, "My sheep listen to my voice; I know them, and they follow me" (v. 27). So, listen! Really listen! And follow Jesus!

But perhaps you already are a Christian. If that is the case, then this applies to you also. You say, "But I already believe that Jesus is God and that his words are truthful. I do not doubt what the Bible says." Good! But that is not in itself the full definition of those who have been called to be his sheep by the Father. Jesus says that those who are his sheep both hear his voice and follow him.

So, do you hear? Do you *really* hear? And do you follow? If you are going your own way, what right do you have to think that you are one of his sheep? If you will not listen to God's truth, what right do you have to think that you belong to him?

In the eleventh chapter of Hebrews we are told about some of Christ's sheep and of what they did when they heard the voice of their Shepherd and followed him. Abel heard and *offered* a better sacrifice. Enoch heard and *pleased* God. Noah heard and *built an ark*. Abraham heard and *obeyed*. Isaac *blessed Jacob* concerning things to come. Jacob *blessed* the *sons of Joseph* in accord with God's promises. Joseph *gave instructions* about his bones. Moses *chose* rather to suffer affliction with the people of God than to enjoy the pleasures of sin for a season. Rahab heard and *received* the spies in peace. Others, we are told *conquered* kingdoms, *administered* justice, *gained* what was promised, *shut* the mouths of lions, *quenched* the fury of the flames, *escaped* the edge of the sword, had weakness *turned to strength, became powerful* in battle, *routed* foreign armies. Women *received* back their dead raised to life again. Others *were tortured* and refused to be released so that they might gain a better resurrection (vv. 33–35).

In each of these cases life was different because the one involved had heard God's call and followed his leading. Do we hear? Do we follow? God grant that it might be so increasingly for Jesus' sake.

128

Christ, the Calvinist

John 10:27–29

"My sheep listen to my voice; I know them, and they follow me. I give them eternal life, and they shall never perish; no one can snatch them out of my hand. My Father, who has given them to me, is greater than all; no one can snatch them out of my Father's hand."

One time, after I had preached a sermon from John touching on some of the main points of the Reformed faith, I found a copy of that week's bulletin on which someone had scribbled his opinion of the message: "I'm sick of Calvinism in every sermon."

The message did not particularly bother me. Notes like that seldom do. But I found it surprising that the person who wrote the note somehow regarded Calvinism as a system of thought that could well be dispensed with while, nevertheless, as he assumed, still preserving Christianity. In other words, this person, like many others, somehow regarded the doctrines that go by the name of Calvinism as at best an addition to the pure gospel and at the worst a system that is opposed to it. Is this true? Are the doctrines of grace wrong? One proof that they are not is seen in the verses to which we come in this chapter.

Historic Calvinism

The verses I have in mind are those in which the Lord Jesus Christ spoke plainly to his enemies, saying that those who do not believe on him do not believe because they are not his sheep, that those who are his sheep believe and follow, that this is true because they are given to him by the Father, that these who are given to him by the Father inevitably come to him and, finally, that these who come will never be lost. This is a message of man's complete ruin in sin and God's perfect remedy in Christ, and it can be expressed in the distinctive points of Calvinistic theology. Before we look at these points in detail, however, we should see that far from being an aberration or addition to the gospel, these truths have always belonged to the core of the Christian proclamation and have been characteristic of the church at its greatest periods.

To begin with, the doctrines of grace that have become known as Calvinism were most certainly not invented by Calvin, nor were they characteristic of his thought alone during the Reformation period. As we shall see, these are the truths taught by Jesus and confirmed for us in Scripture by the apostle Paul. Augustine argued for the same truths over against the denials of Pelagius and those who followed him. Luther was a Calvinist. So was Zwingli. That is, they believed what Calvin believed and what he later systematized in his influential *Institutes of the Christian Religion*. The Puritans were also Calvinists; it was through them and their teaching that both England and Scotland experienced the greatest and most pervasive national revivals the world has ever seen. In that number were the heirs of John Knox: Thomas Cartwright, Richard Sibbes, Richard Baxter, Matthew Henry, John Owen, and others. In America, thousands were influenced by Jonathan Edwards, Cotton Mather, and George Whitefield, all of whom were Calvinists.

In more recent times the modern missionary movement received nearly all its direction and initial impetus from those in the Calvinistic and Puritan tradition. The list includes such men as William Carey, John Ryland, Henry Martyn, Robert Moffat, David Livingstone, John G. Paton, John R. Mott, and many others. For all these the doctrines of grace were not an appendage to Christian thought but were rather that which was central and which most fired and gave form to their preaching and missionary efforts.[1]

This, of course, is precisely why I am reviewing this history—to show that the doctrines known as Calvinism are not something that emerged late in church history but rather are that which takes its origins in the teachings of Jesus, which has been found throughout the church in many periods, and which has always been characteristic of the church at its greatest periods of faith and expansion. It follows from this that the church of Jesus Christ will again see great days when these truths are widely proclaimed, and proclaimed fearlessly.

Jesus is our example. We sometimes think of these doctrines as household doctrines; that is, as truths to be proclaimed only to those who already

believe. But this was not Jesus' procedure. He taught them also to his enemies. In this case, they had come to him with the implication that he was
responsible for their failure to believe; they had said, "If you are the Christ,
tell us plainly." He answered this, not so much with a statement concerning
his identity as the Messiah (although he did say that his words and works
authenticated him), but much more importantly by a full statement of man's
utter inability to choose God and of the necessity for divine grace in each
step of salvation. Did they want it told plainly? Well, this is the truth told
plainly: "You do not believe because you are not my sheep. . . . My sheep listen to my voice; I know them, and they follow me. I give them eternal life,
and they shall never perish; no one can snatch them out of my hand. My
Father, who has given them to me, is greater than all, and no one can snatch
them out of my Father's hand" (vv. 26–29).

State of the Lost

First of all, Christ's words reflect the desperate state of the lost; that is, the
state of all men as they are apart from Christ. The teachings on this point
are not so much direct as indirect. Still they underlie the positive points made
in this passage.

In reference to man's desperate state apart from Christ, these verses show
that he has lost spiritual life; otherwise it would not be necessary for Christ
to speak of it as a gift. Originally, man had life. When the first man and
woman were created by God they were created with that life that shows itself
in communion with him. Consequently, we learn that they communed with
God in the Garden in the cool of the day. When they sinned, this life was
lost, a fact evidenced by their hiding from God. This has been the state of
people ever since. Consequently, when the gospel is preached, those who
hear it turn away unless God intervenes to do a supernatural work of regen-
eration in their hearts.

Moreover, the desperate state of people apart from Christ is suggested by
the fact that no one can recover this life except as a free gift from God. Jesus
calls it a gift, for it is undeserved and unearned. If it were earned, it would
be wages; if it were merited, it would be a reward. But eternal life is neither
of these. It is a gift, which means that it originates solely in God's good will
toward men.

As a last thought on this subject, it is also true, is it not, that men and
women will perish except for this gift. Jesus says of those to whom he gives
life that "they shall never perish." But since he makes this promise, it must
be because we will perish if he does not intervene. We are sinners. Sin makes
us heirs of God's wrath. If God does not intervene, we stand under divine
judgment, without hope, facing the punishment due us for our own sins.
According to these verses, we cannot even come to Christ, for we are not of
his sheep and so lack the ability to hear his voice and turn to him.

Grace

This brings us to the next thought. For while it is true that in ourselves we cannot come to Christ and so lie under God's just condemnation, the main point of these verses is that God has nevertheless acted in grace toward some. Earlier this was expressed by saying that Christ died for the sheep; in other words, by the doctrine of a particular redemption (v. 11). In this section we are told that Jesus has given eternal life to the same people (v. 28), and that these are those whom God has given him (v. 29).

You cannot trace the origins of our salvation farther back than that. In this, as in all things, the origins are to be found in God. Some say, "But surely God called them because he foresaw that some would believe." But it does not say that. Others say, "He chose them because he knew in advance that they would merit salvation." It does not say that either. What it does say is that the initiative in salvation lies with God and that this is found, on the one hand, in God's electing grace whereby he chooses some for salvation entirely apart from any merit on their own part (which, of course, they do not have) and, on the other hand, in Christ's very particular atonement by which he bore the penalty for the sins of these people.

I need to say also, however, that there are aspects of the death of Christ that apply to the world at large. I am not denying that. The death of the Lord Jesus Christ is a revelation of the nature of God. It is a revelation of his hatred of sin in that Christ died for it. It is most certainly a revelation of God's love, for love lay behind it. It is an example to the race. These things are true. But in addition to these there is also a sense in which the Lord Jesus Christ died particularly and exclusively for his own, so that he literally bore the penalty for their particular sins, that they might be forgiven.

These truths do not make us proud, as some charge. Rather they increase our love for God who out of pure grace saves some when none deserve it.

An Effective Call

The third of the reformed doctrines presented by Jesus is the effective call: that is, that God's call of his people is accompanied by such power that those whom he calls necessarily come to him, believing on Christ and embracing Christ for salvation. Jesus expresses this by saying: "My sheep listen to my voice; I know them, and they follow me" (v. 27). It is a mark of the sheep that they both hear and follow their shepherd.

In the Puritan era it was the habit of many preachers to play on these two characteristics, calling them the marks of Christ's sheep. In days when there were many flocks of sheep it was necessary to mark the sheep to distinguish them. In our day, at least on cattle, this is done by branding. On sheep it was often done by cutting a small mark into the ear. "Well," said the Puritans, "each of Christ's sheep has a double mark—on his ear and on his foot. The mark on his ear is that he hears Christ. The mark on his foot is that he follows him."

This is true, of course. It leads us to ask, "Do we hear? Do we follow?"

How many of those who come to church on a typical Sunday morning really hear the voice of Christ or have ever heard it? They hear the voice of the preacher; they hear the voices of the members of the choir. But do they hear Christ? If they do, why are they so critical of what they hear? Why are their comments afterward so much more about the Lord's servant than the Lord? Those who are Christ's hear *Christ*. And they follow him. But how many who come to church are really following? Most seem to make good leaders— in their own cause—but they are poor followers. They make good critics— of the Bible and of Christ's people—but they are poor disciples. They make respectable wolves, for they ravage the flock, but they do not have the traits of the sheep and would even be contemptuous of them if they had an understanding of what those traits are.

Do not presume on your relationship to Christ. You are not his unless you hear his voice and follow him. Jesus said, "If you love me, keep my commandments" (John 14:15). He said, "He who has an ear, let him hear what the Spirit says to the churches" (Rev. 2:7).

Never Lost

Finally, notice that these verses also speak at length of God's perseverance with his saints. That is, they teach us that none whom God has called to faith in Christ will be lost. Indeed, how can they be, if God is responsible for their salvation? Jesus says, "I give them eternal life, and they shall never perish; no one can snatch them out of my hand" (v. 28).

"But," says someone, "suppose they jump out of their own accord?"

"They shall never perish," says the Lord.

"Never?"

"No, never," says Jesus. "They shall never perish; no one can snatch them out of my hand."

This does not mean that there will not be dangers, of course. In fact, it implies them; for if Jesus promises that no one will succeed in plucking us from his hands, it must be because he knows that there are some who will try. The Christian will always face dangers—dangers without, from enemies, and dangers within. Still the promise is that those who have believed in Jesus will never be lost. We may add that the Christian may well be deprived of things. He may lose his job, his friends, his good reputation. Still he will not be lost. The promise is not that the ship will not go to the bottom, but that the passengers will all reach shore. It is not that the house will not burn down, but that the people will escape safely.

Do you believe this promise, that you are safe in Jesus' hands, that you will never be lost? Are you able to trust God for this as you have for other truths? I suppose there is a way of explaining away almost everything, but I must say that I do not see how the opponents of eternal security can explain away this text. Am I Christ's? Then it is he who has promised that neither I nor any who belong to him shall perish. If I do perish, then Jesus has not kept his word, he is not sinless, the atonement was not adequate, and no one in any place can enter into salvation.

I wish that all God's children might come to know and love these truths. I wish that many might be saved by them.

We live in a day that is so weak in its proclamation of Christian doctrine that even many Christians cannot see why such truths should be preached or how they can be used of the Lord to save sinners. This was not always so. It was not always the case that these truths were unused by God in saving sinners.

Did you know that it was these doctrines, particularly the doctrine of God's perseverance with his people, that God used to save Charles Haddon Spurgeon, one of the greatest preachers who ever lived? Spurgeon was saved when he was only fifteen years old, but before that time he had already noticed how friends of his, who had begun life well, made shipwreck of their lives by falling into gross vice. Spurgeon was appalled by such things. He feared that he himself might fall into them. He reasoned like this: "Whatever good resolutions I might make, the probabilities are that they will be good for nothing when temptation [assails] me. I [will] be like those of whom it has been said, 'They see the devil's hook and yet cannot help nibbling at his bait.' I [will] disgrace myself." It was then that he heard of the truth that Christ will keep his saints from falling. It had a particular charm for him and he found himself saying, "If I go to Jesus and get from him a new heart and a right spirit, I shall be secured against these temptations into which others have fallen. I shall be preserved by Him."[2] It was this truth along with others that brought Spurgeon to the Savior.

I wish it might be the same with you! I do not preach a gospel that has a shaky foundation. I do not proclaim a religion of percentages and probabilities. I proclaim the message of Christ, Paul, Augustine, Luther, Calvin, and all others who have found God to be their pure hope and salvation. It is the message of man's complete ruin in sin and of God's perfect remedy in Christ, expressed in his election of a people to himself and his final preservation of them. God grant that you might believe it wholeheartedly.

129

The Hands of God

John 10:28-29

"I give them eternal life, and they shall never perish; no one can snatch them out of my hand. My Father, who has given them to me, is greater than all; no one can snatch them out of my Father's hand."

If you have ever watched a carpenter do rough construction work, you may have seen him do something that will illustrate what the Lord was doing as he was speaking these words to the disciples. Since he had been a carpenter Jesus may have done this same thing himself. Sometimes in rough carpentry a workman will drive a long nail through a thinner board so that the point sticks out the back. Then with a blow of his hammer he will drive the point of the nail over sideways, embedding it in the wood. This is called clinching the nail. It makes the joint just a bit more firm since the nail cannot work itself out from this position.

Two Nails, Four Hands

In a sense this is what Jesus did in these verses. He was so interested in getting the doctrine to stick in his disciples' minds that he not only drove one nail, he drove two, and clinched them both. This is what I mean. First, he taught that those who are his own have been given eternal life. This alone makes the truth fast; for eternal life is life that can never be lost. If it could be lost after a few years or even after many years, it would not be eternal. Nevertheless, Jesus knew that there would be many who would find this difficult to accept and who would attempt to explain it away by saying perhaps that eternal life is a quality of life rather than a life of unending duration. Lest they succeed in doing that, he went on to drive the nail over sideways, thereby clinching it into the wood. "They shall never perish," he said.

"I give them eternal life"—that is the nail. "They shall never perish"—that is the clinch by which the doctrine is reinforced and made fast.

One nail, however well fastened, does not always make a good joint. So Jesus went on to drive a second nail and clinch that. His second nail is found in the phrase "no one can snatch them out of my hand." The clincher is this—"My Father who has given them to me, is greater than all; no one can snatch them out of my Father's hand." It is hard to see how anyone can be safer or any doctrine clearer than that.

Moreover, there is the matter of the hands. First, Jesus says that we are secure in his hand. We can imagine ourselves as a coin around which his fingers have folded. That is a secure position for any object, but especially for us, considering whose hand it is that holds us. But then, lest we think that this is not enough, Jesus adds that the hand of God is over his hand so that we are enclosed in two hands. We are therefore doubly secure. If we feel insecure, we should be reminded that even when we are held in this manner, the Father and Son still have two hands free to defend us. I wish that all Christians might enter into an assurance of that security. "They shall never perish," says Jesus. Believe it! Believe it, too, when he tells us that no man will ever pluck us out of those hands.

"But," says someone, "it may be true, but to teach it is dangerous. If people believe that nothing can ever snatch them from Christ's hand, then surely they will feel free to sin. If I thought so, I would sin."

Would you? If so, I feel sorry for you. I even doubt that you know the Lord, for my experience indicates that it is a knowledge of the love and grace of God that, more than anything else, keeps a believer from sinning.

"Even if there is a possibility of these truths encouraging sin, would it not be better not to preach them? Would it not be better to tell Christians that they might be overcome by sin and so perish?" No, it would not! Moreover, how could I tell what I do not believe? Shall I slander God with falsehoods? Let me put it in terms that you will surely understand. Shall I come to your house and tell your children—little Mary, just two years old, or Michael, just six—that if they disobey you they will cease to be your children and that you will throw them out into the streets? If I were to do that, you would be angry, and rightly so. Rather, you would want me to say, "Children, do you not know that your father loves you, that he will never stop loving you? Therefore, do not disappoint him. Love him and do what he says."

Do you understand that illustration? If so, do not impute lesser motives or lesser love to God. Believe these truths, and allow them to become a great incentive to godly conduct in your life. Moreover, do not be afraid to have them preached, and do not fear to share them with other believers.

Hands of the Father

Let us be specific about the words of our text, particularly about the hands. Jesus said that we are secure in his hand and in the hand of the Father. What do we know about these hands? We recognize, of course, that to talk in this way is at least in part to use poetic language. But the truths are not less true because they are expressed poetically; and in the case of the Lord Jesus Christ the reference to the hands is not even primarily poetic. His hands were real hands. So what do we know about them? And what do we know about the hands of the Father?

Well, the hands of the Father are *creative hands,* for one thing. These are the hands that made the world, that formed man from the earth's dust. The Book of Genesis says: "The LORD God formed man from the dust of the ground and breathed into his nostrils the breath of life, and man became a living being" (Gen. 2:7).

In biblical thought three truths are closely tied up with this teaching. First, God knows us. He knows us because he made us. So nothing that is within us ever surprises him. That is what David had in mind when he said, "For he knows how we are formed, he remembers that we are dust" (Ps. 103:14). We do not need to fear that something in us will suddenly rise up to startle God and cause him to change his attitude toward us.

Second, the fact that we have been made by God means that we have been made for a purpose and that it behooves us to realize that purpose. To realize God's purpose is to find fulfillment and joy, not to find misery. Moreover, it is not for us to question the purpose any more than a pot should question the shape it has been given by the potter. This image is used by the apostle Paul in Romans in order to justify the ways of God in his dealings with Israel.

Third, the fact that we have been made by God means that we should acknowledge that and worship him thankfully. One of the Psalms says: "Come, let us bow down in worship; let us kneel before the LORD our Maker, for he is our God and we are the people of his pasture, the flock under his care" (Ps. 95:6–7).

Loving Hands

The hands of the Father are creative hands, then. But they are also *loving hands.* That is, they are hands that continue to care for and provide for that which they have made.

My favorite picture of this is found in Hosea. It is of God, as a literal father, caring for Israel, pictured as a child who is just learning to walk. The child can also represent ourselves in spiritual infancy. God says, "When Israel was a child, I loved him, and out of Egypt I called my son. . . . It was I who taught Ephraim to walk, taking them by the arms; but they did not realize it was I who healed them. I led them with cords of human kindness, with ties of love. . . . How can I give you up, Ephraim? How can I hand you over, Israel?"

(Hosea 11:1, 3–4, 8). God says that he has been as a father to us, teaching us to walk. His hands have held us up while we were learning and have caught us when we were about to fall down. Moreover, he tells us that this is proof of his love and that he will not give up on those who are his true children.

Angry Hands

Finally, we need to see something that is not so pleasant to contemplate. God's hands are creative hands. They are caring hands. But they can also, so says the Scripture, become *angry hands*. They are hands by which judgment can be administered and by which it will be administered to all whose sin is not covered by the blood of Christ and who are therefore not among the company of God's people. John the Baptist spoke of this, saying that when Christ came it would be with fan in hand and that he would thoroughly purge his floor (Matt. 3:12). John was thinking of the way by which, in Mediterranean lands, wheat was separated from the chaff. Usually this was done by tossing the two into the air so that the wind could blow the lighter chaff away. If the wind did not blow, the winnowing would have to be postponed. However, in Christ's day, says John, Christ will provide his own wind; he will use his fan to separate the righteous from those who will not have him as Savior.

It is of the same judgment that the author of Hebrews writes, saying, "The Lord will judge his people," and then adding by way of stern warning, "It is a dreadful thing to fall into the hands of the living God" (Heb. 10:30–31).

There is a progression at this point. The hands of God are hands that have created. The hands of God are hands that have loved and cared. But man in general has despised the creation and turned from God's love. There is therefore nothing ahead for such men but God's righteous anger and judgment. This thought so possessed Jonathan Edwards that he preached often upon it. In fact, his best known sermon is on precisely this theme. It is "Sinners in the Hands of an Angry God," a title taken from the text that I have just mentioned. The text of the message is Deuteronomy 32:35—"in due time their foot will slip." The point of the sermon is that nothing withholds a man who will not have Christ from God's judgment except God's sovereign will, by which for a time he withholds punishment.

I am told that such truths cannot be preached today, that such teaching will drive listeners away. That may be. At any rate, I am sure that at least one of three things will happen. Either these truths will drive the people away, or the people will drive the minister away, or there will be a great awakening, as there was under Edwards's preaching.

Some say, "Where is revival today?"

I say, "Where are the faithful teachers of God's Word?" I say, "Let the angry God be proclaimed, as well as the God of love, and men's hearts will be stirred to repentance. They have been before. Do it, and many will flee out of a true sense of need to the Savior."

The Hands of Jesus

Look now at the hands of the Son. What do we know about these hands? Well, first, they are the hands of a workman; they are *rough hands*. These hands know labor; they understand toil. He is not remote, this Jesus. He understands us and feels with us in our infirmities.

Moreover, I see this truth and then turn to a text like John 14:2–3 and find an even greater truth there. We are told: "I am going to prepare a place for you. And if I go and prepare a place for you, I will come back and take you to be with me that you also may be where I am." Jesus tells us that he has gone to prepare a home for us. Well, then, I will not worry about the condition of that home or even whether it is going to be finished by the date of occupancy, for the greatest carpenter that ever lived is going to build it for me. In the same way, I do not worry about the condition of my resurrection body. For Paul tells us that if our earthly body "were destroyed, we have a building from God, an eternal house in heaven not built by human hands" (2 Cor. 5:1).

The hands of Jesus are also *outstretched hands*. I see the outstretched hands of Jesus everywhere in the New Testament. They are outstretched in healing, for example. I see him reaching out to touch and heal the leper when no one else would touch him (Matt. 8:3). I see him reach out to heal Peter's mother-in-law when she lay sick of a fever (Matt. 8:15). I see him reach out to restore life to the young daughter of the ruler, recorded in Matthew 9 (vv. 18–26). He touched the son of the widow of Nain to restore his life (Luke 7:11–18). His outstretched hands restored sight to the man who had been born blind (John 9:6–7).

Christ's hands also are outstretched to save such as are floundering. I love the story of Peter walking on the water toward Christ. The disciples were in the boat on the Sea of Galilee when they saw Jesus. He was walking toward them on the water. When Peter saw it he concluded rightly that if Jesus could do it, then by the power of Jesus he could do it also. So he said, "Lord, can I come?" When Jesus agreed, Peter started out. But soon he took his eyes from Jesus, looked at the water instead, and began to sink.

"Lord, save me," he cried.

Immediately, we are told, "Jesus reached out his hand and caught him" (Matt. 14:31). Sinking into the waves? That seems to be a picture of losing salvation. But then we see the outstretched, saving hands of the Lord Jesus. Peter's faith failed, but Jesus did not fail to save Peter.

These hands are stretched out also in blessing. We see the Lord blessing the children, even when the disciples in a fit of self-importance wished to keep them away (Matt. 19:13–15). We find the same thing at the end of Luke's Gospel, in the last picture we have of the Lord Jesus while on earth— "When he had led them out to Bethany he lifted up his hands and blessed them. While he was blessing them, he left them and was taken up into heaven" (Luke 24:50–51).

Wounded Hands

The last thing we need to see is, in some respects, the most obvious truth of all. The hands of Jesus are also *wounded hands*. The imprint of the nails of the crucifixion is in those hands, and it is for us that they were wounded. God told us that they would be. It is prophesied in Psalm 22, in which the crucifixion of the Lord is presented: "A band of evil men has encircled me, they have pierced my hands and my feet" (v. 16). Isaiah wrote: "But he was pierced for our transgressions, he was crushed for our iniquities; the punishment that brought us peace was upon him, and by his wounds we are healed" (Isa. 53:5). Zechariah foretold that this would be a sign by which the true prophet, the Messiah, would be recognized (Zech. 13:6).

It is by this that we recognize him. Thomas is our pattern. Thomas had not been present on that first occasion when Jesus appeared to his disciples. The others told Thomas about it afterward, but Thomas replied, "Unless I see the nail marks in his hands and put my finger where the nails were, and put my hand into his side, I will not believe it" (John 20:25). A week later Jesus appeared again, Thomas being present, and offered to fulfill the conditions of Thomas's test. But the mere sight was enough for Thomas. Thomas fell at Christ's feet and worshiped, saying, "My Lord and my God" (v. 28).

Is that sight not clear enough for you also? Are Jesus' wounded hands not evidence enough for you of his love?

God says that his action in Christ is perfectly clear, so much so that there is no excuse for a failure to believe it. In fact, he says that the way of salvation in Christ has been "made known" (Rom. 3:21). The way of salvation has been made as clear as a striking hand or a blow to the face. Today it is the hand of a gracious God who holds out the way of salvation to you. If you reply that you cannot see it, he asks you to look at the hand itself; for it is a wounded hand, one bearing the print of the nail received by Jesus in dying for your salvation. By faith you may put out your hand and touch that wound. You may know that it is evidence, irrefutable evidence, of God's great love for you. That hand was struck for you. The one extending that hand died for you. Allow him to enclose your hand, to enclose you, and to bring you into that great company of those who possess eternal life and who shall *never* perish.

130

The Issue in Six Words

John 10:30–39

"I and the Father are one."

Again the Jews picked up stones to stone him, but Jesus said to them, "I have shown you many great miracles from the Father. For which of these do you stone me?"

"We are not stoning you for any of these," replied the Jews, "but for blasphemy, because you, a mere man, claim to be God."

Jesus answered them, "Is it not written in your Law, 'I have said you are gods'? If he called them 'gods,' to whom the word of God came—and the Scripture cannot be broken—what about the one whom the Father set apart as his very own and sent into the world? Why then do you accuse me of blasphemy because I said, 'I am God's Son'? Do not believe me unless I do what my Father does. But if I do it, even though you do not believe me, believe the miracles, that you may know and understand that the Father is in me, and I in the Father." Again they tried to seize him, but he escaped their grasp.

The Gospel of John is filled with statements of the full divinity of Jesus Christ, but no statement is clearer than the one to which we come now. The opponents of the Lord asked him to speak plainly, implying that his lack of candor was the cause of their unbelief. So Jesus did speak plainly: first, to say that he had already spoken and acted plainly (it was their sin rather than a lack of evidence that caused their hostility) and, second, to outline the doctrines of God's grace whereby men and women are saved entirely apart from any merit in themselves and are kept secure entirely by God's unchanging good pleasure. It is this latter teaching that leads to the statement of Christ's total divinity with which the discourse closes.

Is Jesus God? That is the great question of John's Gospel. Is he fully divine? In this verse, Jesus declares that he is, doing so in just six words. "I and the Father are one," he says (v. 30). Because of their obvious importance, these words and their sequel deserve both careful study and a personal response.

One in Essence

First of all, what do these words mean? What did Jesus mean when he stated, "I and my Father are one"?

We may begin by saying that at the very least Jesus was claiming to be one with the Father in the matter of his will. This grows out of the context, for he had been speaking of the security of believers and had added that the will both of the Father and of himself was to that end. Believers would never perish, first, because no one could snatch them out of his hand and, second, because no one could snatch them out of the Father's hand. Someone might imagine that the will of the Father and Son in the matter of preserving believers might not be in perfect agreement. But lest they think this, Jesus immediately adds that it is precisely in this that they are united. Because of this unity we know that when we see Jesus working we see God working, and we know that God is like Jesus.

On the other hand, the phrase "I and the Father are one" obviously also means more than this, for only a full claim to divinity by Jesus explains the way in which the leaders reacted to Jesus' statement. What was their reaction? We are told that "the Jews picked up stones to stone him" (v. 31). Why did they do this? Clearly, because they saw that his statement was not only a claim to be one with the Father in respect of his will but also to be one with him in power—"no one can snatch them out of my Father's hand," and, "no one can snatch them out of my hand"—and that this latter was the same thing as claiming to be fully divine. In theological terms, this is the same as saying that the Son is one in substance with the Father and that they are equal in power and glory.

Four important conclusions follow from this truth concerning Jesus' nature: (1) we have the knowledge of God in him, for he is God; (2) we have forgiveness of sins in him, for his death had infinite merit in atoning for sin; (3) we have victory over circumstances in him, for he lived above circumstances; and (4) we have triumph over death in him, for he rose from the dead and has promised to so raise all whom the Father has given to him, that is, all who believe on him and have eternal life (John 6:39–40, 44, 54).

This is not a "pie-in-the-sky" philosophy. It affects our life now. Let me illustrate this by the following poem written by a good friend of mine who recently died of cancer. The death of this woman was a prolonged affair, accompanied by great pain. But she was not bitter. On the contrary, her speech was full of praise as she thought of Jesus, the one through whom she had come to a knowledge of God and who was even then preparing a place for her in heaven. Her son Peter recorded this testimony six months before her departure:

> I read the Psalms when yet my eyes could read
> And I discovered, oh, so many ways,
> That the great psalmist felt the urge and need
> To magnify his God in songs of praise.
>
> Praise is an effort—both when times are good
> And happiness fills our hearts
> And in dark times not fully understood.
> Then it is hard to say: "I'll praise, I will."
>
> I will—a conscious effort. I will praise!
> I will love Thee! I will extol!
> I will rejoice and make a joyful noise!
> Yes, I will praise Thee, Lord, with heart and soul.
>
> But once the songs of praise roll off my tongue
> I'll serve the Lord with gladness and with joy.
> But more than that—I may not praise alone.
> Praise ye the Lord; ye nations, praise His name.
> Sing of His mercy. Make His goodness known.

A testimony like that does not come easily to the tongue. But it does come through a knowledge and love of God as he is seen and known in the Lord Jesus.

Three Arguments

The fact that Jesus made a claim to be God is not the same as proving it, of course. And the fact that it needed to be proved is seen by the reaction of his listeners. They dismissed it outright and were ready to stone Christ for having spoken it. But was there proof? Was there evidence that Jesus is who he said he is? In the verses that follow Jesus responds to these questions with three lines of argument.

First, he told his opponents that he had done nothing to merit stoning. He said, "I have shown you many great miracles from the Father. For which of these do you stone me?" (v. 32). This was a perfectly valid argument. We recognize the force of it when we refuse to judge a person until we see what he can do. A man may claim to be a good worker, but we do not conclude that he is one until we see him at work. A child may claim to have been good while the mother was out shopping, but the mother does not accept the claim at face value until she sees the condition of the living room. So it was with the Lord Jesus Christ. He had made a great claim. All right! What was the evidence? Was the claim unverified or was it backed up by works? We all know the answer. Jesus had healed the sick, raised the dead, cured lepers, taught the multitudes. For which of these works did they reject his claim, then? For which of these were they attempting to stone him?

Strangely enough, his opponents reacted to this argument by reversing it, which we know to be wrong. "We are not stoning you for any of these," they said, "but for blasphemy." In other words, they were willing to skip over the issue of whether his works backed up his words, so intent were they on his destruction.

Today there is not quite the same movement to do away with Christ physically—he is not here to be crucified—but the argument is voiced by many who will not have him to be God in their lives. They will admit that he did good works, but they will not accept him as God; they will not consider whether his works support his claim to be divine. One woman who thought this way, declared, "I do not doubt that Jesus was a good man and did many wonderful things, but I will not accept the claim that he is God. I will not follow him."

Because the Jewish leaders thought this way, Jesus introduced another argument. What they were doing was willfully rejecting his words. So Jesus next showed that there was nothing about his words for which they could fault him either. Here's how he put it, "Is it not written in your Law, 'I have said you are gods'? If he called them 'gods,' to whom the word of God came—and the Scripture cannot be broken—what about the one whom the Father set apart as his very own and sent into the world? Why then do you accuse me of blasphemy because I said, 'I am God's Son?'" (vv. 34–36).

I want to admit, before we get into these verses, that the argument that they contain is a difficult one for most contemporary people to understand. For one thing, it is obviously a rabbinic argument, which means that it depends upon distinctions that were of great importance to the rabbis but that seem at best to be of minor importance to people today. For another thing, the drift of the argument seems to be in the opposite direction from what we understand Christ to have been saying previously. He was claiming to be God in a unique and absolute sense; but in these verses he seems to be watering down the claim by saying that he meant no more by it than what the Old Testament means when it applied the word "gods" to men. What are we to do in the face of these difficulties? How do we begin to understand Christ's argument?

We need to turn to the text he is quoting and see what the words mean there. Jesus is quoting from the eighty-second psalm, and when we turn to it we discover that the phrase "You are gods" (v. 6) is used of the judges of Israel. The judges in this psalm are called gods, not because they are divine but because they act as God in their role as judges. They are consecrated to a special task, indeed a holy task; and in God's name they exercise authority and power. "Now," says Jesus, "I too have been sent into this world by God the Father and that for a specific task. In that task I exercise authority and power, just as the judges of Israel did. If the word 'gods' can be used of mere men because of their function—if judges can be called gods—then how much more should I be called God in the full sense since I have received a unique commissioning and exercise unique power?"

In other words, Jesus was not denying that he is God in a unique sense—far from it. He was only denying that he had spoken words that were improper. The words are proper enough if spoken merely in relation to man. How much more appropriate are they then of Jesus, who is more than man? Do you see the force of the argument? To our way of thinking it may not be entirely satisfactory, but it should be understandable. We can express it by saying that, not only is there nothing in Christ's *works* to merit stoning, neither is there anything in his *words* to merit stoning.

Finally, we come to Christ's third argument, that to which the others lead up. It is this. Since there was nothing in Christ's words to which these men could properly object and since they acknowledged his deeds, these deeds alone should have led them to faith in him. Jesus put it in these words, "Do not believe me unless I do what my Father does. But if I do it, even though you do not believe me, believe the miracles, that you may know and understand that the Father is in me, and I in the Father" (vv. 37–38). Christ's works should lead men to faith in him. It is as simple as that.

Belief and Good Works

This argument confronts you. If you are not yet a believer in Jesus, this argument is one approach to your heart. Can you accuse Jesus of sin or of an inadequate lifestyle? Hardly! It is rather that he, by his life, accuses you. Do you find his works inadequate, his words unsupportable? Certainly not! Instead, you confess with the many of Christ's own time, "No one ever spoke like this man. . . . No one ever did what this man has done." Well, then, let the facts impel you to belief. Throw aside your rebellion and commit yourself to him as his disciple.

Above all, believe on him. I like to distinguish among three different levels of belief. The first level is that on which someone simply believes *something*. It has to do with factual knowledge. A second level of belief is what we might intend when we say that we believe *in something*. In some expressions that word "in" suggests the addition of a value system so that we are saying that the thing we believe in is important. In this sense we may believe in America, in motherhood, in apple pie. The third level of belief is that expressed when we say that we believe *on someone*. This level of belief involves trust and action. It is the kind of faith we exercise when we step onto a bridge, believing that it will hold us up, or when we get into a boat, believing that it is seaworthy and will not go down. This is saving faith. It is the kind of belief Christ calls for on the basis of who he is, what he has done, and what words he has spoken.[1] If you will accept the facts and commit yourself to him in this way, he promises to save you from your sin, give you peace and victory over the circumstances of life, and eventually take you to be with himself in heaven in a place that he has prepared for you. Will you come to him? Will you believe on him as your Savior?

We need to see, too, that there is an application in these verses for the Christian. In these verses the Lord Jesus Christ laid stress upon his works—not his words but his works—and his point was that these should point men to him. That is a wonderful argument. But if it is true for Jesus, it also is true in some sense for his followers. If you are a Christian, you claim to have been saved by Jesus in such a way that his spirit now lives within you and directs your life and life choices. Do you live like it? Is there anything in your life that is evidence of his spirit within you? Jesus indicated that this should be true of you, for when some marveled at his deeds he answered, "I tell you the truth, anyone who has faith in me will do what I have been doing. He will do even greater things than these, because I am going to the Father" (John 14:12).

"Full Moon" Revival

We need to acknowledge that even at best there will always be a great difference between the works of Christ and our works. But for that reason we need all the more to turn to him and draw strength from him. Or, to change the metaphor, we need to turn to him so that we may reflect his brilliance to others. He is the sun. When he was in the world he said, "I am the light of the world," and when he was thinking of leaving this world he turned to those whom he was leaving and said, "You are the light of the world." But they were not suns; they were moons. They, like ourselves, could shine only by reflecting his light.

Now is this world's night, for the sun is gone. But here is the moon, the church, composed of those who know the Lord Jesus. How will it shine? Will it shine as a full moon or a new moon? A waxing or a waning quarter? I want it to be a full moon. I think of the early church, the church of the apostles. The church was just a new moon then. But it grew and came to reflect the glory of its departed Lord to such a superlative degree that the entire world eventually sat up and took notice. It can happen again, if we turn our faces toward him. Let us confess that we have no brightness in ourselves. Let us admit our inability to do works worthy of his presence within us. But then, by his grace, let us also allow him to use us to reflect his glory to the world. Let us have a full moon of revival once again.

131

Word of the Living God

John 10:35

"If he called them 'gods,' to whom the word of God came—and the Scripture cannot be broken . . ."

In the midst of Christ's reply to the religious leaders of his day, who were accusing him of blasphemy, there is a reference to the nature of Scripture that is so important that it deserves special consideration.

The leaders had accused Jesus of making himself the Son of God, and he had replied by a reference to Psalm 82:6 in which the word "gods" was used of the judges of Israel. "If the word can be used of mere men, how much more can the word be used of me?" was his argument. If Jesus had said nothing more at this point, his use of the psalm would be important; for he was basing his argument on a single word of the Old Testament that he clearly accepted as trustworthy. But he did say more, and what he said are the words we want to study. He said that "the Scripture cannot be broken" (v. 35). In our terms this was an affirmation of the Bible's total inspiration, inerrancy, and utter indestructibility. A great statement! It needs to occupy our attention in this study.

Early Christianity

However, before we look at the precise meaning of the phrase "cannot be broken" we need to see that the high view of the Bible expressed by Jesus

795

in this and many other statements has always been the accepted view of the church—until relatively modern times. In the last two centuries or so the orthodox view of the Bible has been denied by large segments of the church so that for many the Bible has become man's word about God rather than God's word to man, and its authority has been lessened. But this was not always so. In fact, when we turn to past ages we discover that until recently all who claimed to be Christians, even heretics, acknowledged that the Bible was infallible and authoritative.

In the documents of the early Catholic Church there are many statements to substantiate this claim. Cyril of Jerusalem, who lived in the fourth century, said, "We must not deliver anything whatsoever, without the sacred Scriptures, nor let ourselves be misled by mere probability, or by marshalling of arguments. For this salvation of ours by faith is . . . by proof from the sacred Scriptures" (*Cathechetical Lectures*, IV, 17).

In a letter to Jerome, the translator of the Latin Vulgate, Augustine said, "I have learned to hold the Scriptures alone inerrant." And in his "Preface to the Treatise on the Trinity" he warned, "Do not follow my writings as Holy Scripture. When you find in Holy Scripture anything that you did not believe before, believe it without doubt; but in my writings, you should hold nothing for certain." He wrote: "I believe most firmly that no one of those authors has erred in any respect in writing" (*Epistles*, 82, 1, 3).

The same position holds good for Luther. It is common today, in surveying works that deny a high view of Scripture, to find Luther's reference to the Bible as "the cradle of Christ" quoted as proving that Luther believed in a revelation within the Bible, not identical with it, and held the Scriptures, which speak of Christ, in less esteem than the Christ whom they contain. For some this means that the "cradle" may be discarded in order to reach its treasure. For others it means that not all of the Bible is the Word of God. It is obvious, however, that this is not what Luther meant. Luther's evaluation of the Bible as the "cradle of Christ" occurs at the end of the third paragraph of his "Preface to the Old Testament." And there, as the late Lutheran scholar J. Theodore Mueller has ably demonstrated, Luther is actually defending the value of the Old Testament for Christians. Far from deprecating Scripture, Luther is actually concerned "to express his most reverent esteem of Holy Scripture, which offers to man the supreme blessing of eternal salvation in Christ."[1] Luther himself says in this context in speaking of the Old Testament, "I beg and faithfully warn every pious Christian not to stumble at the simplicity of the language and stories that will often meet him there. He should not doubt that, however simple they may seem, these are the very words, works, judgments, and deeds of the high majesty, power, and wisdom of God" ("Preface to the Old Testament").

He says elsewhere, "The Scriptures, although they were also written by men, are not of men nor from men, but from God" ("That Doctrines of Men Are to be Rejected"). And again, "We must make a great difference between God's Word and the word of man. A man's word is a little sound, that flies into the air, and soon vanishes; but the Word of God is greater than heaven and earth, yea, greater than death and hell, for it forms part of the power of God, and endures everlastingly" (*Table Talk*, xliv).

In some places, Calvin is even more outspoken. Commenting on 2 Timothy 3:16, he maintains: "This is the principle that distinguishes our religion from all others, that we know that God hath spoken to us and are fully convinced that the prophets did not speak of themselves, but as organs of the Holy Spirit uttered only that which they had been commissioned from heaven to declare. All those who wish to profit from the Scriptures must first accept this as a settled principle, that the Law and the prophets are not teachings handed on at the pleasure of men or produced by men's minds as their source, but are dictated by the Holy Spirit." He concludes, "We owe to the Scripture the same reverence as we owe to God, since it has its only source in Him and has nothing of human origin mixed with it."[2]

John Wesley says the same thing: "The Scripture, therefore, is a rule sufficient in itself, and was by men who were divinely inspired at once delivered to the world" (*A Roman Catechism*, Q. 5). "In all cases, the Church is to be judged by the Scripture, not the Scripture by the Church" (*Popery Calmly Considered*, 1, 6).

It was the glory of the church that in its first sixteen or seventeen centuries all Christians in every place, despite their differences of opinion on theology or on questions of church order, exhibited at least a mental allegiance to the Bible as the supreme authority for the Christian in all matters. It might have been neglected. There might have been disagreements about what it actually teaches. It might even have been contradicted. But it was still the Word of God. It was the only infallible rule of faith and practice.

An Infallible Bible

The fact that the Christians of an earlier day thought along these lines is not an accident of history or, still less, a product of wishful thinking. Christians of an earlier century had a high view of the Bible because the Bible has a high view of itself. Or, to put it in other language, Christians regarded the Bible as the infallible Word of God because the Lord Jesus Christ himself so regarded it.

This is where our text comes in. For when Jesus Christ said, somewhat as an aside, "the Scripture cannot be broken," he was saying (at the very least) that the Scripture cannot be "broken into" or "faulted." That is, Scripture cannot be wrong. Leon Morris comments: "The term 'broken' is not defined, and it is a word which is not often used of Scripture or the like. . . . But it is perfectly intelligible. It means that Scripture cannot be emptied of its force by being shown to be erroneous."[3]

This attitude of Jesus to Scripture is confirmed by other statements of his. For one thing, Jesus often appealed to Scripture as an infallible authority. When tempted by the devil in the wilderness, Jesus replied with three quotations from Deuteronomy (Matt. 4:1–11). By quoting Exodus 3:6 ("I am the God of your father, the God of Abraham, the God of Isaac and the God of Jacob"), he rebuked the Sadducees for questioning the heavenly status of marriage and the reality of the resurrection (Luke 20:27–40). He taught that "not the smallest letter, not the least stroke of a pen, will be any means disappear from the Law until everything is accomplished" (Matt. 5:18). On many occasions he appealed to Scripture in support of his actions—in defense of his cleansing of the temple (Mark 11:15–17), in reference to his submission to the cross (Matt. 26:53–54).

In the second place, Jesus saw his life as a fulfillment of Scripture and consciously submitted himself to it. He began his ministry with a quotation from Isaiah 61:1–2—"The Spirit of the Lord is on me, because he has anointed me to preach good news to the poor. He has sent me to proclaim freedom for the prisoners and recovery of sight for the blind, to release the oppressed, to proclaim the year of the Lord's favor" (Luke 4:18–19). He taught that he had not come "to abolish" the law and the prophets "but to fulfill them" (Matt. 5:17). On the night of his arrest he foretold the scattering of the disciples. This would occur because, he said, "It is written: I will strike the shepherd, and the sheep will be scattered" (quoted from Zech. 13:7 in Mark 14:27). You "search the Scriptures," he told the Jews, "[because] you think that by them you possess eternal life. These are the Scriptures that testify about me" (John 5:39). Even after the resurrection, he chides the disciples for being "'foolish . . . and slow of heart to believe all that the prophets have spoken! Did not the Christ have to suffer these things and then enter his glory?' And beginning with Moses and all the prophets, he explained to them what was said in all the Scriptures concerning himself" (Luke 24:25–27).

On the basis of these and other passages it is beyond doubt that Christ highly esteemed the Old Testament and constantly submitted to it, as to an authoritative revelation. Because they are the words of God, Jesus assumed their complete reliability even to the smallest point of grammar.

Infallibility

Unfortunately, the idea of an infallible Bible is widely rejected in our day, even among some evangelicals—first, by those who allege specific errors in the record, and second, by those who interpret the doctrine incorrectly. There are those, for instance, who interpret the claim of infallibility to mean that the Bible cannot report sin or errors. This is not correct. Many people in the Bible spoke lies and acted sinfully, and the Bible records it. But the Bible does not endorse either their lying or their sin. The Bible quotes the devil, but it does not suggest that we believe him.

In the same way, infallibility does not imply completeness, as though the biblical writers were under an obligation to tell all that happened in any given moment. In fact, sometimes they explicitly disavowed this aim (John 20:30). The doctrine of infallibility does not mean that all the existing manuscripts of the Bible are free from error; they certainly are not. The Holy Spirit inspired the original manuscripts, not the scribes who copied them. The doctrine of infallibility does not imply the infallibility of interpretations of the Bible. These views are misconceptions. The doctrine of infallibility simply means that in their original form the books of the Bible are free from factual errors and that they possess absolute, binding authority when they present teaching that purports to be from God.

Recently the heart of the debate over infallibility has shifted to the function of languages as a vehicle of truth. Some scholars imply that truth transcends language or that Scripture truth resides only in the thoughts, not the words, of Scripture or in the subjective experience of the hearer. But this is nonsense. If the Bible is inspired at all, it must be inspired verbally. And verbal inspiration means infallibility.

Of course, there are parts of Scripture where the choice of a word may make little difference in the recording of a fact or doctrine. The wording of some verses can be changed, as translators sometimes do to convey the proper meaning. But there are other places where the words are supremely important and where the understanding of a doctrine will inevitably suffer if we fail to take the words seriously. Certainly, if we are to have an authoritative Bible at this point, we also must have a verbally inspired and therefore an infallible Bible, a Bible that is infallible at this point and consequently at other points as well.

What happens when the function of language as a vehicle for truth is denied may be illustrated by this story. In one of the classes of one of our prominent theological seminaries a professor had been denying that words have a one-to-one relationship to meaning and had concluded that all truth is subjective. One of the conservative students challenged his professor. He argued that while it is true that we often misunderstand what is meant by a word or words, nevertheless words do have meaning and do convey literal content. The word "airplane" makes all who speak English think of a certain kind of object flying through the sky, he argued. If you say, "Look, an airplane!" people will look up. He gave other illustrations. Finally, the student said to his professor, "If language is what you say it is, then conversation is meaningless. In fact, this class is meaningless: There is no point in our being here."

There was a moment of silence as the truth of his words sunk in. Then someone said, "If this is meaningless, what shall we do for the rest of the hour?"

"Let's play squash," someone suggested. So the class got up and walked out, leaving the professor alone in his classroom.

God's Hammer

Through the ages men and women have sought to discredit Scripture and remove it as a force in their lives. But it has been those who have sought to destroy the Bible who have been destroyed, not the Bible. There are many images for the Bible in its own pages. It is called a lamp, a mirror, a sword, a seed. Notice that it also is called a fire and a hammer, a fire because it will burn in judgment and a hammer because it will break in pieces all who will not bow before it. "Is not my word like fire?" wrote Jeremiah; "and like a hammer that breaks a rock in pieces?" (Jer. 23:29).

Will you resist that Word? If so, then you will be broken; for the Scripture cannot be broken. Or will you submit to it and to the Christ who upheld it?

The Bible is not just another book. It is God's book, and as such it is powerful. It will change you, if you will let it. It was a section of the thirteenth chapter of Romans that changed the life of Augustine as he turned to the Bible in the garden of a friend's estate near Milan. Luther tells how in meditating upon the Scripture he felt himself to be "reborn," and relates how Romans 1:17 became for him "a gate to heaven." Wesley's meditation upon Scripture led to his conversion in the little meeting in Aldersgate.

Here is a modern example: "Some years before the publication of the *New English Bible*," writes J. B. Phillips, "I was invited by the BBC to discuss the problems of translation with Dr. E. V. Rieu, who had himself recently produced a translation of the four Gospels for Penguin Classics. Towards the end of the discussion Dr. Rieu was asked about his general approach to the task, and his reply was this:

"'My personal reason for doing this was my own intense desire to satisfy myself as to the authenticity and the spiritual content of the Gospels. And, if I received any new light by an intensive study of the Greek originals, to pass it on to others. I approached them in the same spirit as I would have approached them had they been presented to me as recently discovered Greek manuscripts.'

"A few minutes later I asked him, 'Did you get the feeling that the whole material is extraordinary alive? . . . I got the feeling that the whole thing was alive even while one was translating. Even though one did a dozen versions of a particular passage, it was still living. Did you get that feeling?'

"Dr. Rieu replied, 'I got the deepest feeling that I possibly could have expected. It—changed me; my work changed me. And I came to the conclusion that these words bear the seal of—the Son of Man and God. And they're the Magna Charta of the human spirit.'"

J. B. Phillips concludes, "I found it particularly thrilling to hear a man who is a scholar of the first rank as well as a man of wisdom and experience openly admitting that these words written long ago were alive with power. They bore to him, as to me, the ring of truth."[4]

132

Blessing before the Storm

John 10:40–42

Then Jesus went back across the Jordan to the place where John had been baptizing in the early days. Here he stayed and many people came to him. They said, "Though John never performed a miraculous sign, all that John said about this man was true." And in that place many believed in Jesus.

Those he Bible says, "There is a time for every thing and a season for every activity under heaven" (Eccl. 3:1). There is a time to advance, regardless of the opposition, and there is a time to retreat. We see an example of the latter in the actions of the Lord Jesus Christ that close the tenth chapter of John's Gospel.

Jesus had been in Jerusalem for some time, according to John's account. But he had not been well received there, and the time for his earthly ministry was running out. We do not know all Christ's movements during this period, but we do know that he had gone to Jerusalem from Galilee in the fall of his final year, at the time of the Feast of Tabernacles (John 7:2, 10), and that he had presumably been there after that for most of the winter. During these months he had preached widely and sharply, and opposition had grown, particularly on the part of the Jewish leaders. They had disliked him initially because of his views about the Sabbath. Now their dislike of him had grown into hatred and attempted murder. Once in chapter 8 and now twice in chapter 10 they have tried to kill him.

Clearly, the door to an effective ministry in Jerusalem was closing. So we read that Jesus left Jerusalem. He "went back across the Jordan to the place where John had been baptizing. There he stayed" (10:40).

It is hard to imagine an action more simple than that. Yet this decision on Christ's part is filled with lessons. For one thing, it is an illustration of the value of returning to places that have been of great blessing in our lives; for beyond the Jordan was where Christ had been baptized, John had preached, and the first disciples had followed Jesus. It was not far from the place in which Christ was tempted by the devil. For another thing, it is an illustration of the value of working at all times; for even though this was a time of retreat from Jerusalem it was not a time of inactivity.

Any one of these themes could be developed. But what I want to focus on particularly is the fact that this became a time of great spiritual blessing, so much so that we read, "and many people came to him. They said, 'Though John never performed a miraculous sign, all that John said about this man was true.' And in that place many believed in Jesus" (vv. 41–42). Driven out of Jerusalem? Yes, in a sense. But not out of a place of God's blessing. In the first chapter of the Gospel, John tells us that the name of this place was Bethabara, which means "place of passage." This undoubtedly referred to a place where a ferry could be used to cross the river; but in these days Bethabara became a place of passage in another sense, for many passed from death to life as the result of Christ's ministry.

The storm is coming. In a short while Christ again will be in Jerusalem and this time he will be crucified. But here is blessing before the coming storm. As we look into the characteristics of this time, which led to blessing, let us pray that these might increasingly become characteristics of our own time and that blessing might follow.

A Quiet Place

We should notice, as we do this, that not every time is a time of blessing. Nor is every place. Jesus had just come from Jerusalem, and that, far from being a place of blessing, was actually a place of persecution. Are there some who have been going through a time of persecution, testing, a dark night of the soul? So did Jesus. He was not always successful in his preaching. So, do not despair. Take heart. The time is coming when night's shadows will pass and the day of blessing will dawn.

What made this time, as opposed to other times, a time in which the Spirit moved and many believed on Jesus? First, we can notice that it was a quiet time. Jerusalem was a city of great bustle and activity, as cities are. But here was a quiet spot and little activity. In Jerusalem Jesus had come to men and had preached to them, but we sense that it was a situation in which he had to fight for their attention. He used dramatic events, like crying out on the last great day of the Feast of Tabernacles as water was being poured on the altar, "If any-one is thirsty, let him come to me and drink" (John 7:37), and miracles, like the healing of the man who had been born blind. Then (we sense it, do we not?) he found his hearers quickly returning to the activities that pressed in upon them. Here, beyond the Jordan, it was different, and those who came to him came not to do things but to hear what he said and reflect upon it.

Let me encourage you to be quiet and to think of spiritual things. If you do not, how can you expect any blessing? One of the earliest preachers from whom we have any substantial writings, Chrysostom, once preached a sermon on these verses in which he commented on the fact that more women than men seem to receive Christ's teachings. Why is it? he asked. He then suggested that in his opinion it is because women for the most part are at home during the day and have time to think, while men are so often entirely caught up in the world's business. Is that true? Perhaps in part, I do not know. But I do know that there will never be blessing unless we take time to think about spiritual things.

So do it. Do it now and also throughout the week in your times of personal Bible study and prayer. Spurgeon once wrote, "Surely, heaven is worth a little thought if it is to be gained."[1] That is certainly true of all spiritual blessings. So be quiet; wait upon God.

A Large Congregation

The second characteristic of this period is that Jesus had a large congregation. "Many people came to him," we are told. Therefore, we are not surprised to read one verse later that "many believed in Jesus."

I do not want to let this point get out of proportion, and I do not want to spend too much time on it. But at the same time I do not want to overlook the fact that Jesus often preached to large crowds. He did not neglect small numbers; in fact, his closest disciples, those with whom he worked most closely and whom he trained, numbered only twelve. But Jesus would also preach to the multitudes, and it is in times like these that we often read of great blessing. Let me state this in simple language. If God chooses to save but one or two, we are glad. If he assigns us to just a small group, we are content; for we are content to do his will, whatever it may be. But if there are no restrictions—and indeed there hardly seem to be any at this moment—then how can we be fully content or experience the fullest measure of delight unless many come to him? There is no special virtue in small numbers. There is nothing honorable in poor results. So let us have great blessing! Let us bring many to hear the faithful preaching of God's Word, and let us have many faithful men to proclaim it.

If we are to have many converts, we must obviously have many hearers. Let us bring them to hear the Word. Whom have you brought to hear God's Word this week? this month? this year? Is there no one whom you can bring? Of course, there is! Then bring him or her, and ask God to send blessing.

A Faithful Testimony

A third feature characterized these days spent in the wilderness beyond the Jordan. It was the memory of John the Baptist's preaching. Jesus preached, but his preaching was not sowing. It was reaping because another faithful minister had sown seed before him. This was where John had preached. Many remembered his teaching and, hearing Jesus, said, "Though John never performed a miraculous sign, all that John said about this man was true" (v. 41). Oh, that this might be true for us as it has been true of others! Do we reap? It is because others have sown. Will we sow? We must, if those who follow us are also to gain a harvest.

These verses also tell us what characterized John's testimony. That is, they tell us why his testimony was fruitful.

To begin with, John *spoke of Christ*. This does not mean, you will understand, that he did not speak of other things too. John spoke to the moral corruption of his time. He rebuked the Pharisees and Sadducees, when they thought to come for baptism without having truly repented of sin. He counseled priests and soldiers and many others, always giving sound biblical instruction and speaking to the times. John did and said many things, but his main work and testimony was to speak of Christ. And this is what remained in the minds of his listeners. John made it his business to speak of Christ— first, last, and always. Consequently, when others looked back on his testimony they remembered that he had taught them of Jesus.

What great preaching this was, this preaching of John. John stood on the far side of the cross and the empty tomb, but he understood what was coming and did not fail to proclaim it. He said that Jesus was the Son of God and gave this testimony, "I have seen and I testify that this is the Son of God" (John 1:34). Is that in your testimony? That Christ is a man is also true. But if his humanity is taught without the addition that he is also God, there will be no blessing. John saw his divinity, rejoiced in his divinity, proclaimed his divinity. We should do so also.

Then, too, John testified that Jesus was the Lamb of God who would take away the sin of the world (John 1:29). Here John had the full sacrificial system of Israel in mind, and he was declaring Christ to be that Lamb sent by God of whom all the other lambs were but figures. Jesus was to die the death of the substitute. He was to die for sin, and not only for sin in general but for the sin of his people. Do you proclaim that message? You may talk about love and grace and social needs and prophecy and countless other items, all of which are good, but if the message of the substitutionary death of the Lord Jesus Christ for sin is missing, the other points will count for nothing. Christ crucified! That is the gospel. It is that which men and women remember.

We have already seen that John spoke of Christ. Notice secondly that *what he spoke about Christ was true*. This was acknowledged by those who had both heard John and met Jesus.

Here we see a great weakness in much preaching. Some preach anything but Christ. They talk of civil rights, about corruption in government, about politics, and seldom speak of Christ. But it is also true that some do speak about Jesus and yet fail in their task because they do not preach the truth concerning him. They have a limited Christ—one who is man but not God, one who died but who did not rise in triumph, one who came once but who will not come again, one who spoke in love but who will not speak out in judgment. Do not give me a Christ whittled down to man's measure. Do not throw me a truncated Jesus. I want the Christ of the Gospels—the One who is both man and God, who died but who also rose again in triumph, who came once but who is also coming again, who is love but who is also filled with wrath against sin. In short, I want the true Jesus, preached by John and by all who are faithful in their teaching of God's Word.

Do we preach such a Christ? Are we known for such testimony? God grant that it might be said of us after we have gone and men reflect on our testimony: "He did no miracle, but all that he said about Christ was true."

John spoke of Christ. What he spoke concerning Christ was true. But then, let us also notice, *all that he spoke concerning Christ was true.* It was not merely that some of his words concerning Christ were true and that some were not. All that he spoke concerning Christ was true. Shall we strive to do less? Shall we be satisfied with facts plus error?

"No," you say. "Let us have the truth, the whole truth, and nothing but the truth."

All right! But how shall we avoid error? There is only one way: by a diligent study of God's Word and a faithful adherence to it. We must not trust our own understanding. Our reasonings must be judged by this book. There is much of human opinion in Christianity in our century. God grant that such a trend might be changed, and that we might be in the vanguard of those who change it. Shall we have a slogan? Then let it be this—"Christ, the true Christ, and only Christ." And may he do the great work of drawing men and women to faith.

Results of Sound Preaching

In conclusion, let me also point out that on the occasion of Christ's ministry beyond Jordan this is precisely what happened. It was a time of blessing because (1) it was in a quiet place, (2) there was a large congregation, and (3) the work of the present was being built upon a strong testimony. But what precisely happened? Three things!

First, we are told that many *came to Jesus.* He was not in a popular place. In fact, he was in an out-of-the-way place. But there was that in him and his message that drew people. The drawing power of the Lord is not lessened. Many may also come to him today.

Second, those who came began to *consider him* and weigh the issues. They may not have done it before. Perhaps they resisted it, because it is often hard work and because the conclusions, at least where one's opinion of oneself is concerned, are uncomfortable. But here, standing right where John had stood and thinking of his words, these people considered Christ and reached sound conclusions. John was a prophet; all men admitted that. John had pointed to Christ as the Savior and Messiah; that was common knowledge. Christ had fulfilled all John's predictions; that they also admitted. "Well, then," they concluded, "Jesus must be the Christ, and we must follow him." I wish that you might reason so soundly today. This is a matter of great importance. I dare say that if one hour ago you had received word that you were dying of cancer, your mind would be entirely taken up with that thought so that you would hardly give attention to anything else. But that would be a matter of the body only, while what I am talking about is a far more important matter of the soul. Eternity is at stake. Your destiny hangs upon your commitment to Jesus. Will you not at least think about it? Will you not at least ask yourself whether these things are so?

And do not stop there. For in the third place we notice that, not only did many come to Jesus and not only did they consider him, but many also *believed on him.* It was good to have come. It was better yet to have considered John's testimony. But neither of these was enough, for the object of the coming and of the testimony was that they might believe on Jesus, accept him as the Son of God and as the Lamb of God and then commit themselves to him on that basis. Should we not have similar results today? Should not *some* believe? Indeed, should it not be *many?*

The last verse of our text says "in that place." "In that place," we are told, "many believed in Jesus." And where was that? Obviously, where they were and without delay! Well, then, do not say, "That was an impressive discussion I just read. I must think about it." Believe on him now. Do not say, "I must pray about this." God is not calling upon you to pray. If you are not yet a Christian, he is calling upon you to believe on Jesus.

Spurgeon once wrote on this last word of the text: "The devil wants you to wait, for he knows that he can then come and steal away the good seed of the kingdom; but if the Lord should give you the grace to decide for Him at once, if you were to believe on Jesus now, what joy there would be among the angels, and the spirit of just men made perfect! They would 'ring the bells of heaven,' and rejoice over lost ones found. What peace there would be in your own heart; and what thankfulness and delight there would be among the people of God when they heard of it."[2]

133

Those Who Loved Him

John 11:1-2

Now a man named Lazarus was sick. He was from Bethany, the village of Mary and her sister Martha. This Mary, whose brother Lazarus now lay sick, was the same one who poured perfume on the Lord and wiped his feet with her hair.

The final argument against God by sinful men is that God has not done enough to convince them of the truth of his revelation. God has done much, but it is not enough. He has acted, but not sufficiently. In Christ's day the argument went, "If you are the Christ, prove it. Do a miracle great enough to convince us that you are who you claim to be."

The facts on the subject are that man has sufficient evidence and, if he does not believe, it is because he will not believe, not because the evidence is lacking. In spite of this, however, we now come to the most impressive miracle in the Gospel—the resurrection of Lazarus from the dead. How are we to take it? Is this a miracle given by Jesus as one last attempt to convince his enemies that he is indeed God? If so, it was unsuccessful, for the narrative ends with an even greater determination by Christ's enemies to have him killed. Or was it performed largely out of a compassion for Christ's friends?

On the surface this seems most acceptable; but if this is the case, why did Jesus delay his return to Bethany for two days, as the record indicates (v. 6)?

As we plunge into the story we find that the real motive was that "God's glory" might be revealed and that "God's Son may be glorified through it" (v. 4), in other words, precisely the motive that John gives elsewhere for the other miracles. In this case the miracle is given to reveal Christ as "the resurrection and the life." It is only incidental to this that some believe and that other hearts are hardened.

A Turning Point

Of the three friends Martha is the last one mentioned. But we begin with her; for in many senses she was the most prominent person, and the effect of the miracle on her was most pronounced. In fact, the resurrection of her brother Lazarus seems to have been a turning point in her life.

Fortunately, we know more about Martha than what is told in John 11. The information is contained in the story of a visit by Jesus to Mary and Martha's home, told in Luke 10:38–42. Jesus had gone to Bethany and was invited to the house of Martha, Mary, and Lazarus for dinner. Lazarus is not mentioned in this story, but we are told that Mary sat at Jesus' feet to learn from him while Martha was encumbered by much serving. Finally Martha began to scold. She came to where Jesus and Mary were sitting and said, "Lord, don't you care that my sister has left me to do the work by myself? Tell her to help me!"

Jesus answered, "Martha, Martha, you are worried about many things, but only one thing is needed. Mary has chosen what is better, and it will not be taken away from her." It is not the fact that she was serving that was the problem but that she was all worked up about it and was being unkind to others as a result. Here was *one* guest, the Lord Jesus Christ, but Martha was so worked up about his visit that she wanted Mary to leave him alone in the living room until the chores were done.

With this story in mind we now turn to another story, the story mentioned by John in the opening verses of chapter 11 but actually told by him in chapter 12. It is also told by Matthew in chapter 26, and by Mark in chapter 14. Once again the setting is Bethany, the town of Martha and Mary, but the home is not Martha's home. It is the home of Simon, identified as "the leper" by Mark, a man who had undoubtedly been healed by Jesus. Again the occasion is a dinner party. The verses in John begin: "Six days before the Passover, Jesus arrived in Bethany, where Lazarus lived, whom Jesus had raised from the dead. Here a dinner was given in Jesus' honor. Martha served" (John 12:1–2).

Notice two things. First of all, it was a large party. On this occasion Jesus was present with his disciples—that alone makes thirteen—and in addition to these there were Simon, Mary, Lazarus, and Martha. That is, there were seventeen, sixteen if Martha is not counted. Second, notice that once again Martha is serving but that on this occasion she does not appear in the least to be troubled but rather seems to be serving with a light spirit. On the former occasion she had one guest and was troubled. Here she has sixteen guests and is not troubled. What made the difference? Obviously only the resurrection of her brother, which comes between the two suppers, in which she learned to get her mind off herself and onto the Lord.

We are not left merely to surmise this, for there is a clue to this interpretation in the earlier story. It is the use of the pronouns "my" and "me" in her complaint to Jesus. In all they are used three times. Martha said, "Lord, don't you care that *my* sister has left *me* to do the work by myself? Tell her to help *me!*" Martha did not have her mind on Jesus at this point or even on the welfare of Mary. She had her mind on herself; and because she had her mind on herself, she felt unappreciated, neglected, and abused. Later, when she had gotten her mind off herself and onto the Lord, she lost those feelings and did what she did buoyantly.

Shall we apply that to ourselves? It is easy to do it, particularly if we are ones who (like Martha) have a gift for serving. There is nothing wrong with serving. That much is clear. So the question is not, should I or should I not serve? It is rather, whom am I serving? and how? Are you serving yourself? Are you trying to build up a reputation for yourself? Or are you serving the Lord Jesus Christ? Is your mind on him? I can assure you that if you are bothered about many things (as Martha was bothered) or if you feel neglected, your mind is on yourself, and you need to meet afresh the One who imparts new life and who causes us to forget ourselves. If you are truly serving him, you will count such service a pleasure; and if others are not helping—well, that is all right, because you are not serving either them or yourself primarily, you are serving Christ.

A Silent Witness

This brings us to the second of these three friends—Lazarus, the man whom Christ raised from the dead. I wonder if you have noticed from your own reading of these stories that never once is it recorded, either in John or in the other Gospels, that Lazarus says anything. We see Martha talking. Mary talks. But Lazarus says nothing; he is perfectly silent. Yet, when we come to the end of the story of the supper at Simon's house, recorded in John 12, we find that Lazarus had become a great and effective witness to Jesus. For "the chief priests made plans to kill Lazarus as well, for on account of him many of the Jews were going over to Jesus and putting their faith in him" (vv. 10–11).

How did Lazarus become such a great witness if, in fact, he said nothing? It is evident that he became a witness in the first instance by the very fact that Jesus had raised him from the dead. Everyone knew that Lazarus had died. In Christ's time funerals were public affairs and were well attended. We read several times of the crowd that had joined Martha and Mary in mourning for Lazarus and that accompanied Mary when she left the house to go to Jesus. Now Lazarus was alive, and anyone who wished could see him. Hundreds, perhaps thousands, came to Bethany and left marveling.

Moreover, Lazarus was a witness to Christ in that he was with Christ and was identified with Christ. In the story of the dinner given in the house of Simon, we are told that Lazarus "was one of them that sat at the table with him." In other words, where he was as well as what had happened to him was a testimony, for by his presence at the table he indicated that his life was identified with the One who had accomplished his resurrection.

This, too, is easy to apply. Neither you nor I have been raised from a physical death by Jesus. But if we understand the miracles in this Gospel—which we should by now—we can understand the raising of Lazarus as an illustration of a spiritual resurrection, none the less real, in which we have all participated if we are Christians. The Bible teaches that before believing in Christ men and women are spiritually dead—"dead in transgressions and sins," as Paul indicates in his letter to the Ephesians (Eph. 2:1)—but that after believing in Christ they are made alive. If you are a Christian, you have been made alive spiritually; that is, Jesus has performed a resurrection within you. Do you give evidence of it? Do you identify yourself openly with the One who performed it, as Lazarus did?

I believe that every Christian should be able to give a verbal witness to what Jesus has done and that we should do it often. But I also recognize that not everyone gives a witness by words easily. You may be one of these. If so, God is not calling you to be a Luther, a Whitefield or a Wesley. You do not have to speak well or all the time. But you should be especially careful that your life demonstrates the reality of that resurrection that Jesus has performed in you so that others might turn to him and believe in him because of what they see.

It is possible to have a great verbal witness and yet bear little fruit because the life counts for nothing. On the other hand, it is possible to say little and yet have a deep and lasting witness because the life is itself evidence of Christ's great grace and power.

Mary Poured

Finally, we come to Mary who is, in some respects, the most delightful and rewarding character of all. We are going to be seeing more of her later in our study both of this chapter and of chapter 12. Nevertheless, even at this stage it is worth noting some of the important things about her.

For one thing, the Gospels nearly always present Mary as being at Jesus' feet. In the first of these three stories, the story that involves Martha's rebuke, we see Mary listening to Jesus and learning from him. The story says that Mary "sat at the Lord's feet listening to what he said" (Luke 10:39). In John 11 we find the same thing, only here we find her expressing belief. Lazarus had died. Jesus had come and talked to Martha. Then he called for Mary, who came running at once and fell at his feet. We are told, "When Mary reached the place where Jesus was and saw him, she fell at his feet and said, 'Lord, if you had been here, my brother would not have died'" (John 11:32). Earlier, when Jesus had talked to Martha, Martha had said nearly the same thing; but her words must be understood as having expressed a complaint—"Lord, if you had been here [instead of wasting time with your work beyond Jordan], my brother [would not have had to die]." Mary, however, expressed her faith: "Lord, if you had been here, my brother would not have died," implying that even then Jesus could do a miracle. Finally, we see Mary in the house of Simon, where she had just broken the alabaster box full of ointment, again at his feet, anointing his head and feet, and then wiping his feet with her hair (John 12:3).

This leads us to another thought about Mary, for if we ask why Mary anointed Christ with the ointment, the answer is that she did it in view of his coming death (John 12:7). Jesus says so himself. And this means that of all those who were with Jesus during the final months of his life only Mary understood that he was going to die for sin. Moreover, if we then ask, "But how did Mary come to know this when the others apparently failed to understand it?" The answer obviously is found in the first of the points made about her, namely, that she had spent time learning at the feet of Jesus.

The use of the ointment suggests one thing more. It suggests that because Mary understood what Jesus was about to do and because she loved him for it, she was prepared to give him her all. Two details of the story indicate this. First, the value of the ointment. This impressed everyone who was there at the dinner, for the ointment was assessed at a value of three hundred denarii, which (if we remember that one denarius was a normal day's wage for a working man) was the equivalent of approximately thirty-five hundred dollars in our economy. We are not surprised, then, that it seemed a shocking waste to many. The second detail is that Mary broke the box that had contained the ointment. Mark tells us this (Mark 14:3). In other words, Mary gave her most valuable possession and gave it so completely that she even broke the box lest some of the precious substance should remain.

I wonder if you have given your most precious possession to the Lord Jesus Christ? Or, to put it in other words, I wonder if you have given yourself? If not—if you are holding something back—is it possible that you have never understood that he actually gave his life for you? Or, is it possible that you do not really love him above all else? I know that you may be thinking, as many do, that if you give your life to Christ, your life will be wasted. But it will not be wasted. It will be invested. Moreover, Christ, the greatest banker who ever lived, will pay great dividends.

We find one obvious dividend in Mary's story. Mary had broken her box and had poured the ointment over the head of Jesus. Some of it ran down to his feet. Then, so we read, Mary "wiped his feet with her hair. And the house was filled with the fragrance of the perfume" (John 12:3). But why was the house filled with the perfume? It could have drifted about naturally, I suppose. On the other hand, if Mary had wiped Christ's feet with her hair and if she moved about, then the odor may well have spread through the house because of her. That is, it clung to her and spread from her. If this is so, then it indicates that in giving her all to Christ, Mary had become identified with Christ and had become a blessing.

A Memorial

This message can be applied by a series of questions. Here were three persons, all different, yet all were affected by their close contact with Jesus Christ. Are you like them? Have you been likewise affected?

First, there is Martha. Martha served. This was her special function, and she did it well. But initially she served for what it would do for Martha and only later did she learn to do it for Christ. Are you like her in her second condition? When you work for the Lord, are your eyes really on Jesus? Second, there is Lazarus. Lazarus only sat. But where he sat mattered, and what he stood for mattered. Are you like him? Can others see that you are with Jesus and that he has changed you? Are you among his resurrected ones? Finally, there is Mary. Martha served. Lazarus sat. But Mary poured. She poured out the perfume of her life and so became a blessing. Are you like her? Have you broken your box? Have you poured out your all upon him?

Dr. Donald Grey Barnhouse, who tells this story far better than I have in one of his radio sermons, concludes at this point by asking whether you, the listener or reader, have experienced the joy of being at the feet of Jesus. "If not," he observes, "the difficulty is that you have kept your perfume sealed in a box. You have not poured it out at the feet of Jesus Christ. What is your perfume? Your perfume is a surrendered life. Only when you break your box and pour out your life upon him, only then will your life cease to be narrow and ingrown, and only then will you cease to clutch your perfume and say, 'But this is mine! This is mine!' When you break the box and give it all and anoint his feet, the whole house will be filled with the fragrance of the ointment, and you will know what it is to be in the glory of the presence of Christ."[1]

Jesus said that what Mary had done would be remembered throughout the whole world as "in memory of her" (Mark 14:9). There are many kinds of memorials—monuments, buildings, books, tombstones. But the greatest is to be remembered as one who gave everything to the Lord Jesus.

134

He Who Loved Them

John 11:3

So the sisters sent word to Jesus, "Lord, the one you love is sick."

We have already looked at the characters who figure in the eleventh chapter of John's Gospel—Martha, Mary, and Lazarus—and we have learned something from them. The story begins, however, not with their past associations with Jesus nor even with expectation of their future blessings, which we have considered. It begins with a problem. The problem is that Lazarus was dying.

This is a problem with which we can all identify, for either it has come to us already or it will at some future time. In this life most people develop at least some close relationships—family relationships or friendships. We prize these highly. We would give anything to maintain them. Still from time to time the natural calamities of life intrude into our happiness, and we find our closest friends wrenched from us by accidents, sickness, and eventually death. Death takes the father of a young family. A mother is taken. A spiritual counselor or leader is taken from us just at the moment when we feel that we most need his presence and advice. One who has been most useful is laid aside by a lingering illness. In such moments some question the presence or love of God. Others, even those who do not doubt God's love and faithfulness, find their faith tested.

What are we to think in such circumstances? What should we do? There is probably not a better example of what we are to do in the entire Bible than the example given to us by Martha and Mary at the beginning of our story. It is simply that the sisters told Jesus of their problem. We are told that "his sisters sent word to Jesus, 'Lord, the one you love is sick'" (v. 3). That they did this is significant. How they did it is even more significant.

Beloved, Yet Afflicted

Before we look at the way in which Martha and Mary approached Jesus, however, we need to notice an obvious point, for it is often forgotten. The point is simply that even those whom Jesus especially loves get sick and eventually die. When the sisters approached Jesus, they did so on the basis of his love for Lazarus. They loved Jesus; his love for them was even greater. Nevertheless, Lazarus was sick and failing. The Greek word that John uses here (there are two principle words for "sick" in Greek) implies that he was "deathly sick" or "sinking." In other words, we are to learn from this that sickness in a believer is in no way incompatible with the Lord's love for him.

It may be that Mary and Martha, knowing as little of God's ways at this point in their lives as many Christians seem to know today, were surprised that someone whom Jesus loved could be sick. There is just a suggestion of this surprise in the word "behold." But they need not and should not have been surprised.

In the first place, they need not have been surprised for the simple reason that the man whom Jesus loves is after all *still just a man*. It is in the nature of being a man to suffer bodily ailments. In one excellent sermon on this text Charles Haddon Spurgeon wrote, "The love of Jesus does not separate us from the common necessities and infirmities of human life. Men of God are still men. The covenant of grace is not a charter of exemption from consumption, or rheumatism, or asthma."[1] So let us learn from this and not be surprised when we ourselves or those we love suffer illness. The Bible says (in the words of one of Job's "comforters"): "Man is born to trouble as surely as sparks fly upward" (Job 5:7). It also says with absolute clarity, "Man is destined to die once, and after that to face judgment" (Heb. 9:27).

Moreover, we should not be surprised at illness, for we know that it often is God's way of speaking to our hearts and of leading us on in the Christian life. That is, it often is *used by God for our good*. Many have known this. David knew it, for he wrote in one of the psalms, "It was good for me to be afflicted so that I might learn your decrees" (Ps. 119:71). Sickness helped him to love and understand the Scriptures. Elizabeth Prentiss, the hymn writer, apparently felt that it had helped her to love Christ more. She wrote:

> Let sorrow do its work,
> Send grief and pain;

> Sweet are thy messengers,
> Sweet their refrain,
> When they can sing with me,
> More love, O Christ, to thee,
> More love to thee,
> More love to thee!

So it has been for thousands who have been tested. Sickness has been a trial. But it has been a trial that was used by God for good. We know, do we not, that "in all things God works for the good of those who love him, who have been called according to his purpose" (Rom. 8:28)?

We should also note that sickness in us is also sometimes *used by God for the good of others*. For this reason too we should not be surprised by it. This point does not need to be elaborated here, for we will come to it again farther on in the chapter. But it is obvious that this is what is involved when Jesus says as he later does, "This sickness will not end in death. No, it is for God's glory, so that God's Son may be glorified through it" (v. 4). If God is glorified by a Christian's illness, then the illness is for God's good and for the good of all who see this particular demonstration of his glory. In the case of Lazarus, to give just one example, for twenty centuries believers have been getting good from it; and even today, as we study it, we are the richer because the beloved brother of Mary and Martha died.

Our Help in Trouble

That we should not be surprised at sickness and death does not mean, however, that we are to desire sickness. Nor does it mean that we cannot tell Jesus of our desire to have the sick one made well. At this point the words of the two sisters provide an example to us of what we may do in sickness and of how we may pray about it.

Notice, in the first place, that the sisters did pray. Or, as we should more properly say in their case, they brought the matter to Jesus. It is always good to bring troubles to Jesus. In fact, it is good to be always in communication with him about everything.

Do we act as they did? Arthur W. Pink observes on this text, "It is written, 'God is our refuge and strength, a very *present* help in trouble' (Ps. 46:1); yet, to our shame, how little we *know* Him as such. When the people murmured against Moses, we are told that, 'he cried unto the Lord' (Exod. 15:25). When Hezekiah received the threatening letter from Rabshakeh, he 'spread it before the Lord' (Isa. 37:14). When John the Baptist was beheaded, his disciples 'went and told Jesus' (Matt. 14:12). What examples for us! We have not an High Priest who cannot be touched with the feeling of our infirmities. No, he is full of compassion, for when on earth he, too, was 'acquainted with grief.' He sympathizes deeply with his suffering people, and invites them to pour out the anguish of their hearts before Him."[2] Mary and Martha showed great wisdom in acquainting Jesus with their problem. And so do we, when we do likewise. True, Jesus already knows our problem. He knows everything about us. Still, he invites us to come to tell him and to receive that heart-relief which only he is capable of giving.

God's Love

This leads us, however, to the second characteristic of the sisters' prayer: the basis of their appeal. What was the basis of their appeal? Was it that they had often had Jesus in their home and that he therefore owed them something? No. Was it that they had served him faithfully and had been true to him when others of the disciples had dropped away? No. Was it that they loved him? No. The basis of the appeal was that he loved them. That is, it was in God's love rather than in the love of man that they took refuge.

There is no comfort in the reverse. Suppose for a minute that their appeal had been that they or Lazarus had loved Jesus. That would have been true at least in part, for they did love him. But if they had appealed on that basis, they would soon have been asking, "But have we loved him enough? Has our love been a pure love? Have we offended him?" and the honest answers to those questions would have thrown them into a morass of self-doubt. But this is not what they did. They did love him, but they knew that their love for Jesus would never in a million years be an adequate basis for their appeal. So their appeal was not that they loved him, but that he loved them. He had loved them freely, when there was nothing in them to commend them to him. He had loved them faithfully, when they were faithless. He had loved them with an everlasting love as, indeed, only God can love. This, then, was the basis. Indeed, it is the only grounds that any of us can ever have in approaching the Almighty.

Moreover, in coming to Jesus in this way, the sisters came, not seeking their own will but rather the will of Jesus. For one thing, they did not actually make a request. I do not think that it is fair to say on this basis that no request was implied. Clearly there was the implication that they would like Jesus to come to their aid, and there was certainly the suggestion that he might help them by healing Lazarus. If this is not implied, there was no point even in sending Christ the message. But at the same time, we cannot miss feeling that when they phrased the report as they did—"Lord, the one you love is sick"—they indicated by the form of it that they were seeking his will rather than theirs in the matter.

I wonder if you do that in your prayers. It is not so much the words you use—I am sure you understand that. It is the desire of your heart. Certainly you would like the trouble removed, the sick one healed. But is that your fundamental desire? Or is it that God's will might be done regardless of the outcome? It is only when we pray in the latter way that we are enabled to make our requests so known unto God that "the peace of God that passes all understanding" keeps our hearts and minds in Christ Jesus.

"It Is Well with My Soul"

Moreover, we need that peace of mind if only because God does not always act in the way we think he should act, or when.

Nothing is clearer than this from the story. No doubt when Mary and Martha first acquainted Jesus with the fact of Lazarus's sickness, they looked to see him recover as soon as the messenger reached Jesus. Or else they expected Jesus to come immediately to their aid. But neither happened. Instead of getting better, Lazarus became worse and died. Instead of coming, Jesus tarried for two more days and then arrived in Bethany at least a full four days after their brother's death. From this we learn that Jesus may be completely informed of our trouble and yet act as though he were indifferent to it. We learn that prayer for the sick may not be answered. Indeed, if this were not the case, no one would ever become sick or die so long as he had a friend or relative to pray for him.

No, the comfort in our prayers is not in the fact that Jesus always answers them as we wish. For he does not. It is that he, who made us and controls all circumstances, knows best and is well able to direct even sickness and death to his glory.

Do you object, "But that is easy to say in the case of Lazarus, for God raised him from the dead. That was obviously to his glory"? But shall we not be raised? Is Jesus not the resurrection and the life to us also? The story says, "Your brother will rise again." Then so he shall, and so shall we all. Thy brother shall rise again. Thy sister shall rise again. Thy mother shall rise again. Thy father shall rise again. Thy children shall rise again.

In the year 1873, a Christian lawyer from Chicago, named Horatio Spafford, placed his wife and four children on the luxury liner *Ville de Havre* sailing from New York to France. Spafford expected to join them in about three or four weeks after finishing up some business, but with the exception of his wife he never saw them again. The trip started out beautifully. But on the evening of November 21, 1873, as the *Ville de Havre* proceeded peacefully across the Atlantic, the ship was suddenly struck by another vessel, the *Lochearn*, and sank a mere thirty minutes later, with the loss of nearly all on board.

On being told that the ship was sinking Mrs. Spafford knelt with her children and prayed that they might be saved or be made willing to die, if such was God's will. A few minutes later, in the confusion, three of the children were swept away by the waves while she stood clutching the youngest. Suddenly the youngest child was swept from her arms. She reached out and caught the baby's gown. Then the baby, a little girl, was lost again. Mrs. Spafford became unconscious and awoke later to find that she had been rescued by sailors from the *Lochearn*. But the four children were gone.

Back in the United States Horatio Spafford was waiting for news of his family, and at last, ten days later (after the rescue ship had reached Cardiff), it came. "Saved alone" was his wife's message. That night Spafford walked the floor of his room in anguish, as anyone would have done. But this was not all. For as he shared his loss with his Lord, a loss that could not be reversed in this life, he found, as many have, that peace that indeed passes all under-standing. Toward morning he told a friend named Major Whittle, "I am glad to be able to trust my Lord when it costs me something." Then, sometime later, as he reflected on the disaster at sea, he wrote:

> When peace, like a river, attendeth my way,
>   When sorrows like sea-billows roll;
> Whatever my lot, thou hast taught me to say,
>   It is well, it is well with my soul.
>
> Though Satan should buffet, though trials should come,
>   Let this blest assurance control,
> That Christ has regarded my helpless estate,
>   And has shed his own blood for my soul.
>
> My sin—O the bliss of his glorious thought!—
>   My sin, not in part, but the whole,
> Is nailed to the cross and I bear it no more;
>   Praise the Lord, praise the Lord, O my soul!
>
> O Lord, haste the day when the faith shall be sight,
>   The clouds be rolled back as a scroll,
> The trump shall resound and the Lord shall descend;
>   "Even so"—it is well with my soul.

The text tells us that Jesus loved Lazarus, as he also loved Martha and Mary. Does Jesus, in a special sense, love you? Are you aware of that love? You say, "But how can I be?" I will tell you how. You can know it if you love him; for we are told, "We love because he first loved us." Do you love him? Is there that love-bond that is evidence of the fact that you are one of his sheep, one of those for whom he died? If there is, then let me encourage you to live in a way that demonstrates the reality and depth of his love. If you are well, serve him vigorously. If you are sick, let the world see how you are able to glorify God in your sickness.

On the other hand, if you are not aware of that love, learn that you are without the brightest and most cheering love in the entire universe and begin to seek God. Do not pass into the next world without the love of the Lord Jesus.

135

A Sickness Not unto Death

John 11:4

When he heard this, Jesus said, "This sickness will not end in death. No, it is for God's glory so that God's Son may be glorified through it."

Everyone wants to know how a story will end, at least if the story is a good one. Children will say to their mothers, as their mothers are reading a bedtime story, "Don't stop now, Mother. Read just one more chapter. I want to know what's going to happen next." Adults will stay buried in a book until they finish it or will stay glued to a television screen until a program ends. The same characteristic also works to keep us reading the daily newspaper until the latest political scandal fades away, the war ends, or the election results are finally tabulated.

Obviously, men and women also have this desire where their own personal stories are concerned, and this accounts for the eternal popularity of fortune-tellers (all ages have had them), oracles, mystics, futurologists, and even the kind of journalistic pundit who is not afraid to announce in print where the world is headed. Unfortunately, as those who follow such leads often discover, men do not know the future. So it is impossible to find out what will happen to us tomorrow or next week, not to mention what will happen to us at life's end. Many who do not know what is coming, therefore, fear the future and shrink from it.

Does anyone know how your life story will end? Surely no *human* knows. But there is One who does know. God knows. In this text Jesus, who is God, referred to a situation in which a friend of his was dying and he announced the outcome. Moreover, it was a good outcome. The text says, "When he heard this [that his friend Lazarus was sick], Jesus said, "This sickness will not end in death. No, it is for God's glory, that God's Son may be glorified through it" (John 11:4). As we read the story we discover that by the time Jesus had received the message Lazarus had probably already died. So Jesus was actually announcing that the final outcome was to be a demonstration of the glory of God through his resurrection.

Only God Knows

The place to begin with this verse is with the fact that God does know the future—as I have already said—and that only God knows it. Furthermore, because he knows and because he loves us and is concerned for us, he delights to reveal at least parts of that future to us.

Think of the Book of Isaiah, for instance. In the center section of that book, in a series of chapters dealing with the nonvalidity of the pagan gods (chapters 40–48), God taunts the idols on the basis of their inability to tell the future. In one place he says this: "Present your case. . . . Set forth your arguments. . . . Bring in your idols to tell us what is going to happen. Tell us what the former things [that is, what did happen] were, so that we may consider them and know their final outcome. Or declare to us the things to come, tell us what the future holds, so we may know that you are gods. Do something, whether good or bad, so that we will be dismayed and filled with fear. But you are less than nothing and your works are utterly worthless; he who chooses you is detestable" (Isa. 41:21–24). The point of this passage is that no one but God can tell the future because no one but God controls it. And the fact that he does tell it is one of the proofs that he alone is the true God.

God does not only reveal the future to demonstrate that he is God, however, though this is one reason. He also does it to warn the ungodly of judgment and to encourage those who are his own.

We find this thought as early in the Bible as the third chapter of Genesis. God had placed the first man and woman in the Garden of Eden and had warned them of death if they should eat of the fruit of the forbidden tree. They ate. So, when God came to them, he came with words of judgment that were, nevertheless, at the same time words of promise. He told of years of hardship—pain for the woman in childbearing and toil for the man as he would work to earn a living. But the same words also told of the coming of One who would eventually destroy the works of Satan. "He will crush your head," he said to the serpent, "and you will strike his heel" (Gen. 3:15). The promise so captivated Eve that she named her first son Cain, meaning (in a very rough translation), "Here he is," because she thought (wrongly) that Cain was the one whom God had promised to send.

In Hosea we find the same thing. God used the story of Hosea's life to illustrate the pending judgment upon and scattering of the children of

Israel—the symbolic names of his three children were to indicate this future: "Scattered," "Not-Pitied," "Not-My-People." At the same time God told of the blessing that would come after the scattering, thereby encouraging those who would have to live through the years of chastisement. We read at the beginning of the story (but as a description of the end), "Yet the Israelites will be like the sand on the seashore, which cannot be measured or counted. In the place where it was said to them, 'You are not my people,' they will be called 'sons of the living God'" (Hosea 1:10).

The Glory of God

Having established this background, then—the background that God foretells the future in order (1) to demonstrate his power to control it, (2) to warn the unsaved, and (3) to encourage believers—return to the text in which Jesus foretold the outcome of the sickness of Lazarus, saying that it would be for the glory of God and that he might be glorified by it.

First, Jesus said that the outcome would be glorifying to God. Notice that while this was true—we are going to see in a moment how it was true—it was not true in the way that the sisters might naturally have expected. I suppose that Christ's words were immediately reported back to Martha and Mary and that they came about twenty-four hours after Lazarus had passed away. I can picture the sisters saying, "But Jesus is mistaken. If he had been here earlier, he might have cured our brother; that would have been glorifying to God. But now Lazarus is dead, and it is too late. At any rate, if any glory is to come of this it will have to be at the time of the final resurrection, and by that time we will all be gone. So far as we are concerned, it is too late." It would have been natural for them to have thought in this manner; but if they did, it was wrong. In fact, the outcome, though different from their plans, was actually going to result in far more glory to God than they could ever have imagined.

The resurrection of Lazarus was itself glorifying to God. That much is obvious. To glorify God means to acknowledge him as being who he truly is; and, since one of God's attributes is omnipotence, clearly the resurrection of Lazarus caused many to acknowledge that great power and so glorify him.

At the same time, however, the glory of God was seen in an even greater sense in the changed lives of those who either took part in or witnessed the miracle. We see the effect on Lazarus, for instance, as we pointed out in the first study of John 11. Nowhere in the entire story are we told that Lazarus said anything. But we are told toward the end of the story that he became a great witness (vv. 10–11). How did this happen? We know that when a man comes to the place where he is going to die, especially if he is a spiritual man, it has an effect on him. So when Lazarus died and rose again, undoubtedly he emerged as one who had experienced a profound transformation and who showed it by his demeanor. Have you been changed? You will be when you come to the place where you have died to self and have been made alive unto Christ, when you have truly become "a new creation" in him. In this, though you may have to suffer greatly, the end (as Christ says) will be to God's glory.

The resurrection also had an effect on the sisters. We saw some of this also in the earlier study. Before it, Martha had been a scold when she was serving just one guest. Afterward she served a whole houseful of people gracefully.

And Mary? Mary came to understand that Jesus was going to give his life so that all the Marys, Marthas, and Lazaruses of this world might not have to die spiritually but might instead enter into newness of life and enjoy an eternity of God's blessing in heaven. Mary indicated this when she anointed Christ's head with the ointment, for Jesus said that she did it in anticipation of his death and burial.

Notice, too, that the death and resurrection of Lazarus had an effect on the disciples and that this was God-glorifying. We are not told in so many words, at least after the miracle, what the effect was. But before it, when Jesus was explaining to them what he was about to do, he said, "Lazarus is dead, and for your sake I am glad I was not there, so that you may believe" (vv. 14–15).

Taken by itself, the first half of that second sentence is astounding: "Lazarus is dead, and . . . I am glad."

"Glad?" we say. "Lazarus dead and Jesus glad? How can that be?" But then we read on and find Jesus saying, in effect, "Do not be surprised at my saying, and do not be dismayed at circumstances. Nothing ever happens to you that I have not first approved, and nothing is approved from which I have not previously appointed good results. Lazarus has died. Yes. The sisters are sorrowing. Yes. But the end will be good, even for you. For in your case the outcome will be a strengthening of faith in me, and you will influence thousands."

Learn from this for the times when trouble comes to you. Do not complain. But take this message seriously. Say, "Lord, I do not see it; but I know that this trouble may have come upon me for the sake of some friend. So use it that way, if it so pleases you. And help me to trust you and grow through the experience."

In the fourth place, notice that the death and resurrection of Lazarus had an effect on the immediate friends of the family. Here Donald Grey Barnhouse, who has developed this sequence well, observes, "Since they were a large family, they had many friends. In John 11:19, it says, 'Many of the Jews came to Martha and Mary, to comfort them concerning their brother.' These were the family friends. We know that whenever there is a death, the friends gather around the family. As an act of courtesy, friends send flowers, they go to the viewing, they shake hands with the loved ones and express sympathy. This is a part of our lives, and it was a part of their lives. And what happened? It says in verse 45, 'Then many of the Jews which came to Mary, and had seen the things which Jesus did, believed on him.' They came to sympathize, and they remained to believe. So the effect of Lazarus' death now is seen in the family friends.

"We go a little further still to the acquaintances when the Lord Jesus Christ reaches the tomb site of Lazarus. As He's praying He says, 'Father, I thank thee that thou hast heard me. And I knew that thou hearest me always; but, because of the people which stand by'—that would be the curiosity seekers—'I said it, that they may believe that thou hast sent me' (John 11:41–42). Here was a circle of people just standing by. They knew that Lazarus was dead. They knew that Jesus had come. Many of them were 'the' important people of the community."[1] Did these people believe? Some did. Others apparently did not. We are told that these merely "went to the Pharisees and told them what Jesus had done" (John 11:46).

To these last unbelievers Lazarus's resurrection was in the nature of a condemnation; for, though it was irrefutable evidence of Christ's power, they would not accept it, and it therefore increased their guilt. Even here, however, God was glorified. For he has been patient in demonstrating his great love and power to sinners.

Jesus Glorified

We return to the text and find there a last phrase that deserves consideration. Jesus had said that the sickness of Lazarus was not unto death in the final sense but rather that it was for God's glory. He then added, and "that God's Son may be glorified through it." How was Jesus glorified by Lazarus's death? There are two obvious answers and one that is not so obvious.

First, since Jesus is God, obviously anything that brings honor to God the Father brings honor to him also. This is made clear if we compare John 2:11, the verse that concludes the account of Christ's first miracle, with John 11:40, a verse that aptly sums up this one. In the former verse we are told, "This, the first of his miraculous signs Jesus performed at Cana in Galilee. He thus revealed *his glory*." In the latter we discover him saying to Martha, "Did I not tell you that if you believed, you would see the *glory of God?*" Christ's glory and God's glory! They are one and the same, for Christ is God. Therefore, "All may honor the Son just as they honor the Father" (John 5:23).

Second, Jesus was glorified in that the death and resurrection of Lazarus revealed him as One who is able to deal with any situation. The story tells us that Jesus delayed his return to Bethany until Lazarus had died and had been buried four days. In other words, Jesus got himself into a predicament. But he got himself into a predicament only so that he might get himself out. On this point Barnhouse writes: "I quite believe that God does that with everyone of us—all the time. That is the Lord's way. If God wants you to trust in Him, He puts you in a place of difficulty. If He wants you to trust Him greatly, He puts you in a place of impossibility. For when a thing is impossible, then we who are so prone to move things through by the force of our own being can say, 'Lord, it has to be you. I am utterly, absolutely nothing.' . . . And the Lord [will say], 'It is for you that this happened, for your disciples, for your family, for your friends, for your acquaintances and the bystanders, but it's also for me; it's for me.' And God is saying. 'I am in the midst of an invisible war. The repercussions of what I am doing will be known in eternity.'"[2]

Finally, there is a point that is not so obvious. Jesus, so he himself said, was to be glorified by what was to come. But what was to come was not only the resurrection of Lazarus; it was also the cross, to which the term "glorify" often refers in John's Gospel. Think of John 7:39, for instance. There we are told that the Spirit had not been given at this time because "Jesus was not yet glorified," that is, had not yet died. Or again, when the Greeks come to him, as recorded in the next chapter, Jesus declares, "The hour is come for the Son of Man to be glorified" (John 12:23). It is obvious that he is thinking of his death in this passage, for he immediately goes on to speak of the corn of wheat that must fall into the ground and die. In the same way, just a few verses earlier, we read that the disciples did not understand these things at first but "after Jesus was glorified [that is, had been crucified and had risen again] . . . they realized that these things had been written about him" (v. 16).

The raising of Lazarus was to result in Christ's death, therefore. And it did. This was the final spark needed to explode the accumulated hostility of the leaders against him and to propel them toward the ultimate sacrilege. As for Jesus, he foresaw the outcome and still moved toward it.

You may be saying, "I understand from this story that the ills of this life are no accident for the one who is a true child of God; and I am pleased that God, who knows the future, has chosen to reveal the outcome to me. But it is still hard to suffer." Yes, it is always hard to suffer. But the Lord Jesus Christ went through it all before us. He asks us to suffer. Indeed, he ordains it. But he does not ask us to do anything that he has not done first. Nor does he ask us to suffer without at the same time promising to go with us through the testing. The fact that he has done it is itself an encouragement. He died, yet rose again. He suffered, but he triumphed gloriously.

And so shall we. This present sickness—whatever it may be—is not unto death, but for the glory of God, that the Son of God might be glorified by it.

136

The Delays of Love

John 11:5-6

Jesus loved Martha and her sister and Lazarus. Yet when he heard that Lazarus was sick, he stayed where he was two more days.

I wonder if you have ever noticed in your study of the fourth Gospel that the disciple whom Jesus loved—John, the author of the Gospel (John 21:20, 24)—is not at all reluctant to record that Jesus loved others also. Already we have been told that Jesus loved Lazarus. Now, in verse 5, we find that he also loved Martha and Mary, Lazarus's sisters. The verse says, "Jesus loved Martha and her sister and Lazarus."

The interesting thing about these statements concerning Christ's love is that they are given in a context that might cause us to doubt them—at least if we did not know better. We have already seen one such context and are about to see another. The problem we have seen lies in the fact that Lazarus was sick, in spite of the fact that Jesus loved him and could heal him. On the surface this seems difficult to accept, just as it sometimes is difficult to accept sickness or death when they enter into our experience. "If Jesus really loves us, how can he let this happen?" is the question we ask. In looking at that problem we saw some answers and learned that sickness and death are not incompatible with Christ's love.

But we have another problem at this point. No sooner are we told that "Jesus loved Martha and her sister and Lazarus" than we also find the report, "When he [Jesus] heard that Lazarus was sick, he stayed where he was two more days"

(v. 6). This means that Jesus delayed his return to Bethany rather than immediately rushing either to help Lazarus or comfort the sisters. Moreover, we are
to understand that the delay was in some sense connected with his love for
these friends and flowed from it. How can this be? If we were in Christ's place,
we would immediately have returned to Bethany—or at least we acknowledge
that this is what we should do if we were in these circumstances. Yet Jesus does
not. He stays where he is. It is only after two days that he finally does go back
to Bethany, arriving there four full days after Lazarus's burial.

Here, then, is a text for careful study, particularly if we have ever experienced God's delay—in answering our prayers, showing us the path we should
take, removing a difficulty, or some such thing. Does God delay? Yes, he does.
But he delays always for a purpose.

In developing this text I am following a three-point outline given to it
years ago by Alexander Maclaren of Manchester, England: (1) Christ's delays
are the delays of love, (2) the delayed help always comes at the right time,
and (3) the best help is not delayed. The discussion is mine, but the points
are from Maclaren's excellent exposition.

Because of Love

To begin with, Christ's delays are the delays of love. If the verse teaches
anything, it teaches this; for the point is that Jesus stayed where he was for
two days *because* he loved them. We may not understand this. We cannot see
the end from the beginning, as God can; therefore, we cannot see how Christ's
delays contribute to an overall plan. Moreover, in the grief that we sometimes have we often cannot see clearly, even though God might have made
his plan clear. It is hard to see through eyes filled with tears. The point, however, is that even though we cannot see how the situation will end or why it
has come upon us, we can know that it flows from Christ's love and is controlled by it. Christ's delays are the delays of love. Therefore, his delays are
to be interpreted in the light of his love and not the other way around.

This truth suggests several related points. First, if Christ's delays are the
delays of love, then they are not the delays of *indifference*. He does not delay
because he does not care.

We recognize that delays often flow from indifference in human affairs.
In fact, Jesus once told a story based on this principle (see Luke 18:1–8). It
concerned a judge and a widow. The judge was a hard man who lived for
himself and who feared neither God nor man. The widow was the victim of
injustice. She came to the judge with her case, but he refused to hear her.
There was nothing in it for him. But because the widow persisted, the judge
eventually rendered justice, reasoning that it was better to act and be done
with the case than to be wearied with the widow's unending requests. Jesus
concluded, "Will not God bring about justice for his chosen ones, who cry
out to him day and night?" (v. 7). The story does not mean that God is like
the unjust judge, of course; its point lies rather in the contrast. But the story

does recognize that God sometimes delays in answering a particular prayer and that in human affairs this often is the product of indifference. It teaches that indifference is never a characteristic of God.

Second, if Christ's delays are the delays of love, then they are not the product of a *preoccupation* on Christ's part. That is, he does not delay his answer because he is too busy to deal with our problem.

There is a story in the Old Testament in which the pagan gods are contrasted with the true God on just this point. It concerns Elijah. Elijah was troubled with the apostasy of Israel in a day when the majority of the people had become worshipers of Baal. So he challenged Ahab the king and the king's prophets, the prophets of Baal, to a contest. The prophets were to prepare an altar upon which a bull was to be sacrificed; Elijah was to do likewise. In each case there was to be an altar, wood, and a sacrifice, but no fire. The true God was to provide fire. The 450 prophets of Baal built their altar, made their sacrifice, and then began to call on Baal to send fire. Nothing happened. They began to cry louder. Still nothing happened. Finally, they began to throw themselves upon the altar and even cut themselves with knives. Although they kept it up for the better part of the day, no flame descended.

At this point, Elijah began to mock them over the supposed preoccupation of their god. "Perhaps he is busy," he said. His actual words were, "Shout louder! Surely he is a god [that is, at least you say he is a god]. Perhaps he is deep in thought, or busy [this phrase is even a bit racy, for it means that perhaps Baal is busy in the bathroom], or traveling. Maybe he is sleeping and must be awakened" (1 Kings 18:27). Obviously, nothing happened. Baal was unable to respond to his worshipers. At last, after they had given up, Elijah called upon his God, Jehovah; and Jehovah, who is never preoccupied, responded with a fire that consumed not only the sacrifice but also the wood and stones and lapped up twelve barrels of water that Elijah had caused to be poured upon them.

We learn from such stories that the delays of God are never the delays of indifference or of preoccupation. They are the delays of love.

Love and Circumstances

To say that Christ's delays are the delays of love is also to say something positive, however. His delays are purposeful. Love has a purpose. Therefore, we are right to seek purposes in God's delays. I must confess that it would be presumptuous to pretend to be able to say always and in detail what God's purposes are. His ways are not our ways. His thoughts are not our thoughts. We cannot see the end from the beginning, as he can. Still, we can look for purposes. And we can suggest, at least in general terms, what some of them might be.

For instance, one of the goals reached by God through his delays is that of molding our errant wills to conform to his perfect will. When God answers us immediately, it often is the case that we then rush on to formulate our own plans for whatever comes next. When God delays, by contrast, we are forced to ask, "Am I right in what I am trying to do? Do I have the will of the Lord on this matter? Does he have more to teach or tell me than I have heard?" An example of such a purpose is seen in God's dealings with the people of Israel during the days of their desert wanderings; for God kept them in the wilderness for forty years, teaching them obedience, until they had become the kind of disciplined fighting force he was going to use one day to conquer Canaan.

Another of God's purposes in delays is to strengthen faith. Our faith does not grow much if we always get an immediate response, though we might think that it would. Rather, our faith grows when we are forced to wait, trusting that God knows what he is doing and that he will fulfill his promises toward us eventually and in the proper time. Abraham's faith grew in this manner. God had promised him a son through whom he was to have a great posterity; but Abraham grew old—in fact, he was nearly a hundred years old—before the son came. What happened to his faith during these long years? Did it weaken and die? Not at all. On the contrary, the years of delay were the years in which Abraham's faith grew most—so much so that at the age of ninety-nine he was willing to change his name from Abram which means "father of many," to Abraham, which means "father of a multitude," as a sign of his faith in the promise of God concerning the son who even then was not given. It was in the year following this that Isaac was born.

God uses delays to mold our wills and strengthen our faith. May I suggest one thing more? Sometimes he also does it simply to bring honor to his own name and to honor Jesus (v. 4). Those who do not know Jesus may find this puzzling or even offensive. I have heard people say, "What kind of God is he who has to be honored?" But those who know him do not find this puzzling. Jesus is glorious. Consequently, to honor him is the only proper and desirable thing to do. In their best moods, Christians rejoice that God is able to honor himself through their circumstances.

Let me summarize this in a challenge that I hope you will remember. *Learn to interpret circumstances by the love of Christ and not Christ's love by circumstances.* Christ's delays are the delays of love; therefore, they should be interpreted by love. If we do it the other way around, we will be even farther from understanding the circumstances, and we may question the love. Begin with Christ's love. Say, "I know that Christ loves me. He died for me. Therefore I will do my best to see his purpose in the things that are happening." If you do that, you will begin to interpret circumstances in the light of love; and, as God gives light, you will begin to see how he is using them to perfect your will, strengthen your faith, and bring glory to his own wonderful name.

Help in God's Time

The second point that Maclaren makes is that the delayed help always comes at the right time. He writes: "Do not . . . forget that Heaven's clock is different from ours. In our day there are twelve hours, and in God's a thousand years. What seems long to us is to Him 'a little while.' [Therefore] let us not imitate the shortsighted impatience of His disciples, who said, 'What is this that he saith, A little while? We cannot tell what he saith.' The time of separation looked so long in anticipation to them, and to him it had dwindled to a moment. For two days, eight-and-forty hours, he delayed his answer to Mary and Martha, and they thought it an eternity, while the heavy hours crept by, and they only said, 'It's very weary; he cometh not.' . . . How long did it look to them when they got Lazarus back?"[1]

No, we must not judge God's actions by our conception of time. We must learn that he always acts immediately and decisively when the time is right.

We have an illustration of God's mastery of time and circumstances in the deliverance of Peter from prison following his arrest by King Herod. Herod had killed James, the brother of John; and, since this had pleased the leaders of the people, Herod planned to kill Peter also. The church prayed. But while they prayed Peter still remained in prison. He had been imprisoned before the Passover, and Herod intended to kill him after it. So for at least seven days the Christians were praying, during which time God delayed. Each day went by, one by one, until it was the night before Peter's pending execution. The time was up. But that night, not a moment too soon or too late, the angel entered the prison and freed Peter.

Moreover, the liberation was done deliberately. Nothing was hurried. It is true that when the angel appeared the chains immediately fell off Peter's hands and the gates swung open. But there was no hurry. Instead, Peter was told to put on his sandals. The angel waited while he did so. Then he was told to throw his robe about him. After that the angel and Peter simply walked out of the prison, past the guards and into the streets.

Again let me quote Maclaren. "God is never in haste. He never comes too soon or too late. 'The Lord shall help them, and that right early.' Sennacherib's army is round the city, famine is within the walls. Tomorrow will be too late. But tonight the angel strikes, and the enemies are all dead men. So God's delay makes the deliverance the more signal and joyous when it is granted. And though hope deferred may sometimes make the heart sick, the desire, when it comes is a tree of life"[2]

No Delays

We have one more point to our study. We have seen that Christ's delays are the delays of love. We have seen that the delayed help always comes at the right time. Notice finally that the best help is never delayed.

The principle we have been looking at is an important principle. But we need to notice that at best it applies to only one half—and not even the most important half—of our prayers to God and of God's answers. We ask for some things in which God delays. He delays guidance, healing, the changing of circumstances, and so on. But in the most important things—those that concern spiritual help, growth, salvation, and blessing—there is no delay. Rather in these the help comes instantly. We might say that if the text for the former circumstances is the one we have been studying—"He stayed where he was two more days"—then the text for the latter is Isaiah 65:24—"Before they call I will answer; while they are still speaking, I will hear." If you are praying for spiritual help, insight, salvation, or a deeper relationship to God, then you can be sure that God hears you and that he is moving even now to meet your need.

Here again Peter becomes our example. Do you remember that scene in which Peter saw the Lord Jesus Christ walking toward him over the water, approaching the boat in which Peter was riding? Peter was sometimes cowardly, but he was sometimes brave, too. So when he saw Jesus he reasoned that if Jesus could walk on the water, then by the power of Jesus, Peter could walk on the water also. "Lord," he said, "if it's you, tell me to come to you on the water."

Jesus said, "Come." So Peter got down out of the boat and began to walk toward Jesus.

The sea was in turmoil. There had been a storm. Soon Peter began to look at the waves rather than at Jesus. He began to lose faith; when he began to lose faith, he became afraid and began to sink. "Lord, save me," he cried. We then read—this is beautiful—"*Immediately* Jesus reached out his hand and caught him . . . and when they climbed into the boat, the wind died down" (Matt. 14:30–32). Immediately! This was no time for delays. Help was needed, and help came instantly.

Let us learn these great lessons: (1) If God delays, it is because he has a purpose in his delays, and (2) when we need help immediately, he is there and helps instantly. Moreover, in that help we always find what we most need.

137

Christ's Disciples Tested

John 11:7–10

Then he said to his disciples, "Let us go back to Judea."

"But Rabbi," they said, "a short while ago the Jews tried to stone you, and yet you are going back there?"

Jesus answered, "Are there not twelve hours of daylight? A man who walks by day will not stumble, for he sees by this world's light. It is when he walks by night that he stumbles, for he has no light."

Years ago, when I was growing up in an evangelical Sunday school, I learned a bit of doggerel that expresses a great truth. It goes like this:

> Only one life! 'Twill soon be past;
> Only what's done for Christ will last.

The lines are not much as poetry. Nevertheless, the thoughts they contain are good, and they deserve attention. Life is short. Time is valuable. How we spend our time is important. These thoughts lie behind the verses to which we now come in our verse-by-verse exposition of John's Gospel.

Jesus had delayed for two days after learning from Mary and Martha that their brother Lazarus was sick. "Then he said to his disciples, 'Let us go back to Judea.' 'But Rabbi,' they said, 'a short while ago the Jews tried to stone you;

831

and yet you are going back there?' Jesus answered, 'Are there not twelve hours of daylight? A man who walks by day will not stumble for he sees by this world's light. It is when he walks by night that he stumbles, for he has no light in him'" (11:7–10).

Time Matters

In approaching these verses we must remember that they occur in a Gospel that shows an unusual interest in time. We noticed this first in the opening chapters. There John presents the first great opening week of Christ's ministry, noting in a series of seven significant days how John the Baptist first denied that he himself was the Messiah, how he pointed to Jesus, how the first disciples followed Christ, how those disciples brought others, how Jesus traveled to Galilee, and then, finally, how he turned water into wine at the marriage feast in Cana. The week ends with the significant statement, "This, the first of his miraculous signs Jesus performed at Cana in Galilee, He thus revealed his glory; and his disciples put their faith in him" (2:11).

The same attention to time is seen in other ways also. For instance, John pays particular attention to time references by which the events of Christ's ministry are marked. Thus, we find him dating Christ's first return to Jerusalem as occurring at the time of "the Jewish Passover" (2:13). Or again, Jesus goes back to Jerusalem a second time, having in the meanwhile left it, at "a feast of the Jews" (5:1). In chapter 6 when Jesus multiplies the loaves and fish in Galilee the "Jewish Passover Feast was near" (v. 4). In chapter 7 he is in Jerusalem for the "Feast of Tabernacles" (v. 2). In chapter 10 we are told of "the Feast of Dedication" (v. 22). The events of the last week of Christ's life take place at the final passover (12:1).

One of the Gospel's most important words is "time," used in connection with Christ's death and resurrection. Early in the Gospel we find expressions like these: "My time has not yet come" (2:4) or "his time had not yet come" (7:30; 8:20). Later, on the verge of the crucifixion, John records: "The hour has come" (12:23), "Jesus knew that the time had come" (13:1), "A time is coming, and has come" (16:32), and "Father, the time has come" (17:1).

We should find ourselves asking: What do I do with my time? Is my time used wisely? Who controls it? Do I really trust God to give me the time needed to do the work that needs to be done?

Who Controls Time?

Expressed in this way our questions about time become a test of our trust in God. This is significant, for it is precisely in this way that the subject is introduced by Jesus in John 11.

To see this we need to notice that when Jesus announced his decision to go to Bethany to help Lazarus, he announced it by inviting the disciples to go with him "to Judea." Apart from the context this was a strange thing to say. We might have expected him to say, "Let us go to help Lazarus" or, perhaps, "Let us go to Bethany." But in saying "Let us go back to Judea," he was deliberately choosing a word that would remind the disciples of what awaited them in the area of the capital. This was where Jesus' enemies lived. It was here that he had almost been stoned. Should they return to Judea? Was this wise? Should they place themselves once again within reach of their enemies? Clearly, by expressing the matter in this way, Jesus was testing his disciples to see whether or not they really trusted God with the ordering of their lives and whether or not they were really willing to spend whatever time might be given to them in Christ's service.

Were the disciples willing? They seem to have been. Thomas says later, "Let us also go, that we may die with him" (v. 16). But whether they were willing or not, at least this much is clear—they recognized the danger. They said, "A short while ago the Jews tried to stone you; yet you are going back there?" (v. 8). Obviously, it is in time of danger that we most need to trust God. So we can learn from these men. Whatever the danger, it is better to be with Jesus. Whatever the outcome, it is comforting to know that our times are controlled by God.

Sufficient Time

To say that the disciples recognized the danger of going to Jerusalem and chose, nevertheless, to stay by Jesus is not to say, however, that they understood the issues involved. In fact, they did not. They feared the Jewish leaders. And they had not yet learned that all of Christ's times (as also their own) were divinely determined. So Jesus began to teach them about time. He did so first by a question. He asked, "Are there not twelve hours of daylight?" (v. 9). This question was intended to set them thinking—and to set us thinking. It suggests three truths.

First, God gives each of us a certain amount of time, and *nothing can shorten it*. The day of our life will not finish before it ends. This applied to Jesus, of course. On an earlier occasion, when he was warned about the hostility of King Herod, he said, "Go tell that fox, 'I will drive out demons and heal people today and tomorrow, and on the third day I will reach my goal'" (Luke 13:32). Jesus' life was not going to be cut short by his enemies one minute before the time appointed by the Father. And neither is ours. I am not going to die too soon. You are not going to die too soon. If we are God's children, he has given us a certain number of days, and we shall have them.

An important conclusion follows from this. We need not fear what people can do to us. Or, let me say it in another way. If the prolonging of our days is in our own hands, then we must be extremely careful in all we do. We must be cautious. For instance, are you sure that you really want to take that trip by auto that you have planned for next summer? Many die on the roadways. You may be safer at home. Or again, are you sure you want to eat the kind of food you are often served in local restaurants? Perhaps it is not good for you. You may want to get on to health foods. Or again, are you sure that you have had sufficient medical checkups? Perhaps you should have a checkup each month.

Or perhaps you should just check into a hospital permanently. Above all, be sure that you do not anger any one. The person you anger may be the kind that kills people. Be careful not to stand for anything.

You see my point. If God is not in control—if you are in control—then be fearful. On the other hand, if God orders the duration of your days and if nothing can cut them short, then you can be bold to serve him, as Jesus was. Indeed, you can be a Luther. He did not fear men, for he knew that there was God-appointed work to be done and that he would have sufficient time to do it.

Second, Christ's question to the disciples suggests that if God gives us each a certain amount of time and if nothing can shorten it, then *there is time enough for everything that needs to be done.* The conclusion to be drawn from this truth is that we need not be frantic. We are a fairly frantic people, we Americans. Work seems pressing. Necessities crowd in upon us. Time seems to be slipping away. It is a common picture, as we all know. But it is a picture we have painted for ourselves—this is my point. It is not of God. And since it is not of God, we do not have to be in it.

The principle of sufficient time is one by which we may establish priorities in our lives. If you are God's child and if you seem to have twenty hours of work to do in just sixteen hours, then obviously four hours of that work is not given to you by God. And you should not do it. Moreover, you can ask: What are the dispensable items? Perhaps you do not need that second job. You may, but perhaps you do not. Perhaps God simply does not want you to have the extra income. You may not need to belong to that club, or to that monthly bridge party, or maybe even to that extra committee of the church or that church board. You will not want to cut out your time of personal Bible study, prayer, worship, and fellowship with Christian friends; but there are items you can cut out. Or you can stop wasting time. If we are frantic, it is our fault; we should reorder our priorities. We have sufficient time for all that God has given us to do.

The third truth suggested by Christ's question—"Are there not twelve hours of daylight?"—is that, even though we have sufficient time to do all that God has given us to do, nevertheless, *we have only that time, and the time should not be wasted.* Are there twelve hours to the day? Yes! But there are not thirteen. So we cannot afford to waste even sixty minutes.

William Barclay makes points similar to these in his commentary and at this point calls attention to a famous passage from Christopher Marlowe's play *Doctor Faustus.* Faustus, as most people know from the Faustus legend, had struck a bargain with the devil by which for twenty-four years the devil would be the doctor's servant and in which his every wish would be granted. But, at the end of that time, the devil would claim his soul. At this point in the drama the time has almost come, and Faustus, seeing what a terrible bargain he has made, is grieving:

> O Faustus,
> Now hast thou but one bare hour to live,

> And then thou must be damned perpetually!
> Stand still, you ever-moving spheres of heaven,
> That time may cease and midnight never come;
> Fair nature's eye, rise, rise again and make
> Perpetual day; or let this hour be but
> A year, a month, a week, a natural day,
> That Faustus may repent and save his soul!
> *O lente, lente currite noctis equi!*
> The stars move still, time runs, the clock will strike,
> The devil will come and Faustus must be damned.

No one can make a bargain like that. All people start by being condemned, a position from which we escape only by turning in faith to the Lord Jesus Christ (John 3:16–18). Nevertheless, the verse makes a true point about time. Time is precious. Nothing can lengthen it. Hence, it must be used wisely. Christians must "make the most of every opportunity, because the days are evil" (Eph. 5:16; Col. 4:5).

I am convinced that if we could think this way consistently, any one of these truths would effect a transformation of our lives. We would see many things we do dropping out. We would find many items of higher priority taking their place. And there would be less time wasted. "Only what's done for Christ will last." It is true. So we should spend our precious time in his service.

Christ's Comments

Having asked his question and having thus stimulated the thoughts of the disciples along the lines we have just followed, Jesus wrapped up his teaching by elaborating briefly upon the question and drawing some conclusions. We need to do the same. He said, "A man who walks by day will not stumble because he sees by this world's light. It is when he walks by night that he stumbles because he has no light" (vv. 9–10).

This is true on two levels, of course; and Jesus intended both of them. On the physical level, it refers to the sun. In Jesus' day there were no streetlights to illumine the cities. In fact, there was little artificial lighting of any kind. So when the day ended, a man's work had to be done. To be abroad after nightfall was to stumble and risk injury. On this level the words encourage a person to use time wisely.

On the other hand, there is also a spiritual meaning that can hardly escape any perceptive reader of John's Gospel. Here Jesus speaks of "the light of this world." But who can read the phrase without at once thinking of Jesus himself? He is the light of this world. This was one of the designations he gave to himself (John 8:12; 9:5). He is the sun in whose light a man may walk and not stumble. He is the One without whom we are in darkness. In making these observations, therefore, Jesus clearly wanted to raise our thoughts from the physical level (which, however, is valid and important in itself) to the spiritual level, and to cause us to ask: Am I in the darkness, or do I walk with Christ who is the light of life?

Ask that question of yourself. Is your life illuminated by the Lord Jesus Christ? Or is it in darkness? Is your path growing brighter and brighter? The Bible says, "The path of the righteous is like the first gleam of dawn shining ever brighter till the full light of day" (Prov. 4:18). Or does it grow darker with each milepost along it?

If you are in darkness—your own heart will tell you whether you are or not—let me warn you that there is a great danger of falling. Even a Christian may stumble when he turns his back upon Christ. He will stumble but not fall. The Bible speaks of God's power to "keep [him] from falling and to present [him] before his glorious presence without fault and with great joy" (Jude 24). He will not fall, but he may stumble. This is bad enough. But what if you are not a Christian? In this case the danger is greatly intensified; for if you will not turn to Christ, the time is coming when you will inevitably fall and that so hard that you will not be able to rise again. You will fall eternally.

What is Jesus warning of if it is not this danger? What was the apostle Paul describing when he said of those who refuse to believe, "for they stumbled at that stumbling stone," if it was not that a man or a woman can stumble spiritually and be lost? Jesus was not threatening people. He loved people and attempted to draw them to himself. But he was warning of what would happen if his call was neglected. I wish that you might heed that warning if you are running away from him. Do you sense the darkness? Return to him. Confess your sin. Confess your rebellion. Say, "Lord, I want you to be my Savior." If you do, you will find that he will make your path plain and fill your life with light.

Horatius Bonar, one of our greatest hymn writers, knew this and wrote of his experience:

> I heard the voice of Jesus say,
>   "I am this dark world's Light;
> Look unto me, thy morn shall rise,
>   And all thy day be bright."
> I looked to Jesus, and I found
>   In Him my Star, my Sun;
> And in that light of life I'll walk,
>   Till trav'lling days are done.

It is better to enter into that experience than to come at the end of life's journey to that place described as being shrouded in eternal darkness where all who inhabit it are lost.

138

How Christ Viewed Death

John 11:11-15

After he had said this, he went on to tell them, "Our friend Lazarus has fallen asleep; but I am going there to wake him up."

His disciples replied, "Lord, if he sleeps, he will get better." Jesus had been speaking of his death, but his disciples thought he meant natural sleep.

So then he told them plainly, "Lazarus is dead, and for your sake I am glad I was not there, so that you may believe. But let us go to him."

There is an openness about death today. Once it was not talked of. Now it is, and with increasing candor.

One person who has contributed to this new openness is a member of my congregation in Philadelphia. His name is Dr. C. Everett Koop, and he is known not only for his leadership in pediatric medicine (where he is a pioneer) but also for the way in which he deals with the subject of impending death in his contacts with the parents of his patients. His writings on this subject have appeared in the *Reader's Digest* and in other publications. The Nurses Christian Fellowship, to give another example, is now conducting seminars on the subject of caring for the dying patient. These seminars are well attended. In the secular world, others, such as the late newspaper columnist Stewart Alsop, have made the subject popular. Alsop, while dying of leukemia, wrote of his struggle with death in a book entitled *Stay of Execution*. Once again, this is evidence of the new openness I am talking about.

But this brings us to an interesting question. For if we are finding out what the doctors, nurses, and columnists think of death today, certainly we also find ourselves wanting to ask, "But what did Jesus Christ think about death?" He was in contact with death—his own, which he clearly saw coming, and that of others. How did he regard it? Did he accept death? Or did he long for a stay of execution? What Jesus thought on the subject is important, obviously, as we all realize. For he had information that we do not have, and his views should illuminate our own.

Two Deaths

We must begin with the fact that Christ's answer to the question was twofold, depending upon whether the death in view was the death of an unbeliever or a believer. If the death was the death of an unbeliever, Jesus was not encouraging. In fact, he warned men against dying in this state. To die without faith in himself as the Savior was to enter hell, he said. He spoke of this as a place of "eternal fire" (Matt. 25:41) or "eternal punishment" (Matt. 25:46). He said that it was a place of "weeping and gnashing of teeth" (Matt. 13:42). At one point he told a story of a rich man who was suffering in hades and who appealed to Abraham to send someone to cool his tongue (Luke 16:19–31). He said on another occasion: "Do not be afraid of those who kill the body but cannot kill the soul. Rather, be afraid of the One who can destroy both soul and body in hell" (Matt. 10:28).

The explanation of Christ's sternness at this point is not hard to find. For in the teaching of the Bible death is separation, and the death of an unbeliever is a separation of the soul and the spirit from God. God is light. So a separation from God in death means darkness. God is the source of all good gifts. Death means a deprivation of those gifts. It is this dimension, not suffering alone, that makes death the fearful thing it is for unbelievers.

On the other hand, Jesus was most encouraging about the death of believers. In fact, he was as encouraging on this aspect of the question as he was discouraging on the other. Here he spoke of entering into Abraham's bosom, or paradise (Luke 16:22; 23:43). He spoke of a land filled with many mansions, which he was going to prepare for those who followed him (John 14:2). In the passage that we are about to study he called death "sleep" and said that he was glad that it had happened to his friend Lazarus. This passage reads: "After he had said this, he went on to tell them, 'Our friend Lazarus has fallen asleep; but I am going to wake him up.' His disciples replied, 'Lord, if he sleeps, he will get better.' Jesus had been speaking of his death, but his disciples thought he had meant natural sleep. So then he told them plainly, 'Lazarus is dead, and for your sakes I am glad I was not there, so that you may believe. But, let us go to him'" (vv. 11–15).

Lazarus Dead and Jesus Glad

What a striking expression this is—"Lazarus is dead, and I am glad." We might understand it better if Jesus had said, "Lazarus is sleeping physically, and I am glad," for we would then have thought as the disciples thought when they apparently first misunderstood Christ's meaning. We would have thought that sleep is a good thing and that Lazarus might therefore recover. But this is not what Christ said. He said, "Lazarus is *dead,* and I am glad." So we find ourselves asking, "How can Jesus be glad? How can death possibly be a cause for rejoicing?"

There are several answers to this question, and they are all in the passage. First, Jesus was glad at Lazarus's death because Lazarus was a believer and he understood what the death of a believer was. It was not to be feared. It was a homecoming. In these verses he terms it a "sleep," which it is, and implies that not only is it not to be feared but rather that it is to be regarded as something beneficial.

We understand this better when we begin to reflect on sleep itself and of the good that comes from it. Notice first that sleep is *harmless.* So also is death for the believer. David knew this. He wrote in the Twenty-third Psalm, "Yea, though I walk through the valley of the shadow of death, I will fear no evil" (v. 4). Or again, Paul wrote, "The sting of death is sin, and the power of sin is the law. But thanks be to God! He gives us the victory through our Lord Jesus Christ" (1 Cor. 15:56–57).

Let me give this illustration concerning death's shadow. In Scotland an old man lay dying. He was afraid of death. The minister who was attending him was trying to comfort him. The minister asked if he had not been a shepherd. "Aye," answered the Scotsman, "I have waited upon the sheep many a day."

"And," asked the minister, "did you never stand on the hillside and watch the wind blow a cloud across the valley?"

"Many a time," said the dying man.

"And when the shadow of that cloud came racing across the heather toward you and the flock, were you afraid?"

The old shepherd drew himself up slightly from his pillow and cried, "What! Afraid of a shadow? Jamie has covenanters' blood in his veins, and he has never been afraid of anything."

The minister then turned to his Bible and read the Twenty-third Psalm as the truth broke over Jamie: "Even though I walk through the valley of the shadow of death, I will fear no evil."

For us death is indeed a shadow. But it is a shadow only because the grim reality of death with all its horror laid hold of our shepherd. Is death separation, separation from God? This is what Jesus bore for those who are his sheep. He was separated from the Father. He cried out, "My God, my God, why have you forsaken me?" He was separated so that for us death might be a shadow.

May I make that even plainer? In the year 1776, the year of the signing of the American Declaration of Independence, an English minister, the Reverend Augustus M. Toplady, was walking across a field in Somersetshire when he was suddenly overtaken by a storm. He was still several miles from home. The place was exposed. But he noticed a cleft running down a mass of rock beside a road, and in that cleft he took refuge. There he stayed till the storm passed. Toplady was a godly man. He had been converted in 1740, at the age of sixteen, while sitting in a barn listening to a man preach who could not even write his name. Toplady had since had a very fruitful ministry. Now, sitting in the cleft of the rock, he thought of spiritual things and, picking up a playing card that he found lying on the ground at his feet, he began to write the words of a hymn that has since become one of the most popular of the English-speaking world.

> Rock of Ages, cleft for me,
> Let me hide myself in thee.

This is why the death of a believer is harmless. It is not that death itself is harmless, but rather that Christ has tasted death fully in place of those who believe on him. He was struck for us in order that we might hide in him as the storms of death pass by.

Second, we may note that sleep is *restful.* It is a relief from the work of the day. The Book of Ecclesiastes notes that "the sleep of a laborer is sweet" (Eccl. 5:12). The disciples said of Lazarus, "Lord, if he sleeps, he will get better" (v. 12). It is the same with death. Thus, in Revelation we read, "Blessed are the dead who die in the Lord from now on. 'Yes,' says the Spirit, 'they will rest from their labor, for their deeds will follow them'" (14:13).

Let me say that I do not believe this means that there will be nothing to do in heaven. In fact, I believe that the opposite will be the case. I believe that the life of heaven will be filled with activity; for God is active himself—he is the Creator after all—and we shall be like him. Heaven will not be restful in the sense that there will be no work to do. But it will be restful in the sense that what we do will be done without toil; that is, without the strain, labor, and sorrow that work involves in this life because of sin's curse.

There is one more thing about the resemblance between death and sleep. Sleep is *temporary.* That is, we sleep to rise again. In the same way, death is temporary. We die, but we do so in order to rise to a world prepared for us by our heavenly Father.

Moreover, on the spiritual level death is so temporary that it can hardly be described by time-words at all. How long is death? It has no duration. It is a passage rather, a passage from this world to the next. It is a doorway. Thus, to be absent from the body is "to be at home with the Lord" (2 Cor. 5:8).

There is a wonderful illustration of this truth in a detail from the funeral of Sir Winston Churchill. At one point in the funeral service a bugler, stationed high in the dome of St. Paul's Church in London, where the funeral took place, sounded taps while everyone waited in hushed silence. Taps signifies the end of the day in military circles. So this was a way of marking the end of Churchill's long and distinguished life. To some extent it was the passing of an era. It was sad, even a bit mournful. But then—and this is the point for which I tell the story—no sooner had the notes of taps died away in that great cathedral than the bugle sounded again. But this time the tune was not taps. The tune was reveille, the call by which the military world begins a new day. Churchill wished to give testimony to the truth that death is only a gateway into God's presence, into a life lived in his eternal day.

Since this is what death is, it is no wonder that Jesus could say, "Lazarus is dead, and I am glad."

A Resurrection

There was a second reason why Jesus could say that he was glad, however. In some ways it is the most obvious. Jesus was glad because he knew that he was going to raise Lazarus from the dead. This is what he implies in the same verse that speaks of Lazarus sleeping; for he says, "I am going there to wake him up" (v. 11).

Death could not exist in the presence of Jesus. There is no indication anywhere in Scripture that Jesus ever met a dead person and failed to raise him. On one occasion, when he was passing the little village of Nain, in Galilee, he met a funeral procession coming out of the city. A man had died, the only son of a widow. Jesus went to the bier, touched the dead man, and restored him to life. On another occasion, Jesus raised the daughter of a certain ruler of the synagogue, named Jairus. Here it is Lazarus who is raised. Jesus never met a funeral that he did not stop. In fact, I would be willing to state that he never came across an illness of any kind without making the situation right. So he was always glad. As here, he could rejoice at the outcome.

May I add one more thought? Jesus is able to raise the dead, as I have indicated; but, note this, *only* he can do it. No one else can. If a person is sick but not yet dead, there is a place for physicians. Medicine coupled with the skill of doctors and the natural rejuvenating powers of the human body can do wonders. But if the person is dead, then the doctors are useless. Only the voice of the divine Christ can call forth life in resurrection.

If only Jesus can call forth the dead, do you know the voice that will call them? Not everyone knows Christ's voice. Jesus said of many of his day, "You cannot hear my word" (John 8:43). He said that only those could hear who had been given to him by the Father. Only his sheep could respond (John 10:27). Are you one of his sheep? Have you been given to Christ by the Father? If you cannot answer that question with a firm yes, perhaps you should put yourself in a place where, by the grace of God, you may hear Christ's voice even now. Begin to read the Bible. Expose yourself to the preaching of the gospel by faithful men. Converse with those who already know Christ. Begin to attend church services. It may be that Jesus will speak to you, bringing forth spiritual life in your otherwise dead heart, and begin to prepare you for that second call that will raise you to the life of heaven.

A Strengthening of Faith

Jesus was glad that Lazarus had died, for a third reason. He was glad because he knew that he would raise Lazarus. He was glad because he knew that the resurrection would result in a strengthening of the faith of many. He indicates this by saying, "And for your sake I am glad I was not there so that you may believe" (v. 15). The faith of the disciples was to be strengthened. The faith of Martha and Mary was to be strengthened. Indeed, many who at that time did not even have faith were to come to it as a result of this dramatic resurrection.

The last point can be applied to you who are Christians by asking whether the resurrection that Jesus has performed in you has had that effect on other persons. Has your resurrection helped others to find Jesus? Perhaps you are saying, "What do you mean, my resurrection? My resurrection has not yet occurred. It will occur at the last day." Are you sure of that? Are you sure that this is the only resurrection you can talk about?

You must remember at this point that while all the miracles recorded are true, nevertheless these are recorded (rather than others) because these miracles are superb illustrations of salvation. Thus, the impotent man is a picture of each of us before we are restored spiritually. We are helpless, unable to move, unable to take even the first step toward Jesus. The man born blind is another example. He was unable to see Jesus. If Jesus had told the man to seek him and that he would then help him, the man could not have done it. Yet Jesus saved him. In the same way, the story of Lazarus is included to show what it means to be "dead in trespasses and sins" and why it is necessary that the voice of Christ sound forth to rouse us from this spiritual slumber. We will not awaken spiritually unless Christ calls. But when he calls we do awaken. This is your experience if you are a believer in the Lord Jesus Christ. And so the question holds: Has your resurrection helped others to find Jesus?

This is what Paul wanted as a result of his transformed life. Do you remember that verse in the third chapter of Philippians in which he expresses the hope that he might "attain the resurrection from the dead" (Phil. 3:11)? The phrase does not suggest that Paul was uncertain about the ultimate outcome of his salvation, as though he might one day discover he was lost. The one who wrote in Romans, "For I am convinced that [nothing] will be able to separate us from the love of God that is in Christ Jesus our Lord" (Rom. 8:38–39), does not mean that. What Paul meant was that he wanted to attain unto the resurrection now; that is, to live as a resurrected one among the millions who are spiritually dead, so that they might have a preview of eternal life in action and that some at least might come to faith in the Savior.

That is what I desire for you, if you are a Christian. You have been dead spiritually. You have been made alive in Jesus. Well, then, can others see it? That is one way in which Jesus would like to express joy in your death and resurrection.

139

The Shadow of Death

John 11:16

Then Thomas (called Didymus) said to the rest of the disciples, "Let us also go, that we may die with him."

I do not know why a man's failures are often long remembered and his attainments forgotten, but that is the way things are. And it is not only in our own time that they are like this. Shakespeare phrased it perfectly when he had Antony say at the funeral of his friend Julius Caesar, "The evil that men do lives after them; the good is oft interred with their bones."

The same thing is true of one of the minor characters of John's Gospel. His name is Thomas. Such is our opinion of him that no sooner do we hear that name than we immediately remember that one incident for which he is least praiseworthy. "Doubting Thomas!" That is the phrase that comes into our minds, for we automatically think of the story in which Thomas expressed disbelief in Christ's resurrection. Jesus had already appeared to the other disciples, Thomas being absent. But when Thomas was told about it, he replied, "Unless I see the nail marks in his hands, and put my finger where the nails were, and put my hand into his side, I will not believe" (John 20:25). We forget that the other disciples did not believe until they had seen Christ either. But we remember this story and by it form our one-sided opinions of Christ's doubting disciple.

What a different picture we might have of Thomas if we could only remember the incident that occurs in the eleventh chapter of the same Gospel!

The Story

To understand this story we must remember that Jesus had announced his intention of returning to the area of Jerusalem and that only a few moments before this he had reminded his disciples of the danger that awaited them there. The danger was no illusion. The disciples were understandably frightened. Christ's enemies had tried to stone him on several occasions and in different places. But the opposition at Jerusalem had been extremely fierce; and the last incident, which had taken place only weeks before, was the most frightening of all. We sense the true danger when we recall that on this occasion Jesus actually left Jerusalem for the area of the Jordan River.

Now he was going back, and the disciples were frightened again. They knew that they could not stop Jesus if he had determined to return. But what were they to do? I can imagine them looking around at one another, then at the ground, then at Jesus. I can imagine them wondering, "What will happen to Jesus if he goes to Jerusalem? No doubt he will die. What will happen to us if we follow him? No doubt we will die also." Perhaps there was a long pause. But at last one of the disciples spoke up with precisely the right words for the occasion. That disciple was Thomas. Thomas said, "Let us also go, that we may die with him" (11:16).

I must admit that this was hardly a cheery statement. It was melancholy, even a bit grim. Thomas did tend to look on the worst side of things after all. Still, I cannot help admiring his words. For one thing, they were honest. The way to Jerusalem *was* the way to death. Second, they were loyal. Thomas was saying that no matter what lay ahead it was better to be with Jesus. And so it is. It is always better to be with Jesus. Finally, the words were courageous. In taking this stand Thomas was literally stating his willingness to walk with Christ into the lion's den.

I know that the time came when Thomas, as well as the others, forsook Christ and fled from him. I also know that the death in Jerusalem was not the whole story, that there was a resurrection beyond it. But all this was before Thomas, and at the time (regardless of what the future held) he did the right thing. So let us remember this and try to be like Thomas in his best moments.

Death and Denial

We might be helped in remembering this incident from the life of Thomas if we remember that it is only one expression in Scripture of an important and pervasive principle. It is the principle of *death and denial*—of dying, of saying no to oneself and to the world in order that we might say yes to Christ. This principle is found throughout the New Testament. For instance, in Romans 6 we read, "If we have been united with him like this in his death, we will certainly also be united with him in his resurrection. For we know that our old self was crucified with him so that the body of sin might by done away with, that we should no longer be slaves to sin" (vv. 5–6). Or again, in Galatians 2:20, "I have been crucified with Christ." Or, later on, "May I never boast except in the cross of our Lord Jesus Christ, through which the world has been crucified to me, and I to the world"(Gal. 6:14).

Let me say again, then, that this is a very important principle, and not the least because we do not naturally want to fit into it. Who wants to die, after all? No one! Who wants to deny himself? Who wants to turn down a chance to fulfill his desires? No one! Moreover, we live in the midst of a world that says no to nothing. No is unpopular. Yet this is where Christianity begins, in one sense, and it is the sole way that victory in the Christian life may be established. In other words, to know victory in the Christian life we must become like Thomas. Like him we hear Christ's call, and like him we are at once aware of many other things that we would rather do or become. But we must not do them. Like Thomas we must turn our backs on these things and follow Jesus.

One Principle, Two Applications

This should not be difficult for us to understand, if we are Christians. For this is where Christianity began for us, as I have indicated. What does it mean to have become a Christian? It means to have turned your back on any attempt to please God by your own efforts and instead to have accepted by faith what God has done in Christ for your salvation. No man can save himself. So we must stop trying. We must die to our efforts. We must say no to them. It is only after we have done this that we can receive God's salvation as a gift.

Let me give an illustration of this from the testimony of Paul. Before his conversion Paul had been trying to please God by his personal achievements. After he had met Christ on the road to Damascus, he said no to this course of action and instead lived for Christ. His own words on the matter are expressive. He wrote, "But whatever was to my profit I now consider loss for the sake of Christ. What is more, I consider everything a loss compared to the surpassing greatness of knowing Christ Jesus my Lord, for whose sake I have lost all things. I consider them rubbish, that I may gain Christ and be found in him" (Phil. 3:7–8). This is where the Christian life begins. So, as I say, the principle of death and denial should not be a difficult one for any true Christian to understand.

The difficulty, however (as in many other areas in life), is not with understanding so much as it is with application; and it is here that most of us fall down. The first application of the principle is to the moment of faith in Christ, and we have both understood and applied the principle at that point— if we are Christians. But then—this is so common—we have forgotten that the principle must also be applied to the living of the Christian life, if we really are to live it. Life? Yes. But only after death. Blessing? Yes. But only after we have taken up our cross.

Let me be explicit at this point. If we are really going to experience death and denial that, in one sense, is the basis of the Christian life, then we must be willing to say no to anything that is contrary to God's will and way for us.

First, it means saying no to anything that is contrary to God's revelation of himself; that is, anything contrary to the Bible. This is the way in which we are to approach the law, for instance. We are not under law in the sense of being under a list of rules and regulations. We are free from that. But we are to obey the law in the sense that it reveals to us the nature of God and shows us those areas of life in which by the power of God we are to say no in order that we might go on with Christ. The first of the Ten Commandments is an example: "You shall have no other gods before me." Here is a negative, an obvious one. It tells us that we are to say no to anything that would take God's rightful place in our lives. Is it an actual idol? We must say no to the idol; we must burn it, destroy it, as many primitive people have done when they have responded to the gospel. Is it money? If so, we must get rid of the money; for it is better to be poor and a close follower of Christ than rich and far from him. Do not misunderstand. Money is not something that necessarily takes the place of God in a life. It is possible to be a devoted and deeply spiritual Christian and rich at the same time. But if it is or has become a god, then we must say no to it, for "You shall have no other gods before me." Is it another person who has taken the place of God for you? Is it a business? An ambition? Your children? Fame? Achievement? Whatever it is, you must say no to it, if it is keeping you from Christ. This is the negative principle, the principle of dying. It must be taken seriously.

If you want to test yourself on this, you may do so with each of the other commandments. "You shall not murder." This means that we are to say no to any desire to take another's life or slander his reputation. "You shall not commit adultery." We are to say no to any desire to take another man's wife or another woman's husband. "You shall not steal." We must say no to the desire to take another person's property. If we have not said no at these points, then we can hardly pretend that we are living in the newness of Christ's resurrection life. Indeed, we are not living the life of Christ at all.

Second, if we are going to experience death and denial, we must also say no to anything that is not the will of God for us. In one sense, this point is related to the previous one about the law. But it also goes beyond it in that not everything permitted in the Word of God is God's will for us. For instance, there is nothing at all wrong with marriage. In fact, the contrary is true. Marriage was created by God and has his blessing. Still, marriage may not be the will of God for you; and if it is not, then you must say no to marriage, consciously and deliberately. Until you do you will not really begin to live the life God has for you. The same thing holds true for a profession, for your own conception of yourself, and for many other matters.

Two quick questions before we go on. First, how can I learn to say no? The answer: watch Jesus, follow him. He is the supreme example of self-denial, for he said no even to the glories of heaven in order that he might become man and die for our salvation. We can learn from him. It was certainly from watching Christ that Thomas was able to say what he did on the occasion of their joint return to Jerusalem.

The second question: How can I know when I have said no? The answer is: when you have stopped complaining. If you are murmuring, as the Israelites murmured in the wilderness, you have not really turned your back on Egypt. But if you have stopped murmuring, then you are ready to go on, as Paul was when he said, "Brothers, I do not consider myself yet to have taken hold of it. But one thing I do: Forgetting what is behind and straining toward what is ahead, I press on toward the goal to win the prize for which God has called me heavenward in Christ Jesus" (Phil. 3:13–14).

Resurrection

I have emphasized the principle of death and denial—first, because it is the major lesson of our text, and second, because it is not often taught to today's Christians. However, I do not want to leave the text at this point, for as it stands it is still one-sided. Death *is* a great principle. It is this that Thomas's words so clearly teach us. But there is also more. In the biblical scheme of things death is always followed by life, crucifixion by the resurrection. It is this that is truly exciting and for which we are willing to die.

Let us go back for a minute to the texts I quoted earlier. "If we have been united with him like this in his death, we will certainly *also* be united with him in his resurrection" (Rom. 6:5). True, we must die to self; but we do so in order that we might live to Christ. We die "that the body of sin might be done away with, that we should no longer be slaves to sin" (v. 6). We read something similar in Galatians: "I have been crucified with Christ and I no longer live, but Christ lives in me. The life I live in the body, I live by faith in the Son of God, who loved me and gave himself for me" (Gal. 2:20). We also find the truth just one chapter farther on in John's Gospel. Jesus is speaking. He says, "Unless a kernel of wheat falls to the ground and dies, it remains only a single seed. But if it dies, *it produces many seeds.* The man who loves his life will lose it, while the man who hates his life in this world will keep it for eternal life" (12:24–25).

What does this mean practically? It means that when we give up trying to run our own lives or when we give up those things that seem so precious and so utterly indispensible to us, then (and only then) do we find the true joy of being a Christian and enter into lives so freed from the obsessions that we can hardly understand from that point on how they could have had such a strong hold on us.

So what is the difference between a joyless Christian and a joyful Christian, a defeated and a victorious one? Death and resurrection! The joyless Christian may have died and risen with Christ in some abstract, theological sense, so that he can in the same sense be termed "a new creature in Christ." But he has certainly never known it in practice. On the other hand, the joyful Christian has found satisfaction in whatever God dispenses to him and is truly satisfied, for he has said no to anything that might keep him from the richness of God's own blessing and presence, and has risen into new life.

A Word to Others

One final thought comes from these ten brief words of Thomas. Have you noticed that Thomas was not only willing to deny himself in order to follow Christ but that he also invited others to do so? His exact words were, "*Let us* also go, that *we* may die with him." He wanted the others to do as he did. And he was successful in his invitation, for a little later in the chapter we find that the disciples are all still with Jesus. Are you like Thomas in that? You may already have learned these lessons. Of course, you may not have; and if this is the case, you must begin there. But if you have, if you have really learned to say no and have thereby also entered into the joy of new life in Christ, then this is the point at which you in particular must imitate Thomas. If you have learned these things, teach others. If you have found joy, invite them to follow the One who taught you how to find it.

Thomas! The word means "twin" in Hebrew; it is the equivalent of Didymus, which means "twin" in Greek. Thomas was a twin. I wonder who the other one was. He was not one of the other disciples certainly. He may not even have been a man; the twin may have been a woman. We cannot know. Yet there is a sense in which I would like you to find him. I would like you to find him every time you look into the mirror. Only I would like you to find, not "doubting Thomas," but rather the one who said to others, "Let us also go, that we may die with him."

140

"I Am the Resurrection and the Life"

John 11:17–26

On his arrival, Jesus found that Lazarus had already been in the tomb for four days. Bethany was less than two miles from Jerusalem, and many Jews had come to Martha and Mary to comfort them in the loss of their brother. When Martha heard that Jesus was coming, she went out to meet him, but Mary stayed at home.

"Lord," Martha said to Jesus, "if you had been here, my brother would not have died. But I know that even now God will give you whatever you ask."

Jesus said to her, "Your brother will rise again."

Martha answered, "I know he will rise again in the resurrection at the last day."

Jesus said to her, "I am the resurrection and the life. He who believes in me will live, even though he dies; and whoever lives and believes in me will never die. Do you believe this?"

About fifty years before the birth of Jesus Christ a letter was written by a well-known Roman, Sulpicius Severus, to the great orator Cicero on the occasion of the death of Cicero's beloved daughter Tullia. It is a magnificent letter. It expresses deep sympathy. It reminds the orator that his daughter had only experienced a lot common to mankind and had passed away only when the freedom of the Republic was itself failing. It is warm and moving. But in spite of these great qualities the letter contains nothing of a hope of life beyond the grave. In reply, Cicero thanks his friend for his sympathy and enlarges upon the measure of his loss.

849

A century later the apostle Paul was in contact with Christians who had become similarly discouraged by the death of their friends, as the result of which he too has left us a letter. But Paul's letter is different. True, it acknowledges sorrow; but it also breathes hope. It deals with death, but it also knows the comfort of a resurrection. In it Paul writes, "Brothers, we do not want you to be ignorant about those who fall asleep, or to grieve like the rest of men, who have no hope. We believe that Jesus died and rose again and so we believe that God will bring with Jesus those who have fallen asleep in him. . . . Therefore encourage each other with these words" (1 Thess. 4:13–14, 18).

These letters present a remarkable contrast, for they throw into relief that new awareness of the future life introduced by Christianity. Cicero was not unaware of Plato's arguments for immortality or of any of the other arguments advanced in his day, but these were poor comfort in face of the cruel horror of death. Paul, on the other hand, moves in a new spirit of hope and confidence.

A Troubled Believer

Before we look at Christ's statement regarding the resurrection and of himself as "the resurrection and the life," we need to look at the one to whom he spoke it. For the person to whom he spoke was Martha, and Martha is an excellent example of a certain type of believer, of whom we have many today. These do not distrust the Lord, but neither do they believe with that full confidence that would allow them to lay aside their care and rest in his good provision. They believe, but they are always troubling themselves with questions of "How?" and "Why?" and "What if?" and so miss the blessing that could be theirs if they would only believe more simply.

Such faith always *attempts to limit God* or, which is the same thing, to scale down his promises. Notice that Martha limited the Lord's working both to time and place, for she said, "Lord, if you had been here, my brother would not have died" (v. 21).

We need to recall here that Jesus had deliberately delayed his return to Bethany for two days so that he eventually arrived in Bethany four full days after Lazarus' burial. Some have felt that Jesus delayed until Lazarus had died (and have imagined this to be cruel), but a careful thinking through of the days will show that this probably was not true. If we number the days one through four, we can reconstruct what happened. On the first day, as Lazarus was getting worse, the sisters sent to Jesus. Apparently Lazarus died some time after the departure of the messenger and was quickly buried, so that this day counts as the first of the four in which he lay in the tomb. Quick burials were customary in such a hot climate. The next two days Jesus stayed in the area of the Jordan; that is, days two and three. Then, on the fourth day, Jesus returned to Bethany and performed the resurrection.

Lazarus was therefore already dead by the time word of his illness reached Jesus; Jesus knew of it and therefore delayed his return, not that Lazarus might die but for an entirely different purpose. The reason Jesus delayed his return from the Jordan was that there might be no doubt that Lazarus was dead and that there might therefore be no cause for doubting the miracle. Thus we know that from the beginning he intended to perform it.

Martha did not see this, however, so when Jesus returned to Bethany her first words were a bit of rebuke. And they expressed her own limited faith, as I have indicated. "If you *had been* here," she said. That is, she felt that Jesus could have done something four days earlier but that he could not do what was obviously necessary now. True, one verse later Martha says, "But I know that even now, God will give you whatever you ask" (v. 22). But we know that her "whatever" did not include a resurrection, for she was quick to rebuke Christ later when he asked that the stone be rolled away from the tomb of Lazarus. Moreover, Martha also clearly tried to limit Christ by place; for she said, "If you had been *here*," that is, in Bethany. It implied that Jesus could not have healed her brother from a distance. A little later she does the same thing when she reacts to Christ's promise concerning her brother—"Your brother will rise again"—by saying, "I know he will rise again in the resurrection at the last day" (v. 24).

In the same way many of us also seek to limit Jesus. We believe that he is able to do all he says he will do—but not now and not here. At least we do not expect him to and are genuinely surprised or disbelieving when he does.

The second characteristic of Martha's strange faith is that she *treated the words of Christ impersonally.* The first recorded words of Jesus after his return to Bethany were a tremendous promise. He said, "Your brother will rise again" (v. 23). But instead of taking this in the best and most personal sense— as a promise that Jesus was about to restore her brother to her—Martha pushed the words off into the future as though to say that they had no relationship either to herself or her situation.

This is also what we do with Christ's promises, many of us. We believe them, in a sense, that is, as they apply to others or to a far distant time. But we do not receive them personally. For us, the glorious promises of God become something like a mighty fleet that has been put in moth balls, or like antiques in the attic. They have value, we suppose; but practically we get nothing out of them. The story is told of a gentleman who visited the home of a poor French couple a long time ago where he saw a note for one thousand francs papered to the wall. He asked them how they got that particular piece of paper. They answered that they had found a poor soldier, who had been wounded, and that they had nursed him in their home until he died. He had given it to them. It was such a nice memorial of him, they thought, that they had caused it to be plastered to the wall where they would always be able to see it. Naturally they were surprised when they were told that it would be worth quite a little fortune to them if they would turn it into money.

Unfortunately many Christians do that with God's promises. But they should not—that is the point. As Spurgeon once wrote, they should have "grace to turn God's bullion . . . into current coin."[1]

A New Revelation

We have looked at Martha, then. Let us now look at Jesus and at the way in which he dealt with her. She had come expressing a poor kind of faith, a faith that was half faith and half doubt. Even her words had a hint of rebuke about them. But Jesus did not get angry with her for her weak faith, or rebuke her in turn for her attitude. He could have said, "Martha, Martha, what poor thoughts you have of me. I have been with you for a long time and you still do not know that I am both willing to and will raise your brother." He could have said something like that, but he did not. Rebuke in a time of great sorrow is not helpful, and is uncalled for. Besides, it would even have been misunderstood; for Martha thought she was expressing great faith in Jesus when she said, "But I know that even now, God will give you whatever you ask" (v. 22).

Instead, Jesus used the opportunity to teach Martha more of himself. He said, "I am the resurrection and the life. He who believes in me will live, even though he dies;. and whoever lives and believes in me will never die" (vv. 25–26).

What did Jesus teach Martha? His first words were words to her condition specifically. She had attempted to push the resurrection off to the last day. Jesus replied by saying that he himself was the resurrection and that, therefore, wherever he is there is life. In this case, the Lord Jesus Christ was present physically; so there was going to be physical life. Lazarus would live again. When Jesus returns physically at the end of this age, there will be a physical resurrection then also. At other times, as today, Jesus is present spiritually; so there is a spiritual resurrection rather than a physical one. If you are a believer in the Lord Jesus Christ, you have experienced this resurrection. You were dead in trespasses and sins, but you have been brought to life by Jesus.

Likewise, all who know the Lord Jesus Christ will experience a physical resurrection. So at this point, having spoken directly to Martha's situation, Jesus goes on to develop his teaching. "He who believes in me will live, even though he dies; and whoever lives and believes in me will never die" (vv. 25–26).

These comments can mean any of three things. First, both halves of Christ's saying can be taken spiritually. If we do this, the sense would be, "Whoever believes in me, though he were spiritually dead, yet shall he become spiritually alive. And whosoever is spiritually alive and continues to believe in me shall never die spiritually." The advantage of this interpretation is that it takes the terms in the same sense. If it is followed, the major thought is that the one who believes in Christ, having received the eternal life of God, will never be lost.

The second interpretation is one that takes the first half of Christ's words physically and the second half spiritually. It would give us a meaning somewhat like this: "He who believes in me, even though he should die physically, yet he will live physically [that is, there will be a final resurrection]. And whosoever is spiritually alive and believes in me shall not die spiritually." The advantage of this interpretation is that it relates to Martha's problem directly—the problem of physical death answered by physical resurrection.

The disadvantage is that the terms, particularly the term "life," must be taken in different senses.

The third interpretation takes both halves of Christ's statement physically, that is, as applying to the time of Christ's second coming at which time those who are alive will be caught up to meet the Lord in the air while those who have died will be raised physically. This, while true, does not seem to relate to the situation in John 11. But if it were the meaning of the verses, we would have to read them like this: "He who believes in me, though he shall have died physically by the time of my return, yet shall he be raised. And whoever is a believer and is still living at the time of my return, shall never die physically but shall be caught up to heaven." This was the interpretation of C. H. Spurgeon and some other commentators.

Which of these is to be preferred? It is probably impossible to say with certainty; for, since the statements involved in each view are true in themselves, each could be possible. In my opinion the second is the most likely in that it begins with Martha's situation but then goes on to present a higher principle. If this is the case, then Christ's promises are all-inclusive. There is a promise of spiritual life and physical life. There is a promise of life now and also life to come. Moreover, it is clearly stated that this life is only for those who believe on Christ and who are therefore members of his covenant people.

A Direct Application

This brings us to our conclusion, which is at the same time (let us note) the conclusion that Jesus pressed upon Martha. It is a conclusion in the form of a question: "Do you believe this?" (v. 26). Jesus had made a statement ("I am the resurrection and the life"); he had elaborated upon it. Now he asks, "Do you believe this? Do you really believe it?" This is the question I would like to leave with you also. Do you believe Christ's teaching?

As you think about it, notice that Jesus speaks of faith and not feeling. He did not say to Martha, "Do you feel better now, Martha? Have you found these thoughts comforting? Do you feel your old optimism returning?" According to Jesus it was not how she felt that was important, but what she believed. Feelings are deceiving. Moreover, they come and go. On the other hand, faith is an anchor fixed in bedrock. To believe the words of Jesus is to believe in One whose promises are absolutely trustworthy.

Notice also that Christ was specific. He did not say, "Martha, do you believe generally?" He said, "Martha, do you believe *this?* That is, do you believe the specific truths I have taught you?"

I ask that question of you. I trust that your answer may be different. Do you believe this? You should be able to say, "Yes, Lord, I believe it. I believe all that is written in your Book.

"I believe in one great God, who has made this earth and has placed me upon it. I believe that I am sinful. I believe that this same God in love and wisdom sent the Lord Jesus Christ to die for me that I might be saved. I believe that Jesus existed with God and as God from the beginning, that he became man, that his death was a substitutionary death for me by which my sin has been removed as far as the east is from the west and on the basis of which it will be remembered against me no more. I believe in Christ's historical, literal, and bodily resurrection, by which God has demonstrated that Christ's sacrifice on the cross is acceptable to him as an all-sufficient atonement for the sin of his people and in which he has also given a foretaste of the coming resurrection of all who believe on him. I believe in the person and power of the Holy Spirit. I believe that he opens blind eyes to see Christ and moves rebellious wills to embrace him to their salvation. I believe that he illuminates the written Word of God so that those who are saved can understand it and obey it. I believe in the fellowship of the saints. I believe in the church. I believe in God's providence, by which nothing enters the life of the Christian that is not the product either of God's direct or permissive will. I believe that God chastises his children. I believe that he is determined to perfect the character of Jesus Christ in all who are united to Christ by faith. I believe that Jesus will one day return from heaven even as he was seen to go into heaven—bodily and in time. I believe that in that day there will be a final resurrection of believers to the life of heaven and of unbelievers to judgment. In hell there will be suffering. In heaven there will be a life of blessing prepared in advance by God for those whom he has chosen in Christ before the foundation of the world."

There is much more that can be said, of course. But every Christian should be able to say at least that. "Do you believe this?" You should be able to echo the teaching of the written Word in answer to the question of the living Word, rounding it off with a hearty, "Yes, Lord, I believe all that is written in your Book."

141

Faith's Foothold

John 11:27

"Yes, Lord," she told him, "I believe that you are the Christ, the Son of God, who was to come into the world."

In our last study, as we were looking at Christ's question to Martha on the occasion of his return to Bethany soon after Lazarus had died, we saw what our answer should be to the question, "Do you believe this?" We should be able to respond, "Lord, I believe everything you say. I believe what is written in your Book." This involves the truth that God is the creator and sustainer of life; that we are sinners; that God has redeemed us in Christ Jesus, his Son; that Jesus rose bodily from the dead, ascended into heaven, and is coming again; that there will be a final judgment; and many other doctrines. However, it may be that some will hear this and say, "I know that is good, and I wish I could affirm all those things. But I haven't come that far. I cannot say them for certain. What should I do?" If that is the case in your life, then the verse to which we now come is for you personally.

Jesus had asked Martha, "Do you believe this?" Her answer is the verse we are considering. She replied, "Yes, Lord, I believe that you are the Christ, the Son of God, who was to come into the world" (v. 27).

We should notice that Martha did not reply directly to what Christ had asked, for her answer did not include her assent to what he had been teaching. Still, it was a good reply. She did not affirm more than she knew, but she affirmed what she did know. Moreover, I am sure that from this point she went on to even greater understanding.

I call her words "faith's foothold," for they were a sure support from which she could climb higher. I have often seen a mountain climber make his way up an outcropping of rock, which someone else might consider unclimbable, simply by finding small footholds in the rock's surface. They are not big, but they are firm; and one who will rest his whole weight on them can move up and on from that position. This is what Martha did. Her sphere of knowledge was not large, but it was firm. So she built upon it. It is my desire that many might begin as she began, as a result of this study.

The Words of Jesus

When we consider her answer a phrase at a time, we notice, first of all, that she gives the *basis* of her understanding. The basis is the word of Christ. We have it in her affirmative response: "Yes, Lord, I believe." This does not mean that she understands everything he has been saying—in fact, she did not—but rather that she accepts it, whatever it is, because she knows that his words are trustworthy. This is an ideal starting point for anyone. This should be true of your spiritual understanding.

Moreover, it is not only that Jesus' words are absolutely trustworthy. It is also the case that *only* his words are fully trustworthy. With anyone else the question of truth is relative. A person may speak what is true at one time but what is false at another. Or he may speak partial truth; that is, truth mixed with error. Or he may not know what is true. With Jesus it is different. Jesus spoke the truth, the whole truth, and nothing but the truth. Moreover, he claimed to be the truth; for he said in John 14:6, "I am the way and the truth and the life." In other words, according to Jesus, the only valid starting point in any religious matter is what he himself has said and done, and not the words or deeds of some other person.

Why is it that in a discussion of religious questions someone will frequently express an opinion on something of which he has no knowledge at all and others will at once adopt his opinion, while the words of Jesus on the same subject (about which he has knowledge) are ignored?

Let me give an example. Someone says, "I believe in reincarnation. If you do well in this life, you will reappear as a person with a good position in life—perhaps someone rich or in a position of authority. If you do badly, you may reappear as an animal or insect. Eventually, if you do well enough, you may progress up and out of the system into a blessed state." Someone who is listening replies, "That sounds good to me. I'll believe in reincarnation too." But why should he? There is no evidence for that view of the afterlife whatsoever; so any opinion about it is groundless. On the other hand, Jesus, who came from eternity and who returned to it, who demonstrated the truth of his claims by means of a resurrection, taught the conscious continuation of the individual soul beyond death, in which state he either suffers for his sins as the result of a punishment imposed by God or else enjoys the bliss of heaven on the basis of Christ's death for him, which he has received by faith—and this is neglected. Why? Generally it is because men and women do not like what God says to them. The Bible says simply that it is because they do not like to retain God in their knowledge and so prefer lies.

When we are talking about the words of Jesus in this way, we must realize that we are also talking about the whole of Scripture, for he inspired Scripture. Indeed, his Spirit stands behind the particular words and books that have been written.

Let us be clear about the fact that we live in a day when men and women have grown unhappy with this book and have therefore thrown it off. Let us also note that they have done so because they do not like what it says, not because it has been shown to be untrustworthy. The standard view is that modern biblical criticism has shown that the Bible contains errors. This quotation expresses it: "The scientific development of the last century has rendered untenable the whole conception of the Bible as a verbally inspired book, to which we can appeal with absolute certainty for infallible guidance in all matters of faith and conduct."[1] But the fact that this is *not* the major reason why the Bible is neglected is seen in the truth that most people who neglect the Bible cannot give you even one example of an alleged error in Scripture, let alone prove it to be an error. So it is not the supposed errors that have turned them off, but the Bible's teaching. It is that the Bible reveals men and women to be sinners in need of a Savior and that most persons do not like to be told this. If men and women were praised by God, biblical truth would be popular.

What shall we do then? Shall we also throw off the Bible and with it the words of Christ? How can we? If we were to do that, we would be abandoning the only sure source of spiritual knowledge available to fallen man, and we would be rendering an answer to the question "Do you believe this?" impossible. Without a sure word from God we cannot believe anything. Indeed, all is uncertain and there are no answers to the great spiritual questions that confront us. On the other hand, with the Bible as a base we can go on to sure knowledge and expanding faith, as Martha did.

It is my firm conviction that we will not have a true revival in today's church until the church as a whole returns to this high view of Scripture. "Yes, Lord, I believe." This should be our starting point, and we should say both to God and others that we do believe all that the Scriptures teach. Indeed, the Word should become our starting point and thus also our only infallible rule of faith and practice.

A Threefold Confession

The second important thing we should notice about this verse is that it also gives a statement of *content* as regards Martha's confession. The first notable feature is the basis upon which she believes. The second is the content or *what* she believes. Clearly this is also important, for faith without content is meaningless. If a person says, "I believe," we want to ask, "But what do you believe?" If he has no answer to that question, we must conclude that he does not know what belief is in the biblical sense and that he is deluding himself in spiritual matters.

Martha was not like this, however, Martha said, "Lord, I believe." Then she immediately went on to say what she believed: "I believe that you are the Christ, the Son of God, who was to come into the world." This confession has three points, but the most important thing to be said is that all three points have to do with Jesus. In other words, he himself is the content of her confession. There are other matters in the Christian faith, of course. But in a sense they all focus in Christ, so that he really is the content of Christianity. Therefore, in this as in the matter of the basis of Christian faith Martha becomes a valuable guide for ourselves and our contemporaries.

God's Messiah

First of all, then, Martha expressed belief that Jesus is "the Christ." *Christ* means "Messiah," or "the Anointed One." So, by saying this, Martha was affirming that Jesus was the one prophesied to appear in the end time as God's specially appointed servant.

We must admit that there were different expectations in Judaism regarding the Messiah, just as there are different views regarding him by Jewish thinkers today. Some expected an otherworldly Messiah. Some expected a great teacher. The society that produced the Dead Sea Scrolls is an example of this. Still others, perhaps the majority, expected a political or warlike Messiah whose primary work would be to drive out the Romans who then occupied the Jewish lands. Many such views were current, but the expectation that tied them together was the belief that one day God would send a specially anointed individual who would be the herald of salvation. Martha believed that Jesus was this anointed one, and so should we all; for it is through him alone that we have salvation.

Second, Martha called Jesus "the Son of God." By this she acknowledged his divinity. If you were to ask me how much about Christ's divinity Martha really understood at this time, I am not sure that I could give a firm answer; for she does not explain her own statement. Did she recognize that Jehovah, the God of Israel, was actually incarnate in Jesus of Nazareth? Did she know that he was the God-man, a totally unique person in whom all the attributes of God and all the attributes of man, except a sinful nature, were present and combined? I am not sure. I am certain that Martha wanted to confess his divinity in some sense, however. And I am certain that all these truths are implied in the general use of the term "Son of God" in John's Gospel.

It is important that Jesus be divine. For only if he is divine is he able to do that which he has been sent to do and that which we need. If Jesus is not God, then his words are to be trusted no more than any other man's. They might be right—in part—but we cannot build upon them. We cannot trust the question of our eternal destiny to his teaching. If Jesus is not God, then his death on the cross has no more meaning than the death of any other individual. It may have been courageous. It may be an example to others who are subjected to persecution and suffering. But it is not an atonement for sins, and those who trust in it are deluded. If Jesus is not God, then he did not rise from the dead; and those who preach the resurrection are of all men most miserable and are deceivers of others. If Jesus is not God, then he has not gone to prepare a place for his own, will not return again for them, and is not now present to guide and assist those who trust him. All this depends upon the affirmation that Jesus is fully divine. So this affirmation must be part of our testimony.

Finally, Martha confessed that Jesus is the one "who should come into the world." What did she mean by this? She meant that Jesus is the one who had been promised in the various Old Testament Scriptures and who had therefore come to fulfill them. Jesus is the one promised to the fallen and dejected Adam and Eve in the Garden, the one who should crush the head of Satan though Satan should wound his heel (Gen. 3:15). He is the seed of Abraham through whom all families of the earth should be blessed (Gen. 22:18). He is that prophet whose coming God foretold to Moses (Deut. 18:15, 18). He is the suffering one of Isaiah's prophecy (Isaiah 53), the crucified but resurrected one of the Psalms (Pss. 16:10; 22:1–18). He is the one who shall rule forever upon the throne of his father David (2 Sam. 7:16).

Do you believe that Jesus is all these things, as Martha believed that he was? If you do, a great consequence will flow from it; namely, that you will stop looking elsewhere for the answers to life, history, and salvation. Some people claim to be Christians, but they act like pagans where their lives are concerned. They say they believe in Jesus, but they do not expect him to help them. Instead, they trust science, politics, education, ecology, or whatever else seems to have caught the fancy of their contemporaries.

Understand that I am not opposed to such endeavors. We must have them. But they are not themselves the answer to society's problems. Shortly after his solution to the immediately pressing problems in the Middle East in the spring of 1974, someone said to Dr. Henry Kissinger, the secretary of state of the United States, "Dr. Kissinger, thank you for saving the world."

Kissinger replied, "You're welcome."

But Kissinger did not save the world, though he may have helped a bit. This is proved by the fact that the guns were soon sounding once again in new conflicts. Clearly, men can work toward solutions; but they can never provide final solutions. Only Jesus can do that. He has already provided the final solution to the problem of sin. He is the only answer to present peace and victory for the individual in this life. In time he will return to solve all problems as he reigns on earth in righteousness for one thousand years. Do you seek solutions? Then this is where you should look—to Jesus, who is "the Christ, the Son of God," the One "who was to come into the world."

An Anchored Faith

Let me ask these final questions. Is your faith like Martha's? Is it based on a knowledge of God's Word, and is it centered in the person of Christ? Or is it without substance, without content, and therefore essentially no more than a state of your mind?

In India there is a tradition that some magicians are able to take a coil of rope, throw it up into the air in the midst of an open field, have a boy start climbing up it, and then have the boy disappear into the sky after which the rope falls back to the ground. It has been shown by many people that this does not actually happen. No one has ever seen it done. But it has become a persistent and fascinating tradition, much like our stories of Paul Bunyan or similar figures. This makes a good illustration of the nature of some people's faith. Their faith is like a rope coiled beside them. They are proud of it. If we ask what they intend to do with it, they reply that they are getting it ready and that when the time comes for them to die they intend to uncoil it, throw it toward heaven, and then climb it into salvation. If we reply that this is impossible, that faith must be attached to something, they object that we are unreasonable and that their faith could never be so limited.

True faith is different. This faith comes down from heaven, for we are told that even faith is not of ourselves, it is the gift of God (Eph. 2:8). In this situation faith comes close to the earth, but does not touch it. So we need only to lay our hand upon it and climb. It is not of man, for it is let down from heaven. It is not groundless, for it is fixed in God and in the truth revealed in his Scriptures. This should be the nature of your faith, as it was of the faith of Martha.

142

Mary

John 11:28-32

And after she had said this, she went back and called her sister Mary aside. "The Teacher is here," she said, "and is asking for you." When Mary heard this, she got up quickly and went to him. Now Jesus had not yet entered the village, but was still at the place where Martha had met him. When the Jews who had been with Mary in the house, comforting her, noticed how quickly she got up and went out, they followed her, supposing she was going to the tomb to mourn there.

When Mary reached the place where Jesus was and saw him, she fell at his feet and said, "Lord, if you had been here, my brother would not have died."

W e are going to look at an invitation of Jesus Christ that is not recorded in the Bible. It was spoken—we can read it between the lines—but not recorded. It is an invitation of Christ to Mary; and I want to study it for what we can learn from the bearer of the invitation, from Mary's response to the invitation, and from the way in which the invitation comes to us.

In this chapter Jesus had come to the area of Bethany, near Jerusalem, because Lazarus, the brother of Mary and Martha, had been sick and subsequently died. By the time Jesus got to the area a great crowd of mourners had collected. So Jesus did not go into the city. He stayed on the outskirts. Word came to Martha that Jesus was there, so she went out to meet him. Jesus then had that conversation with Martha that is recorded in the central part of this chapter in which he reveals himself to be the resurrection and the life. At this point—although it is not recorded—Jesus must then have said to Martha, "Go, call Mary. Ask her to come to me." We know he must have said this because, as we are told in verse 28, Martha "went back and called her sister Mary aside. 'The Teacher is here and is asking for you.'"

I want to apply the invitation by pointing out that the Master has come and calls for *you*. Do you hear his voice? Will you respond to him?

High in the Alps, at the historic Saint Bernard Pass, there is a hostel that is run by monks. They keep the great Saint Bernard dogs there. In the last century, in the winter, when the snow would be coming down and the air would be so filled with flakes that a person could not see the trail, the monks used to ring a great bell so that the traveler who was making his way up the trail through the snow could almost be led to the hostel by the sound. That is what I want to do. I want to sound the bell. Life is sometimes so filled with the mist of afflictions or sorrows (or whatever it may be) that we cannot see the way clearly. But here is a bell that all can hear and follow. Come to me! Come to me! It is the invitation of the Lord to anyone who will hear, leave present occupations, and come to him. To those who will hear there is the promise that if they will come Jesus will not cast them out.

The Messenger

First, we need to look at the bearer of the invitation, Martha. Martha is still in the story, as we can readily see; and she is still a prominent figure. Mary was quiet. But Martha seems always to have been prominent. She had met with the Lord Jesus Christ and had been given this task—to go and *call Mary*. And so she does.

There was a time—we read about it in Luke 10:40—when Martha tried to keep Mary from Jesus. It was the occasion of the supper in her home. Mary was sitting at Jesus' feet, learning from him. Martha was doing chores and was troubled. She asked Jesus to rebuke Mary. In other words, she tried to get Jesus to make Mary get up from his feet and go into the kitchen to help her. But that was before! Here Martha goes to call Mary to be with Jesus. What has happened? What is the difference? The difference clearly is that Martha herself has met with Jesus and has been stirred by his teaching.

Are you a Christian? "Yes," you say, "I am." Well, then, do you go to call others to Jesus Christ? Do you bear to them that invitation that first came to you? If you find yourself admitting, "No, I am afraid I do not," is it not that you have not spent sufficient time with Jesus and have not been stirred by him? You will never be a great soul winner unless you do spend time with Jesus. Unless you do that, all you will be talking about is a theory or doctrine. If you spend time with Jesus, you are talking about a person whose invitation you can bear to other people.

There is a second noteworthy thing about Martha's action. She called Mary *secretly;* that is, *personally* (v. 28). The story tells us that, and the action suggests it. For instance, when Mary arose quickly and went to Jesus, the Jews did not understand where she was going (v. 31). Clearly, this is because Martha had whispered the invitation to Mary. When Martha came into the house, the friends must have been clustered around Mary. So if Martha had shouted in a loud voice, "The Master has come and is calling for you," they would have heard and would have understood. Instead, Martha must have whispered the message: "Mary, the Master is here, and he is calling for you." There is an important principle involved here. It is the principle of "one-to-one" evangelism. I am not saying here that there is not a place for mass evangelism. Certainly there is, though even in mass evangelism the strength lies in the fact that God the Holy Spirit takes the Word to the individual heart. But I am saying that the best evangelism, the most effective evangelism, is when you, the individual Christian, take the Word of the Lord Jesus Christ to one who does not yet believe him.

If you do that, the actual words of Christ will help you. Years ago, when my wife and I were engaged in a Bible study ministry, we had a young woman attend who at that time had difficult marital problems. She and her husband had fights. As we understood it, they did not just argue; they actually hit one another. Sometimes she was bruised as a result. Christians had been trying to get her to our Bible study for a long time, and for one reason or another she had been unable to come. But on this particular occasion she came. We were studying Matthew. We had begun with chapter 1 and had by this time gotten to the Sermon on the Mount. We started to read, and the first Scripture that was read was Matthew 5:39. "Do not resist an evil person. If someone strikes you on the right cheek, turn to him the other also." There was a long pause, the longest pause I have ever experienced in a Bible study. Finally the girl herself spoke up. She said, "I think I understand what this means. It means that if someone hits you and you hit him back, then he will hit you again. But if he hits you and you don't hit back, then the fight will end." We all mumbled something to the effect that this is true. Then she said something very profound. She said, "But it is not so easy to do, is it?" Indeed, it is not! So we had an opportunity to speak to her of the power of the Lord Jesus Christ to make such things possible and to heal relationships.

Let me give you another story of how God speaks to the individual. It is the story of a man who lived next door to a church in St. Paul, Minnesota, which was then pastored by one of my assistants. This man did not believe the gospel, and he did not want to go to church. In fact, he refused all invitations. However, one week the church had a series of special meetings featuring exceptional music. The neighbor heard the music and was so taken with it that he decided to go in and hear it. He said to himself, "I'll go, but I'll go just for the music. When it is over, I'll leave." So he went in and sat down in the back of the church. When the musical portion of the evening was over and the preacher was standing up to preach, the man tried to slip out, but he could not. The church was too full. He said, "I'll do the next best thing; I'll put my fingers in my ears so I can't hear him." So there he was with his fingers in his ears while the preacher was bringing his message. That sort of thing does not really bother God very much. He controls all things. In this case he sent a little fly to buzz around the man's nose. The man ignored the fly as long as he could. But finally that little fly buzzing around his nose got to be too much for him. He took his finger out of one ear and smacked at the fly. But as he did that the preacher said, "He that hath ears to hear, let him hear what God says."

There is a third feature about Martha's activity. First, she called Mary. Second, she called her personally. Notice, third, that she did it on *orders from the Lord Jesus Christ.* Does that apply to us? Certainly it does! For we are under orders to take the gospel into all the world to every creature. This is our Great Commission, and it comes to every believer. It is not a commission to ministers alone. It is not a commission for missionaries exclusively. It is a command for all who know Jesus Christ as Savior. Furthermore, it is repeated many times. I sometimes make the point that anything that is repeated in Scripture is obviously of great importance. If God says something once, we ought to sit up and pay attention. But if he repeats it again and again, the truth should literally seize us and command our thinking. The Great Commission occurs at the end of every one of the four Gospels and at the beginning of the Book of Acts. So we should take notice. Our task is to take the gospel to every creature and teach each one concerning Christ. This is what the Duke of Wellington called "marching orders for the Church."

Ears to Hear

Next, I want us to look at Mary's response to Martha's invitation, because Mary's response is a pattern for us also. If Martha's work in bearing the invitation is a pattern for Christians in communicating the gospel to non-Christians—which it is—then Mary's response is a pattern for what non-Christians should do when they hear the word of Christ.

What did Mary do? We are told, first of all, that Mary *ran* to Jesus. That is, she went to him quickly. In order to do that she had to leave the others who were with her. Other people are often a great hindrance to belief. Here was Mary, mourning in her home. Her friends and acquaintances had come, as was the custom in biblical times and still is to a large extent today. They had sympathized. They had surrounded her with comfort. They had brought in food. Mary could have said to herself, "Jesus has called me, but I have these friends to think of. What will they think of me if I leave them and rush off to Jesus?" Many people think that way today. They hear the gospel. They hear that they are sinners. They hear that they need a Savior. They hear that Jesus Christ is that Savior, and they even believe it. But they say to themselves, "What will my friends think of me if I become a Christian? My friends will say, 'What a fanatic he has become!' I don't want to offend them." So they postpone the day of decision, and the opportunity passes by. Do not do that. Do not let the opinion of others hinder you from coming to Jesus.

Moreover, do not even let them delay you. Not long ago, when I was speaking at a Bible conference, I was asked why I was not giving invitations. Actually

I was. But the questioner was asking why I had not invited people forward or asked them to speak to me afterward. On this occasion I had a good way to answer the question. For just that morning, after I had concluded by asking any who were not Christians to turn from sin, believe in Christ and follow him, another man stood up and asked people to come forward afterward. He thought he was giving an invitation. He said, "If you want to believe on Jesus, come and talk to us." But actually he was delaying the decision, for he was suggesting that the listener postpone his decision until after he had talked to a minister. I told this and then asked my questioner what he thought the best approach was. He acknowledged that the first was better. *Now* is the accepted time. *Now* is the day of salvation.

Someone once asked a little girl whether she obeyed her mother. She turned to her mother and asked, "Mother, do I always obey you?"

"You know the answer to that better than I do," the mother replied.

"Well, I never disobey you," the child said. "I always do what you tell me, but sometimes I go slow." Many people are like that with the Lord Jesus Christ. But not Mary! Mary ran to Christ immediately!

Second, Mary fell down at Christ's feet and *worshiped* him. This too should be true of us. When the Lord Jesus says, "Come unto me," and we do, our next act should be to fall at his feet to worship him.

Every time we see Mary in the Gospels she is at the feet of Jesus. In Luke, in the story I referred to earlier, she is at his feet learning from him. Here she is at his feet worshiping. On the third occasion she is at his feet serving, having broken over him the alabaster box full of ointment. That should be true of us. We sit at Christ's feet first to learn from him. Next, we fall at his feet to worship him. And then we serve him. Have you done that? Perhaps you have learned of Christ but you have not worshiped him. If not, you should acknowledge him as God Almighty, your Savior and your Lord, and then serve him, because we are called to do that also.

Finally, after Mary had run to Christ and had worshiped him, she *expressed her faith verbally*. This is what we find in verse 32: "When Mary reached the place where Jesus was and saw him, she fell at his feet and said, 'Lord, if you had been here, my brother would not have died.' Anyone who reads this closely will notice that Mary said the same thing as Martha—"If you had been here, my brother would not have died." But most persons who read closely will also recognize a difference in the cry. Martha had debated with Jesus. Mary fell at his feet, and her comment was made in the context of total trust and confidence. Mary's words meant, "Lord, you are everything; you can do everything. I trust you totally." Can you say that? Is that your confession?

He Calls for You

Let me sound the bell of the monks once again, as clearly as I am able. Martha called Mary by telling her, "Mary, the Teacher is here and is asking for you." Now the Teacher calls for *you!* Do you hear him?

Notice that he calls for *you,* not someone else but for *you!* You are the one who is to respond. Do you say to yourself, "I am far too unimportant for the Lord Jesus to call me. I am no one"? Mary was the no one of the story. She was the quiet one. The only thing she says in this entire chapter are the words we have here—"Lord, if you had been here, my brother would not have died." Mary was the quiet, overlooked one. Yet Jesus called Mary.

Perhaps you say to yourself, "I am too important; I am too prominent. Jesus could not expect me to come to him." If you are saying that, I want you to hear this story told by Bishop John Taylor Smith, a former chaplain general of the British army. On one occasion, when he was preaching in a large cathedral on the text "You must be born again," Bishop Smith said by way of illustration, "My dear people, do not substitute anything for the new birth. You may be a member of a church, even the great church of which I am a member, the historic Church of England, but church membership is not new birth, and our text says that you must be born again." The rector was sitting at his left. He continued, "You may be a clergyman like my friend the rector here and not be born again, and you must be born again." On his right sat the archdeacon. Pointing at him he continued, "You might even be an archdeacon like my friend in this stall and still not be born again, and you must be born again. You might even be a bishop like myself and not be born again, and you must be born again."

The bishop finished his message and went on his way. But a day or two later he received a letter from the archdeacon that read in part, "My dear Bishop: You have found me out. I have been a clergyman for over thirty years, but I have never known anything of the joy that Christians speak of. I never could understand it. But when you pointed to me and said that a person could be an archdeacon and not be born again, I understood what the trouble was. Would you please come and talk to me?" Naturally Bishop Smith did talk to him, and the archdeacon, important as he was, responded to Christ's call.[1]

There are none too low or too high for whom the gospel does not apply. Nor are there any who do not need to hear Christ's call.

143

Jesus Wept

John 11:33–37

When Jesus saw her weeping, and the Jews who had come along with her also weeping, he was deeply moved in spirit and troubled. "Where have you laid him?" he asked.

"Come and see, Lord," they replied.

Jesus wept.

Then the Jews said, "See how he loved him!"

But some of them said, "Could not he who opened the eyes of the blind man have kept this man from dying?"

In reading the Bible I have often been displeased by the work of those men who divided the text into verses. Done for liturgical reasons originally, often it is harmless. But sometimes the divisions have made the text difficult to understand or have destroyed its meaning. The beginning of Ephesians 2 is an example of this; for the words "and you" (v. 1) rightly continue a thought found four verses earlier in chapter 1 and belong to it. In the division we have, the connection is lost. Similarly 1 John 2:1–2 really belongs with 1 John 1:5–10. There are other examples.

There is a handling of one verse of the Bible by these men for which I have nothing but praise, however. The verse is John 11:35, our text for this and the next three studies: "Jesus wept." The text is only two words, which makes it the shortest verse in the English Bible. Yet it is of such importance that it rightly deserves to stand alone. Underline it! Mark it with red ink! Add an exclamation point! Print it in capital letters! "JESUS WEPT!" Spurgeon, who preached two sermons on this passage in the course of his ministry, wrote, "There is infinitely more in these two words than any sermonizer, or student of the Word, will ever be able to bring out of them, even though he should apply the microscope of the utmost attentive consideration."[1]

I agree with Spurgeon. We shall never exhaust these words. But let us try. If we do, we may well find John 11:35 to be a window through which we shall see into glory beyond. It is a small window; but if we place our eye close to it, we will see much. Let us look at these words for what they teach about the Lord Jesus Christ, about God the Father, about ourselves, and finally about the love of the Lord Jesus Christ for us, which is to be our example.

The first of these, what the words teach about the Lord Jesus Christ, shall concern us in this study.

Truly a Man

What do these words teach about Jesus? The first answer is that they teach us that Jesus was truly a man. Indeed, it is primarily as a man that he wept on this occasion.

There are other facts that reveal the full humanity of our Lord, of course. Many of them are physical. We read that Jesus was born of a woman, that he was wrapped in swaddling clothes. We are to suppose that he was nursed like other babies. We read in Luke that he increased in knowledge. The full text says, "And Jesus grew in wisdom and stature, and in favor with God and men" (Luke 2:52). We read that Christ hungered. This was true many times, obviously, but especially on that occasion when he fasted for forty days in the wilderness and was tempted by Satan to turn stones into bread. After the resurrection Jesus ate broiled fish and a piece of honeycomb to demonstrate that even then he had a real body. Jesus knew thirst. On one occasion, being wearied with his journey, he sat on Jacob's well and asked the woman of Samaria for a drink. On the cross he cried, "I thirst," and they gave him vinegar. Jesus grew tired. One time he was so tired that he fell asleep in a wildly rocking boat, and even the wind and waves failed to rouse him.

The Lord's humanity is seen also in his emotions. At times he was angry, though he differed from us in most of our anger in that he grew angry without sinning in the process. In such times he denounced the hypocrisy of the religious leaders of his day, calling them "blind leaders of the blind," "whited sepulchres," "a generation of vipers," and "children of the devil." Jesus also showed pity, as in his compassion for the multitudes whom he termed "sheep without a shepherd." At times their hunger moved him, for he fed them in Galilee on at least two occasions.

These facts from the life of Christ all speak of his humanity. Yet we compare them with the verse before us and confess that they do not speak to us as this text does. Jesus wept! From this we know that his body had glands, as ours do—tear glands. And we know that he felt as we feel. What a Savior! He is a Savior who became as we are so that we might become like him. Can you not identify with such a One? Can you not love him? Hold fast to Christ's divinity by all means. A Savior who is not divine is no Savior at all. But while you hold to his divinity do not give up the fact that he is also truly human; for it is as a man, as well as God, that he presents himself to perishing men and women.

Acquainted with Grief

Second, the fact that Jesus wept teaches us that Jesus experienced grief, as we do. In this we find him fulfilling Isaiah's prophecy, for Isaiah said that he would be "a man of sorrows, and acquainted with grief" (Isa. 53:3). It may be that Jesus could have come to this earth and died for our sin without having entered into the grief that we experience, but he did not avoid sorrow. We conclude, therefore, that, whatever our grief may be, Jesus knows of it and has entered into it.

We have a problem at this point, however, for the word that is translated "deeply moved" in most of our Bibles is one that is difficult to understand. It is the word *enebrimēsato*. Part of the problem is that the word occurs only three other times in the New Testament and that even then it has a meaning that does not seem to fit this situation. We find the word in Matthew 9:30 and in Mark 1:43 and 14:5. In the first two instances it is translated "strictly charged," in the sense that Jesus strictly commanded a person whom he had healed to tell no one. In the third instance it is used of those who witnessed the anointing of Jesus with costly ointment by a certain woman and who were said to have "murmured" about it. Neither of these translations—"strictly charged" or "murmured"—seems to fit the context of John 11.

In each of these uses there does seem to be what William Barclay calls "a certain sternness, almost anger" to Jesus' expressions. And since this is true, some commentators have placed the idea of indignation or even anger in John's passage. They would translate the verse, "Jesus was moved to anger in his spirit." If we ask why Jesus should be angry, they answer either that he was angry with the supposed unbelief or hypocrisy of those who were weeping over Lazarus (so Morris, Plummer, Loisy, Hoskyns) or else with death, which he would have viewed as a tool of Satan and a great enemy (so Chrysostom, Zahn). It may have been that some of the weeping of the crowd was less than sincere, but this is not said or implied in the passage. Besides, whatever may have been the case with the crowd, it was certainly not the case that Mary and Martha were faking. So we reject the idea of anger, at least at the hypocrisy of the crowd. Anger may have produced shouts of an outraged sensibility, but it certainly did not produce tears on this occasion.

The other possibility is to translate the word in a way that suggests deep emotion. This is made possible by the fact that one other known use of the word *enebrimēsato* in the Greek language is to describe the snorting of a horse, as in the excitement of battle or under a heavy load. Thus—and this is far better than the former interpretation—Jesus may be said to have groaned with the sisters in deep emotion, emotion out of which an involuntary cry was wrung from his heart. This is the view captured by Phillips, who renders the phrase, "He was deeply moved and visibly distressed," or by the translators of the New International Version, who say, "He was deeply moved and troubled."

Some Christians have found this unacceptable, for they imagine that it is just not proper for Jesus to have been moved to such a degree, particularly by the grief of others. They say that he had to have been moved by something no less great or terrible than sin. But this does not satisfy me. I am willing to grant that Jesus grieved over sin, even more so than he grieved over death, which is the consequence of sin. I also grant that he was saddened by unbelief, as he was on that other occasion when he looked out over unbelieving Jerusalem (Luke 19:41). But how can these be separated from the grief of the sisters? And how can we read the passage without seeing that Jesus wept with them? At the least these items must be taken together—grief, sin, unbelief, death, sorrow. For, as Lightfoot says, "The expression used . . . implies that he now voluntarily and deliberately accepts and makes his own the emotion and the experience from which it is his purpose to deliver men."[2] Morgan writes, "He . . . gathered up into his own personality all the misery resulting from sin, represented in a dead man and broken hearted people round him."[3]

What does all this mean? It means that Jesus was acquainted with grief, as we are, that he understands it and is therefore able to comfort those who sorrow. The author of Hebrews knew this, for he commends the suffering of Christ to Christians as a point of identification. "For surely it is not angels he helps, but Abraham's descendants. For this reason he had to be made like his brothers in every way, in order that he might become a merciful and faithful high priest in service to God, and that he might make atonement for the sins of the people. Because he himself suffered when he was tempted, he is able to help those who are being tempted" (Heb. 2:16–18).

It is not an impassible, insensitive, unmovable Christ that is commended to you and me in Christianity. It is One who has entered into our grief and who understands our sorrows. Are you suffering? He knows it. Are you in tears? He has been there before you. Are you distressed? So was he. But he went on to overcome these things so that we might overcome them. Meanwhile, he is One who understands you and to whom you may come.

Not Ashamed

This verse teaches us a third truth about Jesus. It teaches us that he was not ashamed to be human. Here we note that he could have repressed his tears rather than giving vent to them. He can do all things; he could have done this as well. Moreover, he could have given himself good reasons for doing it. He could have said, "If I show tears, my tears will be misunderstood; they will be taken as a sign of weakness." Indeed, this is exactly how some reacted; for it is what they meant when they said, "Could not he who opened the eyes of the blind have kept this man from dying?" (v. 37). They interpreted his tears as a confession that he could do nothing. Or again, Jesus could have argued that it was foolish to cry when he was about to raise Lazarus. "Why weep now?" he might have pondered. "In a few minutes everyone will be rejoicing." I suppose, finally, that he might even have viewed his tears as inappropriate in that the whole episode was going to redound to God's glory (v. 4). But he did not use this excuse either. True, the miracle would result in the giving of glory to God, but that was still minutes away. Now the sisters and their friends were weeping; and if they were weeping, he would weep with them. Jesus knew how the story would end, but in the meantime he was not ashamed to be one with his brothers.

Identified with Others

This leads us to our fourth point. For not only does the weeping of Jesus teach us that he was truly man, that he was acquainted with grief, that he was not ashamed of his humanity; it also teaches that he was pleased to thus identify with his brothers. He could have remained aloof (as we often do), but he did not. Instead, he identified with us in all things, thereby becoming our example.

Why is it that we who are Christians so often fail to do this? Why are we so strong in our crusades against sin but so weak in our identifications with the sinner? Are you one who has launched a crusade? Are you disturbed, for instance, by the declining moral tone of our nation? If you are, I am glad. I wish you well. We need fighters and prophets. But as you declaim against corruption do not fail to weep for those who are caught up in it. Does the current widespread visibility of homosexuality disturb you? Are you against it? Good! But as you strike out against homosexuality do not forget to weep for the homosexual. Are you troubled by the traffic in habit-forming drugs? Splendid! Fight it with every weapon at your disposal. But as you strike out at drugs do not forget to weep for the victims and even for those who victimize.

Os Guinness gives us a biblical example of this principle toward the end of his impressive book *The Dust of Death*. It is the example of Moses. Moses, you will recall, suspected that he was to be the liberator of the Jewish people. But the first time he attempted to liberate them it was from a position of privilege and superiority, and he was a failure. He was a member of the household of Pharaoh. He killed an Egyptian who had been beating an Israelite. But when he came back the next day he was rejected by the very people whom he was trying to serve. "Who made you ruler and judge over us?" was their question (Exod. 2:14). Years later, however, after he had chosen "to be mistreated along with the people of God" (Heb. 11:25), Moses was able to identify with them, to share their hunger, danger, and problems. And they followed him. In the same way, Guinness concludes, "It is when Christians have at least partially entered into the profundity of identification that the Christian community has been at its most human and most sensitive and that its message has been most credible and compelling."[4]

Jesus Loves

Finally, the fact that Jesus wept at the grave of Lazarus also teaches us that he loves. This is what the people of Christ's day saw in his tears; for they observed him and said, "Behold, how he loved him!" (v. 36). Did Jesus love Lazarus before that? Of course he did! He also loved Mary and Martha and the others. But it was his tears that actually got through to at least some of them and convinced them of his love. They knew that he loved when they saw him weep with the sisters over Lazarus.

Is there not in the story of Christ's tears that which will touch your heart and teach you to love him if you have never done so? Perhaps you are one who has heard the gospel? You have heard it presented doctrinally and experientially and in every way the preachers and teachers of the Word know how to present it. But it has remained a theory for you. It has never become that which could touch your heart. Is there not something in the picture of the weeping Christ to reach you? He is God; yet he became man, entering into all the grief and suffering that you know, including tears; and then he died intentionally and willingly for your salvation. If this cannot reach you, what can?

Finally, you may be a Christian. If this is so, then let me ask if there is not in this picture of the weeping Christ that which will convict you of your own cold indifference toward the lost and compel you to bear the gospel to them. Our hearts are cold. We must admit that. But there is in Christ that eternal flame of true love that will enkindle them if we but expose ourselves to it.

We sometimes sing in our Sunday services "Oh, how I love Jesus," and we mean it, up to a point. But do we love him enough to show love to other people? Do you love him enough to leave the affluence of our country to cross the seas to a land where men are starving and in which even on your missionary allowance you will have to live without much that you are now accustomed to in order to present the gospel? Do you love him enough to be a missionary? Do you love Jesus enough to leave your suburban home—I will not say for good, but "once a week"—to cross your town to love and serve those whose state of life is not actually much different from those you might find in many foreign cultures? Do you love him enough to help an inner-city mission? Do you love Jesus enough just to cross the street to your neighbor in order to love him and win him to the Savior?

Humanity! Sorrow! Pride! Identification! Love! All are in these verses, and more besides.

144

Our Tears in God's Bottle

John 11:33–37

When Jesus saw her weeping, and the Jews who had come along with her also weeping, he was deeply moved in spirit and troubled. "Where have you laid him?" he asked.

"Come and see, Lord," they replied.

Jesus wept.

Then the Jews said, "See how he loved him!"

But some of them said, "Could not he who opened the eyes of the blind man have kept this man from dying?"

There is a strange law of biblical exposition that says that the longer the text to be taught, the shorter the amount of time necessary to deal with it. Or, conversely, the shorter the text, the more time necessary. I find that if I have only ten minutes to speak, I can, if necessary, deal with an entire book. I have done that on occasion. If I have only ten seconds, I can cover the Bible. In fact, I can do it now in just ten words. The message of the Bible is: "Man's complete ruin in sin/God's perfect remedy in Christ." Thus it is that a long text takes a short time. On the other hand, a verse as short as John 11:35—"Jesus wept"—takes weeks.

We have already had one study of this text, in which we looked at the words for what they have to teach us about Jesus Christ. But they can also teach us about God the Father, about ourselves, and about the love of Christ, which is to be the pattern of our love both for God and for one another. It is the first of these remaining subjects—the teaching about God the Father—that we want to turn to now. We can see how this follows from the fact that the text teaches us about Jesus; for if Jesus is God (as he is) and if Jesus wept, then there must be a sense in which we can say that God the Father weeps too. We must be careful how we say this, of course. I will introduce some qualifications later. Nevertheless, even with these qualifications, we must say that if Jesus weeps, then we are to learn that the God of the universe weeps in the sense that he cares about us, identifies with us, and shows us mercy.

A Compassionate God

We should notice before going further that this was a novel and even shocking idea in Christ's day, particularly among the Greeks to whom John was writing. Today, conditioned as we are by a culture that has taken on some Christian ideas and values, we find the idea of a compassionate God natural. Why wouldn't he be like this? we reason. But in John's day, among the Greeks, God was thought to be above all such emotions.

Barclay presents the situation well in his commentary, showing that to most pagan thinkers the primary characteristic of God was what they called *apatheia*. This is the word from which we get our English word "apathy," but it does not mean precisely what we mean when we see the word in English. "Apathy" means "a lack of feeling" or "indifference." *Apatheia* means a total inability to feel any emotion whatever. By it the Greeks meant that God could not feel anger, love, pain, disappointment, hope, or any of the other emotions that so totally make up our existence. How did the Greeks come to attribute *apatheia* to God? They reasoned like this. If a person can feel sorrow or joy, gladness or grief, it means that someone else can have an effect upon him; for it is someone else who causes these emotions. If another can have an effect upon him, it follows that he must also have power over him, at least for the moment. But no one can have power over God. That is impossible, and if this is so, then it must mean that God cannot have feelings. He must be lonely, isolated, compassionless. He can be approached through reason perhaps, but not on the basis of his love or pity.[1]

The Jews should have had the right picture, for the Old Testament reveals God as a God of love and compassion. But even the Jews had lost this element as a result of the formal and legalistic religion that had been developing in Israel in the centuries before Christ's birth. Jehovah had become cold and distant, just as he had always been to the Greeks. But Jesus wept and thus revealed a God who enters into the anguish of his people and grieves with them in their afflictions.

A Suffering God

I wrote a few moments ago that I would need to introduce some qualifications in this whole matter of speaking of the sufferings of God, and I must do that now. For we must not think that we are saying precisely the same thing when we say we suffer and when we say that God suffers.

For one thing, when we suffer, weep, or grieve we never do so entirely in innocence. Our sorrows are linked to sin, and we are never entirely sinless in any situation. This is not true of God. If he sorrows with us, it is because of our sin and its consequences and never because of some sin or shortcoming in himself. Second, when we say that God suffers with us, we do not mean that there is therefore a change in God, as though he were not suffering before but now suddenly grieves because of what we have done. In their aversion to this idea the Greeks were right. God *is* the eternal one. He is the same yesterday, today, and forever. In God there is no variableness, neither shadow of turning (James 1:17). So while saying that God enters into our suffering we do not mean that God has ever been surprised or has altered his feelings or plans because of anything we have done. Third, we must notice that, while we are told that Jesus wept on three separate occasions (at the grave of Lazarus, over Jerusalem, and in the Garden of Gethsemane), strictly speaking we are never told that God the Father weeps, either in the Old Testament or in the New Testament.

So we must be careful as to what we infer from John 11:35. We may say that God weeps, perhaps. But as we do we must remember that this is not true for him precisely as it is for men and women.

The Tears of His People

What, then, may we say about the tears of God? The answer is that we may say anything that is both suggested by the tears of Jesus and substantiated by other verses. Let me give a few thoughts on this.

First, we may say that *God notices our tears.* Nothing is more apparent than this in the story of Christ's weeping at the tomb of Lazarus, for the text tells us that Jesus wept when he saw the others weeping—"When Jesus saw her weeping, and the Jews who had come with her also weeping, he was deeply moved in spirit and troubled" (v. 33). Jesus wept because he noticed their weeping. In the same way, many texts tell us that God the Father sees our tears. They tell us that he is not oblivious. They tell us that he takes notice of them.

One example of this is found in the story of God's dealings with aged King Hezekiah. Hezekiah was sick and about to die, and Isaiah was sent to tell him to put his house in order. Instead of doing this, Hezekiah began to weep. He cried to God, saying, "Remember, O LORD, how I have walked before you faithfully and with wholehearted devotion and have done what is good in your eyes" (2 Kings 20:3). The Bible says that he wept very much. What did God do? Surprisingly we read that God spoke to Isaiah at once and told him to return to Hezekiah with a new message. "Go back and tell Hezekiah, the leader of my people, 'This is what the LORD, the God of your father David says: I have heard your prayer and seen your tears; I will heal you. . . . I will add fifteen years to your life'" (vv. 5–6). As we read the story we may feel that the king's tears were unwise, for the fifteen years he lived after this were not good years. Nevertheless, the point of the story is that God heard him, as he also hears us. In the same way, Job declared: "He hears the cry of the needy" (Job 34:28). Likewise, David testified: "The LORD has heard my weeping" (Ps. 6:8).

These last verses also introduce us to a further thought, for they really mean, not only that God knows of our tears but also that *he is touched by them.* Jesus was touched by the tears of Mary and the others; it is because of this that he wept with them. In the same way, the Father is touched. It is this that we mean above all when we say that God weeps with his people.

Here again a number of Old Testament texts are helpful. Job said, in the verse that we have already quoted: "He hears the cry of the needy" (Job 34:28). David wrote: "He does not ignore the cry of the humble" (Ps. 9:12). He said again, "The eyes of the LORD are on the righteous and his ears are attentive to their cry" (Ps. 34:15). Here are three verbs—hears, does not ignore, are attentive—each of which suggests that God is genuinely touched by our sorrow. Should we fear, then, to pour forth tears before him? Should we ever fear that, if we come to God earnestly, we will find him unmoved?

This should be a great encouragement in our prayers. Of course, we will not want to pray foolishly, as Hezekiah did. But neither will we want to pray coldly, particularly when it is another's interest that concerns us. Did Jesus weep before his loving Father? Then so can we. And we will find our tears effective. Spurgeon wrote: "No prayer will ever prevail with God more surely than a liquid petition, which, being distilled from the heart, trickles from the eye, and waters the cheek. Then is God won when he hears the voice of your weeping."[2]

Notice one thing more about our tears and the concern that both the Father and Son have for them. We have seen that God notices our tears and is touched by them. Notice also that *God remembers our tears* and that they are therefore precious to him.

In the Psalms there is a wonderful verse that expresses this truth in a metaphor; it has given us the title of this study. David is writing, telling on this occasion of the many griefs he has had as the result of the deeds of his enemies. They fight against him. They slander him, distorting his words. They hide themselves in order to fall upon him by surprise and destroy him. But, he cries out to God, "Put thou my tears into thy bottle. Are they not in thy book?" (Ps. 56:8 KJV). What is the bottle about which David speaks? We know that the Romans frequently had little glass bottles called tear bottles, in which they collected their tears. But that is not what David is thinking here. The only bottles he knew were large leather bottles, the kind that Jesus later termed wineskins. He is saying that God possesses such a bottle into which he puts David's tears. It is not that David presents his tears to God, as though to prove something. Rather, it is God who collects David's tears, and he does so in a bottle so large that he will lose none of them. In other words, God notices the tears of his people, is touched by them, and places them up in remembrance before him. If you are God's child, know that he treasures your tears and that he remembers them after you have long forgotten.

Tears Wiped Away

Finally, I want you to see that *God acts to remove our tears.* That is my fourth point. God notices our tears, is touched by our tears, remembers our tears; yes, but God also acts to remove our tears forever.

Here again, the example of Jesus is instructive. Suppose for a minute that the eleventh chapter of John had ended with the verse we are studying— "Jesus wept." Or suppose we should read, "Jesus wept and returned to the area of the Jordan." That would not be much of a story. There would be no comfort in it. If that were the case, I doubt if John would have included the story in his Gospel. But this is not what happened. Instead we read that Jesus first wept, but then acted to raise Lazarus and restore him to his sisters. He wept, but he moved to remove the tears and bring joy to the sisters.

It is the same with the Father. He notices our tears, but he also acts to remove them. Thus, we read in the Old Testament, "For you have delivered . . . my eyes from tears" (Ps. 116:8). Or again, "Those who sow in tears will reap with songs of joy" (Ps. 126:5). Or, as in this verse from Isaiah, "He will swallow up death forever. The sovereign LORD will wipe away the tears from all faces" (Isa. 25:8).

We should note that this last verse is picked up twice in the Book of Revelation, once in chapter 7 and once in chapter 21, to speak of the final blessedness of God's saints. There we read, "'These are they who have come out of the great tribulation; they have washed their robes and made them white in the blood of the Lamb. Therefore, "they are before the throne of God and serve him day and night in his temple; and he who sits on the throne will spread his tent over them. Never again will they hunger; never again will they thirst. The sun will not beat upon them, nor any scorching heat. For the Lamb at the center of the throne will be their shepherd; he will lead them to springs of living water. And God will wipe away every tear from their eyes'". . . . I saw the Holy City, the new Jerusalem, coming down out of heaven from God, prepared as a bride beautifully dressed for her husband. And I heard a loud voice from the throne saying, 'Now the dwelling of God is with men, and he will live with them. They will be his people, and God himself will be with them and be their God. He will wipe away every tear from their eyes'" (Rev. 7:14–17; 21:2–4).

Do Something

So where do these truths end? They end with these conclusions. First, do not look at sorrow and death as an unbeliever might do, but see them rather through eyes that have been accustomed to dwell on such promises. This does not mean that we will not sorrow. Sorrow is still sorrow; death is still an enemy. But it does mean that we must sorrow differently, our sorrow being mixed with faith and expectation. Thus, as Paul acknowledged, we will sorrow, but not as those "who have no hope" (1 Thess. 4:13).

Second, do not be afraid to feel with those who feel sorrow. What was proper for our Lord and his Father is not improper for us who are his servants. If Jesus wept for others, we may weep. Indeed, it is as we weep that we most identify with others and exhibit our right to speak the comforting word of the gospel to them.

I think of two great examples of this point, one from the Old Testament and one from the New. The Old Testament example is Moses, whom I have mentioned in another context earlier. Moses had learned to weep with his people, so much so that he was actually willing to be sent to hell if it could mean that they would experience salvation. The story is a simple one. Moses had gone up onto Mount Sinai to receive the law. But as he was receiving it the people who remained below in the valley were breaking it. God asked Moses to step aside while he destroyed them. Moses was horrified and frightened, horrified at the sin of the people and frightened because he knew that God meant business. He went down the mountain. He dealt with the sin. Then on the next day he returned with an offer that must have welled up from a heart nearly broken with grief. In Hebrew it is even choppy, and one sentence is incomplete. We read: "So Moses went back to the LORD and said, 'Oh, what a great sin these people have committed! They have made themselves gods of gold. But now, please forgive their sin—but if not, then blot me out of the book you have written'" (Exod. 32:31–32). Here is a cry from the heart of a man who so identified with his people that he was willing to be sent to hell if only it could mean their salvation.

The other story is from the New Testament. It involves the apostle Paul. He, too, grieved for Israel, and wrote: "For I could wish that I myself were cursed and cut off from Christ for the sake of my brothers, those of my own race, the people of Israel" (Rom. 9:3). Paul is saying the same thing Moses said. Only, unlike Moses, Paul knew that the thing for which he was asking was not possible. This is what it means to be godlike or godly. It is to those who are willing to be like this that God most entrusts the work of spreading the gospel.

145

God's "Valuable" People

John 11:35–37

Jesus wept.

Then the Jews said, "See how he loved him!"

But some of them said, "Could not he who opened the eyes of the blind man have kept this man from dying?"

I t is possible to examine a subject from different points of view. For example, the American Revolution can be studied from the viewpoint of what was happening in England or America in the eighteenth century or from the viewpoint of economics, political theory, or other matters. If it is studied from the viewpoint of England, it can be expected to throw light on such questions as: What was England's relationship to the colonies at this time? What was King George doing? What were the policies of the court? Why were the cries of the colonists unheeded? If it is studied from the American perspective, the examination might tell in part how the revolutionary ideas originated, what the settlers desired from England and from their regional governments, and so forth. Each of these approaches is valid, and the answers derived will be valid depending upon the amount and quality of work done in each area.

In a similar way, the text we have been studying may also be looked at from diverse points of view. In fact, we have already looked at it from two of these viewpoints. The verse is John 11:35—"Jesus wept." It may be looked at for what it teaches us about Jesus, about the Father, about ourselves, and finally about the love of Jesus for us, which is to be our pattern in loving others. It is the third of these, what the text teaches us about ourselves, that will now be our subject.

In an earlier study I compared this text, the shortest in the Bible, to a little window through which, if we get close enough to it, we may see much. At this point we may perhaps compare it to the hole in an old-fashioned pinhole camera, in which the picture becomes sharp only when the hole is small.

What does John 11:35 teach us about ourselves? It teaches that we are precious in God's sight, that we have gotten ourselves into such a state that even God weeps over us, and that we need God. We need to look at each of these points carefully.

God's Treasures

First of all, the text teaches us that we are precious in the sight of God. In fact, this is one of the most obvious lessons of John 11:35, since it is only because we are precious to God that Christ weeps over us. Suppose for a moment that you are walking down a street in your town or city and that you step on a bug. Do you stop and cry over the bug? Not at all. The reason is obvious: the bug is not precious to you. In the same way, most of us do not weep over broken pottery, a torn shirt, a run in a stocking, a dented fender on the car, or thousands of other things. They may have value. Their loss may be an inconvenience to us. But they are not precious, and so we do not weep over them. On the other hand, we do weep over the loss of a friendship, the death of a friend, and similar heartbreaks or disappointments.

God considers us precious in just this sense. Moreover, in case we should miss the point through our slowness in understanding his actions, God actually tells us that we are valuable to him; not, to be sure, because of anything that is in us inherently, but because of what he has made us and will yet make of us.

Made in God's Image

Why are we precious to God? Here we get into an important area of biblical studies, for the answer takes us back to the earliest chapters of Genesis, where man is said to have been made "in God's image." This is actually stressed in Genesis so much that it can be said to be the most important characteristic of the man and the woman. It is what makes them different from the animals and from the plants. Genesis puts it like this, "Then God said, 'Let us make man in our image, in our likeness, and let them rule over the fish of the sea and the birds of the air, over the livestock, over all the earth, and over all the creatures that move along the ground.' So God created man in his own image, in the image of God he created him; male and female he created them" (Gen. 1:26–27).

In speaking of the fact that man was created in God's image I have sometimes referred this to the three-part nature of man's being. We say that God is a Trinity: Father, Son, and Holy Spirit. So when we say that man was created in God's image we mean that in an analogous way man is also a trinity. In man's case this means that he consists of a body, soul, and spirit.

We tend to think that the body is what differentiates man from God; we have a body, while he does not. But in view of the fact that God became incarnate in a human body in Christ, this is not as obvious as it might seem. Which came first in the mind of God, the body of Christ or Adam's body? Or to put it another way, did Christ become like us by means of the incarnation or did we become like him by means of God's creative act? I would say that we were made like Jesus. And if this is so, then our bodies are of great value and should be honored in the way we treat them. Indeed, we can say, as Paul does, that our bodies were made to be "temples" of God.

The soul is the part of man that we would call the personality. It centers in the mind and includes all likes and dislikes, special abilities or weaknesses, emotions, aspirations, and anything else that makes the individual different from all others of his species. Here again we are made in God's image. And here again what we do with our souls is important. Are they being trained to desire the best that God gives? Or do they wallow around in the worst things we know? Do they strive to think God's thoughts after him and so grow intellectually and spiritually and in every other way? Or are they captivated by sinful thoughts and values? In this area we are dealing with the fact that God has what we would call personality and that we have our personalities because of him. It is because we are created in God's image in respect to our souls that we are able to have fellowship, love, and communication with one another.

Finally, man also has a spirit. This is the part of his nature that communes with God and partakes in some measure of God's own essence. God is nowhere said to be body or soul, but he is defined as spirit. "God is spirit," said Jesus. Therefore, "his worshipers must worship in spirit and in truth" (John 4:24). Because man is also a spirit he can have fellowship with God and love him.

Here, then, is a remarkable thing. Man is made in God's image and is therefore valuable to him. God loves him, as he does not and cannot love the animals or plants or inanimate matter. Moreover, he feels for him, identifies with him, grieves over him, and intervenes to make him into all that he himself has determined that a given man or a given woman should be. We get some idea of the special nature of this relationship when we remember that in a similar way the woman, Eve, was made in the image of man. Therefore, though different, Adam saw himself in her and loved her as his companion and corresponding member in the universe. It is not wrong to say, therefore, that men and women are to God somewhat as the woman is to the man. They are God's unique and valued companions in the universe. In support of this we need only to think of the teaching concerning Christ as the bridegroom and the church as his bride, which we find throughout the Old and New Testaments.

One more thing needs to be added before we move on. We have said that man has been made in God's image and that this gives him value. We need to add to this that it is true even after the fall. Even in the state that man is in now he preserves something of the image of God and so remains valuable to him.

We see this in several places in the Bible. For instance, in Genesis 9:6, the verse that records God's institution of capital punishment as a proper response to murder, we read, "Whoever sheds the blood of man, by man shall his blood be shed; for in the image of God has God made man." Or again, in James 3:9–10 in verses that forbid the use of the tongue in cursing other men, we find, "With the tongue we praise our Lord and Father, and with it we curse men, who have been made in God's likeness. . . . My brothers, this should not be." Here the murder of another or cursing of another is forbidden precisely on the grounds that the other person (even after the fall) retains something of God's image and for this reason is to be valued by us as God also values him.

Evangelicals especially need to recognize this and proclaim it widely. It is not intentional, of course, but evangelicals often so stress man's sinful and depraved nature that they end in dismissing the value of man altogether. They look at men with horror-filled eyes and then cease to care for them. In seeing the sin, they lose sight of the sinner and cease to love him. Such things ought not to be. Indeed, if we allow them to be, it will be but a short time until we return again to the dark ages out of which only the Christian ethic, with its emphasis upon the unique value of man, has rescued us.

Some years ago in Philadelphia an expanded surgical team at the world-renowned Children's Hospital separated a pair of eighteen-month-old Siamese twins, Clara and Alta Rodrigues, who had come to the hospital from the Dominican Republic. We had a great deal of interest in this at Tenth Presbyterian Church, which I serve as pastor, because the head of the surgical team, Dr. C. Everett Koop, his first assistant, Dr. Louise Schnauffer, and the head of the anesthesiology team, Dr. Eugene Betts, were members of the church. This operation involved eighteen doctors and five nurses, just for the operation itself. And in addition to this there was a week of tests and at least a month or two of postoperative care. The family came from the poorest area of their country. Literally, they had no income at all. If they had need of something, they would take some of their homegrown vegetables down to the village and exchange them for what they needed. Yet here was an operation done on their children by the best pediatric surgeons in the world at a cost which observers placed at upward of $100,000, yet was cost free to them.

What produces such compassion, such effort? It is not the so-called "spirit" of Western man. For at one time babies like these would have been discarded on a remote hillside to die from exposure or from the ravages of beasts. Or, to bring it closer to home, it is not so long ago that they would have been placed in circuses so that some unscrupulous promoter could make money at their expense. What accounts for this effort? The only adequate answer is the inherent value of man revealed to him by God through Judaism and Christianity and now embodied, at least for a time, in the best of Western ideals and institutions. Take away such a revelation and such values and the age of barbarism will return upon us.

A Shattered Image

We have dealt at length with the matter of man's value, the first of the lessons about man that the phrase "Jesus wept" suggests, because it is the most neglected. But it would not be right to deal with this subject without going on to point out also that man has marred God's image and is therefore in a state to be wept over. Thus, as I said earlier, the text teaches that we have gotten ourselves into such a state that even God, who might be thought to be above tears, weeps for us.

Do we need another example than that of Christ before the tomb of Lazarus? If so, we find one in an event that comes shortly after this in Christ's ministry. A few days after the raising of Lazarus, on what we call Palm Sunday, Jesus entered Jerusalem riding on a donkey. He had sent his disciples to find it; and when they had brought it to him, he sat upon it and rode toward Jerusalem while those disciples who were with him and those who came out of the city at his approach threw their clothes in his pathway and paved the way with branches stripped from the palms. In such a context we might expect Jesus to have been filled with excitement and even joy. We might expect him to have rejoiced in the fact that so many were apparently following him. But this is not what we find. Rather, we find Christ weeping, for he knew that the cheers of the people were shallow and that unbelief rather than faith characterized the multitudes that filled the city. Valuable? Yes, the people were valuable. But they were also so submerged in sin that their eyes were blinded to that which could have been their blessing and spiritual peace (Luke 19:41–44).

It is a terrible thing, this shattering of the image of God in man. It is catastrophic both for the individual and for those with whom he is in contact. Paul tells about it in Romans, showing that sin has broken relationships—with God, first of all, then with others, and finally of the individual with himself. He puts it this way: "For although they knew God, they neither glorified him as God nor gave thanks to him, but their thinking became futile and their foolish hearts were darkened. Although they claimed to be wise, they became fools and exchanged the glory of the immortal God for images made to look like mortal man and birds and animals and reptiles. Therefore God gave them over in the sinful desires of their hearts to sexual impurity for the degrading of their bodies with one another. They exchanged the truth of God for a lie, and worshiped and served created things rather than the Creator—who is forever praised. Amen" (Rom. 1:21–25).

This should cause weeping. Indeed, as we look at man through God's eyes, our text should be Ecclesiastes 3:4, which tells us that there is "a time to weep." Or perhaps Luke 23:28, which contains Christ's words to the women of Jerusalem as they followed him on his way to the cross: "Do not weep for me; weep for yourselves and for your children."

A Needy People

My final point is that we need God. We are valuable to God, yes. But we are so marred by sin, so unable to extricate ourselves from the bondage into which our sin has plunged us, that there is no hope for any of us unless God saves us. Here is the unique quality of Christ's tears at the tomb of Lazarus. If the situation had been redeemable by human effort, Christ would not have wept. If sin could have been overcome or if death, the product of sin, could have been eradicated, we should expect Jesus to have said, "Dry your tears. Stop feeling sorry for yourselves. Get on with the work. Solve your problems." But he does not do that. Instead he weeps, because from man's point of view man is hopeless and his problems unsolvable.

But with God all things are possible. Jesus says to Martha just five verses later, "Did I not tell you that if you believed, you would see the glory of God?" (v. 40).

Martha did see God's glory, for her brother was raised. But so do all who come to Christ as their Savior. We need him. Sin, suffering, and death ably testify to that. But God in Christ is able to meet our need; indeed, he has met it, for he has given his life and then been raised from the dead in order to deal with the entire sin question.

Isaiah told about it a thousand years before Christ was born, stressing that we who had been made in his image so bruised and battered him that physically, at least, his image became even more deformed than our own; but he endured this and all suffering in order that he might restore in us that perfect image of God that we had before we rebelled against him. "But he was pierced for our transgressions, he was crushed for our iniquities; the punishment that brought us peace was upon him, and by his wounds we are healed" (Isa. 53:5). Here is the ability and great love of our God. For these and only these take us from the depths of our sin and restore to us that lost image of God, through faith in Christ Jesus.

146

"Behold How He Loves"

John 11:36–37

Then the Jews said, "See how he loved him!"

But some of them said, "Could not he who opened the eyes of the blind man have kept this man from dying?"

The last of our studies of the phrase "Jesus wept" brings us to the reaction of the spectators to Christ's tears. There were two reactions. On the one hand, there was the reaction of those who were obviously unbelievers. These thought that Jesus' tears were a proof of his weakness; so they concluded, "Could not he who opened the eyes of the blind have kept this man from dying?" (v. 37). These persons were surprised that Jesus had not been able to do something about Lazarus's sickness earlier, but they reasoned that obviously he had not been able to help out or he would have done it. It did not even begin to enter their minds that Jesus was about to raise Lazarus from the dead.

The other reaction to Christ's tears was neither an expression of belief or disbelief. It was just an observation. These people looked at Christ's tears and concluded rightly that Jesus loved Lazarus. They said, "See how he loved him!" (v. 36).

Many people, perhaps most of those who will be reading these words, know the Lord well enough to know that he loves others. And most of these know that he also loves them. But if this is so, then it is surely right to take the text personally and say, "Behold how he loves us!" Or, to make it even more personal, "Behold how he loves me!" This is a cause for great wonder. Spurgeon, in an excellent sermon on this text, once wrote, "Most of us here, I trust, are not mere onlookers, but we have a share in the special love of Jesus. We see evidences of that love, not in his tears, but in the precious blood that he so freely shed for us; so we ought to marvel even more than those Jews did at the love of Jesus, and to see further into his heart than they did, and to know more of him than they could in the brief interval in which they had become acquainted with him."[1]

Let us say, "Behold how he loves us!" and then think quietly over what we know to underlie that statement.

An Everlasting Covenant

As the eyes of our mind ponder all we know concerning Jesus, from the past to the present, where is it that we first see his love? Is it when we first became aware of his love? Or when he died for us? Or when he created us? None of these points represents a true beginning; indeed, there is no beginning. For as far as we can look back into the past we find him loving us. It was in eternity past that he so identified himself with us that he took up our cause and determined to redeem his fallen people.

In his divine foresight Jesus looked upon the race that, as yet, was not created and saw it ruined through sin. We see everything through the blinders of time. For us life is past, present, and future. But it is not this way with God; he is above or beyond time so that to him, in some sense, all things are present. It was in this way, then, that Christ looked out upon what was to come and saw the ruin into which our sin would plunge us. Who was there in that moment beyond time to take our side, espouse our cause, and pledge himself to redeem that fallen temple? There was no one but Christ. As Isaiah wrote concerning God's search for a redeemer, "He saw that there was no one, he was appalled that there was no one to intervene" (Isa. 59:16). It was Jesus, then, who took up our cause.

Moreover, in that moment he also pledged himself to be the surety of his covenant people; that is, he took man's part in the creation of an eternal covenant between God and man, pledging to fulfill man's part. For he knew that the demands of that covenant could never be met by human beings.

The nature of God's covenant with man in Christ is seen in the record of a similar covenant that God later established with Abraham. In Abraham's day a covenant was sometimes made through a strange ceremony in which animals were cut in two along the backbone and placed in two rows over against one another, thereby forming a space in which the parties to the covenant stood while they exchanged their vows. The shed blood of the animals made the covenant particularly sacred. Since this was the form Abraham was used to, God used it in promising Abraham that he would bless him. In this case, however, there was one significant variation. Abraham became a spectator to the covenant—he was on the sideline seeing it in something like a dream or vision—while God, represented by a smoking furnace and a lamp, passed alone between the pieces. The point was that God was establishing the covenant apart from any participation on the part of Abraham. Therefore, it was unilateral, eternal, and undeserved.

In a similar way, Jesus established a covenant on our behalf and for our good, long before we were able to have any part in it personally. He pledged himself to die for us, thereby giving his life as a ransom and an atonement for our sins. The pledge was unilateral, for he did it by himself and without our asking. It is eternal, for what he has begun he will most certainly bring to completion. It is undeserved, for we are lost in sin and therefore have no claim upon him. Moreover, it is sealed with Christ's blood; for we are saved, as the author of the letter to the Hebrews says, "through the blood of the eternal covenant" (Heb. 13:20). Jesus pledged himself to do what we could never do, so uniting himself with us that his death became our death, his life our life, his resurrection our own resurrection. And when did he do this? Before we were even born; indeed, before there was even a physical creation. So great was his love for us!

God's Servant

It also is true that in time the Lord Jesus Christ loved us enough to leave the glories of heaven and take the form of a man upon himself. In this form he endured all temptations, disappointments, and suffering that we are heir to. Paul writes about it in Philippians: "[He], being in very nature God, did not consider equality with God something to be grasped, but made himself nothing, taking the very nature of a servant, being made in human likeness" (2:6–7). This is the essence of the incarnation. It is one of the greatest wonders of all time; but it means, simply, that Jesus became like us in order that we might become like him.

How was he like us? He became like us in temptations; for the author of Hebrews writes that he "has been tempted in every way, just as we are—yet was without sin" (4:15). Have you been tempted? Are you being tempted? So was he; yet he was victorious over it. Now he reigns with the Father in heaven so that you might turn to him to find mercy and have grace to help in time of need.

Jesus also became like us in disappointments. A friend betrayed him. Others let him down. No one really understood him. His own countrymen, whom he had tried to help, killed him. Clearly, Jesus knew disappointments, but these did not defeat him. They did not make him bitter. Instead he triumphed over them.

He also knew suffering. Did anyone ever suffer as much as Jesus did? In a physical sense I suppose it is possible that some persons could have, though there are few forms of suffering as great as that endured in crucifixion. But in a total sense, that is, in a sense that involves mental and spiritual anguish as well as physical suffering, no one can match him. He who knew no sin was made sin for us. He who had never experienced so much as one second of broken fellowship between himself and the Father was separated from him so that he called out in great agony of soul, "My God, my God, why have you forsaken me?" No other suffering was ever as great as his. Yet he endured all this, because his love for us was so immeasurable!

Our Sin-Bearer

This leads to our next point, for we may certainly say, "Behold how he loves us" when we reflect on his death by crucifixion. Jesus loved us so much that he became our sin-bearer. It is as Paul says, "God made him who had no sin to be sin for us, so that in him we might become the righteousness of God" (2 Cor. 5:21).

I am sure that we will never understand the full extent of this action on the part of Christ, certainly not in this life. I even doubt that we will understand it fully in the life to come. For how can it be that the One who had existed with God the Father from eternity and who was himself God could become man and suffer even unto the point of spiritual death, so that he was actually made sin for us and was separated from his Father? I cannot understand it. Yet that is what the Scriptures teach, and I believe it. Moreover, I marvel at it. To look to the cross of Jesus Christ is to marvel at the extent of his love for us. We see there the height and depth of his love. We see the length and breadth of it. Does Jesus love us? Yes, he does. The cross is the proof of his love. He, who knew no sin, was made sin for us, so great was his love for us.

Christ's Call

Jesus also loved us so much that he called us personally and individually, persisting in his call until by the force of his love he drew us to him.

Jesus died for us; that is true. But what was that to us until he called us to him? At best it was an exemplary death, but it meant little. When first we heard of it we were indifferent. If we had been in Jerusalem at the time of the crucifixion, we would not have intervened to save him, nor would we have thought much about it once the death had been accomplished. Now, after the passage of two thousand years, it has meant even less than a little. But Jesus pursued us. We failed to understand the meaning of his death, but he carefully explained it to us. We grew tired of the explanation, but he changed his methods of instruction and taught us differently. We said no to his call, but he would not accept our no. At last, when we could resist him no longer, we yielded to what Spurgeon called "the sweet compulsion of his grace." And we found him forgiving our sin, justifying us from all iniquity, adopting us as his sons and daughters, filling us with his Spirit, and imparting to us all the riches of his abounding grace.

Moreover, this is not just our experience of him in the days before we became his children. Even after we believed, his grace continued. For we were not faithful. He was faithful to us; but we each went our own way, despising his will and pursuing a course of sin marked out by our own stubborn hearts. If Jesus had cast us from him at this point, at least from the point of view of our sin, he would have been justified. But Jesus did not cast us off. Rather, he loved us even in our willfulness and strove by every means to melt our cold indifference and restore us to him. Sometimes Jesus calls loudly. Sometimes he calls softly. But always there is his call. So great is his love for us.

Do We Love Him?

Let us turn the statement around. Up to this point I have been writing of the love of the Lord Jesus Christ for us and have called upon each one who knows that love to marvel at it. When we look at his espousal of our cause in eternity past, his incarnation, his death on the cross, his call to us to come to him, and his bestowal of all spiritual riches upon us, we may well say, "Behold how he loves us!" But turn it around. Do we love him? Has anyone ever said of you, "Behold how he loves Jesus"?

Spurgeon asks that same question in the sermon I referred to earlier, and he answers it like this. "Listen for a minute or two while I tell you of what some saints have done to show how they loved their Lord.

"There have been those who have suffered for Christ's sake. They have lain in damp dungeons, and have refused to accept liberty at the price of treachery to their Lord and His truth. They have been stretched upon the rack, yet no torture could make them yield up their fidelity to God. If you have read *Foxe's Book of Martyrs,* you know how hundreds of brave men and women, and children too, stood at the stake, gloriously calm, and often triumphantly happy, and were burnt to death for Christ's sake, while many of those who looked on learned to imitate their noble example, and others who heard their dying testimonies, and their spiritual songs (not groans), could not help exclaiming, 'Behold how these martyrs love their Master!'

"There have been others, who have shown their love to their Lord by untiring and self-sacrificing service. They have laboured for him, at times under great privations and amid many perils, some as missionaries in foreign lands, and others with equal zeal in this country. Their hearts were all aglow with love for their dear Lord and Savior, and they spent their whole time and strength in seeking to win souls for him, so that those who knew them could not help saying, 'Behold how they love their Lord!' Some of us can never hope to wear the ruby crown of martyrdom, yet we may be honored by receiving the richly-jeweled crown from the hand of Christ as he says to each of his laborers, 'Well done, thou good and faithful servant . . . enter thou into the joy of thy Lord.'

"Then we have known some saints who showed their love to their Lord by weeping over sinners and praying for their conversion. There have been gracious men and women, who could not sleep at night because of their anxiety about the eternal welfare of their relatives and friends, or even of lost ones who were personally unknown to them; and they have risen from their beds to agonize in prayer for sinners who were either calmly sleeping, and not even dreaming of their doom, or else at that very hour were adding to their previous transgressions . . .

"Others have proved their love to their Lord by the way in which they have given of their substance to his cause."[2]

These paragraphs by Spurgeon are a good statement of what others have done because of their great love for the Lord Jesus Christ, and they may serve as a challenge to us. But the question remains: Do *you* love Jesus? Has anyone ever said of *you,* "Behold how he loves his Master"?

Years ago a woman missionary went to North Africa and settled in Tunis where she began to try to win Moslems to Christ. She met with little success, as seems often to be the case in Moslem lands. But she persisted, above all continuing to love those to whom she was witnessing. One young Moslem lad came to her home every week for English classes. She had been giving such classes as a way of getting to know some of the Tunisians and of helping them. So, as she taught him English, she tried to tell him of Jesus. The student listened, but he was unmoved. Months passed. Finally, the summer before he was to go away to university came, and the lad dropped his classes. The summer passed. One day, just before his departure, the young man came to say good-bye to the missionary for the final time. The two of them had tea together, and the woman told of Jesus for what seemed to be the final time. Still there were no results. The Moslem was polite but adamant. At last the moment came for final farewells, and the student left the missionary's door and walked down the path leading through the garden to the outside gate. Here he stopped and looked back, and saw his teacher standing in the doorway looking after him with tears streaming down her face. He could resist no longer. Her tears conquered the rebellion in his heart, and he returned up the path and into the living room where he received the Lord Jesus Christ as his Savior.

Could that be a picture of you? Could it be you, standing there in a foreign land weeping for the lost? Could it be a picture of you at home weeping for a husband, a wife, a son, a daughter, a neighbor? Such a thing should be possible. For many should be able to see the tears of Christ in you and say "Behold how he loves Jesus!"

147

The Seventh Miracle

John 11:38-44

Jesus, once more deeply moved, came to the tomb. It was a cave with a stone laid across the entrance. "Take away the stone," he said.

"But, Lord," said Martha, the sister of the dead man, "by this time there is a bad odor, for he has been there four days."

Then Jesus said, "Did I not tell you that if you believed, you would see the glory of God?"

So they took away the stone. Then Jesus looked up and said, "Father, I thank you that you have heard me. I knew that you always hear me, but I said this for the benefit of the people standing here, that they may believe that you sent me."

When he had said this, Jesus called in a loud voice, "Lazarus, come out!" The dead man came out, his hands and feet wrapped with strips of linen, and a cloth around his face.

Jesus said to them, "Take off the grave clothes and let him go."

The raising of Lazarus from the dead is the climactic miracle of John's Gospel—by any standard of measurement. Its position in the Gospel alone indicates this, for it is the last of seven miracles and is inserted just before the beginning of the final week of Jesus' earthly ministry. The length of the narrative (forty-six verses) and its detail also reveal its importance; it is the longest and most elaborately described of the miracles. Only the miracle of the restoration of sight to the man born blind is of comparable length, but the miracle in John 9 is still shorter than this one. The results of this miracle are more momentous than those of any other sign, primarily in the increased determination of the religious leaders to eliminate Jesus. Finally, and most importantly, the deeper or spiritual meaning of the miracle is striking and is essential to the book's theology.

The first of the miracles in the Gospel of John is the turning of water into wine (2:1–11). It is a small miracle, as miracles go, but it reveals Jesus to be the true source of joy and of life in abundance. It concludes with the observation, "This, the first of his miraculous signs, Jesus performed at Cana in Galilee. Thus he revealed his glory; and his disciples put their faith in him" (v. 11). The second miracle is the healing of the son of a nobleman (4:46–54). It shows Jesus to have power over human sickness and, by extension, over that sickness of the spirit caused by sin. The third miracle is the healing of the invalid (5:1–16). Here the spiritual meaning of the miracle is obvious, for the invalid is an eloquent symbol of the helpless spiritual state to which sin has brought all men and women. The feeding of the five thousand (6:1–14) reveals that Jesus is "the bread of life." The story of his walking upon the water (6:15–21) points to his power over nature. The sixth miracle is the restoration of sight to the man who had been born blind (9:1–41). This shows the effect of sin on the mind—the sinner is spiritually blind and walks in darkness—and the need for Christ who alone can restore sight. The story is summarized in advance in Christ's saying, "I am the light of the world. Whoever follows me will never walk in darkness, but will have the light of life" (8:12).

In each of these stories there is a real miracle, but it is told by John primarily because of the spiritual meaning found in it. The same is also true of the raising of Lazarus from the dead, the seventh miracle. Lazarus was certainly raised from the dead; in fact, as John indicates, it was the report of this astonishing miracle that led the religious leaders to the conclusion that they would have to dispose of Christ immediately. In addition to this it is also a picture of how a man or woman who is dead in sin is brought to spiritual life by Jesus. It may well be studied for what it has to teach about sin, faith, the power of Christ, and evangelism.

Believing Is Seeing

The story begins, "Jesus, once more deeply moved, came to the tomb. It was a cave with a stone laid across the entrance. 'Take away the stone,' he said. 'But, Lord,' said Martha, the sister of the dead man, 'by this time there is an odor for he has been there four days.' Then Jesus said 'Did I not tell you that if you believed, you would see the glory of God?'" (vv. 38–40).

The lesson Jesus had for Martha, and therefore for us also, is that in spiritual matters believing is seeing. He said, "Did I not tell you that if you *believed*, you would *see* the glory of God?" These words, "seeing" and "believing," sound natural to us because of the expression "Seeing is believing." But we can hardly miss the fact that Jesus puts it the other way around. "Seeing is believing," we say. "Believing is seeing," says the Lord Jesus.

Both are right so long as we realize that in our expression we are talking about human affairs while Jesus in his expression was talking about a relationship to God. In human affairs the expression means simply that men and women are untrustworthy. Some are more trustworthy than others, no doubt. These are the ones we seek to work into positions of responsibility and authority, but even here we are not entirely believing. So corporation heads are bonded, builders are bound by contracts, union heads sign work agreements, and so on. Take as an example a case in which a personnel representative in a company is interviewing a young applicant for a job. "Do you think you can do the work?" the representative asks.

"Certainly," the young man answers. It is obvious that he does not lack confidence.

"Do you know what is involved?"

"Yes, I have read all about it. And, besides, I have had two years' experience doing the same thing in Phoenix."

"And did the job go well there?"

"Very well," is the reply. "And I know I can do well here." The personnel representative is probably pleased to see the young man's confidence. In spite of this he does not take his profession of ability at face value. Instead, he writes for references. Moreover, he does not promise that the job will be permanent even if he offers it to him. "We'll see how it goes," he says. In other words, seeing is believing; and this is right because in human affairs performance has not always followed promise. We want references. Or, to put it in other terms, we want collateral before the loan is made.

How then can Jesus invert the adage and say, "Believing is seeing"? There is only one answer: it is because he is not speaking of men but of God. Men are untrustworthy, but God is not like men in this respect. "God is not a man, that he should lie," the Scriptures tell us (Num. 23:19). God has never made a promise that he has not fulfilled fully. Consequently, to believe God is to put oneself in the place of blessing, from which one will certainly see all that is promised in due time.

Perfect Faith

Jesus' statement links "seeing the glory of God" (which refers here to the raising of Lazarus) to such faith. But the interesting thing about this is that Martha apparently did not have such faith, nor did anyone else so far as we can discern from the narrative. When Jesus said, "Did I not tell you . . . ?" he probably was referring to his message to Martha through the messenger, recorded much earlier in the chapter (v. 4). But when Jesus finally arrived at Bethany four days later, Martha did not expect the resurrection. Moreover, even after Jesus had talked with her face-to-face she did not expect it. For when Jesus said, "Take away the stone," Martha replied that this would be unwise in that the body would undoubtedly have begun to decay. She did not expect a resurrection. She only thought that for some reason Jesus wanted to look at and mourn over the body.

The crowd that was standing by did not believe in the possibility of a resurrection either. For most of them were saying, "Could not he who opened the eyes of the blind have kept this man from dying?" (v. 37).

Where then was the faith that was to result in seeing God's glory? Again there is only one answer. If it is not seen in Martha or Mary or any of the others, the only person left in whom it can be seen is Jesus. He is the One who believed and who therefore saw God's glory. Consequently, his trust in God at this point becomes a model for our own.

What is it that makes Christ's faith in the Father what it is? Or, to put it in other language, what is the nature of Christ's faith? There are several answers. First, it is *personal.* That is, it is not faith in some abstract concept or some mere truth that Jesus knew about God. His faith was in God himself, which he indicates by calling him "Father." John records it this way: "So they took away the stone. Then Jesus looked up and said, 'Father . . .'" (v. 41). Is your faith like that? Is it personal? Faith in the biblical sense most certainly involves propositions, but it is not propositional alone. It is faith in a person. Thus, regarding salvation we should be able to say, "Lord Jesus Christ, I love *you* and want *you* to be my Savior." Or in the matter of prayer, "*Father,* I lay such and such a need before you."

Second, the faith of the Lord Jesus Christ was a *perfect* or totally trusting faith. This is indicated by the fact that Jesus offered God thanks for the miracle even before it had taken place. We find him praying, "Father, I thank you that you have heard me. I knew that you always hear me" (vv. 41–42). I do not know personally how close we can come to that total belief of the Lord Jesus Christ. Certainly we often fail to express confidence that God will hear and answer our prayers. On the other hand, we often pray in ways that are mere presumption. We fail, but we should still grow toward the point of such perfection.

Dr. Harry A. Ironside used to tell the story of one old man who had. He was a Scotsman who on one occasion was making his way by foot to a certain synodical meeting of the Free Kirk in Aberdeen. On the way, he was overtaken by a young theological student, also on his way to the meeting, and as they had much in common they continued on their way together. At lunchtime they turned aside to a grassy embankment to eat their lunch, first thanking God for the food. They had good conversation. Then, before they started out again, the old man suggested that they each pray, asking God for what they would need that evening. The young student was embarrassed; but he agreed, and the older man prayed. He had three requests. First, he reminded the Lord that he was hard of hearing and that if he did not get a seat well up toward the front of the meeting hall, he would get little from the sermon that evening. So he asked that a seat be kept for him. Second, he told the Lord that his shoes were badly worn and that they were hardly fit for the city. He needed a new pair, although he did not have money to buy them. Finally, he asked for a place to sleep that night, for he knew no one in the city from whom he could seek accommodations. As he made each request the old man thanked the Lord in advance for answering them.

The theological student was aghast at what he considered to be the impertinence of the old man, and he determined to check up on him later to see what came of his prayers. That night they reached the meeting a bit late. The hall was crowded. There was not a seat left. The student thought, "We will see now what becomes of such prayers." However, someone came out, and the old man managed to squeeze into a place near the door, where he stood with one hand cupped to his ear.

Just then a young lady in the front row turned and saw him. She called an usher. "Sir," she said, "my father asked me to save this seat for him, saying that if he should be late I should offer it to someone else. Evidently he has been detained. Will you please go and offer it to that old man who has his hand to his ear and is standing just inside the door." The usher followed her instructions, and so in just a few minutes the first request of the old man had been answered.

The time came for prayer. In Scotland in those days some persons always knelt for prayer while others reverently stood. The old man was the kneeling kind. The young woman was the standing kind. Standing thus beside her guest and looking down she could not help noticing the condition of his shoes. Her father ran a shoe store. So afterward she politely raised the subject and asked the old man if she might take him to her father's store, though it was closed for the night, and give him a pair. So petition number two was answered. Finally, while in the store, the young woman inquired where the old man was staying that night; and he answered that God had not yet shown him the room. "Well," she said, "I think we have the room for you. The Rev. Dr. So-and-So was to use our guest room tonight, but he has telegraphed to say that he is not coming. Will you use it?" The next day when the theological student inquired how the old man had made out, he learned the answers and found that God is not indifferent to the believing prayers of his people.[1]

Finally, we notice that the faith of the Lord Jesus Christ was *public*. That is, he did not express his faith quietly in a corner, but rather audibly and openly before men. In this respect we find him praying, "I knew that you always hear me, but I said this for the benefit of the people standing here, that they may believe that you sent me" (v. 42). If we will do likewise, at least on occasion, then others may also come to believe as the result of our indirect testimony and God's action.

The prayer of Jesus leads to the moment of the resurrection itself. Having finished his prayer, Jesus called to Lazarus in a loud voice, so all could hear (Lazarus, of course, would have heard even if he had whispered): "Lazarus, come out." The story continues by reporting with great understatement, "The dead man came out, his hands and feet wrapped with strips of linen, and a cloth around his face. Jesus said to them, 'Take off the grave clothes and let him go'" (v. 44).

Here is the climax of the miracle, and it is here that it must be applied spiritually. The resurrection of Lazarus happened. But we notice that it is also what happens spiritually whenever Jesus speaks to a lost and fallen child of Adam. According to Scripture, anyone without Christ is dead spiritually. He is "dead in trespasses and sins," as Paul wrote to the Ephesians. As such he is helpless. There is nothing he can do to improve his condition. But Jesus comes. He calls. He calls the dead one by name. And the one who hears his voice responds and rises from his grave to meet him. Perhaps he is calling you. Do you hear him? Will you follow?

Finally, the story says this to Christians: Will you also play your part in Christ's miracles? You say, "But what do you mean? Haven't you said that the work is Christ's alone? No one can raise the dead but Jesus." Yes, that is true. But have you noticed that although it was Jesus alone who could bring the dead to life; nevertheless, he delighted to involve the bystanders in the miracle. First, they were told to move the stone. Then, after the miracle, they were told to unbind Lazarus. True, we cannot bring the dead to life. But we can bring the word of Christ to them. We can do preparatory work, and we can do work afterward. We can help to remove stones—stones of ignorance, error, prejudice, and despair. After the miracle we can help the new Christian by unwinding the graveclothes of doubt, fear, introspection, and discouragement.

The miracle is Christ's. But there is work for us to do if we will do it. Will you? Jesus used Ananias to reach Paul, even after he had been struck down on the road to Damascus. He used Peter to reach Cornelius. Philip preached to the Ethiopian. Do you doubt that he would use you if you were ready to do such work? Then get ready! Or be ready! As Pink says, "There is no higher privilege this side of Heaven than for us to be used of the Lord in rolling away gravestones and removing graveclothes."[2]

148

What Shall We Do with Jesus?

John 11:45–50, 53

Therefore many of the Jews who had come to visit Mary, and had seen what Jesus did, put their faith in him. But some of them went to the Pharisees and told them what Jesus had done. Then the chief priests and the Pharisees called a meeting of the Sanhedrin.

"What are we accomplishing?" they asked. "Here is this man performing many miraculous signs. If we let him go on like this, everyone will believe in him, and then the Romans will come and take away both our place and our nation."

Then one of them, named Caiaphas, who was high priest that year, spoke up, "You know nothing at all! You do not realize that it is better for you that one man die for the people than that the whole nation perish." . . .

So from that day on they plotted to take his life.

The resurrection of Lazarus by the Lord Jesus Christ was over, and the people who had been standing by and had witnessed the miracle were left to wonder at it. What was to be their reaction? Would they believe on Jesus? Or would they fail to believe? Would they become his followers or his enemies? As we read the sequel to the story we are not surprised to find that both were true; that is, some believed, while others disbelieved. There were people who had come to Mary, and had seen the things that Jesus did and "put their faith in him" (v. 45). Their case reminds us of the report of the people of Samaria, who had come to Jesus through the testimony of the woman whom Jesus met at the well and who had then believed. They said, "We no longer believe just because of what you said; now we have heard for ourselves, and we know that this man really is the Christ, the Savior of the world" (4:42). Theirs was a wonderful experience and an example. We would do well to be like them. Or again, we would do well to be a channel for faith, like Mary or the woman of Samaria through whom others believed. If we had more time, we could reflect on this profitably.

The story does not allow us to do that, however. For no sooner are we told that some believed, than we are also told that others did not. In fact, these did worse than merely disbelieve. These actually reported on Jesus to the authorities, who then held a council. We are told of them, "But some of them went to the Pharisees and told them what Jesus had done" (v. 46).

An Evil Council

What a strange council this was! And what an evil one! We look at the action of those who had witnessed the raising of Lazarus, then went and told the Pharisees, and we say, "How could they show such ill-will toward Jesus? How could they be so hateful to him and so impervious to his miracles?" But then we look at those to whom they reported, and the hatred of the first group seems mild by comparison. Presumably the bystanders reported to the Pharisees who in turn informed the Sadducees, who then called a meeting (either officially or unofficially) of the great Sanhedrin, the supreme governing body of the nation. Here were the best men of the nation—at least in their own opinion. There were chief priests in their robes; the chief priests were all Sadducees. There were Pharisees, the "holiest" men of all, in their phylacteries. These met in holy council. No doubt they opened their meeting with prayer. Yet, what were they meeting for? They were meeting to oppose a perfectly innocent man. He was a man who had been doing great miracles, so great in fact that a proper council would have been one on how to encourage his work and lead multitudes to follow him.

It was an unlikely coalition. The Pharisees, strictly speaking, were not a political party at all, though they had political power because they were so highly regarded. Actually, they were a religious party or denomination. They were concerned chiefly with observing each minute requirement of the law and with encouraging others to do so. They were sticklers for detail. One example of their outlook is seen in the objection of Nicodemus, who was probably a Pharisee, to proceedings in a council held earlier. Nicodemus is reported to have said, "Does our law condemn anyone without first hearing him and to find out what he is doing?" (7:51).

On the other hand, there were the Sadducees. These were not religious men, though some undoubtedly played at religion for their own ends. These were the politicians. They were wealthy and aristocratic, and they collaborated with the Romans to preserve their privileged position. These men had much to lose, particularly if there should be a civil disorder; for that would bring swift intervention by the Romans. They compromised to preserve their position. If justice and civil order ever came into conflict, the Sadducees would always be found on the side of the Romans in preserving civil order.

The interesting thing is that these two groups were enemies or rivals. That is, they hated each other and often opposed each other bitterly. Yet—and this is the wonder—we find them working together here in their opposition to Jesus. Why was this so? Clearly because their opposition to Jesus was more important than their rivalry with each other. The Pharisees hated Jesus for his religious views; he exposed their sin. The Sadducees hated him for being a threat to their privileged position. But both hated him, and so they collaborated. A little later we find the same thing in connection with Herod and Pilate, who were also enemies but who made common cause in doing away with Jesus. "Then Herod and his soldiers ridiculed and mocked him. Dressing him in an elegant robe, they sent him back to Pilate. That day Herod and Pilate became friends—before this they had been enemies" (Luke 23:11–12).

The situation gives us insight into the hearts of sinful men and women. People would rather unite with their enemies than follow Jesus. Winston Churchill once said facetiously that if Hitler invaded hell, he was sure that he would be able to find a good word to say for Satan in the House of Commons. Many persons are like that spiritually. They will agree with anyone and work with anyone rather than Jesus. I hope it is not true of you. I hope rather that you have seen the folly of such an outlook and have come to him.

An Evil Discussion

We need to notice further that the council of the Pharisees and Sadducees, convoked with such an evil intent, proceeded next to equally evil deliberations. First of all, they muddled about in indecision. "What are we accomplishing?" they said. "Here is this man performing many miraculous signs. If we let him go on like this, everyone will believe in him, and then the Romans will come and take away both our place and our nation" (vv. 47–48).

The most striking thing about this discussion is its unintentional confession of Christ's strength versus their weakness. It is more striking in that it happens on several levels. For one thing, there is no attempt to deny the miracles. "Here is this man performing many miraculous signs" was their testimony. There was an earlier point when these same men sent officers to arrest Jesus and admitted, after the soldiers had returned empty-handed, that they really did not know what he was doing (7:51). But now they do know, and still they deny him. One commentator has written, "They owned the genuineness of his miracles, yet were their consciences unmoved."[1] Another states, "They admitted the miracles, yet opposed the Miracle-worker."[2]

Moreover, they admitted that they had been powerless over a considerable period of time, for this is the effect of the question with which the discussion began: "What are we accomplishing?" The religious leaders were acknowledging that their efforts had for long been ineffective and that they were now at their wits' end. We might capture the force of the question by translating the sentences: "Look how Jesus is growing in popularity. What are we doing about it?" Implied in the question is the admission that a new policy is needed, precisely because the old one is not working. Jesus' plans were working, but theirs were not working. Their efforts were weak, but he was strong.

I said earlier that the fact that the Pharisees and Sadducees collaborated against their natural instincts to do away with Jesus reveals the nature of sin in the heart of man. That is true. But the same point is even more obvious here. Sin had formed them and hardened them. Thus, no matter what others did, no matter even what Jesus did, these men were determined not to believe on him. In fact, they would not even raise the question of whether his miracles ought not rather to be taken as evidence that he was who he said he was, or even that he was a prophet to whom they should listen. They had already shut their ears to such issues and were only seeking a way to stifle his influence or eliminate him.

Does this seem extreme to you? Or foolish? It is foolish, of course, but it is not so different from what many do today. A number of years ago a lady was invited by a friend to go to a gospel meeting. "I am afraid to go for fear I will get converted," she answered. Imagine! She was afraid that she might get straightened out with God. On another occasion a minister said to a certain woman in his congregation, "I have not seen your husband lately. Has he lost interest in the gospel?" She answered, "Well, he is afraid to come; for when he comes and hears the Word, it takes him nearly two weeks to get over it."

What are we to do with such a one? Or again, what are we to do with you, if this is your policy? We will keep preaching the Word. But be careful that you do not slip away forever like these Sadducees.

An Evil Conclusion

What did they do? How did their council end? One of them, named Caiaphas, stood up and counseled sordid self-interest. He did not put it that way, of course. He said, as politicians always do, "We must think of the good of the people." But this is what he meant. He succeeded in swaying the council too; for it was on this level, the level of self-interest, and not on any high level of rule by law or the good of the nation that these malicious men were malleable. Caiaphas said (we shall return to his words in more detail in our next study), "You know nothing at all! You do not realize that it is better for you that one man die for the people than that the whole nation perish" (vv. 49–50).

I am impressed with how cleverly Caiaphas spoke. He began by dismissing all comments by all previous speakers. "You know nothing at all," he dogmatized. That is, "Everything said thus far is foolishness." Then, eloquently and simply, he advised that it was better that one man die (though innocent) than that all should perish. And he won! First, he won in the council. We read, "So from that day on they plotted to kill him" (v. 53). Second, he won before Pilate, for it was when Pilate perceived that a riot was developing and that he could be held responsible before Caesar, and even viewed as an insurrectionist himself, that he released Jesus for crucifixion (John 19:12–13).

Expediency! That was the lever then, as it so often is today. It is in the name of expediency and self-interest that the most terrible things are done.

I am also impressed by the fact that this is not the end of the story. Indeed, we can hardly miss the point that this is not the end or that John especially tells the story as he does to suggest a different end from this beginning. What we have here is a remarkable case of high dramatic irony. Caiaphas had said it was better to kill Jesus than that the entire nation perish. But this is what happened anyway. The very events they dreaded came to pass. True, they eliminated Jesus—in one sense at least. But in the aftermath of the crucifixion and the gradual scattering of the Christians from Jerusalem, the revolutionary spirit began to grow with intensity in Palestine, a war broke out, and the Romans intervened to crush the rebellion. In that great war all the strongholds of Israel were overthrown, Jerusalem was besieged and destroyed, and the temple was left in ruins. In fact, as Josephus tells us, a plow was even drawn across the temple area to stress the desolation. How different events might have been if these men had received their Messiah! But they did not. They resisted him, and the sin of resistance had consequences. As Barclay says, "The very steps they took to save their nation destroyed their nation."[3]

Since the destruction of Jerusalem took place about A.D. 70 and since John was writing about A.D. 90, according to conservative estimates, no one who read the Gospel in John's day would miss this irony. Moreover, they would not miss the irony inherent in a thriving Christianity either. The Sanhedrin had acted as it did in order to put down Jesus. "If we let him go on like this," they said, "everyone will believe in him." But what happened? Men believed on him. They killed him; but it was through his death that the gospel spread, not only throughout Judaism but to all nations (v. 52). Indeed, as John wrote there were Christians in every major city and in every country of the empire.

You cannot frustrate God. You can oppose him, but only you will pay the consequences, as did these men. You may oppose him, but Christianity will spread. The Bible says, "Many are the plans in the mind of a man, but it is the purpose of the LORD that will be established" (Prov. 19:21 RSV).

Three Choices

So let me turn the story of the Jerusalem council around in order to address you personally. It began with a question: "What are we accomplishing? Here is this man performing many miraculous signs." Make this your question. "What am I accomplishing—what am I doing—with the Miracle-worker?"

There are only three choices for you, so far as I can see. The first is to try to ignore him. Many try this, of course. You may be trying it too. But if this is your choice, I do not believe that you get very far with it. Why? Because he does too many miracles. He did them then; he does them today. Do you not fear that if you "let him alone, all men will believe on him"? And if they do, what will you do? How will you survive in such a Christ-centered world? How will you ignore him when your daughter believes, your son believes, your husband believes, your wife believes, your father believes, your mother believes, your friend believes? How will you ignore him on that day when, as we are told, every knee will bow and every tongue confess that Jesus Christ is Lord to the glory of God the Father (Phil. 2:10–11)? Can he be ignored? Is Jesus really One whom you can thus put down?

Your second choice is to oppose him. Many have taken this course too, as we know. Caiaphas was the first but certainly not the only or even the worst persecutor of the Nazarene. History is full of those who opposed the Lord Jesus Christ. But where are they? The church remains, but what has happened to the persecutors?

Not long after the persecution of the early Christians instituted by Caiaphas and the other leaders of the Jews, Rome also tried to stamp the church out. Under Nero the Christians in Rome were gathered up and executed as scapegoats for the great fire. Some were sewed up in animal skins and mauled by bloodhounds. Some were bound to oxen and thus torn to pieces in the arena. Many were crucified. Some were dipped in pitch and set on fire like torches in order to light the gardens of the mentally deranged emperor. Under Diocletian, several centuries later, churches were destroyed, sacred books confiscated, clergy imprisoned, and many believers forced to sacrifice to pagan gods by torture. But the more they were persecuted the more the early Christians thrived, until at last the gods of the heathen were overthrown and Christianity was accepted as the faith of the empire.

Can you oppose him? If you do, do you really believe that you will be successful? Will you not rather be in the deplorable company of those rulers who "take counsel together against the LORD and against his Anointed, 'Let us break their chains,' they say, 'and throw off their fetters,'" of whom we are told, "The one enthroned in heaven laughs; the Lord scoffs at them" (Ps. 2:2–4)?

The last of the three choices is the only sensible one. You can believe on Jesus and follow him. "Follow him?" you say. "But he went to the cross. He was crucified. What is desirable about that?" That is true; his way is the way of the cross. But the cross is the way to victory, for it is only by losing life that a man can save it. It is only by following Jesus that the victory is won. If you reject him, you will not win. In fact, you will lose all that you have, as did the Jewish rulers. But if you believe on Jesus and follow him, though you may lack some things now, you will pass beyond that and share his glory.

149

Why Did Jesus Christ Die?

John 11:51–52

He did not say this on his own, but as high priest that year he prophesied that Jesus would die for the Jewish nation, and not only for that nation but also for the scattered children of God, to bring them together and make them one.

It is no exaggeration to say that, along with the resurrection, the cross of Jesus Christ stands at the center of Christianity. But it is also no exaggeration to say that few people really understand it. Few doubt that he died; indeed, all men must die. Few doubt that he died by crucifixion. But *why* Jesus died or what his death means is a puzzle to them. Why did Jesus die? As we might expect, the answer, being of great importance, is found throughout the Bible—in the illustrations provided by the Old Testament sacrificial system, in prophecies such as Isaiah 53, in narrative, and in explicit doctrinal teaching. But there are few verses that speak of the death of Christ as deeply and in as short a space as our text for this study.

In this text John says of the unwitting prophecy of Caiaphas, the high priest of Israel, at the time of the death of Christ, "He did not say this on his own, but as high priest that year he prophesied that Jesus would die for the Jewish nation, and not only for that nation but also for the scattered children of God, to bring them together and make them one." This is John's comment on Caiaphas's prophecy: "It is better . . . that one man die for the people" (v. 50).

Unwitting Prophecy

It is interesting and somewhat surprising, however, that a prophecy of the meaning of Christ's death should come from this source. For of all the self-seeking and ruthless men who made up the Sanhedrin in that year, Caiaphas must have been the most self-seeking and the most ruthless.

Generally speaking, those who attended the council at which the decision was reached to kill Jesus were just distressed and confused. They confessed that Jesus was doing many miracles. They expressed their fear that unless something was done it was likely that all men would believe on him. But they did not know what to do. We can imagine them trying out various suggestions and then rejecting each one. There was one man in that group who did know his mind, however, and that was Caiaphas. Others may have been confused, but Caiaphas at least was not. "There is one thing to be done," he said. "Never mind about the miracles. Never mind about his teaching. Never mind about his character. The man must die. For, every minute that he lives the danger to ourselves and our prerogatives is intensified." Caiaphas expressed this in terms of the greater good of the people, of course. Politicians always do. Nevertheless, his advice to the council was clearly pure self-interest and expediency. And it carried, for the decision was reached immediately to do away with Jesus (v. 53).

The amazing thing, however, is that John tells us that in giving his ruthless council Caiaphas prophesied unwittingly. For "being high priest that year he prophesied," John says. That is, unintentionally Caiaphas foretold, not only that Jesus would die but also why he would die and the scope of his atonement.

It does seem strange that the prophecy should come from such an evil source, then. But it does not remain strange when we look at it in the light of God's dealings with men throughout biblical history. Maclaren writes, "Did not the Spirit of God breathe through Balaam of old? Is there anything incredible in a man's prophesying unconsciously? Did not Pilate do so, when he nailed over the cross, 'This is the King of the Jews,' and wrote it in Hebrew, and in Greek, and in Latin, conceiving himself to be perpetuating a rude jest, while he was proclaiming an everlasting truth? When the Pharisees stood at the foot of the Cross and taunted Him, 'He saved others, himself he cannot save,' did they not, too, speak deeper things than they knew? And were not the lips of this unworthy, selfish, unspiritual, unscrupulous, cruel priest so used as that, all unconsciously, his words lent themselves to the proclamation of the glorious central truth of Christianity, that Christ died for the nation that slew him and rejected him, nor for them alone, but for all the world?"[1]

We learn from this that God uses even the wrath of man to accomplish his purposes. Indeed, Jesus may well have said to the unscrupulous high priest, as Joseph did to his brethren after he had revealed himself to them in Egypt, "You intended to harm me, but God intended it for good to accomplish what is now being done, the saving of many lives" (Gen. 50:20).

Some commentators have imagined that in verse 51 the evangelist shows himself to be in error and that, as a result, we have here one example of why the Scriptures may not be considered entirely trustworthy. John says that Caiaphas was high priest "that year." "But," they say, "the office of high priest was a permanent office, not an annual one. John is mistaken, and the Scriptures do contain errors." But this is not what John means. John knew as well as anyone that the high priests were appointed permanently. His point, therefore, is not that *Caiaphas* was high priest that year in the sense that someone else had been high priest the year before and that still another would be high priest in the year following. Rather, his point is that in *that eventful year* of the crucifixion of the Son of God, Caiaphas was high priest.

What an irony! What a tragedy! For this was the year in which the great "High Priest for ever" came and stood by the earthly high priest—the reality by the shadow—and by his sacrifice of himself for sin emptied the earthly priesthood and earthly sacrifices of all validity. Caiaphas did not even know it! Consequently, he lost not only his place and his nation, but his office as well, which henceforth passed to that One who alone is worthy of it and who is able to execute it perfectly.

A Vicarious Sacrifice

But Caiaphas did prophesy concerning Christ's death. In the first place, he told the nature of it. From the human side it was a ruthless murder for political ends. The Sanhedrin, on the advice of Caiaphas, plotted to kill Christ in order that there might not be an uprising at the feast. This would endanger their privileges and power. Pilate consented to his death in order that he might not be accused of encouraging an insurrection or an insurrectionist. But from the divine side, which is conveyed to us in the prophecy, the death of Christ was a vicarious sacrifice for sinners. That is, it was Christ taking their place, dying in their stead, taking upon himself the guilt and punishment of their sins, in order that there might be nothing left for them but God's heaven.

We must admit, of course, that the view of the atonement that is expressed in this verse is incompatible with many modern ideas about God and the nature of salvation. Some think the idea of a vicarious sacrifice to be at odds with what we know about God. "Isn't he a God of love?" we are asked. "How then can he require a sacrifice as the basis of man's salvation? Or again, why is one necessary? If God is love and if he is all-powerful, isn't it true that he can simply forgive men outright? Moreover, if this is so, then are we not justified in considering the idea of a sacrifice merely a carryover from an outdated, Hebraic worldview?" To this we must answer that God is not only love; he is also a God of perfect holiness and justice. Therefore, salvation must take place so that none of these attributes is violated.

We are also told that the idea of a vicarious sacrifice is inadequate and immoral. It is inadequate, we are told, because the suffering of one man for only three hours (however intense) can never be equal to the eternal suffering of even one sinner in hell, not to mention a whole race of sinners. And it is immoral, our opponents add, for it is unjust of God to punish one man for others' sin. The answer to these objections is that they do not take into consideration who was dying, nor all that was involved in his sacrifice.

After all, who was dying? Not man, though Jesus was a man and had to be to die, but God. God the Son was dying. Moreover, it was because of the love and holiness of God the Father that he was dying.

One writer puts it like this: "God is not only perfectly holy, but the source and pattern of holiness. He is the origin and the upholder of the moral order of the Universe. He *must* be just. The Judge of all the earth *must* do right. Therefore it was impossible by the necessities of His own being that He should deal lightly with sin, and compromise the claims of holiness. If sin could be forgiven at all, it must be on some basis which would vindicate the holy law of God, which is not a mere code, but the moral order of the whole creation. But such vindication must be supremely costly. Costly to whom? Not to the forgiven sinner, for there could be no price asked from Him for His forgiveness; both because the cost is far beyond his reach and because God loves to give and not to sell. Therefore, God Himself undertook to pay a cost, to offer a sacrifice, so tremendous that the gravity of His condemnation of sin should be absolutely beyond question even as He forgave it, while at the same time the love which impelled Him to pay the price would be the wonder of angels, and would call forth the worshiping gratitude of the redeemed sinner.

"On Calvary this price was paid, paid by *God:* the Son giving himself, bearing our sin and its curse; the Father giving the Son, his only Son whom he loved. But it was paid by God become man, who not only took the place of guilty man, but also was his representative. . . .

"He offered himself as a sacrifice in our stead, bearing our sin in his own body on the tree. He suffered, not only awful physical anguish, but also the unthinkable spiritual horror of becoming identified with the sin to which he was infinitely opposed. He thereby came under the curse of sin, so that for a time even his perfect fellowship with his Father was broken. Thus God proclaimed his infinite abhorrence of sin by being willing himself to suffer all that, in place of the guilty ones, in order that he might justly forgive. Thus the love of God found its perfect fulfillment, because he did not hold back from even that uttermost sacrifice, in order that we might be saved from eternal death through what he endured."[2]

Let me pause here to ask whether this is your faith and whether or not you know that you have entered into a right relationship to God through Christ's sacrifice. Do you know that he did indeed die for you, that he took your place so that you might never have to suffer the consequences of your sin and spiritual rebellion? Do you trust him as your personal Savior? If you cannot answer yes to these questions, do not let this hour go by until you have put your trust in Jesus. The testimony of the entire Word of God is that he was wounded for your transgressions, that he was bruised for your iniquities, that your chastisement was upon him in order that by his stripes you may be healed.

A Definite Atonement

There is more to the prophecy of Caiaphas than a mere statement of the nature of the atonement, however. For John goes on to say that his prophecy was that Jesus should die "not only for that nation but also for the scattered children of God" (v. 52). This verse amplifies his previous statement; for, having informed us of the nature of Christ's death, he now likewise informs us of the power and scope of it.

On this point Arthur Pink is so excellent that I cannot forebear quoting him. He writes: "The great Sacrifice was not offered to God at random. The redemption-price which was paid at the Cross was not offered without definite design. Christ died not simply to make salvation *possible*, but to make it *certain*. Nowhere in Scripture is there a more emphatic and explicit statement concerning the objects for which the Atonement was made. No excuse whatever is there for the vague (we should say, unscriptural) views, now so sadly prevalent in Christendom, concerning the ones for whom Christ died. To say that He died for the human race is not only to fly in the face of this plain scripture, but it is grossly dishonoring to the sacrifice of Christ. A large portion of the human race die *unsaved*, and if Christ died for *them*, then was his death largely in vain. This means that the *greatest* of all the works of God is comparatively a failure. How horrible! What a reflection upon the Divine character! Surely men do not stop to examine whither their premises lead them. But how blessed to turn away from man's perversions to the Truth itself. Scripture tells us that Christ '*shall* see of the travail of his soul and be *satisfied.*' No sophistry can evade the fact that these words give positive assurance that every one for whom Christ died will, most certainly, be saved.

"Christ died for sinners. But everything turns on the significance of the preposition. What is meant by 'Christ died *for* sinners'? To answer that Christ died in order to make it possible for God to righteously receive sinners who come to Him through Christ, is only saying what many a Socinian has affirmed. The testing of a man's orthodoxy on this vital truth of the Atonement requires something far more definite than this. The saving efficacy of the Atonement lies in the *vicarious* nature of Christ's death, in His representing *certain persons*, in His bearing *their* sins, in His being made a curse for *them*, in His *purchasing* them, spirit and soul and body. It will not do to evade this by saying, 'There is such a fulness in the satisfaction of Christ, as is *sufficient* for the salvation of the whole world, were the whole world to believe in Him.' Scripture always ascribes the salvation of a sinner, not to any *abstract* 'sufficiency,' but to the *vicarious nature*, the *substitutional* character of the death of Christ. The Atonement, therefore, is in no sense sufficient for a man, unless the Lord Jesus died *for* that man: 'For God hath not appointed us to wrath, but to obtain salvation by our Lord Jesus Christ, *who died for us'* (1 Thess. 5:9–10). . . .

"For *whom* did Christ die? 'For the transgression of *my people* was he stricken' (Isa. 53:8). 'Thou shalt call his name JESUS: *for he* shall save *his people* from their sins' (Matt. 1:21). 'The Son of man came not to be ministered unto, but to minister, and to give his life a ransom for *many*' (Matt. 20:28). 'The good Shepherd giveth his life *for the sheep*' (John 10:11). 'Christ also loved *the church* and gave himself *for it*' (Eph. 5:25). 'Who gave himself for us, that he might *redeem us* from all iniquity, and purify unto himself *a peculiar people*' (Titus 2:14). 'To make propitiation for the sins of *the people*' (Heb. 2:17). Here are seven passages which give a clear and simple answer to our question, and their testimony, both singly and collectively, declare plainly that the death of Christ was not an atonement for sin abstractly, nor a mere expression of Divine displeasure against iniquity, nor an indefinite satisfaction of Divine justice, but instead, a ransom-price paid for the eternal redemption of a certain number of sinners, and a plenary satisfaction for *their* particular sins. It is the glory of redemption that it does not merely render God *placable* and man *pardonable,* but that it *has* reconciled sinners to God, put away their sins, and forever perfected His set-apart ones."[3]

The Children of God

I am glad that John also wrote, "And not only for that nation" but also for "the scattered children of God." For that includes representatives from among the Gentiles and from our own time also. If Christ had died only for an elect company from among the Jewish nation, he would have been just; for he need not have died for anyone. If he had died only for people who lived in his own time and not for us, that would have been just too. But this is not the case. Jesus died in order that he might bring many sons into glory among whom are men and women from every tongue and race and tribe and nation. These he is gathering. It may be that he is gathering you into the company of his people at this moment.

Will you resist him? Why? He died for you. He loves you. In fact, he commends his love to you on the basis of the fact that he did in truth die for you. Receive him. Yield to the sweet prodding of his Spirit. And find that salvation that is indeed already complete in him and is to be the basis of your assurance before him forever.

150

His Hour Not Yet Come

John 11:54–57

Therefore Jesus no longer moved about publicly among the Jews. Instead he withdrew to a region near the desert, to a village called Ephraim, where he stayed with his disciples.

When it was almost time for the Jewish Passover, many went up from the country to Jerusalem for their ceremonial cleansing before the Passover. They kept looking for Jesus, and as they stood in the temple area they asked one another, "What do you think? Isn't he coming to the Feast at all?" But the chief priests and Pharisees had given orders that if anyone found out where Jesus was, he should report it so that they might arrest him.

The end of chapter 11 marks an important division in John's Gospel, second in importance perhaps only to the close of chapter 12. It closes what has been called by some scholars "the book of signs." According to these commentators, John is to be divided into four parts: the prelude and introduction (involving the whole of chapter 1), the book of signs (involving chapters 2 through 11), the passion narrative (chapters 12 through 20), and the postscript (chapter 21). Thus, the verses we are to study mark the halfway point in the Gospel and form a transition to the beginning of the last and most eventful week of Christ's ministry.

In my outline of the Gospel, the break at the end of chapter 11 is of less importance than the break at the end of chapter 12. For chapter 12 sums up the public ministry, explaining why as a whole the people did not receive Jesus; and chapter 13 introduces us to the entirely different and very private final conversations of the Lord with his disciples. Nevertheless, there is enough of a break at the end of chapter 11 to make the verses that we find here significant. For one thing, the verses reflect a great tension, a tension broken finally only by the dramatic appearance of Jesus in Jerusalem on what we call Palm Sunday. For another thing, they clearly summarize the point to which the three great protagonists in the final struggle had come. These protagonists were the people, the leaders of the people, and Jesus. Therefore, in summarizing the period of Christ's public ministry centered in the signs, we should look at each one.

The Common People

I have said that there were three great protagonists in the final struggle portrayed in the last half of John. But, strictly speaking, the people are hardly *great* protagonists. They are important. They figure in the action in that the Pharisees and the chief priests proceed as they do because of their fear that if they arrest Jesus openly, the people will riot in support of him. Still, they are hardly *great* protagonists, for they seem generally confused. They are onlookers, spectators, as the majority of people have always been.

The situation was this. Jesus had raised Lazarus from the dead, and this was so spectacular and so public that the leaders of the people had proceeded to hold a council at which the decision was reached to arrest Jesus, bring him to trial, and execute him. Jesus, however, knew that his hour was not fully come. True, it was close at hand; within days he would go up to Jerusalem for the final time. Still, it was not yet quite at hand. So, with his disciples, he left the Jerusalem area to go to a place where he could not easily be found. The Scripture says, "Therefore Jesus no longer moved about publically among the Jews. Instead he withdrew to a region near the desert, to a village called Ephraim, where he stayed with his disciples" (v. 54). This city (maybe the one named in 2 Chron. 13:19) was probably near Bethel and thus about fifteen miles north of Jerusalem near the wilderness country that divided the highlands of Judah from the lush Jordan River valley.

All this had happened on the verge of the Passover, however. And this meant that at the time when Jesus left the area of the capital, many Jews from throughout the country were going up to Jerusalem. Before they could attend any feast they had to be ceremonially clean. So, many came to Jerusalem early, with the intention of purifying themselves through the prescribed ceremonial washings and offerings. All this took time, so while they waited they apprently gathered in little groups and eagerly discussed the major topic of the hour. "Where is Jesus?" they asked. "Do you think he will not come to the feast?" The way they phrased the question indicates that they did not expect him to come; for they knew, as Jesus did, that the leaders had determined to arrest and execute him.

Surely this is a deplorable picture. True, they had not yet set themselves in opposition to Jesus, as the Pharisees and chief priests had done. But neither had they come out for him. Moreover, they were content merely to observe the outcome, which they knew might well mean the execution of a perfectly innocent man—and to do it even while they went about the aspects of their ceremonial religion. What matter that Jesus was innocent? They would see what would happen, and enjoy it. What matter that he was God's own Passover who should that very week give his life for the sins of his people? It did not matter to them so long as they could enjoy their own Passover with its delightful ceremonies.

Do you think this is too hard a judgment on these poor sheep? Then what about this quotation from the Babylonian Gemara, dating in its edited form from about A.D. 550? The Gemara is the written commentary on the Mishnah. "Tradition reports that on the evening of the Passover Jesus was crucified, and that this took place after an officer had during forty days publicly proclaimed: This man who by his deception has seduced the people ought to be crucified. Whosoever can allege anything in his defense, let him come forward and speak. But no one found anything to say in his defense. He was hanged therefore on the evening of the Passover."[1]

The Gemara is not inspired, of course. It does not even claim to be. The words quoted may be simply a justification of their action by the leaders. But there is no need to be skeptical of these words, and there is every reason to believe that this is precisely what happened. If this is right, then these people were interested in Jesus, even sympathetic to him, but they would not stick out their own necks in order to be identified with his cause. Moreover, they would even be religious while they watched him be crucified.

I think we see something similar to this today. Throughout America there are thousands of people who, while they are very careful about their church membership and about the details of Christian worship, nevertheless, being in their hearts unwilling to be identified with Jesus, in fact reject him. They may have been baptized. They may faithfully attend the Lord's Supper. They may even be church officers. But they will not come out for Jesus. So God looks down upon their empty rites and pronounces them to be a curse, for they are that by which they bring down judgment upon their own soul.

The Rulers

The second of the protagonists who figure in the events of Christ's last week are the rulers. These were the chief priests and Pharisees, according to our text, and they had given a command that if anyone knew where Jesus was, he should tell them "that they might arrest him" (v. 57). These men were opposed to Jesus and were determined to eliminate his presence from their lives and land.

It is an amazing fact, but a true one, that the raising of Lazarus had intensified the hostility of these rulers to Jesus. We might have expected them to have been convinced by the miracles. At least we would expect them to have been curious. But neither of these things happened. Rather, instead of belief or curiosity, we find hatred. We have seen the same thing before, of course. At the beginning of chapter 5, where their hostility originated, we find that they were angered that Jesus had healed the invalid who had spent thirty-eight years at the pool of Bethesda. Why? Because he had healed the man on the Sabbath. They seem to have been entirely insensitive to the needs of the man and indifferent to the great wonder that had been performed by Jesus. In chapter 9 we find that they become even more angry at the healing of the man born blind. Again, it is because of the violation of their little rules for the Sabbath. They do not even marvel at the great healing. Nor do they rejoice with the one who had been so miraculously delivered from a long nighttime of darkness.

Notice further that these were not acts performed over a period of many centuries by many different men, or in far-flung regions of the Jewish state for which they might therefore be excused if they lacked certain knowledge. These acts were done either in Jerusalem or in the immediate area of the city by one man during a period of just a few years. What is more, they were amply witnessed by many hundreds, if not thousands, of people. Still they would not believe. What a picture of traditional religion—that is, religion without the divine life. It hardens the heart, dulls the conscience, narrows the mind, and sets the will against the true God who is revealed in Jesus.

Are you one? If so, I fear for you. Far better to be an atheist, far better to be the most ungodly among the ungodly, than to be a hypocrite who masks hatred for the Son under the guise of a formal worship of his Father. Will you not fear for yourself? Will you not so shake for fear that you will turn in desperation to the Savior? Do not wait, if this is your status. Turn now. The days hurry on; the moment of grace may be fleeting. God grant that his grace might extend to you and that you might find yourself walking in the steps of Saul of Tarsus, who once opposed Christ but later served him, rather than in the steps of Caiaphas.

The Lord Jesus Christ

The third of the three great protagonists is Jesus. Yet he hardly seems to be a protagonist at this point, so great is his mastery of the situation.

Three factors contribute to that mastery. First, there is his knowledge of people and with that his knowledge of all that was transpiring. This is suggested at the beginning of the passage by the word "therefore." We are told that "Therefore Jesus no longer moved about publically among the Jews. Instead he withdrew to a region near the desert." What does it mean, "*Therefore* Jesus no longer moved about publically"? Simply that he knew of the decision of the council reported just one verse earlier. We have no reason to suppose that someone told him what had transpired. At least nothing like that is suggested. Jesus simply knew what was happening. No wonder John, who witnessed this, told us earlier, "But Jesus would not entrust himself to them, for he knew all men. He did not need man's testimony about man, for he knew what was in a man" (2:24–25). Nothing anyone has ever done has caught him by surprise.

Second, Jesus had a sense of God's timing. Jesus knew that he was to be crucified. He did not shrink from it. In fact, he prays just one chapter later, "What shall I say? 'Father, save me from this hour'? No, it was for this very reason I came to this hour" (12:27). Though the hour was coming, it was nevertheless not yet come. So he waited. At the precise moment and with great determination he entered Jerusalem.

This leads to the third point: his courage. The people, as they waited in Jerusalem, concluded that he would not come. After all, a man would have to be foolhardy indeed to take on the whole might and authority of Jewish officialdom. Of course he would not come. No one could expect him to come to this feast, things being what they were. But the people had underestimated Jesus. He was not fearful. He was courageous under God. Consequently, when the time came for his appearance, nothing, not all the rulers of Israel, no, not even the hosts of hell, would hinder him.

Barclay, who notes the presence of a similar courage in those who follow Jesus, writes thus of Martin Luther: "Luther was a man who hurled defiance at cautious souls who sought to hold him back from being too venturesome. He took what seemed to him the right course 'despite all cardinals, popes, kings and emperors, together with all devils and hell.' When he was cited to appear at Worms to answer for his attack on the abuses of the Roman Catholic Church, he was well warned of the danger in which he stood if he went. His answer was: 'I would go if there were as many devils in Worms as there are tiles on the housetops.' When told that Duke George would capture him, he answered: 'I would go if it rained Duke Georges.' It was not that Luther was not afraid, for often he made his greatest statements with a voice and with knees that shook; but he had that courage which conquered fear," which, we might add, he had learned from Jesus and in which many others, who have also known Jesus, share. Barclay concludes: "The Christian does not fear the consequences of doing the right thing; he fears the consequences of *not* doing it."[2]

An Open Confession

This brings us to our conclusion and leads me to ask: Where are you in this summary of these three great protagonists? Each of us must be identified with one.

To say that it is not your fight, that you are not for Christ or against him, that you have other concerns—these sayings put you in the camp of the common people who were sympathetic but who would not come out openly for Jesus and who therefore missed their moment. Jesus was there, but they could not decide either for him or against him. Thus, one week they were with the mob who welcomed him into Jerusalem with palm branches, shouting "Blessed is the King of Israel, who comes in the name of the Lord," and the next they were the mob that shouted "Crucify him! Crucify him!" These people do not make history. They are victims of history. Moreover, they are victims of their own sin and selfishness, for to such it is just too costly to be identified with him.

What is the cost if you or anyone else is to be identified with him? First, there is renunciation. When Jesus asked people to come to him, the simplest form of his call was "Follow me." But there can be no following without a previous forsaking of all that keeps you from him. The disciples had forsaken all. So they were with Jesus in Ephraim. But these who were in Jerusalem had forsaken nothing. Thus, they were not with Jesus and did not even know where they might find him. Some people are in these shoes today because they will not renounce their sin.

Second, to follow Jesus one must confess him openly. Jesus said, "If anyone is ashamed of me and my words in this adulterous and sinful generation, the Son of Man will be ashamed of him when he comes in his Father's glory with the holy angels" (Mark 8:38). Or again, "Whoever acknowledges me before men, I will also acknowledge him before my Father in heaven" (Matt. 10:32).

If you find yourself in the great camp of the uncommitted and are disturbed by it, this is the way to move into the camp of Christ's followers. First, forsake all that can keep you from him. Second, confess him publicly. Will you do it? Will you say, "Yes, I have been uncommitted, but I will turn from my sin and my own plans for myself and will follow Jesus"? If you do, God will bless you. He will save you. The Bible says that "if you confess with your mouth, 'Jesus is Lord,' and believe in your heart that God raised him from the dead, you will be saved. For it is with your heart that you believe and are justified, and it is with your mouth that you confess and are saved" (Rom. 10:9–10).

What will happen if you do not confess him? Before long you will find yourself in the second category, the category of those who are opposed to Jesus. This will occur because it is impossible ultimately to be neutral. Eventually you will have to decide, and when you decide against him you will be among those of the opposition whose eyes are increasingly blinded and whose hearts are hardened.

On the other hand, what will happen if you do believe? You will increasingly become like Jesus. You may suffer as he did. Jesus warned that his way would be costly. But you also will become like him in insight, timing, and courage—even in this life. You will amount to something. And you will know God's full blessing both in this life and in the life to come.

151

Memorial to a Woman's Love

John 12:1-8

Six days before the Passover, Jesus arrived at Bethany, where Lazarus lived, whom Jesus had raised from the dead. Here a dinner was given in Jesus' honor. Martha served, while Lazarus was among those reclining at the table with him. Then Mary took about a pint of pure nard, an expensive perfume; she poured it on Jesus' feet and wiped his feet with her hair. And the house was filled with the fragrance of the perfume.

But one of his disciples, Judas Iscariot, who was later to betray him, objected, "Why wasn't this perfume sold and the money given to the poor? It was worth a year's wages." He did not say this because he cared about the poor but because he was a thief; as keeper of the money bag, he used to help himself to what was put into it.

"Leave her alone," Jesus replied. "It was intended that she should save this perfume for the day of my burial. You will always have the poor among you, but you will not always have me."

W e now begin a study of the most momentous week in world history, a week that began with the arrival of Jesus of Nazareth at Bethany on his way up to Jerusalem, where he was to be crucified, and that ended with the crucifixion itself on what I believe to be Thursday of the Passion week. No other week is quite like this week, not even the other most important weeks of biblical history. The week of creation is an important week, beginning with God's creation of light and ending with God's resting upon the seventh day. The first week of Christ's earthly ministry is also important. The fourth evangelist is even careful to highlight it in the opening pages of his Gospel. Nevertheless, these weeks do not compare with the block of seven great days with which John and all the other Gospels end. Nearly one-half of John's Gospel is given over to a narration of the events of this week and what follows it (nearly two-fifths of Mark, over one-third of Matthew, and over one-fourth of Luke). And they are right to do so. For the events of this week were brought on by Christ's steadfast determination to go up to Jerusalem, to die for the sin of the world, and thereby to give his life a ransom for his people.

The events of this week contain the anointing of Jesus at Bethany, the entry into Jerusalem on Palm Sunday, the cursing of the fig tree, the Olivet discourse recorded by the Synoptics, the final discourses with the disciples recorded by John, the Last Supper, the arrest, trials, and crucifixion of Jesus, and the embalming and burial of the body by Joseph of Arimathaea and Nicodemus. After three more days the events of this week are climaxed by the resurrection.

Anointed for Burial

Knowing what this momentous week contains, as we do, we are not surprised to find that it begins with the supper given for Jesus in Bethany at which Mary, the sister of Martha and Lazarus, anointed Jesus with spikenard, doing it, as Jesus said, "for the day of my burial." In actual fact, the burial was still six days away. But this was the moment at which Jesus was symbolically set apart for burial by the only one who really understood what was happening, just as in a similar way he was also set apart as God's great Passover Lamb on Palm Sunday.

John does not tell us all that happened as Jesus began his journey to Jerusalem for the final time, but we know some of the details from the other three Gospel writers. For one thing, we know that he did not return to Jerusalem directly from Ephraim, where we last saw him. If Ephraim was to the north of Jerusalem, as it seems reasonable to believe, Jesus could have returned directly southward, entering Jerusalem from the north. Instead of this, we know that he went east into the Jordan River valley, south to Jericho, and then upward to the west through Bethany to the capital. In Jericho, he had stayed with Zachaeus after the diminutive tax collector had climbed a sycamore tree in order to see him (Luke 19:1–10). As he left Jericho, he restored sight to blind Bartimaeus and his friend (Matt. 20:29–34; Mark 10:46–52).

John does not tell us these things, however. He only tells us that "Six days before the Passover Jesus arrived at Bethany, where Lazarus lived, whom Jesus had raised from the dead. Here a dinner was given in his honor. Martha served" (John 12:1–2).

From Matthew and Mark we learn that this was held in the house of Simon the leper, a man whom Jesus at one time had undoubtedly healed of his leprosy.[1] This supper was presumably a celebration for the raising of Lazarus or, if you will, a "thank you" supper; and, as such, it was a brave thing for the friends of Jesus to have done. We remember that the Sanhedrin had given an order that if anyone knew where Jesus was, they should report it to the authorities. To fail to do so would make them more or less accessories to his crime. Still Christ's friends held this supper and held it openly. As a result of it we know that Lazarus at least was placed in danger; for we read just a few verses later, "So the chief priests made plans to kill Lazarus as well, for on account of him many of the Jews were going over to Jesus and putting their faith in him" (vv. 10–11).

What stuck out in everyone's mind concerning this supper, however, was not the presence of Lazarus so much, or even the bravery of Christ's friends. What the disciples remembered of this dinner and wrote about long afterward was the act of Mary who, we are told, "took about a pint of pure nard, an expensive perfume; she poured it on Jesus' feet and wiped his feet with her hair" (v. 3).

One Who Knew

Our text contains a marvelous statement regarding Mary, for it tells us that she knew that Jesus was about to die. He was about to give his life for us on the cross, and Mary knew it. Moreover, she was the only one who knew, so far as we can tell. Jesus had tried to tell the others. Hours before on the way to Jerusalem he had told the disciples, "We are going up to Jerusalem . . . and the Son of Man will be betrayed to the chief priests and teachers of the law. They will condemn him to death and will hand him over to the Gentiles, who will mock him and spit on him, flog him and kill him. Three days later he will rise" (Mark 10:33–34). But the disciples had not understood it, as becomes clear from their conversation with Jesus in the Upper Room (John 13–14) and from their despondent, almost unbelieving reaction to his crucifixion. Only Mary understood. She had understood for some time. Now she broke her box of perfume over Jesus in order to show him that she understood.

How did Mary understand these things when the others, particularly the disciples, failed? The answer is: by being often in the place where we find her now. Where? She is at the feet of Jesus, anointing him and wiping his feet with her hair. Where is she always? At the feet of Jesus! Thus we find her there in the story of the supper held for Jesus in her own home, the supper at which Martha busied herself with much serving, and we find her at Jesus' feet in John 11, at the time of Lazarus's death. In each case Mary is at his feet worshiping him and learning from him.

May I suggest that if you do not know much concerning spiritual things, it is because you have not spent time at the feet of Jesus? Do you want to learn? Do you want to grow strong in a knowledge of God's will and ways? Then you must learn from Jesus.

You say, "But how do I do that? Certainly I cannot sit at his feet literally today."

That is true, but you can do the same thing through studying the Bible. In Hebrew idiom, sitting at one's feet meant only to learn from that person. It was the place of a child learning from a parent, or a pupil learning from his rabbi. Today we do the same thing by studying the Book Christ gave us and in which we find him. Do you study the Bible? Do you really study it? Some people would like to know it, but they will not discipline themselves for the necessary work. Years ago a young boy was riding with a well-known Bible teacher on a train enroute to one of the Bible teacher's meetings. The teacher was reading his Bible. The boy was reading the newspaper. Finally, the boy looked over at his mentor and saw what he was doing. "I wish I knew the Bible as you do," he remarked in a complimentary way.

"You'll never get to know it by reading the newspaper," the teacher answered kindly. The boy got the message, put the paper away, and began to read his own Bible. In time he went on to become a widely known Bible teacher in his own right.[2] Not all will become Bible teachers. But if we are to learn anything about Jesus, then the words about Jesus are essential and we must study them. Will you? I could wish that every one of us might become followers of Mary in this important characteristic.

Love's Extravagance

There is another characteristic also in which we should be like Mary. We should be like her in her love, and that even to the point of extravagance.

Here we get close to the real motivation of this wonderful woman. For when we ask, "Why did Mary pour out this valuable ointment on Jesus?" we cannot really answer adequately that she did it just to show that she knew that he was about to die. Jesus knew that anyway, and she knew that he knew. No, she also did it for something much more simple and more sublime. She did it just to show that she loved him, understood his sorrow at what was coming, and wanted to identify with him in his sorrow even as he had iden- tified with her in her sorrow and in her moments of joy. Did she succeed? Of course, she did. She had sat at his feet, looked into his eyes, and seen his sorrow. She had said to herself, "What can I do to show that I love him and that I understand what he is doing for us?" She had thought of her most pre- cious possession, her ointment. She said, "I'll give him that." She had given it, and he (as is always the case) had understood. In replying to Judas it is as though Christ had said, "Stop annoying the woman, for she alone of all of you has understood what I am about to do and loves me for doing it."

Are you like Mary? Or are you like the Judases of the world, who criticize those who are bountiful in their love? What a contrast there is at this point! Judas's objection to Mary's action contains the first recorded words of Judas in the Gospels. They are a carping complaint: "Why was not this ointment sold for three hundred denarii, and given to the poor?" Mary's first words are a trusting confession, "Lord, if you had been here, my brother would not have died" (John 11:32). Out of his greed Judas eventually sold Christ for thirty pieces of silver, an amount probably equal to 120 denarii. Mary gave Jesus an offering worth two-and-a-half times that amount. Judas kept the bag, from which he pilfered. Mary broke her box in order that all might be given to Jesus. Judas sought to turn attention from Jesus. Mary sought to turn it to him.

So who are you like? Judas? Or the one who gave her all for Jesus? Remember, as you think of this, that Mary gave her most valued possession. Your most valued possession will be different. It may be a comfortable home, a successful self-image, a bank account, a pension, a family, or a dozen other things. But whatever it is, the question holds. Could you (would you) give it for Jesus? Is there a way that you could employ it to serve him, or just to show your love for him? Would you let your children leave the standard of life that you have created for them, and of which you are so proud, to go into Christian work, perhaps in a distant unrewarding place? Would you leave everything to go yourself, if God should so lead you? Would you be able to use your substance to send others?

"But I would be throwing away all that I have worked for," you say. Yes, in a sense you would. At least, that is the way the world will look at it. But, on the other hand, you will be investing in great spiritual dividends with God. Such blessings bestowed on Christ out of love always come home to roost on those who dispense them.

We see this in the case of Mary. Mary had broken her box, giving her all. Then she stooped to wipe Christ's feet with her hair. From her point of view that was the end of the story. But John adds, "And the house was filled with the fragrance of the perfume." How did the house become filled with that odor? It may have spread around all by itself, of course. But on the other hand, if Mary was also helping to serve (as I have no reason for doubting she was) and if the odor of the ointment was now in her hair (as it must have been), then the odor may well have spread from her with the result that her gift to Jesus, given with no thought of herself, nevertheless became the means by which she shared the blessing.

Apply this personally. If you are not a blessing to other people, if seeing you does not make them think of Jesus, if your own life seems dry and unprofitable, then do what Mary did. Get down on your knees before Jesus. Give him your all. Do it now. Pour out your life before him. If you seek to hoard your life and substance, you will not be a blessing to others, and you will lose even those possessions in the end. "You will be saved," as Paul says, "but as by fire." On the other hand, if you give him your life, then you will become enriched yourself and will inevitably become a blessing to all about you.

A Lasting Memorial

There is one final lesson in the story though John does not bring it out verbally. At the end of the story in both Matthew and Mark, after Jesus has explained Mary's motivation in anointing him, the Savior goes on to say, "I tell you the truth, wherever the gospel is preached throughout the world, what she has done will also be told, in memory of her" (Mark 14:9). Mary's act was to become a lasting memorial of her love for Jesus, and so it has. What the others did on that occasion has been forgotten; many of their names have even been forgotten. But Mary—well, Mary is remembered. Indeed, after the passage of two thousand years we are remembering her now.

Do you want to be remembered? Then do not build monuments, build love. Do not be stingy with your possessions, share them. Share yourself. Give yourself away. Jesus said, "For whoever wants to save his life will lose it, but whoever loses his life for me and for the gospel will save it" (Mark 8:35).

And one more thing: Mary loved Jesus and gave her all, but so also did Martha. She did not give her ointment. She had none to give, I suppose. As I read the story and try to understand Martha, I even suspect that Martha was not the kind of person who treasured perfume, or kept it for a special occasion, as Mary did. Martha would not have valued the perfume, but she did value something. She valued hard work. That can be seen in every context in which we find her. So what is she doing? She is working. She is dealing in perspiration rather than perfume. But, more importantly, she is serving Jesus, and she is not complaining about it as she did formerly.

What a joy to serve Jesus! In any form! Ironside tells of an elderly man who had always wanted to be a preacher but who had no gift for it. He was a successful businessman, high up in his company. But he wanted to get involved in Christian work somehow. So he helped open up a small mission hall in the downtown area of one of our big cities. There, after the office had closed for the weekend, he would roll up his trouser legs and shirt sleeves, take a bucket of water and a brush, and clean the chairs and floor. No one in the company knew of his service. Besides, as is often the case when something is done well but quietly, no one even thought to ask who did the cleaning. One day a couple of men from his company went over to the hall on a Saturday to get some songbooks, and they saw him scrubbing. They threw up their hands and said, "Oh, we never knew you were doing this! You shouldn't do it. We will scrub the floor, or at least we will get someone else to scrub it."

The old man objected. "No," he said, "please let me do it. I want to do it for Jesus' sake"[3] That is exactly it. "For Jesus' sake!" It is not so much what is done that is important, though there are specific things that need to be done. It is rather that it be done for Jesus and that it be done by those whose hearts are fully surrendered to him.

152

Inescapable Evidence

John 12:9–11

Meanwhile a large crowd of Jews found out that Jesus was there and came, not only because of him but also to see Lazarus, whom he had raised from the dead. So the chief priests made plans to kill Lazarus as well, for on account of him many of the Jews were going over to Jesus and putting their faith in him.

For those who live in America in the post-Watergate era there is no novelty at all in the idea of people trying to destroy evidence. The Watergate tapes are themselves an example. The famous "eighteen-minute gap" is a further specific. In colloquial language we even speak of burying the evidence. If one is innocent, there is no need to destroy evidence. If one is guilty, this is at least one way of trying to avoid conviction and maintain a facade.

When we think of it we soon recognize that this is nothing new. For one thing, we do it ourselves. We try to cover over facts that present us in a less-than-favorable light. For another, we find similar cases from other periods of world history.

Here is a biblical example. "A large crowd of Jews found out that Jesus was there and came, not only because of him but also to see Lazarus, whom he had raised from the dead. So the chief priests made plans to kill Lazarus as well, for on account of him many of the Jews were going over to Jesus and putting their faith in him" (12:9–11). These verses tell us that as a result of Jesus' miracle of raising Lazarus from the dead, Lazarus had become impor-

921

tant as evidence that Jesus was right in his teaching and that the rulers of the people, the Pharisees and Sadducees, were wrong. The Pharisees and Sadducees were, therefore, seeking to destroy the evidence by killing Lazarus.

One Must Die

It is a sad picture in some ways; such things always are. But it is humorous too, when we remember that the decision to start killing people was reached after Caiaphas had first argued, "It is better for us that *one* man die for the people" (John 11:50). At that time it *was* one. But now the rulers are finding out that one will not do. Jesus is not enough. Now it is "Lazarus also." In time it will be Stephen and James and Peter and then the many other martyrs. Such is the course of trying to cover up evidence for a truth. It is as if the truth were an artesian well or spring. A person can try to hide it if it is a tiny stream. But sooner or later the water will come bubbling through, bearing dirt with it. The efforts to cover it up, no matter how great, will be wasted.

G. Campbell Morgan writes on this point, "Hostility to God as manifested in Christ, has been the characteristic of the world ever since [the days of Jesus and Lazarus], and it has ever been trying to get rid of him. How many have they put to death in the endeavor? Pilate probably thought he had done the business presently when he put Jesus on the cross. When he handed him over it was with a sort of sense of relief, that it was done with. Done with! Within a couple of generations the power he represented had to repeat the martyrdom of Jesus ten thousand times in Rome itself."[1] That is the point (or at least one of two points) of this study: the evidence for the truth of Christ's teaching and of his power to change lives is undestroyable and therefore inescapable.

The other point, since I suppose that we should really separate them, is that those who are Christians *are* the evidence and should therefore be equally undestroyable and inescapable. Are you evidence of Christ's claims? Are you really? If so, you should be like Lazarus, whom we find in this story, and should share his experience.

An Irresistible Attraction

What is it that we learn about Lazarus in these verses? We learn several things, the first of which is that he had become an irresistible attraction. Jesus had raised him from the dead; now people were coming to Bethany, not just to see Jesus (whom most had seen before) but also to see Lazarus and hear his story. The text says, "A large crowd of Jews found out that Jesus was there and they came, not only because of him but also to see Lazarus, whom he had raised from the dead" (v. 9).

I wonder if you are irresistible as evidence of the truth of Christ's teaching. I wonder further if you are really an attraction by which men and women are finding him. Are you good bait? Has your life been made so delicious by

Jesus that others cannot resist biting and thereby getting caught by the greatest of all fishermen?

As I ask those questions I know you may have to admit that you are not irresistibly attractive in the sense about which I am speaking, and you may be concerned about it. If you are, let me point out the two things that made Lazarus attractive and show how they apply to you. First, *Lazarus had been brought to life* by Jesus. He had been dead. He had no hope of making any physical recovery. Others, even his own sisters, Mary and Martha, had no hope of reviving him. But Jesus came and raised him from the dead. He had called with a loud voice, "Lazarus, come out," and Lazarus had come out of the tomb still bound with grave clothes. Granted, none of us has ever been physically dead. We cannot say that we have been brought back to physical life by Jesus. But we have been dead spiritually. The Bible teaches this when it declares that we "were dead in transgressions and sins" (Eph. 2:1). Being dead, we were without hope of recovery, just as Lazarus was. Then Jesus came and called us, as a result of which we were made alive and rose up at his voice to follow him. This is the case of all who are Christians. This is what it means to be a Christian. It means to have been made alive by Jesus. Consequently, we too can be an attraction by which others find Jesus, if we have really been made alive by him.

Another way of saying the same thing is to say that ultimately it is not we who are attractive; it is Jesus. Therefore he must be in us if he is to attract others to himself through us. Is Jesus in you? Are you a thoroughly converted person? If not, remember what Jesus said to Peter shortly before his crucifixion. He said, "When you have turned back, strengthen your brothers" (Luke 22:32). This meant that Peter was in no position to help others until he had himself—after his cowardly denial of Jesus—turned again to Jesus and been changed by him.

The second thing we notice about Lazarus is that he was *with Jesus*. Indeed, John stresses this; for he points out that at the dinner given for Jesus in Bethany "Martha served, while Lazarus was among those reclining at the table with him" (John 12:2). I can imagine Lazarus being constantly by Jesus in those days, so that those who came to see Jesus saw Lazarus and those who came to see Lazarus inevitably saw Jesus. Can anything be plainer? Put yourself in the place of Lazarus and then conclude: I will help others to see Jesus to the degree that I spend time with him.

It is easy to see why this is so; for those who spend time with Jesus become like Jesus, and Jesus is the true attraction. Ralph Keiper wrote that this truth was one factor in his own discovery of the secret of effective witnessing. Before this time, he had looked upon people as fish to be caught, and he was distressed that so many ungrateful people would not cooperate in letting him save them. He imagined, so he says, that their obstinacy would cause him to get an "F" on his report card in heaven. Then he discovered that his first job was not to win souls but rather to be like Jesus. He writes, "Turning to the Scripture, I was stunned by what I found. I discovered that my first duty was not to win souls for Christ. My primary obligation was to live for him in the daily tasks which were mine, so that the people with whom I came in contact might see God's salvation in action."[2] After he had learned the secret of being with Christ and therefore of becoming like Christ, the "job" of witnessing became the "joy" of leading others to him.

I need to point this out in the opposite way too. I have said that as we spend time with Jesus we will become like Jesus and therefore become an attraction for him. But on the other hand, we will be like him only to the extent that we spend time with him. To put it in other words, our time of prayer and Bible study cannot be neglected.

Here I can profitably quote from Hugh Evan Hopkins's excellent little book *Henceforth.* "The practical side to victory over sin lies in the keeping of a Quiet Time with God. It is then that faith is fed and holiness cultivated and victories won. Nothing in the life of the Christian is more attacked than his times alone with his God. Yet nothing is more essential if he is to go forward in the spiritual life. Frequent interviews with his Master are the secret of abiding in him. All the saints of the past have been men who have made time to see their King's face. John Wesley and Charles Simeon were up by four in the morning; Bishop Ken and Samuel Rutherford are reputed to have risen earlier still; Lancelot Andrews spent five hours a day in his devotions; Gordon of Khartoum used to tie a white handkerchief outside his tent door during his Quiet Time and no one was allowed to disturb him." Hopkins acknowledges that such prolonged hours are hardly possible for the average man or woman today, in our much busier times. But he adds, "The essential point is determination and sincerity of purpose rather than length of time. The closed door and the quiet spirit are what the Father requires of his children when they would meet with him."[3]

One other truth follows from the fact that Lazarus spent time with Jesus. He became courageous. It was not easy to be courageous in such times, for the friends of Jesus as well as Jesus were in danger. But if they were near him, they could be bold even though danger threatened.

A Threat to Unbelievers

There is a second characteristic that we learn about Lazarus from these verses. He was a threat to unbelievers. In this case the unbelievers were the chief priests. We read of them, "So the chief priests made plans to kill Lazarus as well, for on account of him, many of the Jews were going over to Jesus and putting their faith in him" (vv. 10–11).

There were two ways in which Lazarus was a threat to these men. First, they were threatened politically. The chief priests were the wealthy, aristocratic rulers of the Jewish people. They were not particularly religious, but they were successful. They were at the top of the social heap; they had much to lose. In Roman times a conquered people were often permitted great freedom in governing themselves, as the Jews were. But let an insurrection start, even a small civil disobedience, and at once the Roman armies cracked down. Usually they executed the insurrectionists and removed from authority those who had been responsible for keeping the peace. These were the days of Passover. Excitement was running high. The chief priests saw Jesus as the leader of a potential rebellion. Everything he did inflamed the situation, so they believed. The raising of Lazarus inflamed it most of all! So they determined to remove Lazarus as a political factor.

The one who spends enough time with Jesus will always become a threat to unbelievers, particularly those whose chief interest is in maintaining their own position, the status quo. This does not mean that believers in Jesus will become revolutionaries in the political sense, at least not with violence. But it means that they will become revolutionaries in a far deeper sense, for by their values they will be a challenge to the established and selfish comfort of mere political authority. Christians have always been a threat in this sense, at least to the degree that they become like Jesus.

Lazarus was a threat to the chief priests in another sense also. He was a threat to their beliefs or theology. We must remember that the chief priests were all Sadducees and that, unlike the Pharisees, the Sadducees did not believe in the resurrection of the dead. It was the Sadducees who tried to trap Jesus with a problem regarding the seven brothers who had each been married to the same woman. They had asked, "Whose wife shall she be in the resurrection?" Here were Sadducees, who did not believe in the resurrection. Suddenly they are confronted with this unknown man Lazarus, who had been raised from the dead. What were they to do? Where could they turn? The irony of the situation is almost humorous, and John does not miss it in telling the story. For he refers here just to the Sadducees and not to the Pharisees and the chief priests as he had in recounting the results of the council earlier. These men were threatened politically, and they were threatened theologically. So, unless they could take decisive action both their power and the influence of their teaching would soon be slipping from beneath their feet.

There was only one course for them to follow. Since they would not believe in Jesus, the only thing they could do was seek to eliminate Lazarus.

Have you become a threat to anyone because of your testimony? If you have, you will know soon enough; for it is likely that you yourself will be threatened. Does your life challenge anyone through its Christlike character? Then prepare to be defamed. Does your testimony with its clear logic and unimpeachable experience strike home to the hearts of those who hear you? Then be prepared to be called a fool for your testimony. Does your love for the lost expose, as it must, the great hate and selfishness of the world around you? Then be prepared to be hated and even spit upon for Christ's sake. Do not be under an illusion as to what it means truly to follow Jesus, for Jesus himself did not allow anyone to be deceived on that subject. He told his disciples that following him meant a cross. As someone has said, "He never hides his scars to win disciples." On the other hand, you can know that to be with him in his suffering is to be identified with him and to allow him to bring glory through you to his own name.

A Blessing to Many

There is one final thing that we learn about Lazarus from these verses. It is for this perhaps above all that Christ's enemies wished to destroy him. He was a blessing; for many, we are told, believed on Jesus because of Lazarus. Here was a man so much alive because of Jesus and so identified with him in discipleship that others believed on Jesus just because of him. The application is obvious. Has anyone believed on Jesus because of you? Can it be said of you, "On account of him [or her], many put their faith in Jesus" (v. 11)?

One year the missionary conference of Tenth Presbyterian Church in Philadelphia was attended by four veteran missionaries. Two were a couple who had given more than thirty years of their lives to working in unevangelized fields in Africa. Another, together with her husband, has done pioneer Bible translation work in Mexico. The last had spent over forty years in Spain. These presented their work at a series of meetings and dinners during the week and then eventually returned to their fields. After they were gone I received this letter from a woman who had been a member of the church for many years and had attended the conference. She wrote, "In 1936, I started attending Tenth Church while in college and have followed ever since then the work of these three missionaries, who had just then left for missionary service. The Wolls have evangelized Kenya in that time. They have trained and sent out workers. They have established churches and Bible schools. Maria Bolet in that same time has been training Spanish missionaries in a Bible school and has sent those trained throughout Spain. She has operated summer camps. She has been persecuted, several times been put out of Spain, and then allowed to return. Now the children of her earlier converts are attending camps, and the mothers are crying out for more camps. In that time the Lathrops have reduced a language to writing, have translated the New Testament into that language, and have evangelized the entire Tarascan area of Mexico. They have established an indigenous church there. I have pursued my profession at home and overseas and have a few years remaining, a satisfying career. But who will greet me in heaven when I arrive there and say, 'I am here because you gave your life to proclaim the gospel of the Lord Jesus Christ'? Who will count me such a blessing?"

I know this person well enough to know that she has been a blessing. Quite a few have come to know and trust in Christ as a result of her testimony. But the question still stands—for me and for you. Have you been brought to spiritual life by Jesus? Can others tell that you have been with Jesus? Have any believed on Jesus because of your testimony? God grant that this might be true of each of us, or that we will allow God to make it true as we spend more time with him.

153

The King Is Coming

John 12:12–19

The next day the great crowd that had come for the Feast heard that Jesus was on his way to Jerusalem. They took palm branches and went out to meet him, shouting,
*   "Hosanna!"*
*   "Blessed is he who comes in the name of the Lord!"*
*   "Blessed is the King of Israel!"*

Jesus found a young donkey and sat upon it, as it is written,
*   "Do not be afraid, O Daughter of Zion;*
*   see, your king is coming,*
*   seated on a donkey's colt."*

At first his disciples did not understand all this. Only after Jesus was glorified did they realize that these things had been written about him and that they had done these things to him.

Now the crowd that was with him when he called Lazarus from the tomb and raised him from the dead continued to spread the word. Many people, because they had heard that he had given this miraculous sign, went out to meet him. So the Pharisees said to one another, "See, this is getting us nowhere. Look how the whole world has gone after him!"

With the exception of the birth, death, and resurrection of Jesus Christ, no incident from his life is better known than his triumphal entry into Jerusalem on what has come to be known as Palm Sunday. Yet, few incidents from his life are more widely misunderstood. For whatever reason—whether the love of mere spectacle, the requirements of church liturgies, or just the misreading of the Gospel accounts—the entry of Jesus into Jerusalem on Palm Sunday has been regarded by many as a last public offer of himself as King to the people of Jerusalem. Up to this point he had avoided allowing himself to be thought of as a King, so the argument goes. But now, with the hostility of the leaders of the people building up against him and with the moment of his destiny rapidly closing in, Jesus makes one last attempt to gain a following. It is only when the Hosannas turn to demands for his crucifixion that Jesus abandons this plan and goes to Calvary.

Unfortunately for this view, the Gospels tell us that Jesus had already offered himself to Israel as King once, early in his ministry (Matt. 4:17). He had been rejected. Now he entered Jerusalem with an entirely different purpose.

He Came to Die

Why, then, did Jesus enter Jerusalem as he did on Palm Sunday? There are several answers to that question, the first of which is that he came to die. Here Mark's account is most explicit, for he tells us that Jesus explained this to his disciples just two days earlier, that is, on the Friday preceding the Passover at which he was killed. "They were on their way up to Jerusalem, with Jesus leading the way, and the disciples were astonished, while those who followed were afraid. Again he took the Twelve aside and told them what was going to happen to him. 'We are going up to Jerusalem,' he said, 'and the Son of Man will be betrayed to the chief priests and teachers of the law. They will condemn him to death and will hand him over to the Gentiles, who will mock him and spit on him, flog him and kill him. Three days later he will rise'" (Mark 10:32–34).

Against this background it is certain that Jesus entered Jerusalem as he did, not to win over the people (the time for that had long passed) but rather to goad the Pharisees and chief priests into action and thus precipitate the events that he knew awaited him.

Scriptures Fulfilled

The second reason why Jesus entered Jerusalem as he did was that he might fulfill Scripture. To us this may seem like an inverted way of doing things. We think that Jesus, as God, should be bound by nothing. But Jesus did consider himself bound by Scripture as an infallible expression of the will of the Father, as many other Scripture-led actions throughout his ministry also indicate. Thus, both Matthew and John refer to the prophecy of Zechariah in which was written, "Rejoice greatly, O Daughter of Zion! Shout, Daughter of Jerusalem! See, your king comes to you, righteous and having salvation, gentle and riding on a donkey, on a colt, the foal of a donkey" (Zech. 9:9). John tells us that the disciples did not understand this at the time but that they came to understand it later.

When Did Jesus Die?

To my way of thinking the most important reason why Jesus entered Jerusalem, particularly when he did, was to show himself to be our Passover. That is, he wanted to exhibit himself as our Passover Lamb who was to take away the sins of the world.

The making of this point depends upon the dating of the events of the Passover week at which Jesus was killed. So it is necessary to deviate from our main theme in order to deal with the problems of that dating. In the traditional view of this week Jesus was crucified on a Friday, which we call Good Friday, and was raised from the dead early on Easter Sunday morning. In terms of the Jewish calendar, this means that the Passover Sabbath was Saturday; so Saturday must have been the fifteenth of the month of Nisan. In this reconstruction Jesus therefore entered Jerusalem on Sunday, the ninth of Nisan, after a Sabbath rest in Bethany, was crucified on the fourteenth and was raised from the dead on the sixteenth.

The strength of the traditional view results from two factors; first, the length of the tradition and, second, the apparent placing of the crucifixion of Jesus on the day immediately before the regular Saturday Sabbath by all four of the Gospel writers (Matt. 27:62; Mark 15:42; Luke 23:54; and John 19:31). In spite of these factors, which are, however, not as obvious as they appear, the traditional view presents us with several major difficulties.

Most people who know anything at all about the Bible are aware of the first difficulty. It is the difficulty of squaring a Friday crucifixion with Christ's prophecy that the Son of Man shall "be three days and three nights in the heart of the earth" (Matt. 12:40). It is true that according to Jewish idiom the phrase "three days" does not necessarily mean a period of seventy-two hours. It can mean merely one whole day plus parts of two others. But while this observation helps us in dealing with texts that actually say "three days," it hardly helps us in dealing with this important prophecy from Matthew. "It is possible that parts of one day and one night are involved, rather than three full days and three full nights; nevertheless, three periods of light and three periods of darkness must be accounted for. And this, regardless of anything else, is fatal to a Friday crucifixion theory. As one writer says, "Add to this indictment of Friday the statement of the two disciples on the way to Emmaus, spoken on the afternoon of Sunday (Luke 24:21), 'Today is the third day since these things were done,' and the case looks black indeed against Friday. Sunday is not the third day *since* Friday."[1]

The second difficulty with the Friday dating is one known to anyone who has attempted to sort out the events of the final Passover week and assign them days. On an average, about one-third of the Gospels is taken up with the events of the last week of Christ's life; we should rightly infer from this that the events of this week, being of great importance, are given to us fairly completely and in detail. Indeed, from the arrival of Jesus in Bethany, six days before the Passover, until the resurrection, every moment seems to be accounted for. Yet when the events of these days are pieced together one whole day, and possibly two, is lacking. One of the silent days can be explained as the preceding Sabbath, a day in which Jesus rested in Bethany and received those who came to see both himself and Lazarus. But what of the other day? Can it really be that in a week as full as this one was, one whole day is unaccounted for?

It should be noticed that the difficulty of accounting for this day has led no less careful a scholar than Frederick Godet to move the events of Palm Sunday forward to Monday, thereby compressing six days of activity into five. However, we cannot help also noticing that the same effect can be achieved by moving the crucifixion backward a day to Thursday rather than by moving Palm Sunday forward.

One more difficulty must be seen before we attempt a solution. It is a difficulty of more recent development. The dating of historical events is a complicated and often uncertain matter, involving the days and times of solar and lunar eclipses and of new moons. But in recent years, thanks to the use of computers, much that was formerly uncertain is known. Thus, to give an example, as recently as 1973, a work entitled *New and Full Moons* by Herman H. Goldstine was published, from which it is possible to calculate the days of the week upon which the Jewish Passover had to fall in any given year during Christ's lifetime or thereafter. If this would establish a Saturday Passover and therefore a Friday crucifixion for any year near the time at which Jesus must have been crucified, it would be excellent support for the traditional theory. But, in fact, it does not. Instead, the day before Passover falls on a Friday only in the year A.D. 26, which is too early, and in the year A.D. 33, which most scholars agree is too late.[2]

What, then, are we to do with these problems? Is there a solution? I believe there is and that it is obviously *the* solution, once we get over the idea that the crucifixion must have been on a Friday, as tradition says. The solution is simply that two Sabbaths were involved in this last week of Christ's earthly ministry. One was the regular weekly Sabbath, which always fell on Saturday. The second was an extra Passover Sabbath, which, in this particular week, must have come on Friday. In this reconstruction, Jesus would have been crucified on Thursday and would have been raised from the dead sometime before dawn on Sunday morning.

April 6, A.D. 30

What does this rearrangement do to the problems we have already encountered as a result of the traditional dating? In a word, it eliminates each one. First, it clearly allows for the required three days and three nights in the tomb in line with Christ's prophecy. Jesus had spoken of a period beginning with daylight and comprising the whole of three days and nights, with the possible qualification that the opening period of day and the closing period of night need not necessarily be a full twelve hours. This is provided for as follows. Jesus died on Thursday afternoon about three o'clock; hence, the hours from 3:00 P.M. until dusk qualify as the first day. This period is followed by Thursday night, Friday, Friday night, Saturday, and Saturday night; that is, a total of three days and three nights in that precise order. In this scheme of things Jesus could have risen from the dead at any point after dark on Saturday evening. We know that he had been raised before the women got to the tomb at dawn on Sunday morning.

It is worth adding here that several minor points tend to reinforce this conclusion. For one thing, when the soldiers invented their excuse as to why they were unable to guard the tomb successfully, they ended up saying, "His disciples came during the night and stole him away while we were asleep" (Matt. 28:13). This would be a natural outcome if the resurrection and the subsequent opening of the tomb by the angels took place during the night.

The second area of difficulty for the traditional view is the absence of one whole day of activities during the final week. This too is overcome if the crucifixion is seen to have been on Thursday. In this scheduling of events we have the following:

Sunday: Jesus enters Jerusalem riding on a donkey after having first made arrangements to secure the animal. He goes to the temple and looks about, but as it is late he returns to Bethany, having done nothing.

Monday: Jesus returns to Jerusalem. On the way he curses the fig tree as a symbol of the barrenness of Israel and as a prophecy of what was coming to the nation. In Jerusalem he cleanses the temple for the final time and returns to Bethany where he spends each night of this week save the last.

Tuesday: On the way back to Jerusalem the disciples find the fig tree withered and receive Christ's explanation. In the city the disciples comment on the magnificence of the temple and are told that the day is coming when it will be torn down. On the way home Jesus pauses on the Mount of Olives to give what has come to be called the Olivet Discourse concerning things to come. Prophecy seems to be the theme of this day from beginning to end.

Wednesday: Jesus sends the disciples to make preparation for the Passover that is, however, eaten that evening without the Passover lamb. Jesus is arrested that same night as he deliberately tarries in the Garden of Gethsemane on what would have been his normal trip back to Bethany.

Thursday: Jesus is tried and eventually crucified. The trial begins on what we would call Wednesday night (but which is actually the early hours of Thursday by Jewish reckoning) and is completed in the morning. Jesus is buried that evening by Nicodemus and Joseph of Arimathaea. The women observe where Jesus is buried and buy spices, but as it is now the start of the Jewish Passover (that is, the Friday Passover Sabbath that began at dusk on Thursday evening), they are unable to attempt to anoint the body until Sunday morning.

Friday and Saturday: The body of Jesus remains in the tomb. The women and disciples observe the two Sabbaths. Jesus rises from the dead sometime between the coming of darkness on Saturday evening and the coming of the dawn on Sunday morning.

The final difficulty with the traditional view is also easily answered in accord with the Thursday Passover theory. We recall that the day before Passover, the fourteenth of Nisan, did not fall on a Friday between the years A.D. 26 and A.D. 33. But how about Thursday? The answer is that the fourteenth of Nisan fell on a Thursday once during those years and that this one time perfectly fits the situation. The fourteenth of Nisan fell on a Thursday in the year A.D. 30, the most probable year of the crucifixion even by other measurements. Therefore, to put it in our terminology, the crucifixion of Jesus may be dated with some certainty as having occurred on April 6, A.D. 30.

Christ Our Passover

But what does this mean for the question with which we began this study, namely, why did Jesus enter Jerusalem as he did on Palm Sunday? Well, if the crucifixion, which we know to have been on the fourteenth of Nisan, occurred on a Thursday as I have just argued, then counting backward we find that Palm Sunday was the tenth of Nisan, which is important, because it was on that day that the thousands of Passover lambs that were to be sacrificed were taken up to Jerusalem and kept for three days in the homes of those who were to eat them.

Not all are aware how many lambs were involved. So it is necessary to note that there was a great number. Josephus, the Jewish historian, tells us that one year a census was taken of the number of lambs slain for Passover and that the figure was 256,500. In other words, with numbers this large, lambs must literally have been driven up to Jerusalem throughout the entire day. Consequently, whenever Jesus entered the city he must have done so surrounded by lambs, himself being the greatest of lambs. Four days later, at the time the lambs were killed, Jesus himself was killed, thereby becoming the ultimate Passover lamb on the basis of whose shed blood the angel of spiritual death passes over all who place their trust in him.

Is he your Passover? Have you received him as your Savior? Say with Isaiah, "He was pierced for *my* transgressions, he was crushed for *my* iniquities; the punishment that brought *me* peace was upon him, and by his wounds *I* am healed" (Isa. 53:5). Truly, "we all like sheep have gone astray," but in accord with his grace "the LORD has laid on him the iniquity of us all."

154

Christ's Hour Come

John 12:20–23

Now there were some Greeks among those who went up to worship at the Feast. They came to Philip, who was from Bethsaida in Galilee, with a request. "Sir," they said, "we would like to see Jesus." Philip went to tell Andrew; Andrew and Philip in turn told Jesus.

Jesus replied, "The hour has come for the Son of Man to be glorified."

As a preacher and public speaker it falls to my lot to see a side of pulpits that congregations seldom see. On the audience side of the pulpit there is usually ornamentation, perhaps a carved figure or a cross. On the speaker's side there are less glamorous things: buttons to push, wires to trip over, stacks of books, glasses, fans, heaters, squeaky boards, and so on. I have been in pulpits held up by hymnbooks. I have been in pulpits equipped with a clock—so the speaker knows when to stop. Sometimes there are signs: "The service ends at 12:00 noon" or "When the red light goes on you will have just two minutes remaining." Obviously, I am not always as impressed with the pulpits as I trust the audiences are with the messages that come from them.

There is one pulpit that I always remember favorably, however. It is the pulpit of the little chapel on the campus of the Stony Brook School, located at Stony Brook, Long Island. I suppose that there are times when the backside of this pulpit is filled with hymnbooks and glasses of water too. There may even be buttons. But I have never noticed these things when I have been there, because of something else. That something else is a quotation from the Bible, which faces the preacher as he stands to address his congregation. It is a short quotation, but an arresting one. It simply says, "Sir, we would see Jesus."

"We would see Jesus!" That is a good word for any preacher. I could wish that every preacher and teacher of the Word of God might have those words before him constantly as he prepares his messages and as he speaks them. But at the same time, the sentence is also a word for all who hear or read messages. Would you see Jesus? If that *is* the case, then in one sense you will never be disappointed; for you will find Jesus. I know that any given sermon may be disappointing. I have been in places where it is almost always disappointing. Still, you will find Jesus if you seek him. He himself said, "Ask and it will be given you; seek and you will find; knock and the door will be opened to you. For everyone who asks receives; he who seeks finds; and to him who knocks the door will be opened" (Luke 11:9–10).

We Would See Jesus

I introduce our study in this way because the verse I have quoted—"Sir, we would see Jesus"—occurs in the midst of a story told in the next few verses of John's Gospel, and it is this story we want to study. Interestingly enough, we are not told that the people who made this request actually did see Jesus, though I do not doubt that they did. Rather, we are told of Christ's reply to their question and, therefore, indirectly of the significance of the fact that they had asked it. The significance of the story for us lies in the fact that we will see Jesus when we properly understand his answer.

We do not know precisely when the incident that is recorded here took place, for John does not give us a time indication. From my reading of the other Gospels I doubt that it was on the same day Jesus made his triumphal entry into Jerusalem, for on that occasion he seems to have returned quickly to Bethany. Perhaps it was the next day, or the next. On the day following his dramatic entry into Jerusalem, Jesus cleansed the temple courtyard of the money changers who were always found there. And, since this was in the so-called "Court of the Gentiles," it may be that the Gentiles who came to Christ—for they were Greeks in the gentile sense, not Hellenistic Jews—saw his actions. At any rate, some time after Christ's dramatic appearance in the capital certain Greeks came to see this great rabbi from Nazareth.

We are told that the Gentiles came first to Philip, though John does not say why. It may be because Philip had a Greek name: *Philipos*. It meant "a lover of horses." The name may also have reminded them of the great Greek king, Philip of Macedon, father of Alexander. At any rate, they came to Philip; and Philip, who did not know whether Jesus would talk to Gentiles or not, went to Andrew. Incidentally, Andrew also had a Greek name, and both men had come from Bethsaida, a town that was located near a Greek area of the ancient east known as Syrophoenicia. Together Philip and Andrew conveyed the Greeks' request to Jesus.

If we ask why Philip hesitated to bring the Greeks to Jesus immediately, we must remember that from the point of view of the disciples there had been some ambiguity in Christ's actions toward the Gentiles. When he had sent them out on their first preaching mission, he had instructed them, "Do not go among the Gentiles or enter any town of the Samaritans. Go rather to the lost sheep of Israel" (Matt. 10:5–6). He had told the Syrophoenician woman, "First let the children eat all they want, for it is not right to take the children's bread and toss it to their dogs" (Mark 7:27). He had told the woman of Samaria, "Salvation is from the Jews" (John 4:22). On the other hand, Jesus had healed the daughter of the Syrophoenician woman at her request, and apparently he had gone out of his way not only to reach the woman of Samaria but also to preach to her entire town. We recognize that Jesus was not bigoted in his more restrictive statements and actions. He simply felt an obligation to proclaim the coming of his kingdom first to Israel, in fulfillment of the Old Testament prophecies. Besides, he knew that the prophecies foretold a turning to the Gentiles after Israel had rejected her Messiah. But Philip and Andrew did not understand this and so must have debated the matter before going to him.

Christ's Hour

I do not know what Andrew and Philip were expecting when they first told Jesus that the Greeks had come to see him. But I am certain they were completely surprised by his answer. They might have expected him to say, "I am not seeing Greeks now." Or, again, "I would be glad to see them." But Jesus voiced neither of these. Instead, he seems to have looked upon the coming of the Greeks as a sign that the climax of his mission had at last arrived; for he said, "The hour has come for the Son of Man to be glorified" (v. 23).

This, then, is the first point of Christ's reply. His hour had come. The phrase makes us think of those other instances throughout the Gospel in which we are told that his hour had not yet come. The first was in chapter 2. There Jesus had been confronted by his mother with the implied request that he do something about the lack of wine at a wedding. He replied, "Woman, why do you involve me? My time has not yet come" (2:4). In other words, though Jesus later provided approximately 120 gallons of the best wine, he was saying that the hour of his crucifixion had not yet come and that he therefore did not want to draw attention to himself by means of a public miracle. In the same way, we read in John 7 that Christ's brothers wanted him to go up to Jerusalem at the time of one of the feasts in order to do miracles there. They did not believe on him, John tells us. But they had noticed that his followers seemed to be slipping away at this particular time and thought that a few strategically performed miracles might recover the lost momentum. Jesus replied that the brothers could go up to Jerusalem any time they wanted, for their time was always at their own disposal. On the other hand, he said, "The right time for me has not yet come" (7:6, 8). Similarily, on two other occassions when the leaders of the people were seeking to arrest him, John the Evangelist concludes, "But no one laid a hand on him, because his time had not yet come" (7:30; 8:20). All through the three years of his public ministry this had been a dominant theme, but now suddenly it changes. Before, "My hour has not yet come." Now, "The hour has come." And all, so John implies, because of the coming of the unnamed Greeks to Jesus in Jerusalem.

What was the significance of the Greeks? Clearly, they were a sign that the turning point had come, as a result of which salvation would now be offered to Greeks as well as to Jews. Indeed, it would be the beginning of the proclamation of the gospel to the entire world.

John indicates this in his own careful way in telling the story. He does it by contrast and irony. The contrast is seen in the picture of the Greeks, on the one hand, and in the picture of the Pharisees given just one verse earlier, on the other. The Pharisees had rejected Jesus. They were Jews, even the most highly regarded of religious figures among the Jews. Yet they had rejected Jesus and were going about to kill him. On the other hand, here were Gentiles, aliens from the house of Israel, seeking him. The irony that I mentioned is also seen in these verses. In verse 19 the Pharisees, who have rejected Jesus, complain, "See, this is getting us nowhere. Look how the whole world has gone after him!" As they say this they are thinking of the great Jewish crowd that had surrounded Christ on Palm Sunday. But they spoke truer than they knew, for this was the point at which literally the entire world, represented by these Greeks, was beginning to go after him.

Christ's Glory

The second point in Christ's response to the question of the Greeks is that now he was to be glorified. "The hour has come," he said. That is, "The hour has come for the Son of Man to be glorified."

There are two senses in which this was true. The first is that it was obviously glorifying to Christ to have the Greeks come to him, indeed, to have all men come to him for salvation. We tend to think in the opposite way, as C. S. Lewis has pointed out in a brilliant little essay called "The Inner Ring." We tend to think that we have arrived when we are exclusive. If we can shut off others in order to preserve what we consider to be a more sophisticated way of life, we think that we are honored and that others will honor us. We notice that it often is hard to get to see and know the so-called "great" of this world. So we try to break into their inner circle, and on the way we exclude others as if to prove to them and to ourselves that we are getting there.

Jesus did not think this way. Rather, his glory consisted in opening the doors wider and wider, so that at the last men and women from every tribe and race would be members of his spiritual family. Indeed, this is almost the last view we have of him. For the same John who gave us this Gospel has also recorded in the Book of Revelation that new song in which those who have been redeemed by Christ praise him, saying, "You are worthy to take the scroll and to open its seals, because you were slain, and with your blood you purchased men for God from every tribe and language and people and nation. You have made them a kingdom of priests to serve our God, and they will reign on the earth" (5:9–10).

If you wish to see Christ glorified, seek to help others find him. Lead them to Jesus. I am sure that if you do not, Jesus is still honored by your praise of him for saving you. At least I hope you are praising him for that. But what if you also lead others to him? In that case, I am convinced that even your praise will be better; and, besides that, there will then be two or more voices to give him glory.

Christ's Cross

The second sense in which the Son of man was to be glorified is obviously by the cross. Jesus said, "The hour has come for the Son of Man to be glorified." But when we ask what that hour was we immediately realize that it was the hour of his death, burial, and resurrection. Consequently, we also recognize that it was by dying for us that he was glorified.

The next verses say this explicitly. "I tell you the truth, Unless a kernel of wheat falls to the ground and dies, it remains only a single seed. But if it dies, it produces many seeds. The man who loves his life will lose it, while the man who hates his life in this world will keep it for eternal life" (vv. 24–25).

I wonder if you have seen this—not so much as it applies to Christians in the living of their own lives, for we shall come to that again in our next study—but as it applies to Jesus. Have you seen that it was only by dying that he could save men and thus draw us to him? What do the verses I have just read mean? They use the image of a grain of wheat that falls into the ground and dies. Clearly that is Jesus himself. So the teaching is that unless he died there would be no fruit, that is, no salvation for any poor sinner and that, on the contrary, if he did die, many would be saved.

It is only the crucified Christ dying in the place of sinners who saves. The *example* of Christ does not save. Jesus is not saying to us that if we will only follow his example and try to live as he lived we will find happiness in this life and salvation in the world to come. That is not his message. No man was ever saved by following Christ. Following is involved, of course. After we are saved we are to follow him; he has left us an example for that. But we are not saved by his example. We are saved through faith in what he has done on the cross. After that we can follow him. Moreover, we are not saved by his *teaching.* Jesus did not say that he could point out the way to God and that if men and women would only follow that way, they would find him. That is what teachers of the other world religions have done, but not Jesus. He did not say, "I will show you the way." He said, "I am the way." Besides, the entire teaching of the Word of God is to the effect that he made the way by dying for us.

Here is Christ's glory, that he died for us; and it is in this above all else that he should be honored. Will you honor him? The best way is by coming to him in faith in order to receive him as your Savior. Or again, if you already know him as your Savior, it is by living as he lived and by bringing others to him.

There is a children's T-shirt that has this inscription: "To know me is to love me." That, as it seems to me, is supremely true of Jesus. To see him as the crucified Savior is to truly know him, and to know him is to love him fervently. God grant that it may be true of many and that those who know him may also glorify him by living their lives in accordance with his Word and in the power of the Spirit.

155

How to Save Your Own Life

John 12:24–26

"I tell you the truth, unless a kernel of wheat falls to the ground and dies, it remains only a single seed. But if it dies, it produces many seeds. The man who loves his life will lose it, while the man who hates his life in this world will keep it for eternal life. Whoever serves me must follow me; and where I am, my servant also will be. My Father will honor the one who serves me."

We live in an age that is conscious of the value of life, at least in some areas. As a result, we have many devices for saving life. We have life preservers, life belts, life rafts, lifeboats, lifelines, life nets, lifeguards, even life insurance, which is a bit of a misnomer since it pays off only at death. And there are also many courses on lifesaving. In all this emphasis upon the saving of life, however, there is probably no instruction as strange as that of the Lord Jesus Christ, who said to the people of his day, "The man who loves his life will lose it, while the man who hates his life in this world will keep it for eternal life" (v. 25). We say, "The one who would save his life must save it." Jesus said, "The one who would save his life must lose it, for only by losing it can he save it for the life to come."

Why should we listen to advice that seems so foolish? For two reasons. First, the One who spoke those words did exactly what he said. He gave up his life, yet in such a way that we can hardly regard his having done so as

939

foolish. Second, by giving his life he was extraordinarily successful; he gained both his own life and also a vast host of followers.

This is instruction that cannot easily be put aside. Therefore, we turn to his words with interest. As we study these words we notice that they contain four elements: (1) a great principle, (2) an application of the truth, (3) a personal invitation, and (4) a reassuring promise.

A Great Principle

To begin with, the Lord Jesus Christ enunciated a great principle drawn, as was often his procedure, from nature. He said, "Unless a kernel of wheat falls to the ground and dies, it remains only a single seed. But if it dies, it produces many seeds." We have already seen this principle in John 11:16; we have also seen that it is found throughout Scripture. It is the principle of death and denial, the truth that life comes only by death. Here Jesus illustrated the principle by referring to a grain of wheat, which remains unfruitful so long as it is kept to itself but which becomes fruitful when thrown into the ground and buried there.

We see this in many areas. The man who works only to put in time and receive a paycheck is not worth much to his employer. On the other hand, the man who gives himself to the work, who is seeking above all to do a good job and to get it done, is invaluable. The family provides us with another application. If a father or mother lives only for himself, or herself the family suffers and the children eventually go astray. On the other hand, if they give of themselves, the family thrives and the children become an honor to their parents and multiply the parents' joy.

If this is true in business and family life and in other areas, as it is, then it is particularly true in spiritual things. For only when we say no to ourselves do we become capable of saying yes to God and so receive his fullest blessing. This is what Paul meant when he said, "I have been crucified with Christ" (Gal. 2:20). He meant that he had died to self in order that he might live for God. Or again, "May I never boast except in the cross of our Lord Jesus Christ, through which the world has been crucified to me, and I to the world" (Gal. 6:14). In saying this Paul meant that his identification with Christ in death made it possible for him to live for Christ and by Christian values and not for the world and its values.

This is the principle then: death and denial. It is only by death that life comes. We see it in many areas and can hardly miss the fact that Jesus demonstrated the principle by his own death and subsequent resurrection.

The Truth Applied

The difficulty with a principle is that it is so often abstract. Or, to put it in other language, we have difficulty relating it to ourselves. We can relate it to other people, but it does not carry the same weight for us personally.

Jesus knew this, of course; so his next words make the application. He had talked about a grain of wheat. Now he says, "The man who loves his life will lose it, while the man who hates his life in this world will keep it for eternal life."

The most interesting feature of this verse is that it contains a contrast that is not apparent in the English translation. We read, "The man who loves (or hates) his life," and he shall keep his "life," and for us there is no way of telling that the words "life" and "life" are different in the original language. Yet this is the heart of what the verse is saying. The first word is *psuche*, which refers to the life of the mind. We call it the ego. It means the human personality that thinks, plans for the future, and charts its course. Jesus is saying that this is what must die. In other words, the independent will of man must die, so that the follower of Christ actively submits his will to him. The other word is *zoe*, which, joined to the adjective "eternal," means the divine life. Every Christian has this eternal or divine life now, but he has it in its fullness only when his entire personality with all its likes and desires is surrendered to Christ. It is close to the same thing to say that the Christian will experience the fullness of God's blessing only when he consciously and deliberately walks in God's way.

For some reason the idea is current today that, because God is gracious and loving, a Christian can therefore enjoy the fullness of God's blessing without at the same time accepting the full lordship of the Lord Jesus Christ in his or her life. This is not biblical. Those who have convinced themselves of this flout God's laws. They disregard his instructions about the permanency of marriage, for instance. So they get divorces. They ignore his instructions about continuing to meet together with other Christians. So they retreat into their own little private shell of Christianity. They ignore the lost and perishing around them, forgetting that Jesus has sent them as witnesses into the world. They do not live by the highest of moral standards. So they are not happy, and they do not know why. Well, this is why. They have not died to their own desires in order that they might live for Christ. They have not been crucified with him. They have not obeyed him. Jesus is their Savior, but he is not truly their Lord.

If this is true of you, I encourage you to learn this lesson. It is not pleasant to be crucified, I know. But you will never truly live in the full spiritual sense until you are. George Mueller could be your example. He lived in England several generations ago and founded many great orphanages, maintaining them solely through prayer. He was extremely effective. But when asked the secret of his effective service, he replied, "There was a day when I died—died to George Mueller, his opinions, preferences, tastes and will; died to the world, its approval or censure; died to the approval or blame of my brethren or friends; and since then I have studied only to show myself approved unto God."

To lose your own life in order to gain it unto life eternal does not mean you must do what Mueller did. But it does mean you must be willing to do *anything* for Christ, if he directs it. It will not be a sad and gloomy thing either. Do not think that. The sad thing is to disobey him. To obey is a joy. Remember that it was "for the joy set before him" that our Lord endured the cross and scorned the shame (Heb. 12:2).

A Personal Invitation

The third element in our Lord's teaching about life through death is an invitation. He has stated the principle and applied it. Now he invites each of us to put it into practice by following him. He says, "Whoever serves me must follow me."

I am sure there is a sense in which any Christian thinks he would like to serve Christ. We read in the Gospels of Jesus going about from place to place without so much as a home to call his own. He slept in the fields. He was weary. At times he was hungry. There were times when he was hounded by his enemies. We read these things and think how we would like to have been there. "For," we say, "if I had been there, I would have taken him in. I would have fed him. I would have seen that he had a place to sleep. I would have shielded him from his enemies." It is possible that we may have done that if we had lived in Christ's time. We may have been like Mary and Martha rather than like the indifferent millions. But I am afraid that whenever we think along these lines much of our thought is mere sentiment. For if we would really serve Christ, that we can do it now. He has even told us how, for he has spoken to all of us at all ages of the church when he said, "Whoever serves me (that is, anyone who really wants to serve me) must follow me."

How can we follow him? Let me suggest some ways. First, you can follow him in the same kind of *self-denial* about which I have been speaking. That is, you can take up your cross and follow him. As I say this, I do not want to suggest that this will necessarily mean a total change in what you are doing with your life. It may be that you are essentially where the Lord wants you. On the other hand, it *may* mean a total change. For none of us is doing all the Lord has for us to do. The real issue, as I have shown, is the issue of the will. Are you willing to do whatever Christ calls you to do? To be poor in his service, if he so leads? To be despised? To be forgotten or nearly forgotten because you are working in some obscure corner of the world? To surrender your leisure time because there is work to be done that you cannot do during your normal workweek and because there is no one else to do it? To surrender a cherished hobby, sin, or pastime? I cannot tell what the details will be in your case. But God knows them, and you know them. Will you obey him? Will you serve Christ by following him in self-denial?

Second, you can follow him in *service*. You say, "But how can I serve him? He is not here to be served." Really? Did he not say, "Whatever you did for one of the least of these brothers of mine, you did for me" (Matt. 25:40)? And what was he talking about when he said this? He was talking about those who fed the hungry, welcomed the stranger, clothed the naked, and visited the sick and those in prison.

Do we do those things? There was a time when the evangelical church led the way in such areas. We founded missions and built hospitals. We launched welfare programs and cared for widows and orphans. But I am afraid that we do not do that so much anymore. Rather we have allowed unbelieving churchmen to drive a wedge between evangelism and social service and then push us into only one half. Moreover, we have convinced ourselves that we are fully obeying the Lord by doing it. Do not misunderstand me. We must evangelize. That too is a command of Christ; and if liberal churchmen will not do it, then we have an even greater burden to carry the gospel to all who have not heard it. Moreover, there is much evangelical social work going on. In my city there are evangelical missions, orphanages, homes for the aged, welfare programs. But I am asking whether these works really involve us or whether, on the contrary, we do not simply allow a small minority to do them while we enjoy the comforts of our middle-class life and use our free time selfishly?

Third, you may serve Christ by following him in *holiness*. He lived a perfectly holy life, so holy that even his enemies could find no fault in him. If you would serve him, you must strive to be like him in that. To do that you must put aside all you know to be sin, spend time with him in order to grow in him, and then seek to practice what you already know.

Fourth, you may serve Christ by following him in *faithfulness to his teachings*. Here I speak especially to those who are ministers or teachers of the Word. Are you faithful to Christ's teaching in your teaching? Or are you seeking to be novel or clever or to gain a reputation for being different from every other teacher? If you are doing the latter, learn that it is not Christ's way. I am aware that our pride wants to serve Christ by striking out in new paths. Spurgeon once wrote, "Proud man has a desire to preach new doctrine, to set up a new Church; to be an original thinker, to judge, and consider, and do anything but obey."[1] But this is no service to Christ. True service consists in faithfulness. It is to tread in the old paths, where he alone leads the way. To follow him in these ways is really to follow him, and to follow is to serve.

Two Incentives

Having given his invitation, the Lord Jesus Christ next offered two incentives to help us respond. They are in the form of promises. First, he promised that he would be with anyone who followed him; second, he promised that God would himself honor such a one. He said, "Where I am, my servant also will be. My Father will honor the one who serves me."

The first half of this phrase, containing the first promise, may be understood in two ways. Probably both ways are intended. On the one hand, it can apply to this life. If we follow Christ here, we can be sure that wherever we are, he will be with us. Indeed, this is self-evident. For if we are with him, then obviously he is also with us. To me this is a great promise. "What is better?"

I ask myself. "To be in the best of circumstances without Jesus? Or to be with Jesus even if being with him means being with him in persecution or suffering?" The only answer I have is: to be with Jesus whatever the circumstances or whatever the cost. He is worth any cost.

The second way Christ's promise that we will be with him may be taken is in reference to the fact that he was going to be with the Father. I know that he said, "Where I am," using the present tense. But this can refer to something in the immediate future and often does. Here it likely refers to his soon return to heaven. It means that if we are with Jesus here, identifying with him in his suffering and sorrow, we will also be with him in glory. It is the equivalent of Paul's statement (which he says was a faithful or true statement often quoted in the early church), "If we died with him, we will also live with him; if we endure, we will also reign with him. If we disown him, he will also disown us" (2 Tim. 2:11–12).

This leads to Christ's second promise: "My Father will honor the one who serves me." In one place Spurgeon imagines how this will be. He imagines a case in which a prince and the prince's servant fall into the hands of bandits, who hold the prince for ransom. The negotiations for the ransom are delayed, and during the interval life goes badly for the one who is of noble blood, and, of course, also for the servant. The prince falls sick. The servant tends him. The servant wipes his master's fevered brow and gives him cool water to drink. There is a point in their captivity when the servant, who is well, finds an opportunity to escape; but he declines his opportunity, preferring to remain with his lord. Finally the whereabouts of the prince are discovered, and both the prince and his companion are rescued. "Now," asks Spurgeon, "who is the man whom the King delights to honor?" Clearly it is the servant. "For," says the King, "this is the man who was with my son in the prison, who cared for him, attended him, who nursed him when he was near death. He shall therefore be with my son in his honor, even above that of the greatest statesman of the realm."[2]

In the same way, Jesus tells us that God will honor those who follow him in this life. In this life his way often involves suffering. Sometimes it involves death for his sake. It always involves self-denial. But, says Christ, the suffering will be followed by honor and the self-denial by praise.

Can we not hear it? I think I hear the King's voice. "Stand back, you angels! Make room, you seraphim! Make way! For here comes the man, here comes the woman, who was with my Son. He was only a poor sinful man. He was born in an ungodly time in the midst of an ungodly people. He did not know much. But he was with my Son. He was like him. He stood by him. Now I will honor him. Come up here. Here, take this crown, and then sit there with my Son on his throne and reign with him. For you shall indeed be with my Son in his glory, even as you were with him in his shame." God grant that this might one day be true for all of us who truly call upon his name.

156

Christ's Soul Troubled

John 12:27–30

"Now my heart is troubled, and what shall I say? 'Father, save me from this hour'?
No, it was for this very reason I came to this hour. Father, glorify your name!"

Then a voice came from heaven, "I have glorified it, and will glorify it again." The crowd
that was there and heard it said it had thundered; others said an angel had spoken to him.

Jesus said, "This voice was for your benefit, not mine."

None of us understands fully what it cost God the Father and Jesus Christ the Son to forgive our sins. We sometimes pray, in saying the Lord's Prayer, "Forgive us our sins as we forgive those who sin against us." But we often do not think of how costly it was to God to make that prayer possible. Nor do others, who are not Christians, appreciate it. Some mock it. On one occasion Voltaire, the famous French agnostic, was asked whether he thought God could forgive some terrible sin, and he replied glibly, "Pardoner? C'est son metier!" ("Forgive? That's his job.") Obviously it had not entered his head, nor has it entered the heads of many, how much salvation cost God.

Will we ever know how much salvation cost him? I do not see how, for I do not see how we can ever enter fully into the experience of Jesus as he was separated from his Father during those hours of suffering in which he was made sin for us. Still, that is not all that can be said. For, while we can never understand it fully, we can nevertheless begin to understand it in part as a result of what the Bible has to tell us. In particular, we can learn from the verses that are before us, which tell us that on the eve of the crucifixion Christ was troubled. "Now my heart is troubled, and what shall I say? 'Father, save me from this hour'? No, it was for this very reason I came to this hour. Father, glorify your name" (vv. 27–28).

As we study these verses we also learn an equally valuable and even more personal lesson. For not only do they teach us about Jesus, they also teach us how we may find comfort when our souls are likewise troubled.

In studying these verses we will look at: (1) the reason why Christ's soul was troubled, (2) the underlying resolve that gave him stability even in the midst of trouble, (3) the divine reassurance in the form of a voice from heaven, and (4) how this may all be applied to ourselves for those times when we also go through testing.

A Cause for Trouble

We look first, then, at the reason why Christ's soul was troubled; and we confess, even before we look for a reason, that the fact itself is startling. If this were a mere man, we would not be surprised. For what man is there who is not sometimes troubled by pressing circumstances or disquieted by fears of what the future may thrust upon him? But this is no mere man. This is the Son of God! This is the Christ! This is the One who stilled the raging waves on Galilee and rebuked the disciples for their lack of faith—"Why are you so afraid? Do you still have no faith?" (Mark 4:40). This is the One who walked through rampaging crowds led by men intent on his death. This is the same Jesus who in a short while will instruct his disciples, "Do not let your heart be troubled. Trust in God, trust also in me" (John 14:1). How can this be? How can the One who turns to us to say, "Let not your heart be troubled," say of himself, "Now is my heart troubled"? It seems incongruous, even inconsistent.

It is not inconsistent when we realize what it was Christ was dreading! We must remember that the coming of the Greeks, recorded just a few verses earlier, had launched a train of thought in Christ's mind that led to musings on his coming crucifixion and on the fact that he would soon bear the sins of the world. He had rejoiced in the coming of the Greeks as an earnest of the many Gentiles soon to come. But their coming presupposed his death—only a crucified Savior could avail for sins—and this meant separation from the Father judicially as he bore the sins of his people. It was not physical death that he dreaded; it was this spiritual death.

How could the One who had never known one second of unbroken fellowship with his Father, had never sinned, peacefully contemplate that hour in which he should be made sin for us and in which the fellowship that he had would, at least for a time, be broken?

Let me give you a remarkable contrast to make this clear. Consider the death of Socrates as it is described by Plato in the *Phaedo*. Socrates had been condemned to death by the council on grounds of teaching the youth of Athens atheism. While he was awaiting the hemlock potion that he was to drink and that would bring about his death, Socrates discoursed on the immortality of the soul and argued forcefully with his assembled disciples that one should not fear death. Rather he should embrace it peacefully. The body and soul belong to different worlds, he argued. Hence, the destruction of the body cannot affect the soul. It sets it free. As he rehearsed this teaching, Socrates did not merely proclaim his theorems; he lived them. So at last when he drank the hemlock potion and lay down to die, he did so peacefully. Socrates' death is a beautiful, though touching death. Nothing is seen of death's horror. Instead, it is not really a horror, for it merely is that which frees him from the body.

On the other hand, we have Jesus. All the Gospels agree in telling us that as the cross drew near, Jesus began to tremble and be deeply troubled (Mark 14:33). He declared that he had a baptism to be baptized with and was "distressed" until it should be accomplished (Luke 12:50). In Gethsemane he prayed three times that the cup he was about to drink might pass from him. And when at last he concludes, "Yet not as I will, but as you will," this does not mean that at the last he attained to some of the faith of Socrates by coming to regard death as a liberating friend. Rather it means that in spite of his particular death being the greatest of all horrors, he was nevertheless determined to embrace it fully in fulfillment of the plan of God for our salvation.

That is the meaning of the sentence "Now my heart is troubled." We cannot plumb its depths. But when we see the death of Christ in these terms we can at least begin to comprehend it.

An Underlying Resolve

There is another thing to notice about these verses. In spite of the depth of Christ's trouble (which is intensified by linking it to the many verses that speak of his soul's trouble, as I have just done), there is nevertheless an underlying strength or resolve that runs through all Christ is saying. To be sure, Christ's soul is troubled. But there is not even a hint of pulling back or changing course. "What shall I say? 'Father, save me from this hour'?" The answer is obvious. Of course not! Because, "for this very reason I came to this hour. Father, glorify your name."

There is something important here. Obviously there is a strong resolve in Christ that sees him through this struggle. But what is the distinct nature of that resolve? Jesus is resolved to die. But why is he resolved to die? We answer, of course, that Jesus is determined to die for our salvation, to save us, and it is true. But notice that Jesus does not give this as his chief reason. To glorify God is his chief end. Thus, although the death he is to die has its horrors, he will not shrink from following whatever way the Father chooses to have the Son glorify him.

God Glorified

Did God glorify himself through Jesus' death? Indeed he did. Moreover, not only was his name glorified, there was even a special voice from heaven to announce that it had already been so and would be so again.

God's name had already been glorified in Christ, for the voice from heaven spoke of the past. Where do we see that past glory? For one thing, in the incarnation. For that, there must be praise to God. The incarnation is the greatest of all mysteries, that the great and holy God of the universe should so take up the cause of his sinful and rebellious creatures that he should become one of them, becoming like them so that they might become like himself. On the occasion of the incarnation the angels did well to sing, "Glory to God in the highest, and on earth peace, good will toward men."

Moreover, there are the years of quiet ministry in Nazareth as the One who once ruled angels now learns to do a humble carpenter's work, to know poverty, to be a friend of sinners, to be despised and rejected by those who would have considered themselves important.

Pass on to the cross and beyond that to the first Easter morning, and find there a glory that was yet to come. Jesus had been crucified. To many, the dream seems over. The disciples are scattering. But then the great name of God is glorified again as God breaks the bands of death that bind his Son and sends him forth to empower his weak disciples to the task of world mission. Soon many believe, and in this God is glorified.

Finally, the day will come when Christ will return in glory to judge the living and the dead and to set up his kingdom, and in this God will be glorified. Indeed, in that day the angels who sang at the birth of the Savior will again sing, "To him who sits on the throne and to the Lamb be blessing and honor and glory and power forever and ever" (Rev. 5:13).

When We Are Troubled

What heights there are in that resolution and prayer, "Father, glorify your name." But now we must step down from the rarefied atmosphere of this third heaven to make this practical in our own earthly environment. It is easy to do. We read that the soul of Christ was troubled. Well, is our soul ever troubled? Is it likely to be troubled in the days ahead? What are we to do in such circumstances? What are we to do when relatives die? When sickness strikes? When we lose our job? When enemies abuse us and friends fail to understand? What shall we do?

We learn from the Master, who when his soul was troubled breathed this prayer, "Father, glorify your name." In other words, if I must lose my health, glorify your name by my sickness. If I must lose my wealth, glorify your name by my poverty. If I must lose my good name, glorify your name by my humiliation. If I must lose my life, glorify your name by my death and send the resurrection.

There is power in that prayer. Look at it a word at a time. The first word is "Father." Anguish is ameliorated, trouble is transformed when we can address God as "Father." We see this in children. A number of years ago when our middle daughter was very small, my wife and I and a group of friends were in Granada, Spain, on a hot afternoon. Earlier we had been up to see the Alhambra, that great monument to Moorish art and culture; but now we were in the bustle of the old city making our way around the great cathedral to a covered market on the other side. There were more adults than children on this particular trip, so there always seemed to be one adult holding each child's hand. Yet suddenly, there we were in the marketplace with the realization that our middle child was missing. Quickly we retraced our steps and at last found her where we had been blocks away. Apparently she had become preoccupied with something and we had gone on, thinking that she was with us. When she noticed that we were gone she had begun to cry, as well she might. For she was lost in a large and frightening city, and there was no one able even to try comforting her in her own language. I got to her first, and at once she came to me, calling out, "Daddy!" She had already stopped crying, and the word "Daddy" was a cry of relief that she had been found.

We may be lost in this world with not a friendly face in sight. We may not know which way to turn. The circumstances may be hopeless. Yet if we will only catch a glimpse of our heavenly Father, though the circumstances remain exactly the same there is a sense in which they will nevertheless be entirely changed, for we will not be lost anymore. And we need not say more. For when we have said, "Father," we have said all that really needs to be said.

The next words are, "Glorify your name." How blessed we will be if we can say those also. "Your name!" The difficulty is that we often substitute *my* for *your* and mean "my name," or at least, "your name and my name together." We want God glorified, but not at our expense or in a way that is not that which we would choose personally.

Ralph L. Keiper illustrates this from his own experience. He was born with very bad eyesight and consequently was greatly handicapped during his years of study for the ministry. He fretted about it and, I suppose, like Paul asked many times that the thorn might be taken away. One day, as he was sitting in the library trying to study, the Holy Spirit began to speak to him. He said, "Keiper, what is the chief end of man?"

Keiper was a student of theology, so he certainly knew the answer to that. He replied, "That's easy. That's the first question of the Westminster Shorter Catechism. Man's chief end is to glorify God and enjoy him forever."

"And is that your chief end?" the Holy Spirit prodded.

"Of course," said Keiper.

At this point, according to Keiper, the Holy Spirit got a bit discourteous. "Which would you rather have," he asked, "perfect eyesight or the privilege of glorifying me?"

This time the young student did not answer so quickly. But at last he said, "There is no comparison. The only possible answer is the privilege of glorifying your name."

"Then," said God through the Spirit, "why worry about the means I have chosen to have you glorify it?"

In Me

Finally, if you have followed me and have prayed the prayer of the Lord Jesus Christ this far, I wonder if you can also add one more thing, to make it inescapably personal. Add the words "in me" or "in my body." Pray, "Father, glorify your name in me; glorify your name in my body." I have biblical warrant for asking you to do this; for, in this form, the words are almost the exact words of the apostle Paul as he reflected on the circumstances of his imprisonment in Rome in writing to the Philippians. He wrote of his hope "that I will in no way be ashamed, but will have sufficient courage so that now as always Christ will be exalted in my body, whether by life or by death" (Phil. 1:20).

Think of what had happened to Paul. He had planned a trip to Rome as a free ambassador of the gospel. He had hoped to have been well received and to have been furthered on his way by the prayers and gifts of the Roman Christians. Instead, there had been an abrupt arrest and imprisonment. There had been a two-year confinement in Caesarea. This was followed by perils at sea, a shipwreck, landing on Malta, another journey by sea, and then the long walk to the city of Rome—in chains, in the company of the condemned. Believers had gone out to meet him, as they would have gone out to meet any great celebrity, and for a time Paul had a degree of liberty in his own rented house in Rome. But then circumstances changed. He must have been confined more closely, for in time the Christians even forgot his whereabouts. We know this because when Onesiphorus arrived in Rome to see Paul, no one seemed able to tell him where Paul was, and it was only after considerable searching that this faithful brother found him (2 Tim. 1:16–17). Paul witnessed in prison, and some of the guards began to believe, with the result that the gospel spread into the courts of the emperor. When word of this got back to some of the Christians in the city, they became jealous and soon began to make trouble for Paul. I believe that it was as the result of this trouble that Paul was eventually executed. These were Paul's circumstances. Yet in spite of them Paul rejoices that God will be glorified in him, whether by his life or his death.

That should be our prayer also. If we have difficulty praying it—as we naturally do—we can be helped by the secret of the surrendered life that Paul offers in the next sentence of his Philippian letter. It is: "For me to live is Christ." To live is Christ! Christ! May that be true of us! If it is, then we will be able to endure either joy or sorrow, sickness or health, bane or blessing, to see him glorified.

157

Jesus, the Great Attraction

John 12:31-33

"Now is the time for judgment on this world; now the prince of this world will be driven out. But I, when I am lifted up from the earth, will draw all men to myself." He said this to show the kind of death he was going to die.

I n the whole of human history nothing, no matter how important or how unusual, has attracted men and women like the uplifted Christ. There have been attractions that have seemed to compete for a time. In the ancient world, men and women turned out by the hundreds of thousands to praise the Roman emperors as they returned from their military triumphs. But the emperors passed on, one by one, and at last even Rome itself fell to the advancing barbarians. In more recent times, millions turned out to praise Hitler and followed him to ruin. Now Hitler is gone, and the day that he ushered in lives on only in bad memories.

What attracts men and women today? Is it sports? Certainly millions are caught up in the excitement of a world series or Superbowl playoff. But this year's winner is soon forgotten. And even at the peak of excitement, even on the day of the Superbowl contest itself, not so many can be found watching the playoff (even with the marvel of television) as can be found on the same day, morning and evening, worshiping the Lord Jesus Christ.

951

The Lord Jesus Christ has attracted more people to Madison Square Garden in New York for more consecutive days and in greater total numbers than any event in New York's history. He has attracted greater crowds for longer periods than any other single personality—in Dallas for Expo 72, in Korea for mass rallies. Christian radio programs have endured for decades where secular programs have succumbed to changing fancies, and Christian churches have remained strong from generation to generation and have even grown both in impact and in numbers.

What is the attraction? It is not the attraction of mere human personalities, for they change. It is not denominational distinctives, for they are all different. It is not slick methods of promotion, for often there is no promotion at all. The attraction is the uplifted Christ. It is the One who said, nearly two thousand years ago in the text that we are now to study, "But I, when I am lifted up from the earth, will draw all men to myself." Jesus promised to draw people to himself, and so he has. Nothing or no one has ever attracted men and women like Jesus.

The Historical Jesus

This remarkable fact deserves some careful consideration. So, taking his promise, let us consider some questions regarding it. First of all, let us ask who is speaking. Who is the "I" of the statement? The answer is Jesus, the Jesus of history.

Notice that it is not an imaginary Christ who draws men and women. Reuben A. Torrey, one of whose greatest sermons was based on the words of this text, has written, "The speaker was our Lord Jesus. He was not the Christ of men's imaginings, but the Christ of reality, the Christ of actual historic fact. Not the Christ of Mary Baker Eddy's maudlin fancy, or of Madam Besant's mystical imaginings, but the Christ of actuality, who lived here among men and was seen, heard and handled by men, and who was soon to die a real death to save real sinners from a real hell to a real heaven."[1]

The situation bears this out, for Christ's words were spoken in the context of the coming of the Greeks to Jesus about which we have been studying. These were real men, who presumably were well acquainted with the religions and philosophies of Greece. But they had come to a real Jesus because they had found mere philosophies inadequate. We must remember that Greece had some of the greatest philosophers the world has ever known. Greece was the native land of Plato, Socrates, Aristotle, Epictetus, and many others. But these were not saviors, nor did their philosophies satisfy. So the Greeks came to Jesus, and Jesus saw in their coming the first fruits of those many millions of all tribes and tongues and nations who would eventually flock to him when he had been crucified as the world's Savior. Let me say it again: It was no myth to whom the Greeks came. It was the flesh-and-blood Jesus, the real Jesus, the Jesus of history. It is this Jesus alone who still draws people today.

Christ Crucified

Our second question is this: In what aspect is this historical Jesus presented? That is, in what guise or stance does he draw people? The answer is found in the phrase "lifted up from the earth" and in the following sentence: "He said this to show the kind of death he was going to die." Clearly Jesus was referring to his crucifixion, and the point of the verse is that it is the crucified Christ alone who draws human beings.

In an earlier study of this theme, in a related verse (8:28), I pointed out that the idea of the uplifted Christ often is taken as an encouragement to lift up Christ in our preaching, with the suggestion that if we will do that, he certainly will draw people. Indeed, Jesus should be lifted up in our preaching, and it is always a shame when any preacher, no matter how conservative or evangelical, allows anything else to take the primary place in his preaching. Jesus should be lifted up in the sense that we must talk about him and seek to present him vividly to the world's gaze. But this is not the primary meaning of this text. The lifting up referred to here is not the lifting up of Christ by preaching but rather the lifting up of the historical Jesus by his enemies in crucifixion. It is the Christ of Calvary who draws. It is the Christ whose blood was shed and whose body was broken. It is the Christ who gave himself in the place of sinners so that he might bear in himself the proper and justified wrath of God.

This is the true reason why the conservative churches are growing and the liberal churches fail. "Preach any Christ but a crucified Christ," says Torrey, "and you will not draw men for long."[2] They may come for a time for a social gospel, but they will not be there for the duration. They may come for a time for bingo or out of fear, but they will not be hearty and joyous followers of the Nazarene. Modernism does not draw. Moral rearmament does not draw. Only the crucified Christ draws men and women, for only the crucified Christ reveals the great love of almighty God and provides that Savior whom we need.

Drawn, Not Driven

The third question is this: What does the historical Jesus so presented promise to do? The answer, as already noted many times, is: draw people.

This phrase involves much sound theology. For one thing, it reveals the need of men and women. If they need to be drawn to Jesus, it follows that apart from this gracious and effective drawing all are separated from him. And if they are separated from him, they are separated from everything good and need a Savior. It is not just a small or insignificant separation either. For, as Paul describes it in writing to the Romans, it is a separation that is our ruination. He shows that although the existence and power of God have been revealed to all people, they have nevertheless turned from him to follow their own wisdom and to pursue those vices that originate in their own rebellious hearts. Paul writes, "For although they knew God, they neither glorified him as God nor gave thanks to him, but their thinking became futile and their foolish hearts were darkened. Although they claimed to be wise, they became fools and exchanged the glory of the immortal God for images made to look like mortal man and birds and animals and reptiles" (Rom. 1:21–23). This is a terrible state. So we learn from Romans and from Christ's own statement that men and women are far off from Christ and that he must draw them to him.

There is another point of sound theology in these words. Not only are men and women separated from Christ, they are also separated from him in such a deep and profound way that they will not even come to him unless he draws them. In other words, their very will is captivated by the sin into which they have plunged themselves. Christ is lifted up. But they will not return to him unless he draws them.

Why is it that we must make such an effort to win people and then in addition pray that God will bless our efforts and convert them? It is because they will not come without his intervention. Spurgeon once wrote on this text: "Sometimes, when I am trying to prepare a sermon to preach, I say to myself, 'Why must I take all this trouble?' If men were in their senses, they would run to Christ without calling. Why must we put this business so temptingly? Why must we plead? Why must we be so earnest? Because men do not want to come, not even to their own Savior. They do not wish to have their sins forgiven. They do not wish to be renewed in heart; and they never will come— no, not one mother's son of them—unless He that sent Christ to them shall draw them to Christ. A work of grace in the heart is absolutely necessary before the sacrifice of the Lord Jesus will be accepted by any one of us."[3]

There is a third great lesson in the words "draw him." We discover it when we notice that people are *drawn* to Christ, not *driven* to him. Some think that people must be driven to him. Therefore, they preach on the law and judgment. They seek to frighten people into Christ's kingdom. But this is not Christ's way. Let me say here, lest I be misunderstood, that the law is indeed our schoolmaster to lead us to Christ (Gal. 3:24) and that preaching from the law, as part of the Word of God, is useful in its way. In fact, many men and women *have* been frightened enough of their sin and its consequences to flee to Christ in desperation. But I have noticed—and I believe that anyone will find this to be true who takes the trouble to poll any true Christian congregation—that an overwhelmingly greater percentage of people are won to Christ by the sweet drawing of his love than have ever been won by fear of his disfavor. What does the Word of God say? "I led them with cords of human kindness, with ties of love; I lifted the yoke from their neck and bent down to feed them" (Hosea 11:4).

Oh, the drawing power of the crucified Christ! How gentle it is! How sweet, how gracious, how quiet, how effective! Men and women are separated from Christ and will not come to him of their own will. Yet he draws them to himself and saves them in spite of themselves to the praise of his glory.

All May Come

There are two more questions that we must ask of Christ's statement. First, who does this historical, crucified Jesus promise to draw? The answer is: everyone. We must understand here that this is not a statement that can be quoted in support of universalism. It is not a promise that every individual who has ever lived will come to Christ and be saved. If it were, it would not be true; for certainly many millions of people go through a lifetime and eventually die without coming to him. It is not a promise that every individual will be won to Jesus, but rather that all types of people—from every level of life and every race and nation—will come to him.

The gospel of the crucified Christ has been preached in palaces and halls of state, and the mighty of this world have come to him. It has been preached in the dirtiest and most dangerous of the back alleys of our cities, and the weak and outcast of this world have come to him. It has been preached to Americans, and Americans have come. It has been preached in the nations of Africa and Asia and South America, and citizens of those nations have come. It has been preached to children, and children have come. It has been preached to the aged, and the aged have come. It has been preached to the intelligent and the not-so-intelligent, to the socially favored and to the socially disadvantaged, to blacks and whites, to Jews and Moslems and Buddhists and total pagans, and men and women from each of these groups have turned to Jesus as the One who is able to cleanse from sin and lead them in the way everlasting.

Will you come? Will you allow the crucified Christ to draw you? It does not matter who you are or what your background is. The text tells us that Christ draws and will draw everyone. Why, then, should not you be among them?

Himself to Himself

The last of our questions is even more obvious than the others. It is this: To whom does Jesus promise to draw such people? The answer is: to himself. It is not said that Jesus will draw men and women to the visible church, still less to one particular expression of it. It is not said that he will draw them to a particular denomination, sect, movement, or program. It is possible that he may bless these endeavors and even raise up leaders for them, but he does not promise that he will draw men and women to any of these. The promise is only that they will be drawn to Jesus. "Himself to himself!" That is the heart of the text. Is it your desire that those you know might indeed be drawn to him?

This brings me to the point at which I can easily conclude this message. I can conclude it by applying it first to believers and then to unbelievers.

First, to believers involved in serving Christ. If you are serving Christ, you undoubtedly are trying to lead others to him; if you are, then you should learn from this study. Learn, first of all, that if you would win men and women for Jesus, you must draw them rather than drive them to him. Some think that people are won by black looks and scowls, but few come to this kind of preaching or witnessing. Do not scowl at people. Do not seek to condemn them. Love them for Christ's sake, and draw them through his love and by gentle invitations.

Second, learn even as you seek to draw them that, nevertheless, it is Christ who draws and who must therefore be the great and sole attraction. Would you win people? Then do not deal too much with more peripheral matters. Of course, you must cover the whole counsel of God in time in your preaching, if you are a preacher. You must also deal honestly with whatever questions are asked you as a result of your witnessing, regardless in what direction they tend. But to win men and women, it must be the case that Christ, rather than these other matters, is central. And, more than this, it must be Christ crucified. Speak of the Christ who died for sinners, and that very Christ will draw sinners to himself in abundance.

Finally, if you are not yet a Christian, learn that if Jesus said he will draw men and women to himself, then he will draw them now as much as at any point in history. He has not changed. The value of his death has not changed. People have not changed. The problems have not changed. The attraction of the Lord Jesus Christ is always present, and he will draw people now. Do you sense that he is drawing you? If so, do not ask, "May I come to Jesus?" Of course you may come, if you are drawn to come. If he is drawing you, come! Resist no longer. Turn from all that might hold you back, and fly to Jesus.

158

Who Is This Son of Man?

John 12:34

The crowd spoke up, "We have heard from the Law that the Christ will remain for-ever, so how can you say, 'The Son of Man must be lifted up'? Who is this 'Son of Man'?"

The existence of God is not a terribly difficult concept for modern man. In fact, if we are to believe the opinion polls, most of our contemporaries do believe in him. The difficulty most people have is in other areas. Take the idea of God suffering, for instance. For many, the existence of God is probable; but the idea that he became a man in order to die for sinners is an offense so great as to be almost blasphemous.

This is not just a problem for men and women of our own day, however. It also was a problem for Christ's contemporaries. No doubt they had all the intellectual difficulties with this idea that we do, but in addition to this, they had a difficulty that arose out of what they knew to be the teaching of the Word of God. In the chapter of John that we have been studying, Jesus had prophesied his death, saying that "the Son of Man [should] be glorified" by it (v. 23). But how could anyone connect the Son of Man with suffering? the people wondered. The Old Testament said, "His dominion is an everlasting dominion that will not pass away, and his kingdom is one that will never be destroyed" (Dan. 7:14). God had told David, "When your days are over and you rest with your fathers, I will raise up your offspring to succeed you, who will come from your own body, and I will establish his kingdom. He will build a house for my Name, and I will establish the throne of his kingdom forever"

957

(2 Sam. 7:12–13). Isaiah had prophesied of the coming Messiah, saying, "Of the increase of his government and peace there will be no end. He will reign on David's throne and over his kingdom, establishing justice and righteousness from that time on and forever" (Isa. 9:7). These and many other texts speak of an eternal and everlasting rule of the Son of Man. So how could the Son of Man suffer? How could he be lifted up? In the Gospel, John reports the people as asking, "We have heard from the Law that Christ will remain forever, so how can you say, 'The Son of Man must be lifted up'? Who is this 'Son of Man'?" (v. 34).

This is a very important question, of course. And it becomes even more important when we recognize that the title "Son of Man" was virtually the only title used by Jesus of himself. He has other titles. He is the Lamb of God, the King, the Messiah, the Beloved, the Word, the Son of God, and many others. But Jesus did not use these titles of himself. They were given him by others. In his own speech, he was always the Son of Man. This title occurs sixty-nine times in the synoptic Gospels and twelve times in the Gospel of John.

Moreover, the title "Son of Man" is a particularly inclusive title, as we shall see. One scholar writes, "The idea of the Son of Man . . . embraces the total work of Jesus as does almost no other idea."[1] To study the term is, therefore, to study not only what Jesus thought of his own ministry—including why he was to die—but also to gain the broadest possible outlook on it.

A Semitic Idiom

The place to begin in a study of the term "Son of Man" is with the simple meaning of the words, which is quite interesting. Our phrase is a direct translation of the Greek words *huios tou anthropou,* but this phrase is based upon original Aramaic or Hebrew expressions. In Aramaic, the phrase is *bar-nasha.* In Hebrew, it is *ben-ish* or *ben-adam.* The first part of these expressions, *bar* or *ben,* means "son." We have it in the proper names Barnabas, Barsabbas, Bartholomew, and others. The second part, *nasha, ish,* or *adam,* means "man." The Hebrew *ben-adam,* meaning "son of man," is known to many English-speaking people through Leigh Hunt's winsome poem "Abou ben Adam," the opening line of which reads, "Abou ben Adam, may his tribe increase."

The significance of this linguistic study lies in the fact that in Aramaic and Hebrew idiom (not Greek), the word *bar* or *ben* often is used in a figurative sense, so that, as in the phrases we are considering, the word following it designates the classification to which one belongs. For instance, for "liar" the Aramaic idiom is "son of a lie" or "son of the lie." Sinners are "sons of sin." A wealthy man is a "son of wealth," and so on. Our term, *bar-nasha* or *ben-ish,* therefore denotes one who belongs to the human classification. That is, it simply means "man." In a sense, therefore, the Greek translation of the term, from which we get our title "Son of Man," is too literal and therefore also just a bit misleading. It misleads us when we miss the fact that by using this term Jesus was on the simplest level just calling himself "a man."

This is important, for it speaks to us both of the great humility of Christ and of the joy he found in being made one with his brethren. To be sure, he was much more than man. He was God. He could have called himself "God." But instead of this, we find that the great second person of the Godhead, that is, the Christ who became flesh, rejoices to be precisely what he became—"a man." In a sense, it is his boast. For he knew that in becoming like us, he would open the way for us to become like him.

The Phrase in Daniel

We must not be misled in our study of the phrase by stopping at this point, however. It is true that the words "Son of Man" do mean "man" in Semitic idiom. But it also is true that they had come to mean more in Christ's time as the result of one unique occurrence of this term in the Old Testament and of a subsequent development of the term in the intertestamental period.

The one Old Testament reference is in Daniel, in the seventh chapter. This is the chapter that relates Daniel's vision of the four great beasts that come up out of the sea and reign in succession on earth for a time. It is clear that they represent world powers. The first was like a lion, representing the kingdom of Babylon. The second was like a bear. It represented the kingdom of the Medes and Persians, who conquered Babylon. The third was like a leopard. It represented Greece. Finally, there was a beast too terrible to be compared with any known animal. It represented the coming Roman empire. Within this empire, different kings competed for prominence, and one king, represented by a "little horn," displaced three of the others.

At this point, the vision shifts to heaven, and Daniel describes a scene in which thrones are set up and the Ancient of Days takes his place upon one of the thrones and renders judgment. In this judgment, the last of the beasts is killed and all have their kingdoms taken away. Daniel then writes of the final conquest and of a new and everlasting kingdom: "In my vision at night I looked and there before me was one like the Son of Man, coming with the clouds of heaven. He approached the Ancient of Days and was led into his presence. He was given authority, glory and sovereign power; all peoples, nations, and men of every language worshiped him. His dominion is an everlasting dominion that will not pass away, and his kingdom is one that will never be destroyed" (Dan. 7:13–14).

In the period following the writing of Daniel and before the coming of Christ, this concept of the Son of Man was taken up in various apocryphal writings (such as 4 Ezra and the book of Enoch) and in the Targums. In these books, "Son of Man" is one term given to the anticipated Messiah.

This is a different situation from the purely linguistic meaning of the Hebrew or Aramaic phrases, therefore. Linguistically, the phrases mean man. But in these sources, they obviously mean man in a very specific sense. That is, they mean "The Man," understood as that eternal or archetypal man who exists eternally with God and who is to appear at the end of time to consummate God's plan of salvation.

One other thing must be said about this Son of Man figure. As we read the apocalyptical writings, we detect that there is not always full agreement as to who the Son of Man is or what he will do. He is a Messianic figure, but a shadowy one. Consequently, there must have been a wide variety of opinions concerning him in Christ's day. Here we probably have a clue as to why Jesus used this term rather than another to describe himself. The other terms—Messiah, Son of God, Deliverer—all had very fixed meanings, and the meanings were not those Jesus wished to have attached to his ministry. To give one example, to most people the word "Messiah" denoted a political figure whose primary work would be the deliverance of Jewish lands from the Romans. Jesus was the Messiah. He acknowledged this indirectly in his conversation with the Samaritan woman (John 4:25–26). But if he had said this publicly, everyone would have expected him to organize an army and lead a liberation movement; and he did not want this. So he did not make an open claim to be the Messiah. However, with the Son of Man concept, it was different. People knew that this was a special Messiah-type figure, but they did not know what to think about it precisely. The question of our text indicates this. "Who is this 'Son of Man'?" Therefore, Jesus used this phrase of himself while at the same time infusing it with whatever content he chose to give it. In other words, it became the supreme title by which he described his own person and ministry.

A Suffering Savior

This leads to the question of how Jesus did use the title, which is the important issue. What did he mean by the Son of Man? What ministry did he conceive for this figure? As we look at the references to this figure, primarily in John's Gospel, we discover several major teachings.

1. Jesus used the term "Son of Man" to teach that he was *preexistent.* That is, the life of the Lord Jesus Christ did not begin at birth, as our lives do. Rather, he is eternal, having existed with God the Father from the beginning, as John declares in the prologue to his Gospel. This is the first clear teaching about the Son of Man in John's Gospel. It occurs in Christ's conversation with Nicodemus. In this conversation Christ said, "No one has ever gone into heaven except the one who came down from heaven—the Son of Man" (3:13). In other words, no mere man can say what heaven is like, because no man has ever been there. But Jesus can because he came from heaven. His life did not begin on this earth. In chapter 6, there is a similar but indirect reference to the same truth. In that chapter, Jesus asks of those who were offended by his teaching, "What if you see the Son of Man ascend to where he was before!" (v. 62). In other words, "What if I should not go to the cross but rather just return to heaven?" In these verses the preexistence of the Son of Man is self-evident teaching.

2. The unique element in Jesus' teaching about the Son of Man is that the Son of Man was to suffer *humiliation and death.* So we naturally find more verses

devoted to this teaching than to any other. For example, in the verse immediately following the one in which Jesus taught Nicodemus about his pre-existence, the Master disclosed, "Just as Moses lifted up the snake in the desert, so the Son of Man must be lifted up, that everyone who believes in him may have eternal life" (3:14–15). Clearly, even at this point in his ministry, Jesus had his crucifixion in view.

There is another reference to his suffering in chapter 8. "So Jesus said, 'When you have lifted up the Son of Man, then you will know that I am the one I claim to be and that I do nothing on my own but speak just what the Father has taught me'" (v. 28). In chapter 12, in the verse that begins the section we are studying, the same truth is suggested, "Jesus answered, 'The hour has come for the Son of Man to be glorified'" (v. 23). Again, in chapter 13, "When he [Judas] was gone, Jesus said, 'Now is the Son of Man glorified and God is glorified in him'" (v. 31).

None of Christ's hearers would have thought that suffering was a part of the Son of Man's ministry. Thus, when Jesus spoke of suffering, they were always puzzled. They looked for glory and power when the Son of Man should come. Jesus taught that glory was to come by suffering, and power by way of the cross.

3. The third point to Christ's teaching about the Son of Man is that he was to become a vital *part of all who should believe* on him. That is, the salvation that he would bring was to be not merely objective or abstract but personal. It was to be applied individually. On this point, the teaching in John 6 is quite clear. "Do not work for the food that spoils but for food that endures to eternal life, which the Son of Man will give you. On him God the Father has placed his seal of approval" (v. 27). "I tell you the truth, unless you eat the flesh of the Son of Man and drink his blood, you have no life in you. Whoever eats my flesh and drinks my blood has eternal life, and I will raise him up at the last day" (vv. 53–54). We have already seen that eating Christ's flesh and drinking Christ's blood is the equivalent of "coming" to Christ or "believing" on him.

4. At several points Jesus refers to the Son of Man in the context of the *final judgment.* This is the fourth doctrine, and it is this that comes closest to the original teaching concerning the Son of Man in Daniel. In John's Gospel, Jesus is reported as saying, "For as the Father has life in himself, so he has granted to the Son to have life in himself. And has given him authority to judge because he is the Son of Man" (5:26–27). In Revelation 14 there is a more elaborate description of this judgment; there the Son of Man appears with a sharp sickle in his hand, and both he and an angel "gathered its [the earth's] grapes and threw them into the great winepress of God's wrath" (Rev. 14:19).

5. Mention of the Book of Revelation leads to a fifth teaching concerning the Son of Man that, although it is not mentioned by Jesus in the Gospels, nevertheless is important. This teaching comes from a vision of Christ that John had on Patmos, which is recorded in the first chapter of Revelation. Here Jesus

is seen, not as a separate figure coming to the Ancient of Days to sit with him on one of two thrones (as in Daniel) but as the Ancient of Days himself. John writes, "I turned around to see the voice that was speaking to me. And when I turned I saw seven golden lampstands, and among the lampstands was someone 'like a Son of Man,' dressed in a robe reaching down to his feet and with a golden sash around his chest. His head and hair were white like wool, as white as snow, and his eyes were like blazing fire" (Rev. 1:12–14). The importance of this vision is twofold: first, it identifies Jesus with God the Father, and second, it regards him as being active on earth in the midst of the seven golden lampstands.

What are the lampstands? A few verses later we are told that the lampstands are "the seven churches" (v. 20). Thus, the picture is of Christ's current *rule over the churches.* Indeed, in the next two chapters, Christ addresses the churches, warning of judgment on some and encouraging those who are still faithful to remain so.[2]

Savior and Lord

We need to apply these truths to ourselves, in spite of the fact that much of what I have said seems to be purely academic. How shall we do this? The best way is by catching a vision of the Son of Man and thereby realizing precisely who it is we worship. When we preach Christ or when we gather as God's people to worship Christ, we are not thinking merely of a figure who lived on earth two thousand years ago. True, he did live on earth; it is because of this that we know him. But more than this, we are thinking of the great and eternal God of the universe, the second Person of the Trinity, the one who existed before all things and through whom all that we know came into existence, the one who will also be there at the end to render judgment. This is a glorious Christ. This is one who rightly demands our worship and deserves our service.

If you are not a Christian, you need to come to him first as Savior. You need to thank him for coming and dying for you, and then trust him and follow him. You will not make a wiser decision in your entire remaining life, no matter what that may hold. On the other hand, if you are a Christian already, you must give him an opportunity to be all he desires to be to you, in order that he who is your Savior might also be your Lord.

159

An Appeal and a Promise

John 12:35–36

Then Jesus told them, "You are going to have the light just a little while longer. Walk while you have the light, before darkness overtakes you. The man who walks in the dark does not know where he is going. Put your trust in the light while you have it, so that you may become sons of light." When he had finished speaking, Jesus left and hid himself from them.

There is something especially poignant about a great man's last public teaching or last words. I remember, for instance, how moved I was as a boy when I memorized General Douglas MacArthur's farewell address to the American Congress after he had been relieved as commander of the armed services. I had memorized this speech for a declamation contest and was personally affected as I got to the closing lines. MacArthur referred to the old military ballad, "Old soldiers never die, they just fade away," then concluded, "And like the old soldier of that ballad I now fade away, a soldier who tried to do his duty as God gave him the light to see that duty. Good-bye." I suppose there was something equally poignant about Napoleon's farewell to his troops from the steps of the hunting retreat at Fountainbleu before his deportation to Elba, and of the last speeches of many other great men.

We come now to the last words of the public teaching of the Lord Jesus Christ, uttered just a few days before his crucifixion. These words were followed by many words of private instruction, of course. Undoubtedly, there were wonderful conversations between Jesus and the disciples at the home of Mary, Martha, and Lazarus at Bethany. John himself records the last discourses of Jesus with the Twelve in those final days in and around Jerusalem and in the upper room. But these last were all private words, spoken only to his own disciples. The words we are to study now were his last public teaching.

At this point the sun of righteousness had all but set. Within two or three days, God would blot out the sun on Calvary. Yet, there was still time to turn to the light. So Jesus, who was always love toward those who were perishing, speaks these last words of solemn appeal and promise. Alexander Maclaren, who provides an excellent sermon on this text, writes, "He loves too well not to warn, but He will not leave the bitterness of threatening as a last savour on the palate; and so the lips, into which grace is poured, bade farewell to His enemies with the promise and the hope that even they may become 'the sons of light.'"[1]

Jesus said, "You are going to have the light just a little while longer. Walk while you have the light, before darkness overtakes you. The man who walks in the dark does not know where he is going. Put your trust in the light while you have it, so that you may become sons of light."

We notice as we read these words that they are not a direct answer to the question that Jesus had been asked in the verse preceding. He had said that he was going to be lifted up from the earth in death, and the people had asked how this could be true of the Messiah. "We have heard from the Law that Christ will remain forever, so how can you say, 'The Son of Man must be lifted up'? Who is this 'Son of Man'?" (v. 34). This was their question, but Jesus did not answer it. Instead, he dealt with a different theme entirely. The people wanted to discuss expectations of the Messiah. Today it would be prophecy. Jesus, on the other hand, wanted to talk about the relationship of an individual to himself. "The darkness is coming," he said. "So seize the light while you have it." The same words apply to our time in which the darkness is even more evident and the light often shines but faintly.

What is our analysis of these verses? From my viewpoint, they provide a perfect last will and testament. They have four parts: (1) a reminder, (2) a challenge, (3) a warning, and (4) a promise. That is the message I would also leave with you in this study.

Christ's Reminder

The reminder is a reminder of a simple truth: namely, that Jesus Christ is this world's light. This is marked in the Greek text, because in four of the five occurrences of the word "light" in these verses, "light" is preceded by the definite article—"*the* light." It is a clear reference to Christ. "You are going to have *the* light a little while longer. Walk while you have *the* light . . . put your trust in *the* light." This is all the more obvious in that in the last occurrence of the word, in reference to men and women rather than to Jesus, the article is omitted. There we read merely of being "sons of light."

This is significant, because it is a teaching found throughout the Gospel and is almost the first descriptive epithet used by John of Jesus. The first descriptive term is "word" or *logos*. It occurs in verse 1. The second is "life." But then, as early as the fourth verse of the Gospel, the term "light" occurs, and this is immediately picked up and repeated so often that it occurs six times just in the next six verses. "In him was life, and that life was the light of men. The light shines in the darkness, but the darkness has not understood it. There came a man who was sent from God; his name was John. He came as a witness to testify concerning that light, so that through him all men might believe. He himself was not the light; he came only as a witness of that light. The true light that gives light to every man was coming into the world" (1:4–9). Later Jesus will himself say, "I am the light of the world" (8:12; 9:5). John writes elsewhere in his Gospel, "This is the verdict: Light has come into the world, but men loved darkness instead of light because their deeds were evil. Everyone who does evil hates the light, and will not come into the light for fear that his deeds will be exposed. But whoever lives by the truth comes to the light, so that it may be seen plainly that what he has done has been done through God" (3:19–21). The last occurrence of the image is in John 12:46, in which Jesus cries out, "I have come into the world as a light, so that no one who believes in me should stay in darkness."

This is a profoundly rich image, of course, which is why Jesus reverts to it here on the eve of his crucifixion. For one thing, it identifies him with God the Father, which means that he is also preexistent and eternal. Light is an ancient image of God. David writes in one psalm, "The LORD is my light and my salvation" (Ps. 27:1). Again he says, "For with you is the fountain of life; in your light shall we see light" (Ps. 36:9). In mathematics, there is an axiom to the effect that "things equal to the same thing are equal to each other." Consequently, if Jesus is light and if God is light, Jesus must be the same as God. He is God. This is certainly the biblical teaching.

Second, the image teaches that Jesus makes God known. Light is as universal an image for the illumination of the mind as it is an image of God. Without illumination, men are in mental and spiritual darkness. They do not know God. Jesus comes; his light shines upon men. Now those who were in darkness have the light of the knowledge of the glory of God in the face of Jesus Christ.

Third, Jesus is unalterably opposed to the darkness. That is, he is opposed to ignorance, sin, and evil, and is determined to destroy them. How does he do this? In the simplest terms, he does it simply by shining. The cross is the focal point of his victory, of course. But in terms of the response of the individual, he overcomes ignorance and evil simply by shining into our hearts and by thus drawing us to him. This is so natural a part of the illumination he gives that John can argue in his first epistle that if we are not drawn away from sin into righteousness, we are not truly Christians (1 John 1:5–7).

Fourth, this image reveals Jesus as a full or genuine light, as opposed to all partial lights. It is what John means when he calls him "the true light" that has come into the world (John 1:9). To call Jesus the light is not to deny that there are other lights, however derivational, misleading, or imperfect. Man is made in the image of God; and, in spite of the fall, some vestiges of that image remain. He aspires to good things. He desires peace, progress, prosperity. None of these things is bad. It is just that they are partial lights. They are good so far as they go, but they do not go far enough. They deal with externals, but they do not provide that inner satisfaction that all men need and so desperately crave. To call Jesus the true light is, therefore, to refer to him as that sole source of full illumination by which men and women can learn the truth about God and about themselves and enter into that close personal relationship to him to which they are called. All this is involved in Christ's reminder that he is the light.

Suppose the people reject him? It does not matter. He is still the light. Suppose they kill him? He is still the light. He is the light for our own time also.

A Challenge

Jesus did not only give the people a reminder, however; he also gave them a challenge that was coupled to it. It has two parts: "walk" in the light (v. 35), and "believe" in the light (v. 36). Here Jesus speaks of walking first and of believing second. Placed in logical order, "believe" should come first and "walk" second. First, we must believe on the light. After that we are to walk in it.

What does it mean to believe on the light? Simply, it means to believe on Jesus, which is to trust him. In the twentieth chapter, John gives this as the purpose of the book: "Jesus did many other miraculous signs in the presence of his disciples, which are not recorded in this book. But these are written that you may believe that Jesus is the Christ, the Son of God, and that by believing you may have life in his name" (vv. 30–31). In the biblical sense, believing on someone means to take that individual at his or her word and then to act upon it. In the case of Jesus, it means to take him at his word when he declares himself to be the Son of God and our Savior and then to act upon that conviction by trusting him as Savior and following him as Lord.

Is Jesus God? Then he must be our God and we must worship him as God. Is he the Savior? Then he must be our Savior. Is he the One who lives to instruct and help and strengthen his people? Then he must be our instructor and helper, and the source of our strength.

This leads to the second part of Christ's challenge. It is the challenge to "walk" in Christ's light. This is a step beyond merely believing, though it is related to it. It involves continuing activity or progression. In other words, a proper response to Jesus involves much more than merely committing oneself to a set of truths and acting upon them once. Rather, it involves committing oneself to Jesus, who is on the move, and following him continuously. It means walking in his steps. It means doing what he does, thinking as he thinks, acting as he acts. To do that is to walk in the light, for he is the light. To refuse to follow him is to fall back into darkness.

The Encroaching Darkness

The third part of Christ's final teaching is a warning: "Walk while you have the light, before darkness overtakes you." This is serious, for it is the teaching that if we do not follow Christ, not only do we remain in darkness, but the darkness in which we find ourselves intensifies. Maclaren has written, "Rejected light is the parent of the densest darkness, and the man who, having the light, does not trust it, piles around himself thick clouds of obscurity and gloom, far more doleful and impenetrable than the twilight that glimmers round the men who have never known the daylight of revelation."[2]

The Pharisees in John's story of the man who had been born blind are the clearest example of this principle. On the one hand, the story of the man who had been blind is the story of Christ bringing light to one who had been born in darkness. This was true both physically and spiritually. The physical miracle is obvious. The spiritual miracle is seen in the blind man's gradual growth in perception as to who Christ was and in believing on him. At the beginning of the story, he knows him only as "the man they called Jesus" (9:11). Later on, he calls him "a prophet" (v. 17). Still later, Jesus is referred to as being "from God" (v. 33). The last we see of the man who had been born blind, he is calling Christ "Lord" and worshiping him as "the Son of Man" (vv. 35, 38). In other words, the story of the man born blind is the story of the coming of spiritual (as well as physical) light to a man who had been born in both spiritual and physical darkness. On the other hand, the story is also the story of a progression into greater darkness by those who would not have Christ's light. The Pharisees could see physically, but they would not see spiritually. Consequently, they come to hate the light increasingly as the story unfolds.

What will it be like in our lives? Will we go from faith to faith and from sight to sight, as was the case in the life of the man who had been born blind? Or will we go from unbelief to unbelief, from darkness to darkness? It all depends upon our relationship to him who is the only genuine light of this world.

A Promise

Finally, we notice that Christ's words also contain a promise. It is the promise that, if we believe in the light, we will be "sons of light." How gracious this is! We notice that, in one sense at least, Christ's final sermon is complete even without this promise. It has contained a reminder of Christ's teaching. It has presented a challenge. It has even possessed a warning of what will happen if the challenge goes unheeded. If Jesus had stopped at that point, who could say that anything is lacking? No one! Yet such is the grace of our Lord, that he seems unwilling to end his public words with a warning and instead closes on a note of promise. True, the darkness is coming. But though it comes, the one who believes on Jesus may, by that very belief, become a child of light and thus reflect the radiance of his departed Master to the darkening world.

This does not mean that the followers of Christ will be lights in the same sense that he is the light. There is only one true light; that is Jesus. But it does mean that they may reflect him and thus become a source of blessed illumination to others.

This, then, is Christ's final message. For some it must be a reminder. If you have heard the truth but have not responded to it, you must be reminded. You must also believe. Others require a challenge. If you are one who needs a challenge, you may remember what Jesus has said and know that you must do something. But you have not done it. Heed the challenge. Jesus commands you to "put your trust in the light" and "walk in it." Still others must be warned. You need to be warned if you have delayed your decision. Learn that you are in danger of slipping away into darkness forever. Learn that there is a true light and a true darkness, and believe on Jesus. Finally, there are those who must be encouraged by Christ's promise.

"Put your trust in the light while you have it, so that you may become sons of light." Believe on him, and enter into that great and promised blessing.

160

The Miracle of Unbelief

John 12:36–40

"Put your trust in the light while you have it, so that you may become sons of light."
When he had finished speaking, Jesus left and hid himself from them.

Even after Jesus had done all these miraculous signs in their presence, they still would
not believe in him. This was to fulfill the word of Isaiah the prophet:
"Lord, who has believed our message
and to whom has the arm of the Lord been revealed?"

For this reason they could not believe, because, as Isaiah says elsewhere:
"He has blinded their eyes
and deadened their hearts,
so they can neither see with their eyes,
nor understand with their hearts,
nor turn—and I would heal them."

Jesus' last sermon to the people of his day—a sermon that contained a reminder of his teaching, a challenge to respond to him, a warning to those who would not respond, and a promise to those who would—properly closes this, the middle section of John's Gospel. It is a section in which Jesus began to call a people to himself out of Judaism. It started with Christ's call to the man who had been born blind; it ends with this final and open invitation: "Believe in the light while you have it, so that you may become sons of light" (v. 36). The next section of the Gospel, chapters 13 through 17, properly contains Christ's private teaching to those who are his own. Therefore, there are no more public invitations to come to him.

In spite of this good ending, however, John seems unwilling to conclude this section of the Gospel without a few summarizing comments. Therefore,

969

in verses 37–50, we find a three-part conclusion. First, there is an analysis of the stark fact of Israel's unbelief (vv. 36–41). Second, there is the acknowledgement that, nevertheless, some did believe, coupled to an explanation of why they did not come forward publicly to defend the Lord (vv. 42–43). Third, there is a résumé of the whole of Christ's teachings, stressing (1) his relationship to the Father, (2) his identity as this world's light, (3) the danger of unbelief, and (4) the nature of his teachings and the blessed result of responding to them (vv. 44–50).

This threefold summary of Christ's public ministry will occupy us in this and the last two studies of the twelfth chapter. The next study, "What Isaiah Saw," is an excursus.

Unbelievable Unbelief

Jewish unbelief has been a recurring theme throughout this Gospel. So we are not surprised to find that, as John brings his account of the public ministry to a close, he reminds us of this once more. He writes, "When he had finished speaking, Jesus hid himself from them. Even after Jesus had done all these miraculous signs in their presence, they still would not believe in him" (vv. 36–37). It is a striking fact, but a true one, that Israel would not receive, and actually killed God's Messiah.

The unbelievableness of Israel's unbelief escapes us today, being separated from the events of those days by nearly two thousand years. But though it means little to us, the strangeness of Israel's unbelief did not escape the early preachers of the gospel, most of whom were Jews, and in fact actually became a source of great puzzlement and anguish for them. These men lived their lives in the light of the Old Testament prophecies and therefore knew that the Messiah of God was to come to bless Israel. Besides, they knew that Jesus was this Messiah. What should have happened? Obviously, Israel should have believed in Jesus and have welcomed him joyfully. But instead of this, Israel seemed as a whole to be rejecting him while the Gentiles seemed to be increasingly responding. How could this be? Did it mean that God had changed his mind, that he had cast off his people? Did it mean that events had taken even God by surprise? The importance of these questions and the struggles that they reflect are seen clearly in Romans 9–11, in which Paul fights his way through such questions forcefully, concluding at the end that God has not cast off his people but rather has allowed them to fall into unbelief for a time in order that his grace in Christ might be extended to the Gentiles as well as to a remnant chosen out of Israel.

This is precisely the problem with which John is dealing. And while it is true that he does not deal with it as analytically as does Paul, nor as fully, nevertheless it is along the same lines (particularly in regard to prophecy) that he answers it. This answer is in the verses before us.

John asks why it is that the nation of Israel as a whole did not believe. The answer he gives is that the unbelief of the Jews is in accord with prophecy.

"Even after Jesus had done all these miraculous signs in their presence, they still would not believe in him. This was to fulfill the word of Isaiah the prophet: 'Lord, who has believed our message, and to whom has the arm of the Lord been revealed?'" (vv. 37–38).

It is a terribly significant prophecy that John refers to, of course. For the verses he quotes are those that open the magnificent fifty-third chapter of Isaiah. The chapter begins with the questions: "Who has believed our message, and to whom has the arm of the Lord been revealed?" The answer is: No one. So the chapter goes on to show the consequences of the failure to believe. The Messiah came, but he was "despised and rejected by men, a man of sorrows, and familiar with grief. Like one from whom men hide their faces he was despised, and we esteemed him not" (Isa. 53:3). This is the more remarkable in that the Messiah was to speak such great words and perform such great deeds. Here Bishop Westcott, one of the most careful commentators on John's Gospel, notes: "The prophecy itself (Isa. 53:1) sets forth the two sides of the divine testimony, the message as to the servant of God which appealed to the inward perception of truth; and the signs of the power of God which appealed outwardly to those who looked upon them. In both aspects the testimony failed to find acceptance. The message was not believed; the signs were not interpreted."[1] John also indicates that Jesus spoke wisely ("These things spoke Jesus," v. 36) and acted powerfully ("He had done so many miracles," v. 37); yet the people of his time did not respond to him.

John's quotation cannot be construed in any way that would lessen the responsibility of men and women for their own disobedience. It is true that by their disobedience the people of Christ's day fulfilled Scripture (v. 38). It is also true, as the next verses will also show, that as a result of their disobedience God increasingly blinded their eyes so that they could not see, or understand, or be converted (vv. 39–40). But this does not mean that they were not responsible before God for their lack of response to Jesus. John does not minimize human responsibility. Consequently, the tone of the passage is actually one of marveling that the people of Christ's day could have disbelieved, particularly after he had taught so persuasively and done so many miracles.

In view of this emphasis it may be well to translate verse 38 by using the second of two possible meanings of the Greek word lying behind the word "that." The word can mean "in order that," which would tend to put the blame for their unbelief upon God. But it can also mean "so that" or "consequently." If that is so, the verses may be translated, "They believed not; consequently the saying of Isaiah was fulfilled." John's point is not that God made them disbelieve, but rather that we should not be surprised by their disbelief in that God had prophesied it even before it happened.

Anyone who is away from God is away from God because of his or her own desires and decisions. Men and women departed from God in Adam, and they remain cut off from God because they prefer their own will to God's will and will not have Christ to be their Savior.

When God Hardens Hearts

"But what of the next verses that quote Isaiah 6:9–10?" someone might ask. "Do they not say explicitly that God blinded their eyes and hardened their hearts precisely so that those involved might not see, understand, or turn to Jesus?" It is a good question. Let me answer it.

Above everything else, we must say that if God chooses to intervene in a specific way in an individual life to harden that life so that the individual cannot believe on Jesus, then God is right in so acting. If this is what he actually does—and notice that I only said "if"—then God is just, and no man (least of all we ourselves) has the slightest ground for rebuking him. As Paul writes, "What then shall we say? Is God unjust? Not at all! . . . Therefore God has mercy on whom he wants to have mercy, and he hardens whom he wants to harden" (Rom. 9:14–18). If God hardens hearts as a result of which men and women cannot believe and are judged for it, then that is just the way it is, and God is guiltless. We are in no position to judge him by our limited wisdom and inadequate standards.

But is this, in fact, what he does? Or, to be more specific, is this what our text teaches? I do not believe so, for these reasons:

First, this is not what the Word of God as a whole teaches. What does it teach? Does it teach that men are able to choose God but that God singles out some, whose minds he closes, who therefore do not believe, and who are therefore damned? Is it this? Or is it that men begin by being unable to choose God, God intervenes graciously to open some eyes to see the truth and embrace it, and, as a result, these objects of God's gracious intervention are saved? Certainly it is the latter. Jesus said, "No one can come to me unless the Father who sent me draws him" (John 6:44), and he pointed out that God does draw some (John 6:37). Consequently, in terms of salvation it is hardly necessary for God to blind anyone; for men begin blind and come to Christ only when God intervenes to give sight to them. If God wishes anyone to go to hell, he needs only to withhold his grace, and the individual will go there as the inevitable consequence of his or her own negative capabilities.

The second reason why this is not the proper interpretation of our text is that an entirely different sequence is indicated even in this passage. We notice here that John does not begin with a quotation from Isaiah 6:9–10. He begins with the statement that even though Jesus did so many miracles, "they still would not believe in him." That is, he begins with their unbelief. It is only after this that he notes that God hardened their hearts lest they should see and be converted. In other words, this is a judicial activity. In the beginning they "would not" believe. Afterwards they "could not."

The third reason why we must not reason from God's blinding of eyes to unbelief (but rather the reverse) is that it is the latter that occurs in the immediately preceding words of Jesus. In that passage Jesus warned his listeners not to reject the light, arguing that if they rejected the light, an even greater darkness than they now knew would come upon them. This is not a dark-ness that causes unbelief but rather a darkness that results from it. It is a working out of God's just laws, by which faith leads to even greater faith and unbelief to even greater unbelief. We think here of Paul's threefold repeti-tion of the phrase "God gave them over" in the first chapter of Romans. "If God withhold abused grace, and give men over to indulged lusts, if he per-mit the evil spirit to do his work on those that resisted the good Spirit, and if in his providence he lay stumbling-blocks in the way of sinners, which con-firm their prejudices, then he *blinds their eyes,* and *hardens their hearts,* and these are spiritual judgments, like the giving up of idolatrous Gentiles to *vile affections,* and degenerate Christians to *strong delusions.*"[2]

In all this there is a most solemn affirmation of human responsibility and an even more solemn warning of what transpires when the light of God goes unheeded. Because of her unbelief God gave Israel up to a deep darkness. Because of unbelief God has also promised to give the gentile world up to a "powerful delusion, so that they will believe the lie" (2 Thess. 2:11). Could that be true of you? If so, be warned by this teaching, and do not trifle with the overtures of God's love for you or his great grace.

Having said all this, one problem remains. We have concluded that God does not specifically keep some men and women from believing on Jesus but rather elects some to salvation as an outflowing of his mercy. God's hard-ening of hearts is a judicial hardening of those who have already turned from the light to walk in darkness. But why, we might ask, does he not save every-one? Why does he not intervene to save all men before they persist in unbe-lief and enter into an even greater darkness?

In the most profound sense, we must say to these questions that we just do not know. "Who has known the mind of the Lord? Or who has been his counselor?" (Rom. 11:34). This is perhaps the greatest of all mysteries; and if our understanding here is not perfect, it is only what might be expected. We must simply confess our limited understanding.

On the other hand, while we do not understand the matter perfectly, there are at least in this particular case some suggestions by which we may discern a little of God's purposes. To begin with, the first passage quoted from Isaiah is from that chapter in which the death of the Lord Jesus is fully prophe-sied. Isaiah shows that he was to be rejected by his people and therefore to be crucified. Moreover, he shows that as a result of this undeserved death the Messiah was to be the Savior of a great number of people. How could Jesus have died as he did unless the nation of Israel had rejected him? We might surmise that it could have happened in some other way. But it is hard to see how Jesus could have died unless he had been rejected. In this case, then, the blinding of Israel becomes the means by which the light of God shines forth from the cross unto salvation.

Moreover, it is also true that it was by the blinding of Israel that the gospel extended to the gentile nations (cf. Rom. 11:25). Had the Jews accepted the gospel it is hard to see how it could have gone out freely to the Gentiles. "But when the Jews rejected it, it became a world religion," as Morris notes.[3] It may be that this is suggested by John's second quotation from Isaiah; for it occurs in a context in which it is said that the whole earth (not just the land of Israel) is filled with Christ's glory.

True Conversion

These are difficult words both because they speak of God's sovereign purpose in the affairs of men and because they speak of our responsibility. The sovereignty of God? That is something over which we have no control, and of which we possess only limited understanding. On the other hand, responsibility is something which must concern each of us personally.

Have you responded to the light you have been given? If not, let me remind you from the Isaiah quotation what should happen. The quotation contains four steps for a true conversion. First, you must *see* with your eyes. That is, you must perceive the reality of divine things and have some knowledge of them. I am well aware that this is impossible except by the grace of God. But perhaps God is thus graciously working in you and you have progressed thus far. If so, it is good. You must begin by such perception. Second, you must *understand* with your heart. This means that you must not only hear the truth and understand it objectively; you must also understand it and receive it personally. Third, you must be *converted*. This means that you must turn from sin to Christ, for conversion is nothing more than such an about-face or turning. It means leaving everything that might exert a contrary claim upon you in order truly to have and follow Jesus. Finally, you must *be healed* by God. This is God's final seal upon conversion and is itself salvation. God's healing involves justification, sanctification, and glorification for which God alone is responsible.

In the first quotation Isaiah asked, "Who has believed our message, and to whom has the arm of the Lord been revealed?" May God give you grace to answer, "I have believed it; I do believe it." To so believe and so answer is to become a son or daughter of light and a recipient of God's healing.

161

What Isaiah Saw

John 12:41

Isaiah said this because he saw Jesus' glory and spoke about him.

The Gospel of John is a book filled with many extraordinary verses. But none is more extraordinary than (and few are equal to) the verse to which we come now. It is a verse in which John refers to one of the most glorious visions of God ever given to a human being—the vision received by Isaiah at the beginning of his ministry as a prophet, in which he saw Jehovah sitting upon a throne, high and lifted up, with his train filling the temple—saying quite naturally, it would seem, that this applies to Jesus. John says, "Isaiah said this because he saw Jesus' glory and spoke about him" (v. 41).

To us the reference may seem natural, for we are conditioned by centuries of Christian theology, in which full divinity has been ascribed to Jesus of Nazareth by many persons. But it was hardly natural to John, who was a Jew. Nor was it natural to his contemporaries. We must remember that for the Jew of Christ's time God had become something almost inaccessible and incomprehensible. God was the Holy One of Israel, and rightly so. He dwelt in glory unapproachable. None actually saw him. When on occasion some extraordinary figure like Moses or Isaiah received a vision of God in his glory, this was not believed even then to be a viewing of God as he is in himself but only what we might call an image of him. And even this was extraordinary and filled with wonder. Moreover, of this limited number of visions, none was more glorious than that received by Isaiah, so that if one wanted to describe what God was like in himself, nothing could come closer than this vision. Yet it is precisely this vision with all its breathtaking splendor that John blithely applies to Jesus. Without questioning, it would seem, John takes this, the most exalted portrait of Jehovah in the entire Old Testament, and says that it is a portrait of the humble carpenter from Nazareth, who was about to be crucified as a result of the hatred of his people and the indifference and calculating political expediency of the local Roman government—so great is his opinion of Jesus.

This is not the only time that Jesus has been called God, of course. He is said to be God in the opening verses of John: "In the beginning was the Word and the Word was with God and the Word was God" (1:1). The same truth is implied by Jesus himself in John 8: "Before Abraham was born, I am" (v. 58). It is at least not denied toward the end of the book: "Thomas said to him, 'My Lord and my God'" (20:28). But nothing quite equals this amazing utterance, for it is so graphic, so dynamic, and so unexpected.

To understand this we need to ask precisely what it was that Isaiah saw when "he saw Jesus' glory and spoke about him." And we need to ask what it teaches about the Lord Jesus.

Four Elements

Here is Isaiah's full record of the vision: "In the year that King Uzziah died, I saw the Lord seated on a throne, high and exalted, and the train of his robe filled the temple. Above him were seraphs, each with six wings: With two wings they covered their faces, with two they covered their feet, and with two they were flying. And they were calling to one another, 'Holy, holy, holy, is the LORD Almighty; the whole earth is full of his glory.' At the sound of their voices the doorposts and thresholds shook, and the temple was filled with smoke" (Isa. 6:1–4). The vision contains four elements. First, there is the vision of the Lord himself, high and lifted up. This speaks of God's sovereignty in the universe. Second, there is the view of his train filling the temple. This has to do with the fact that at this highest point of the universe there is room for no one else. Third, there is a picture of those angelic beings who wait upon God to do his bidding. This speaks of service and of how it should be performed. Finally, there is a demonstration of worship, which teaches us how we should worship the Lord Jesus Christ, who is our great God.

A Sovereign God

The first element, then, is the element of sovereignty, embodied in the picture of "the Lord seated on a throne, high and exalted." It is a dramatization of the fact that he and he alone is in control of things and is always in control of them.

The obvious contrast with Uzziah is important, for it was in the year King Uzziah died that Isaiah received his vision. Uzziah was a good king who had enjoyed a long rule—in all, fifty-two years—during which time the kingdom was restored to a measure of that righteousness and prosperity it had enjoyed under David and Solomon and their immediate successors. Isaiah had grown up under the latter years of the rule of this great king. Unfortunately, however, Uzziah became ill with leprosy and eventually died. His successor was a young man of only twenty-five years of age. Besides this, trouble was brewing in the form of an increasingly belligerent and powerful Syria to the north. In time this kingdom overran the northern kingdom of Israel and threatened Judah. In the year that Uzziah died, Isaiah undoubtedly bewailed the king's loss and despaired over what the future might bring. But it was precisely at this time that God revealed himself to Isaiah as the One who was still on the throne. Uzziah might be dead, but Jehovah was living. Uzziah might have yielded up his throne, but Jehovah reigned. God, not man, was in control. Consequently, Isaiah need not fear but instead could trust God in spite of circumstances.

And, indeed, he did! In fact, trust in the sovereign God lies at the base of all Isaiah's subsequent preaching and is the secret of his great strength. Jeremiah faced many hard tasks. He knew the greatness of Israel's God, as Isaiah did. Yet Jeremiah complained and drew back and sometimes doubted. Isaiah never complained; nor did he doubt. Isaiah had peace even in storm, and the secret of it was his assurance of the sovereignty of God as revealed in this vision.

I wonder if you know God to be a sovereign God to you? Not abstractly but in a personal way? If not, it is a pity; for this is the most important of all the doctrines that concern our God.

In one of his minor writings, Donald Grey Barnhouse, the founder of the *Bible Study Hour,* tells a story from his childhood that illustrates the proper place of this doctrine in any system of theology. It concerns a visit to his home by a member of the U.S. Cavalry. In those days there were very few automobiles and no airplanes; so the army still used horses, and the cavalry was an important and glamorous branch of the armed services. This cavalryman gave the young Barnhouse a troop flag that read "Troop M, 14th Cavalry." One day in boasting about the relative importance of this branch of the service, the soldier said, "The most important thing in the armed forces is a Cavalry General. After that there is a Cavalry Colonel, a Cavalry Major, a Cavalry Captain, a Cavalry Lieutenant, a Cavalry Sergeant, and a Cavalry Trooper. And then there is the Cavalry Trooper's horse, followed by nothing, followed by nothing, followed by a General in the Infantry."

Everyone laughed. But years later Barnhouse remembered it and applied it to the relative importance of the various doctrines in Christianity. What is the most important doctrine in Christianity? The most important doctrine is the sovereignty of God. Our God is the Lord, high and lifted up. Beside him

there is no other God. We might say that after that there is no second doctrine. He is the Lord. Nothing is second to that. So after it there is nothing,
followed by nothing. Then come the doctrines that concern God's attributes,
the person and work of Jesus Christ, justification, sanctification, and so on.
Then there are more blank spaces. Finally there come doctrines about which
the churches are divided. How should the churches be governed? Should there
be bishops? What forms should the ordinances take? Is the Lord's Supper a
mere memorial or does it contain a real presence of the Lord? And so on.

The tragedy of most Christian discussion is that it centers almost exclusively on the third of these categories, rarely considers the second of these
categories, and almost never even appreciates the first category. Isaiah began
with category number one, and it transformed his ministry. So would it trans-
form us all, if we would only see it and believe it wholeheartedly.

No Other Gods before Me

The second thing that Isaiah saw was God's train (or robe), and he noticed
that it filled the entire temple. This suggests that there is room for no one
else at the highest pinnacle of the universe. It is not just that Jehovah reigns,
therefore, but also that no one else reigns beside him or in opposition to
him. It is not just that the Lord Jesus Christ is Lord; it is also that no one else
is Lord. A little later on in Isaiah's prophecy we find God saying, "I am the
LORD; that is my name! I will not give my glory to another" (Isa. 42:8). In the
Ten Commandments he says, "I am the LORD your God, who brought you
out of Egypt, out of the land of slavery. You shall have no other gods before
me" (Exod. 20:2–3).

This causes us to ask whether what is true in this absolute sense is true for
us personally. Jesus is Lord. There is no one beside him. But is he Lord in
our lives? Or is he forced to compete with our own conflicting loyalties? Does
his train fill the temple of our soul? Or does he occupy just a corner of the
throne room while we try to crowd many other items in also?

Some try to crowd many things in. We try to crowd in our own plans for our
lives. We try to crowd in other people. Some of us crowd in our successes or
the good opinion of our friends. Then we are disturbed when our lives seem
cluttered and disorganized and when they seem to have no meaning. If that
is so for you, you need to learn to let other things go. Let Jesus have his rightful place and learn to pray with true sincerity, "Thy will be done on earth, as
it is in heaven." It is rightly said that either Jesus is Lord of all or he is not Lord
at all. So allow him to be what he must be and certainly will be one day. The
Bible says, "For he must reign until he has put all his enemies under his feet"
(1 Cor. 15:25). It also says, "Therefore God exalted him to the highest place
and gave him the name that is above every name, that at the name of Jesus
every knee should bow, in heaven and on earth and under the earth, and every
tongue confess that Jesus Christ is Lord, to the glory of God the Father" (Phil.
2:9–11).

Humility and Service

The third element in Isaiah's vision was a sight of those angelic beings that wait on God to do his bidding. Isaiah calls them "seraphim," the only occurrence of this name in the Bible. He says each had six wings: "With two wings they covered their faces, with two they covered their feet, and with two they were flying" (6:2). Here a great deal is suggested. In saying that they covered their face, he is saying that they were *reverent*, for they did not consider themselves worthy even to gaze upon God. In saying that they covered their feet, he speaks of *self-effacement*. "Seraphim" probably means "the burning ones," so they are glorious also, as is God. Yet they did not want any eyes to settle on them, but on God only. Finally, he speaks of the wings that they used to fly. This speaks of *service*, for they used these to do God's bidding.

Would we serve God? Then here is a picture of what is required: humility, self-effacement, and readiness to respond. The seraphim are a pattern for such service.

Moreover, they are a reminder of the resources that are available to God in accomplishing his purposes and protecting those whom he has promised to protect. For one thing, these angelic powers were available to the Lord Jesus Christ during the days he spent on earth. In the Garden of Gethsemane, after Peter had sought to defend him against the soldiers who had come to arrest him, Jesus said, "Put your sword back in its place, for all who draw the sword will die by the sword. Do you think I cannot call on my Father, and he will at once put at my disposal more than twelve legions of angels? But how then would the Scriptures be fulfilled that say it must happen in this way?" (Matt. 26:52–54).

That same lesson is demonstrated in the story of Elisha and his young servant at Dothan. Ben Hadad, the king of Syria, had been fighting against the king of Israel at this time; but every time he made plans to attack Israel, God revealed the plans to Elisha, Elisha told the king of Israel, and the Jewish armies escaped. Ben Hadad thought that there was a traitor in his camp. But when he was told the truth he determined to capture Elisha. One night, when Elisha was at Dothan with his servant, Ben Hadad surrounded the city so that at daybreak, when the servant went out (probably to get water) he saw the soldiers, horses, and chariots, and was terrified.

"Oh, my lord, what shall we do?" cried the servant.

Elisha responded, "Don't be afraid. Those who are with us are more than those who are with them." Then he prayed, asking God to open the young man's eyes so that he might see the true situation. God opened the eyes of the servant so that he saw "the hills full of horses and chariots of fire all around Elisha" (2 Kings 6:17). We may apply these stories personally, noting that all the glory and power that surrounds the court of our Lord is also available for the defense of those who are his servants.

Holy, Holy, Holy

The fourth thing that Isaiah noticed was the worship given to God by these hosts of heaven. "They were calling to one another," we are told. "'Holy, holy, holy, is the LORD Almighty; the whole earth is full of his glory.' At the sound of their voices the doorposts and thresholds moved and the temple was filled with smoke" (6:3–4). Worship means to acknowledge God's worth, that is, to take up his attributes and to remember them before him one by one. Is it not interesting, therefore, that the attribute of God that most impressed these angelic beings, who knew him so well, was holiness? If you stop any normal person on the street and ask what is the most important of God's attributes, the answer you will almost always get today is "love." Well, that is important; but it is not what most impresses those who see God face-to-face. Those who see God or have a striking revelation of God are always impressed with his holiness. Thus, it was with Isaiah himself. "Woe to me! I am ruined! For I am a man of unclean lips, and I live among a people of unclean lips, and my eyes have seen the King, the LORD Almighty" (v. 5). It was the same with Peter: "Go away from me, Lord; I am a sinful man" (Luke 5:8).

If this is so, then holiness should obviously characterize the lives of those who are God's people. All the attributes are important, of course. We should be wise, as he is wise. We should love one another. We should be merciful. But above all we should be holy. We should be increasingly freed from the power of sin in our lives.

Isaiah's Commission

All this is what Isaiah saw. But it would not be right to stop at this point without at least suggesting the effect of this entire vision on his life. For the point of this is that the same effect will be seen in our lives if we catch a vision of God either through his vision or else directly from the Lord Jesus Christ.

Actually, Isaiah had three visions. The first was a vision of God; we have looked at that most carefully. The second was a vision of himself; for having seen God in his holiness, he recognized afresh that he was a sinner. Finally, there was a vision of service. This came about when Isaiah confessed his sin, was cleansed of his sin by God, heard God's voice saying, "Whom shall I send? And who will go for us?" and then responded, "Here am I. Send me." Moreover, our text tells us what he did when he was sent: "Isaiah said this because he saw Jesus' glory and spoke about him." Isaiah had more to say about the Lord than any other Old Testament writer. He tells of his humiliation and glory, his nature and names, his atonement and future reign. So should it be for us. If we have truly seen Jesus and then have confessed our sin and been cleansed of it, we too will want to speak of Jesus as the faithful incarnation of our God.

162

A Silent Majority?

John 12:42–43

Yet at the same time many even among the leaders believed in him. But because of the Pharisees they would not confess their faith for fear they would be put out of the synagogue; for they loved praise from men more than praise from God.

I s it possible for a person to be a secret believer in the Lord Jesus Christ? Is it possible to believe in Jesus as the Son of God and our Savior from sin and truly to be committed to him and yet be silent about it? Is it possible to believe in Jesus with our whole hearts and not confess him openly?

These questions are pertinent in the light of our text, for it tells us that although the Jewish people as a whole rejected Jesus during the time he was on earth, nevertheless many did believe on him even though they did not confess him publicly. "Yet at the same time many even among the leaders believed in him. But because of the Pharisees they would not confess their faith for fear they would be put out of the synagogue; for they loved praise from men more than praise from God" (vv. 42–43). On the surface, the text seems to say that silent belief is possible, for they "believed" on Christ yet "did not confess him." At the same time the language is such that we naturally wonder if the belief involved was genuine. We can hardly avoid contrasting these verses with Christ's own statement recorded in Luke 12, in which he says explicitly, "Whoever acknowledges me before men, the Son of Man will also ackowldge before the angels of God. But he who disowns me before men will be disowned before the angels of God" (vv. 8–9).

These verses are fascinating and instructive. Yet I must confess that, even after studying them carefully, I am still not sure what final answer they give to our questions. Was the belief of these men genuine? Were they really a believing majority, though silent? If they were, it is certainly an abnormal situation; and we are warned by it. If they were not, we are encouraged to make clear by a public confession whatever faith in Christ we may have.

Secret Believers

It is easy to outline these verses, for the statements depend on three verbs: believe, confess, and love. The first two tell what the men involved did; they seem to be contradictory. The third verb explains the situation.

The first thing that is said of these men, then, is that they believed on Jesus. This is John's usual phrase for speaking of true belief (6:40, 47; 7:38; 9:35; 10:42; 11:45; 12:11, 44, 46; 14:12; 17:20). What is more, they tell us that *many* believed and that these were among the *rulers* of the people and not just among the masses. In light of the verses that come just before this statement, which tell us that the majority did not believe because the Scriptures had foretold a general rejection of Jesus by his people, the statement that some nevertheless did believe is significant. It is John's way of saying that unbelief is never total, that human responsibility persists regardless of the biblical prophecies, and that (regardless of the depravity of the age) God always preserves to himself a remnant. We remember that it is a characteristic of this book that after having spoken of unbelief, John almost always adds that nevertheless some followed Jesus (7:31; 10:39–42; 11:45; 12:10–11).

At this point, then, it would seem that the belief of these rulers was genuine. And if this is so, then the message is the same as the one Paul gives in discussing the unbelief of the masses of Israel in Romans 11. "I ask then: Did God reject his people? By no means! I am an Israelite myself, a descendant of Abraham, from the tribe of Benjamin. God did not reject his people, whom he foreknew. Don't you know what the Scripture says in the passage about Elijah—how he appealed to God against Israel: 'Lord, they have killed your prophets and torn down your altars; I am the only one left, and they are trying to kill me'? And what was God's answer to him? 'I have reserved for myself seven thousand who have not bowed the knee to Baal.' So too, at the present time there is a remnant chosen by grace" (vv. 1–5). I repeat, then, that if the belief of these rulers was genuine, then we have a marvelous illustration of the grace of God in preserving his remnant. For here, even at the time of the crucifixion of the Lord, there were those who believed on him.

On the other hand, suppose that theirs may not have been a genuine faith. Suppose they did not believe to the point of actually committing themselves to Jesus. Still they believed intellectually and were at least sympathetic. Who can tell what they might have done had someone only spoken to them and sought to draw them to a more open commitment?

We should be encouraged by that in our witnessing. At times it seems as if all are openly hostile or at least indifferent to the claims of Christ, and we feel ourselves defeated even before we begin to speak to them of Jesus. But we cannot see their hearts, and it may well be that many of those to whom we speak actually already secretly believe a great deal of what we have to say and only need a small degree of encouragement in order to make an open profession. Here Matthew Henry writes most perceptively: "The truth of the gospel has perhaps a better interest in the consciences of men than we are aware of. Many cannot but approve of that in their hearts which yet outwardly they are shy of. Perhaps these chief rulers were *true* believers, though very weak, and their faith like smoking flax. . . . Some are really better than they seem to be. Their faults are known, but their repentance is not; a man's goodness may be concealed by a *culpable* yet pardonable weakness, which he himself truly repents of. The *kingdom of God comes not* in all *with* a like *observation;* nor have all who are good the same faculty of appearing to be so."[1]

If this is the case, then we who have confessed Christ openly may be greatly encouraged and may make every effort to "lift up the hands which hang down and the feeble knees" and lead many to an open confession of Christ unto salvation.

Cost of Discipleship

At this point, however, we have said everything positive that we know to say about these secret believers. For having said that they "believed on" Christ, the text goes on to add that nevertheless "they did not confess their faith for fear they would be put out of the synagogue." They believed, in some sense; John says so. But, having said this, there is no more good to add.

But perhaps even here some small good may be said. For it is at least true, is it not, that they recognized the true cost of discipleship, even though they were unwilling to pay it. What was the cost? In their case it involved what we would call excommunication. It involved being barred from public worship. It involved being excluded from the religious life of their fellow men. It involved the loss of the sacrifices as an atonement for sin. It involved loss of position. It involved becoming somewhat of a pariah, an outcast, one to be kept from the society of decent people and to be spoken of to children as a warning of the consequences of sin. These were no small items, particularly for those who had been leaders in Israel. They were costly—too costly. So, although these men wished to believe on Christ and confess him, and although they recognized the cost of such discipleship, they would not pay the price and so kept silent.

They were trying to do something that ultimately is impossible—to be secret disciples. Someone has said that secret discipleship is a contradiction in terms; for either the secrecy kills the discipleship, or else the discipleship kills the secrecy. Perhaps it was the latter. Perhaps they eventually came out for Jesus. But we do not know what happened. We only know that they ran a great risk. For, having failed to confess him, there is always the other alarming possibility, that they fell away.

I wonder who those are who are trying to be secret believers today. Are you one? Are you one who believes in Christ but who is willing to have others deny him and never raise a word in his defense?

I wish I could get through to you, if that is the case. I wish I could show you that this is not true discipleship as the Bible speaks of it. Dietrich Bonhoeffer is one who faced precisely this problem in his day and who wrote a book about it. He served in the state church in Germany, a church in which many claimed to be believers and yet never thought of paying the cost of confessing Jesus openly. Bonhoeffer fought such a practice, calling it "cheap grace," and by contrast called for a grace that was "costly." He wrote, "Cheap grace is the preaching of forgiveness without requiring repentance, baptism without church discipline, Communion without confession, absolution without personal confession. Cheap grace is grace without discipleship, grace without the cross, grace without Jesus Christ, living and incarnate.

"Costly grace is the treasure hidden in the field; for the sake of it a man will gladly go and sell all that he has. It is the pearl of great price to buy for which the merchant will sell all his goods. It is the kingly rule of Christ, for whose sake a man will pluck out the eye which causes him to stumble. It is the call of Jesus Christ at which the disciple leaves his nets and follows him. . . .

"Such grace is *costly* because it calls us to follow, and it is *grace* because it calls us to follow *Jesus Christ*. It is costly because it costs a man his life, and it is grace because it gives a man the only true life. It is costly because it condemns sin, and grace because it justifies the sinner. Above all, it is *costly* because it cost God the life of His Son: 'Ye were bought at a price,' and what has cost God much cannot be cheap for us. Above all, it is *grace* because God did not reckon His Son too dear a price to pay for our life, but delivered Him up for us. Costly grace is the Incarnation of God."[2]

As I reason along these lines I find myself thinking that these rulers of the people were not children of God after all. I find myself anxious that all who think they believe should be Christ's true and open followers. Costly? Yes, Jesus never said otherwise. But still it is the only wise thing to do. Remember that our Lord asked perceptively, "For what good will it be for a man if he gains the whole world, yet forfeits his soul?" (Matt. 16:26).

For Men or God?

The third of John's verbs is the verb "love" by which he gives an explanation of what would otherwise be totally contradictory and confusing. These men believed on Christ; yet they did not confess him. Why not? One answer is that they did not want to be excommunicated from the synagogue. But why did they value that so highly? The man who had been born blind was excommunicated; yet he willingly endured that for the joy of knowing Jesus. What was wrong with these rulers? John gives us the explanation by the word "love," explaining that they did not confess Christ because ultimately "they loved praise from men more than praise from God."

There is a wonderful expression of irony in this verse that we will miss if we look only at the English translation. The English says that the believing rulers loved the "praise" of men more than the "praise" of God. This is technically correct as a translation. The difficulty, however, is that the word rendered "praise" is not the normal word for "praise" but rather the word that is almost always elsewhere translated as "glory," the word *doxa*. Why does John use this word? The answer is seen in verse 41, in which John writes of the great vision of Isaiah, saying, "Isaiah said this because he saw Jesus' glory *[doxa]* and spoke about him." Verse 43 refers back to verse 41, as if to illustrate the folly of preferring any earthly glory, however impressive, to that overwhelming and magnificent glory that belongs to God.

John tells us that these rulers had a scale of values into which, on the one side, they put the praise of men and, on the other, the praise of God. There was much to be said for the praise of God. They knew that by confessing Christ they should be praising God and should be approved by him. On the other hand, there was even more to be said for the praise of men, so they reasoned. This is a world in which men and women operate on the basis of mutual esteem. It was good to give deference to those in high positions, and it was enjoyable to receive such deference from others. They wished to be thought well of by their superiors and to be praised by those who were beneath them in the social scale of their culture and age. In this scale the followers of the Nazarene had nothing to offer; they had lowly positions and were looked upon with contempt by all who seemed to be pillars in Jerusalem. In this balance the praise of men predominated; and the rulers concluded, to their eternal hurt, that it was better to be thought well of by men than to be accepted by almighty God.

How sad this all is, and how tragic! "No doubt," as Barclay writes, "these rulers thought themselves wise and prudent men; no doubt they thought that they were playing safe. But their wisdom did not extend to remembering that the opinion of men might matter for the few years in which they lived upon this earth; but the judgment of God matters for all eternity."[3]

A Bold Confession

We come at the end to the question with which we began. Is it possible for a person to be a secret believer in the Lord Jesus Christ? It seems to my mind that the question is still unanswered by this text, though I tend to think that the weight is on the side of secret belief being an ultimate impossibility.

But does it matter? It does to the extent that these questions teach us the meaning of true discipleship and motivate us to take a forthright and public stand for Jesus. What does this text teach about discipleship after all? First, it teaches that belief in Christ and confession of Christ properly belong together. Possibly, just possibly, one can believe in Christ and fail to confess him, whether from fear of what others might think or from some other cause. But this is clearly abnormal and not at all to be praised. In normal belief, confession follows inevitably. So much is this the case that Paul can link the two inseparably, as he does in writing to the Romans. "If you confess with your mouth, 'Jesus, is Lord,' and believe in your heart that God raised him from the dead, you will be saved. For it is with your heart that you believe and with your mouth that you confess and are saved" (Rom. 10:9–10).

Second, the text teaches that even granted the possibility of such secret discipleship, nevertheless belief without confession is dangerous. Belief may win out. But silence may stifle belief instead, as indeed it seems to have done with these rulers. Did they later come out for Christ publicly? Were they among the three thousand who believed at Pentecost or the five thousand who, we are told, believed later? We do not know.

Finally, the verses teach us the relative value of God's approval as over against the variable and passing praise of men. Ultimately only God's approval matters. Who cares if men should mock us? Who cares if we should lose the esteem of this world's beautiful people? What matters if we lose everything, so long as we have God's approval? Do we have these values? Do we think in these terms? God grant that we might and that, as a result, we might be bold to confess Christ openly.

163

What Jesus Said

John 12:44–50

Then Jesus cried out, "When a man believes in me, he does not believe in me only, but in the one who sent me. When he looks at me, he sees the one who sent me. I have come into the world as a light, so that no one who believes in me should stay in darkness.

"As for the person who hears my words but does not keep them, I do not judge him. For I did not come to judge the world, but to save it. There is a judge for the one who rejects me and does not accept my words; that very word which I spoke will condemn him at the last day. For I did not speak of my own accord, but the Father who sent me commanded me what to say and how to say it. I know that his command leads to eternal life. So whatever I say is just what the Father has told me to say."

The most obvious division in the Gospel of John occurs at the end of chapter 12, for up to this point John has been dealing with what the Lord Jesus Christ did publicly—his miracles, public teaching, and healings—while after this, from chapter 13 through the end of the book the ministry of the Lord becomes a private one directed toward his disciples. These last chapters contain the beloved final discourses, plus the record of Christ's death and resurrection.

This makes the verses that end chapter 12 particularly important; for in them John sums up what Jesus has said and done and reflects upon it, thereby also commending the teachings of Christ to any who may not yet be Christians. This has been true of all these final verses, of course, beginning with verse 37; but it is particularly true of the verses to which we come now.

These last verses (vv. 44–50) contain what we can only call a résumé of Christ's teaching. These are not the last words Christ spoke publicly—the last words he spoke publicly are recorded in verses 35 and 36—but they are a final summation of his teaching.

In them, Jesus speaks, first, of his relationship to the Father (vv. 44–45). This involves his deity and is very important. Second, he speaks of himself as the "light of the world" (v. 46). Third, he speaks of the danger of unbelief (vv. 47–49). Finally, in the last verse, there is a command to believe (v. 50).

Knowledge of God

We begin, then, with the deity of Jesus. The importance of this is explained by the Lord himself in saying, "When a man believes in me, he does not believe in me only, but in the one who sent me. When he looks at me he sees the one who sent me." The importance of the deity of Jesus Christ is that we know God only in him; and if the Lord Jesus Christ is not God, then we do not know what God is like because we have no basis for saying anything about him.

If God does not intervene in history to speak of himself (which is what we have in Scripture), and if he does not act to show himself (which is what we have in Jesus Christ), then we have no knowledge of him. We can hold conferences. We can say, "I think God must be a being who cares for us; because we care for one another God must care for us." But that is all inferential. It may be right, but we do not *know* that it is right. On the other hand, when God intervenes to tell us about himself in Scripture—through men who, as Peter says, were "borne along by the Holy Spirit"—then we have sure knowledge about God. That is why the Word is important. And when God intervenes in history in Jesus Christ to give us not just words but also to show us a personality, then we know him personally.

What is God like? The answer is that God is like Jesus. That is the importance of the deity of Jesus Christ. There are other important truths connected with this, of course. If Jesus Christ is not God, Jesus could not have died for our sin. If he were just a man, he had to die for his own sin. That is part of it, and there is more. Nevertheless, in terms of our knowledge of God, which this Gospel, written to a Greek world very much concerned with knowing God, emphasizes, the deity of Jesus Christ is important in that it is the ultimate and only solution to knowing him.

Do you think that God is love? You know that God is love because Jesus Christ is love and showed it by dying for us. Do you think that God is holy and righteous and good? Do you want to know that God is filled with wisdom, that he understands you, that he is able to help you in any extremity? You know that because of Jesus. Therefore we, as Christians, are not left in the dark as to what God is; we do not find ourselves saying, "Oh, I wish I knew what he is like! If only I could know him, that would certainly be satisfying!" We are not in the position of those who make that kind of a statement.

Rather we are those who turn our eyes to the Jesus we find in the Scriptures and say, "There is our God revealed." And we love him and worship him because of it.

Escape from Night

The second thing Jesus says is that he is "a light" come into the world in order that whoever believes on him should not abide in darkness. This is another great theme of the Gospel. John speaks of it in the opening chapter, for instance, describing the Lord Jesus Christ as both light and life. Then in two great texts later on—once in the eighth chapter, verse 12, and once in the ninth chapter, verse 5—the Lord Jesus Christ says explicitly, "I am the light of the world."

What does it mean that Jesus is this world's light? It means several things. First, it means that apart from him this world is in darkness. That does not mean that there are therefore absolutely no glimmerings of what we might call light. Certainly man was made in the image of God and retains something of that image even after the fall, although in a debased form. Our minds, as partial remnants of that image, can think God's thoughts after him. They can provide and disseminate a certain degree of light in human thought and philosophy. But our minds cannot do this in spiritual things. That is the point. And that is why the world is in such deep darkness. The world can understand mechanics, science, art, interpersonal relationships, and many other subjects. But spiritually, it has no light at all. Jesus is the One who came to impart light in order that we might see what goodness, truth, and righteousness are, and above all might see what God himself is.

When the Lord Jesus Christ came into the world and shone as God's light, he exposed the darkness of the world as no one had ever done previously. And, of course, those who had an invested interest in things as they were hated him for exposing their darkness and eventually had him crucified.

It is interesting and helpful to review the claim "I am the light of the world" in the contexts of the two stories in which it occurs in John's Gospel. Take the eighth chapter, first of all. There the sentence occurs in verse 12. But what occurs in verses 1–11? In those verses John tells the story of the woman taken in adultery, which story reveals the hatred and ruthless activity of Christ's opponents more than anything else in the entire Gospel. These men said, "Perhaps we can catch him in this way. We know that he preaches love and forgiveness. We also know that he pretends to speak for God. Let us catch him in a situation in which he will be forced to choose between love and God's law. If he says to forgive, we will say, 'What kind of a prophet is this that speaks against the law of Moses?' If he says to obey the law, we will say, 'What is all this talk about love?' We will discredit him." Eventually someone thought of confronting him with a woman who had been caught committing adultery. It was brilliant, they thought; it fit the bill perfectly. It was a good capital offense by Mosaic law, yet it was also the sort of thing that would draw out sympathy. So they set it up. Probably they enticed the woman; at least one of them did. Then they trapped her, making sure, of course, that they had two eyewitnesses. They peeked through the keyhole. Then they dragged the poor woman off to see Jesus. Imagine going to such lengths just to catch Jesus Christ!

Jesus said, "All right. You want to operate by the law. Let us operate by the law. The law requires two witnesses. Who is going to witness? Who has a pure enough heart to stand up and condemn this woman?" It was certainly not going to be one of those who had seen her, because under Jewish law, entrapment was just as reprehensible as it is under our law. Besides, they were guilty of other sins also. So under Christ's gaze they all just faded away one by one, and in the end there was only one person who could have accused her, the Lord himself. He said, "We have operated under the law, but there is only one witness now. The law cannot function, for it requires two witnesses. Therefore I now choose to operate on the basis of my grace based upon the death that I am going to provide as an atonement for sin." So he forgave her, saying, "Go, and sin no more."

"I am the light of the world." A great light! But that light also reveals the terrible darkness of the human heart.

When one turns to the next chapter of John's Gospel, he finds Christ's statement in another context. Here is a man who had been born blind. He had lived all his life, thirty-eight years, in this state. He had never seen the sun. He had never seen a tree, a stone, a lamb. He had never seen a person. This man had moved around the city of Jerusalem by touch for all these many years. At last, however, the Lord singled him out and healed him. And what happened? The healing had taken place on the Sabbath, and these same leaders were angry that Jesus was breaking their Sabbath regulations. They did not care at all about the man who had been healed. So they dragged the man in, interrogated him, and in exasperation eventually excommunicated him. He had not done anything. He had just been a passive victim of a healing. Yet they threw him out, thereby revealing the darkness of their own hearts. They preferred ecclesiastical rules, regulations, and liturgies to God's transforming work within the life of a man or a woman. Jesus was "the light of the world," but these rulers were in darkness.

Then, too, it is not only that the world is in darkness and that Jesus is the light. This is not the only thing Jesus says here. Jesus also says that it is possible to be delivered out of darkness. If the world is in darkness, we are in darkness. But Jesus Christ does not come just to reveal our darkness, to say, "Look! You are in darkness, and darkness it is." He comes to lift us out of our darkness by means of his marvelous light. He says, "I have come into the world as a light, so that no one who believes in me should stay in darkness."

To believe on the Lord Jesus Christ—that is the solution! He is the light. So if we come to him and depend upon him, we have light and walk in his light. Moreover—because this is not just external, because it is also an internal transformation—we even become, wonder of wonders, what he himself calls us: "sons of light." That is, we come to partake of his nature through believing on him.

Judgment Coming

There is a third point, beginning with verse 47. It is what I would call the danger of unbelief. "As for the person who hears my words but does not believe, I do not judge him," says Jesus. "For I did not come to judge the world, but to save it. There is a judge for the one who rejects me and does not accept my words; that very word which I spoke will condemn him at the last day. For I did not speak of my own accord, but the Father who sent me commanded me what to say and how to say it."

Here Jesus speaks of a future day of judgment. He comes in grace. Indeed, he comes in grace to all of us. This is the day of grace. He offers himself as the Savior. But Jesus does not mince words when he says that if you reject him now, you are going to face his words in a future day that will not be a day of grace but will be a day of judgment, and that in that day you will be required to answer for everything you have done and said. You will have to answer for all your rebellion. Is that not significant—that there is a future day, that the future day is a day of judgment, and that the words of Jesus will judge us in that day?

Some time ago, when I was speaking at a theological conference, a professor in one of our theological seminaries stood up and said, "We have got to get it into our heads that nothing in life is ever going to change. Things are as they are today, and they are going to continue as they are indefinitely. The Lord Jesus Christ is never going to come back." Fortunately, the apostle Peter had warned me what to think about such a person, because he had said several thousand years ago that in the last times scoffers will come saying, "Where is this 'coming'? Ever since our fathers died, everything goes on as it did since the beginning" (2 Peter 3:4). Moreover, he had warned me to pay no attention to them, saying, "Do not forget this one thing. . . . With the Lord a day is like a thousand years and a thousand years are like a day. The Lord is not slow in keeping his promise, as some understand slowness. He is patient with you, not wanting any to perish, but everyone to come to repentance" (vv. 8–9).

Do you think that this world will continue indefinitely? A person has a right to his opinion, I suppose. But I believe the word of the Lord Jesus Christ who said that all things will not continue as they are, that a future day of judgment is coming, and that all men and women will in that day have to answer for what they have said and done.

How will you answer? What will you say when God asks you, "What right do you have to come into my heaven?" Will you say, "I have done many good things"? God will answer, "Not good enough; my standard is perfection." Or will you say instead, "I come not on my own merit but solely on the merit of the Lord Jesus Christ, who died for me. I have nothing in myself by which to commend myself to you. But Jesus died in my place. He paid the price of my sin. He bore the punishment for my transgression. Through believing on him I have received a new life." That is the only basis on which any man or woman will be saved. So we must come to that now, to that commitment to the Lord Jesus Christ about which John speaks.

A Command to Believe

The last point is in verse 50: "I know that his command leads to eternal life. So whatever I say is just what the Father has told me to say." I find the word "commandment" to be most interesting. Jesus says that God's *commandment* is life everlasting. But what commandment is this? What command is life everlasting? Only this: "Believe on the Lord Jesus Christ and you will be saved." That is God's commandment.

Today, in much of our evangelism, we treat the offer of salvation as nothing more than an invitation—an invitation to come and believe on Jesus, to give one's heart to the Savior. This is true in one sense, of course. The Lord Jesus Christ did say, "Come to me all who are weary and burdened." But we must remember that this is not all that can be said. The offer of salvation is an invitation, but it is an invitation that is at the same time a command. When Paul preached at Athens he talked about the spiritual ignorance of the Athenians that, he said, God "overlooked" for a time, but now he "*commands* all men everywhere to repent*" (Acts 17:30). In the same way, on the day of Pentecost, Peter said, "Repent and be baptized, every one of you, in the name of Jesus Christ for the forgiveness of your sins" (Acts 2:38). This is not something to be toyed with; this is not something to be delayed. God is our master, and he orders us to turn from sin and to respond to him.

I do not want to seem harsh. Of course, the call to believe on Jesus is an invitation. It is out of love that the Lord Jesus Christ offers the command, speaks the words. It is out of love that God calls upon us to repent. But, at the same time, the matter of belief is not optional. It is required of us. Therefore, to fail to believe is not just a misfortune. It is sin.

Will you believe? Jesus says, "He who has seen me has seen the Father." He says, "I have come into the world as a light." Will you allow him to be your light, your Savior?

Notes

Chapter 112: Christ and a Man Born Blind

1. Arthur W. Pink, *Exposition of the Gospel of John,* vol. 2 (Grand Rapids: Zondervan, 1945), 59–60.

Chapter 113: The Problem of Pain

1. Donald Grey Barnhouse, *The Love Life* (Glendale, Ca.: Regal Books, 1973), 126.
2. John Calvin, *The Gospel according to St. John, 1–10,* trans. T. H. L. Parker (Grand Rapids: Eerdmans, 1959), 237–38.
3. Donald Grey Barnhouse, *God's River* (Grand Rapids: Eerdmans, 1959), 82.

Chapter 114: Jesus, the Worker

1. Carl F. H. Henry, "What Next God?" *Eternity,* January 1970, 48.

Chapter 115: The Sixth Miracle

1. J. B. Phillips, *Ring of Truth: A Translator's Testimony* (New York: Macmillan, 1967), 86–87.

Chapter 116: "He Is a Prophet"

1. Pink, *Exposition of the Gospel of John,* 78.
2. For a full discussion of the Sabbath problem, see vol. 2.
3. Calvin, *The Gospel according to St. John,* 246.

Chapter 120: Are We Blind Also?

1. See chapter 112.
2. Leon Morris, *The Gospel according to John* (Grand Rapids: Eerdmans, 1971), 497.

Chapter 121: The Parable of the Good Shepherd

1. Brooke Foss Westcott, *The Revelation of the Father* (London and Cambridge: Macmillan and Co., 1884), 84.
2. Pink, *Exposition of the Gospel of John,* 107.

Chapter 123: Life, More Life

1. Phillip Keller, *A Shepherd Looks at Psalm 23* (Grand Rapids: Zondervan, 1970), 35.
2. Ibid., 91.

Chapter 125: The Chief Shepherd

1. Pink, *Exposition of the Gospel of John,* 124.
2. Watchman Nee, *The Normal Christian Worker* (Fort Washington, Pa.: Christian Literature Crusade, 1970), 20.

Chapter 126: One Flock, One Shepherd

1. Charles Haddon Spurgeon, "Other Sheep and One Flock," *Metropolitan Tabernacle Pulpit,* vol. 29 (London: The Banner of Truth Trust, 1971), 187.
2. William Barclay, *The Gospel of John,* vol. 2 (Philadelphia: Westminster Press, 1956), 74–75.
3. D. Martyn Lloyd-Jones, *God's Way of Reconciliation* (Grand Rapids: Baker, 1972), 282–88.

Chapter 128: Christ, the Calvinist

1. For a similar review of this history, see vol. 2 ("Those Who Shall Come," John 6:36–37).
2. Charles Haddon Spurgeon, "Perseverance without Presumption," *Metropolitan Tabernacle Pulpit,* vol. 18 (Pasadena, Tex.: Pilgrim Publications, 1971), 347–48.

Chapter 130: The Issue in Six Words

1. The various levels of belief are also discussed in vol. 2.

Chapter 131: Word of the Living God

1. J. Theodore Mueller, "Luther's 'Cradle of Christ,'" *Christianity Today,* 24 October 1960, 11.
2. *Calvin's New Testament Commentaries,* vol. 10 (Grand Rapids: Eerdmans, 1964), 330.
3. Morris, *The Gospel according to John,* 527.
4. Phillips, *Ring of Truth,* 74–75.

Chapter 132: Blessing before the Storm

1. Charles Haddon Spurgeon, "Jesus and His Forerunner," *Sermons on the Gospel of John* (Grand Rapids: Zondervan, 1966), 84.
2. Ibid., 91.

Chapter 133: Those Who Loved Him

1. The *Bible Study Hour,* 7 September, 1958.

Chapter 134: He Who Loved Them

1. Charles Haddon Spurgeon, "Beloved, and Yet Afflicted," *Metropolitan Tabernacle Pulpit*, vol. 26 (London: The Banner of Truth Trust, 1971), 73.
2. Pink, *Exposition of the Gospel of John*, 160.

Chapter 135: A Sickness Not unto Death

1. Barnhouse, *The Love Life*, 140–41.
2. Ibid., 144–45.

Chapter 136: The Delays of Love

1. Alexander Maclaren, *Expositions of Holy Scripture*, vol. 7, "St. John, Chapters 9–14" (Grand Rapids: Eerdmans, 1959), 78.
2. Ibid., 80.

Chapter 140: "I Am the Resurrection and the Life"

1. Charles Haddon Spurgeon, "Though He Were Dead," *Metropolitan Tabernacle Pulpit*, vol. 30 (London: The Banner of Truth Trust, 1971), 495.

Chapter 141: Faith's Foothold

1. W. L. Knox, *Essays Catholic and Critical* (London: Society for Promoting Christian Knowledge, 1931), 99.

Chapter 142: Mary

1. H. A. Ironside, *Illustrations of Bible Truth* (Chicago: Moody, 1945), 49–50.

Chapter 143: Jesus Wept

1. Charles Haddon Spurgeon, "Jesus Wept," *Metropolitan Tabernacle Pulpit*, vol. 35 (London: The Banner of Truth Trust, 1970), 338.
2. R. H. Lightfoot, *St. John's Gospel* (Oxford: Oxford University Press, 1963), 229.
3. G. Campbell Morgan, *The Gospel according to John* (Westwood, N.J.: Fleming H. Revell, n.d.), 197.
4. Os Guinness, *The Dust of Death* (Downers Grove, Ill.: InterVarsity Press, 1973), 388.

Chapter 144: Our Tears in God's Bottle

1. Barclay, *The Gospel of John*, vol. 2, 113–14.
2. Spurgeon, "Jesus Wept," 343.

Chapter 146: "Behold How He Loves"

1. Charles Haddon Spurgeon, "Oh, How He Loves," *Sermons on the Gospel of John* (Grand Rapids: Zondervan, 1966), 92.
2. Ibid., 98–100.

Chapter 147: The Seventh Miracle

1. Ironside, *Illustrations of Bible Truth*, 97–99.
2. Pink, *Exposition of the Gospel of John*, 209.

Chapter 148: What Shall We Do with Jesus?

1. Pink, *Exposition of the Gospel of John*, 214.
2. Charles Haddon Spurgeon, "The Great Miracle-Worker," *Sermons on the Gospel of John*, 104.
3. Barclay, *The Gospel of John*, vol. 2, 122.

Chapter 149: Why Did Jesus Christ Die?

1. Maclaren, *Expositions of Holy Scripture*, vol. 7, 115.
2. H. E. Guillebaud, *Why the Cross?* (Chicago: InterVarsity Christian Fellowship, 1947), 130, 185.
3. Pink, *Exposition of the Gospel of John*, 219–22.

Chapter 150: His Hour Not Yet Come

1. F. Godet, *Commentary on the Gospel of John*, vol. 2 (New York: Funk & Wagnalls, 1886), 196.
2. Barclay, *The Gospel of John*, vol. 2, 124–25.

Chapter 151: Memorial to a Woman's Love

1. From the accounts of Matthew and Mark we might suppose that the supper took place later in the Passover week, but a careful reading will show that John's dating is the correct one.
2. The story is told about himself by Donald Grey Barnhouse in the booklet "How to Study Your Bible," by Ralph L. Keiper, based on material supplied by Barnhouse (Philadelphia: The Bible Study Hour, 1961), 9–10.
3. H. A. Ironside, *Addresses on the Gospel of John* (Neptune, N.J.: Loizeaux Brothers, 1942), 486.

Chapter 152: Inescapable Evidence

1. Morgan, *The Gospel according to John*, 209.
2. Ralph L. Keiper, "The Secret of Effective Witnessing," in *Share Your Faith*, ed. Russell T. Hitt and William J. Petersen (Grand Rapids: Zondervan, 1970), 12.
3. H. A. Evan Hopkins, *Henceforth* (London: Inter-Varsity Fellowship, 1957), 46.

Chapter 153: The King Is Coming

1. Roy M. Allen, *Three Days in the Grave* (New York: Loizeaux Brothers, 1942), 21–22.
2. Roger Rusk, "The Day He Died," *Christianity Today*, 29 March 1974, 6.

Chapter 155: How to Save Your Own Life

1. Charles Haddon Spurgeon, "Christ's Servant—His Duty and Reward," *Metropolitan Tabernacle Pulpit,* vol. 8 (Pasadena, Tex.: Pilgrim Publications, 1973), 438.

2. Ibid., 444.

Chapter 157: Jesus, the Great Attraction

1. R. A. Torrey, *The Uplifted Christ* (Grand Rapids: Zondervan, 1965), 19.

2. Ibid., 21.

3. Charles Haddon Spurgeon, "The Marvellous Magnet," *Metropolitan Tabernacle Pulpit,* vol. 29 (London: The Banner of Truth Trust, 1971), 240.

Chapter 158: Who Is This Son of Man?

1. Oscar Cullmann, *The Christology of the New Testament,* "The New Testament Library" (London: SCM Press, 1963), 137.

2. Illustrations of the preexistence of the Son of Man and of his work of judgment from the apocryphal literature are particularly well documented by S. Mowinckel, *He That Cometh* (New York: Abingdon Press, 1954), 370–73, 393–99. This book devotes more than one hundred pages to the Son of Man concept.

Chapter 159: An Appeal and a Promise

1. Maclaren, *Expositions of Holy Scripture,* vol. 7, 162.

2. Ibid., 168–69.

Chapter 160: The Miracle of Unbelief

1. Brooke Foss Westcott, *The Gospel according to St. John* (London: James Clarke & Co., 1958), 184.

2. Matthew Henry, *Commentary on the Whole Bible,* vol. 5, "Matthew to John" (New York: Fleming H. Revell, n.d.), 1084.

3. Morris, *The Gospel according to John,* 605.

Chapter 162: A Silent Majority?

1. Henry, *Commentary on the Whole Bible,* vol. 5, 1085.

2. Dietrich Bonhoeffer, *The Cost of Discipleship* (New York: Macmillan, 1966), 47–48.

3. Barclay, *The Gospel of John,* vol. 2, 155–56.

Subject Index

Scripture Index

James Montgomery Boice is president and cofounder of the Alliance of Confessing Evangelicals, the parent organization of *The Bible Study Hour*, on which he has been the speaker since 1969. He is the senior pastor of Philadelphia's historic Tenth Presbyterian Church.